MONARCHIES AND NATIONS

GLOBALISATION AND IDENTITY IN THE ARAB STATES OF THE GULF

EDITED BY PAUL DRESCH
AND JAMES PISCATORI

I.B.TAURIS
LONDON · NEW YORK

New paperback edition published in 2013 by I.B.Tauris & Co Ltd
6 Salem Road, London W2 4BU
175 Fifth Avenue, New York NY 10010
www.ibtauris.com

First published in hardback in 2005 by I.B.Tauris & Co Ltd

ISBN: 978 1 84885 866 4

A full CIP record for this book is available from the British Library
A full CIP record is available from the Library of Congress

Library of Congress Catalog Card Number: available

Typeset in ES_B8 by A. & D. Worthington, Newmarket, Suffolk

CONTENTS

List of Contributors v
Preface vii

Introduction: Societies, Identities and Global Issues
Paul Dresch 1

PART I. CULTURE AND CONNECTEDNESS

1. Channels of Interaction: The Role of Gulf-Owned Media Firms in Globalisation
Naomi Sakr 34
2. Dialect and National Identity: The Cultural Politics of Self-Representation in Bahraini *Musalsalāt*
Clive Holes 52
3. Cultural Construction, the Gulf and Arab London
Christa Salamandra 73

PART II. LOCAL IDENTITIES: THE IMPORTANCE OF NATION-STATES

4. Transnational Connections and National Identity: Zanzibari Omanis in Muscat
Madawi Al-Rasheed 96
5. Neither Autocracy nor Democracy but Ethnocracy: Citizens, Expatriates and the Socio-Political System in Kuwait
Anh Nga Longva 114
6. Debates on Marriage and Nationality in the United Arab Emirates
Paul Dresch 136

PART III. PRACTICAL AND MORAL ORDER

7. Public Order and Authority: Policing Kuwait
Jill Crystal 158
8. Gender, Religious Knowledge and Education in Oman
Mandana E. Limbert 182
9. Political Actors Without the Franchise: Women and Politics in Kuwait
Haya al-Mughni and *Mary Ann Tétreault* 203
10. Managing God's Guests: The Pilgrimage, Saudi Arabia and the Politics of Legitimacy
James Piscatori 222

Notes 247
References Cited 277
Index 301

CONTRIBUTORS

Jill Crystal is Associate Professor in Political Science at Auburn University. She is author of *Oil and Politics in the Gulf: rulers and merchants in Kuwait and Qatar* (1990) and *Kuwait: the transformation of an oil state* (1992). Her primary research focus has been domestic politics in the Arab Gulf, and her current work is on the relationship between general order and maintaining regime-specific order.

Paul Dresch is University Lecturer in Anthropology and Fellow of St John's College, University of Oxford. He is author of *Tribes, Government and History in Yemen* (1989) and *A History of Modern Yemen* (2000) and co-editor with Pierre Bonte and Edouard Conte of *Emirs et Présidents* (2001). His interest in the United Arab Emirates and the Gulf more generally dates to the mid-1990s.

Clive Holes has been Khālid bin 'Abdullāh al-Sa'ūd Professor for the Study of the Contemporary Arab World at the University of Oxford since 1997. He worked for many years in Bahrain, Kuwait, Oman, Algeria and Iraq and has published widely on sociolinguistic change. He is currently working on a three-volume study entitled *Dialect, Culture and Society in Eastern Arabia* to be published by Brill.

Mandana E. Limbert is Assistant Professor of Anthropology at Queens College, City University of New York. She has been a Ford Foundation post-doctoral fellow at New York University and a Sultan post-doctoral fellow at Berkeley. Her article, "Senses of Water in an Omani Town", appeared in *Social Text.* Her interests include sociality, religion and modernity in the Arab Gulf.

Anh Nga Longva is Associate Professor in the Department of Social Anthropology, University of Bergen, Norway. She has done extensive fieldwork in the Gulf (Kuwait and Bahrain) since the late 1980s and researched on labour migration, ethnic relations, human rights, democracy and tribalism. Her publications include *Walls Built on Sand: migration, exclusion and society in Kuwait* (1997).

Haya al-Mughni wrote her doctoral thesis at Exeter in 1990 on the politics of women's groups in Kuwait. She has since published extensively and contributed to a number of books on gender politics, citizenship and women's movements. Her most recent publication is "Citizenship, Gender and the Politics of Quasi-States", with Mary Ann Tétreault, in *Gender and Citizenship in the Middle East* (2000).

James Piscatori is Fellow of the Oxford Centre for Islamic Studies and of Wadham College, Oxford. He was formerly Research Fellow on Islam and Politics at the Royal Institute of International Affairs and Professor of International Relations at the University of Wales. He is the author of *Islam in a World of Nation-States* (1986) and co-author with Dale F. Eickelman of *Muslim Politics* (1996).

Madawi Al-Rasheed is Senior Lecturer in Social Anthropology at King's College, University of London. Her research focuses on history, society and politics in Saudi Arabia. Her books include *Politics in an Arabian Oasis* (1991), *Iraqi Assyrian Christians in London* (1998) and *A History of Saudi Arabia* (2002). More recently, she has conducted research in Oman on transnationalism and Omani heritage.

Naomi Sakr, formerly an editor for The Economist Intelligence Unit, lectures on the political economy of communication in the School of Media, Art and Design at the University of Westminster. She is the author of *Satellite Realms: transnational television, globalization and the Middle East* (2001) and has written widely on media reform and development in the Arab World.

Christa Salamandra received a D.Phil. from the Institute of Social and Cultural Anthropology, Oxford University. She has been a Fulbright Scholar and Visiting Professor of Sociology at the Lebanese American University in Beirut, and is currently Assistant Professor, Lehman College, the City University of New York. Her book, *A New Old Damascus: authenticity and distinction in urban Syria* (2004), was published by Indiana University Press.

Mary Ann Tétreault is Una Chapman Cox Distinguished Professor of International Affairs at Trinity University in San Antonio. Her books include *The Kuwait Petroleum Corporation and the Economics of the New World Order* (1995) and *Stories of Democracy: politics and society in contemporary Kuwait* (2000). Her edited volumes include *Partial Truths and the Politics of Community* (2003).

PREFACE

This volume represents part of the Transnational Communities Programme of the (UK) Economic and Social Research Council. All but one of the papers were presented at a workshop held at St John's College, Oxford, in late September 2001. The intention of this meeting, following the rationale of the broader research programme, was to examine the extent to which cross-border connections – social, political, economic and, importantly, cultural – knitted together an Arab Gulf community. The conclusions that emerged were rather different from what might have been expected, and it became clear to us that when examined "ethnographically" national processes of affiliation and identification were more important than current literature suggests.

Transliteration and standardisation of spelling are always difficult, and we have opted for a combination that presents most Arabic words and names in the form used by the *International Journal of Middle East Studies*, but which uses common English spellings of certain names and places. Words ending in *tā' marbūṭah* are transliterated as *ah* (except in a genitive construction); *aw* and *ay* are preferred for the diphthongs; and long vowels are represented with a macron. The transliteration of Chapter 2 reflects the specific dialects of Bahrain.

A number of individuals have generously assisted us with the general project or this volume in particular: our project colleague, Madawi Al-Rasheed; Steven Vertovec, director of the overall Transnational Communities Programme; our research assistants, Christa Salamandra and Gaelle Le Pottier; Yahya Birt, who produced the figures, and Ali Parchami, who provided valuable help at several junctures. We have benefitted as well from the advice and encouragement of several individuals: Melinda Babcock, Wendy James, Hassan Abedin, John Gurney and Nadim Shehadi. Kay McLeary of the Institute of Social and Cultural Anthropology, Oxford, and Christine O'Sullivan of the Oxford Centre for Islamic Studies were cheerfully efficient in their logistical and administrative support. We owe all of them, not to mention our patient contributors, a debt of gratitude.

James Piscatori and Paul Dresch
Oxford, December 2004

INTRODUCTION

SOCIETIES, IDENTITIES AND GLOBAL ISSUES

Paul Dresch

The Middle East is poorly served by academic literature, and the Gulf particularly ill served. Nor is the problem confined to literature in English. Writers in Arabic, most importantly, face problems gaining critical mass as well of imposed discretion; but the contrast more generally between the prominence of the Gulf in current affairs coverage, as for instance in the London-based *al-Wasaṭ*, and its obscurity in more reflective work is striking. As the countries of the region have taken solid form, indeed, what there was on migration, the nature of the state and pan-Arab considerations has died away.[1]

In local usage "the Gulf" covers usually the Arab oil monarchies.[2] Saudi Arabia is on another scale from its coastal neighbours – the population, including foreigners, is now in excess of 20 million, while Qatar and Bahrain are each under 1 million – and in a common Saudi view such neighbours owe their separate status to Western imperialism. Oman, by contrast, with a "national" population less than 2 million, claims a continuity that far precedes Western influence. Yet Saudi Arabia, Kuwait, Bahrain, Qatar, the United Arab Emirates (UAE) and Oman, despite the differences between them, are treated as relatives by their neighbours and citizens. In Arabic the informal "Gulfy" (*khalījī/khalījīyīn*) has the common-sense status of terms such as Shāmī (a northern Arab) or Maghribī.

The Gulf Co-operation Council, or GCC, which comprises these six states, was founded in 1981, but a shared position in the world, and thus a set of common perspectives, is evident which reworks older patterns of familiarity and runs deeper than immediate decision making. Part of their shared position is simply that the area is rich in hydrocarbons. Flows of goods and wealth across national borders are conspicuous, and local wealth is often felt by Gulf citizens to be pillaged by outsiders (Fandy 1999: 68, Yamani, M. 2000: 36, 80, 119, 130). Gulf finance itself is implicated in wider patterns, as Naomi Sakr

(Chapter 1) shows for satellite television. An unusual degree of exposure to the world economy, and indeed to global imagery, is matched, however, by a large foreign presence locally (see Figure 1): of a total Gulf population close to 30 million, less than two-thirds are nationals (Kapiszewski 2001: 38-40). The net effect, as several papers here suggest, is a huge stress on the status of "citizen" (*muwāṭin*), as opposed to that of migrant, expatriate or foreigner.

Figure 1: GCC General Population Statistics

	Population (thousands) (2000)	Expatriate Population (thousands) (2000)	National Population (thousands) (2000)	Percentage Nationals of Total Population (2000)	Nominal GDP per head/US$ (2001)
Saudi Arabia	20,723	5,595	15,128	73	8,880
Kuwait	1,984	1,300	685	35	14,202
Bahrain	691	256	435	63	11,930
Qatar	585	439	146	25	27,740
UAE	2,905	2,196	709	24	20,670
Oman	2,395	647	1,748	73	8,100

Sources: Anthony H. Cordesmann, "Oil Crash" and "Oil Boom"; Economist Intelligence Unit; Penn World 6.1

As several papers also document, these national societies are related to each other. Clive Holes (Chapter 2) notes connections of roads and bridges, then analyses with a linguist's care the unstated convergence of national dialects evident in "heritage" programmes on local television. More explicit links mark the same partial commonality. Citizenship affects residence, access and even who can marry whom, distinguishing connections among nationals of the GCC, whether formally or informally, from those with other Arabs and with foreigners (*ajānib*). Particular GCC governments, and indeed groups beyond government, have meanwhile had a huge effect elsewhere in the world not only through channels which conventional studies of factions and power would note but through charitable subventions, publishing and television, through images of what a state might be and particular visions of Islam. The focus of the present volume is on the states themselves.

To say this is not, in itself, to say much except that the focus of the work is local. In English "the state" refers equally to government as opposed to people and to both as a unit opposed to others, while the way in which governments manifest themselves as "the state" differs. In France, for instance, the inscription RF and the tricolour adorn government buildings like the tokens of an occupying power; in Britain there is seldom a conspicuous office plaque. Yet even in the French case one need not be a doctrinaire adherent of Foucault to feel that seeking "the state" in the isolable sense that much political science gives the term would mean it was always in the next office down the corridor.[3] The literature of International Relations, most notably, presents an unrealistic view of politics and none of life in the everyday (Piscatori 2000: 88–92), yet so dominates study of the Arab Gulf that political scientists concerned more with local realities are as swamped by a rhetoric of governmental strategy as are people in history, anthropology or human geography. The main alternative is a literature of "coffee-pots and camels" (Dresch 2000a: 119), much of which, as Christa Salamandra shows (Chapter 3), is produced offshore.

This volume does not try to set the academic world to rights. It does suggest, however, that in writing about the Gulf we might try for the standards set elsewhere in the Middle East (e.g. Bourquia and Miller 1999) where the forms of governmental power are seen to connect with society at large. As Muḥammad al-Rumayḥī said 20 years ago (al-Rumayḥī [1983] 1995), "The Gulf is Not Just Oil". Nor, as one might think from much that is published, are the polities of the Gulf simply counters on a strategic game-board. These countries, whether large or small, are entirely real, which itself is of interest in a world that we are told increasingly is characterised by flows of imagery, wealth and people, not by frontiers.

The state and the world

Global capital may well command something like abstract space (Harvey 1989: 147, 164, 228–9, 234–8). Certain resources are territorially specific, however, and everywhere certain places, such as great cities, tie the knot in more general exchanges of wealth and goods (Friedmann 1986). "Hydrocarbon states" are meanwhile an extreme example of a general phenomenon dependent on the state system, that is, on the claim that human affairs can be dealt with between governments and that governments fill the global space politically: to align the state system with a "world system" (in the manner of Wallerstein 1974) might not be difficult. But to stop there would be misleading, for the terms are part of a global "pidgin" (Bayart 1989). John Davis, for instance, in discussing Libya, underlines how inevitable "states" are in a world which the powers of the North Atlantic organised yet how different their domestic logic (Davis, J. 1987: 257ff.), a claim which deserves attention when considering the Arab Gulf and which sits uneasily with International Relations theory, where common denominators such as "regime stability" – indeed, the very term "regime" – reduce difference in kind to difference of degree.

Lisa Anderson (1991, 2000) suggests "monarchies" are well adapted to rapid state formation, and she points more generally (2002: 7–8) to the "primacy of political criteria" over economic development in Arab states' relations with imperial powers. That applies very plainly to the Gulf; recent literature (e.g. Herb 1999) lists the family connections of those ruling. Monarchy itself is no simple category, of course, and is blurred in the Arab World by the phenomenon of *jumlakīyah*, that is, of republics (*jumhūrīyāt*) which transmit power through marriage and descent as does a kingdom (*mamlakah*).[4] The distinction between dignified and efficient parts of government needs examining in either case. But the GCC's specific dynasts make the principle of family rule explicit and the people of these states share a place in the world system that intersects with conceptions of moral order, which rulers in turn claim always to uphold. This combination of issues does much to define Gulf experience.

The propriety of Gulf societies is striking by comparison with, let us say, Jordan or Morocco (both monarchies themselves, of course), let alone with Yemen (cf. Dresch 2000b). The amount of space in which citizens can be, as it were, off-stage varies from case to case. But a concern with public order – quite widely equated with moral order – exceeds what is ordinary in Arab countries. In few other places (perhaps Singapore?) would one find, as one does in Sharjah, a street sign saying, "Please express your civilised personality through the following actions: do not litter in streets and roads …", or in Abu Dhabi an appeal to maintain the "civilisational peculiarity" of a modern city. Parallel texts in Urdu and in English remind us that public life here is largely foreign (see Figure 2): much "local" life is restricted to family compounds. The ideal city-quarter becomes a planner's vision (Nagy 2000, Fuccaro 2001) and the texture of society is seldom displayed in public forms. Outsiders are thus warned of "a world with its own geometry" (Iseman 1978: 44); "laterality" seems a key to "vertically" built cities (Raban [1979] 1987: 153); "networks of exchange supplant territoriality" (Naciri 1997: 140). This suspicion of false appearances affects citizens as much as others, as if what is built in their name is somehow not fully theirs or not fully adequate as a sign of "progress".

In public imagery, wise and far-sighted rulers lead their people on a journey (*masīrah*) to prosperity, power and respect by others, which validates indefinitely old values (Madawi Al-Rasheed in Chaper 4 describes this for Oman). But a feature of discussions generally – well beyond what governments have to say, beyond even educated discourse – is the acceptance of what one thinks of as an "Egyptian" orthodoxy in circumstances very different to those in which terms like *aṣālah* and *ḥadāthah* (authenticity and modernity) and *ḥaḍārah mu'āṣirah* (modern, contemporary civilisation) first had their being (Armbrust 1996).[5]

Figure 2: Population of the UAE (1997)				
Emirate	Total Population (thousands)	Foreign Nationals (thousands)	Nationals (thousands)	Percentage Nationals of Total Population
Abu Dhabi	1,013	771	242	24
Dubai	740	605	136	18
Sharjah	432	325	107	25
Ajman	129	110	19	15
Umm al-Qaiwain	39	29	11	28
Ras al-Khaimah	153	87	66	43
Fujairah	84	27	57	68
Total	2,590	1,954	636	25

Source: *GCC Demographic Report 1998*, p. 77.

The Gulf suffers intellectually from a double displacement. If the rhetoric of certain Third World states condemns them to a felt marginality (to a race run by others' rules, in brief), then those who borrow such rhetoric at second hand are in a still less comfortable position, particularly where, as in the Gulf case, the harbingers of civilisation are social inferiors – mere retainers or paid employees – and their message ambivalent (cf. Raban [1979] 1987: 93–4, 115). Mandana Limbert, in discussing Oman (Chapter 8), thus points to distrust of Egyptian teachers and of Egypt itself as surrogate and exemplar of imperialism. Education, publishing and broadcast media, however, all present a valued language – or rather, competing languages – whose origins are distant from Gulf experience. A common effect is of competing claims misfitting sociology as if the borrowed terms account for less than does the act of borrowing – by whom, from where, with what ends in view.

The place of women in society is a case in point. Most states, even Saudi Arabia, make an issue of women's role in national development, and well-known figures such as Thoraya Obaid (of the UN population fund) spread the message abroad (Obaid 2002). Some constituencies in the Gulf oppose to this a nativist or traditionalising view that separates domestic space from "politics" (see e.g. Doumato 1992). Such divisions, always questionable analytically, are important practically (Eickelman and Piscatori 1996: 7, 18, 81–2, 97–8). They can also be highly charged. As Anh Nga Longva points out in Chapter 5, deviation from an "international" norm – which is largely a norm of the North Atlantic states' middle classes – draws criticism. Local claims align therefore with far larger global claims as to right and wrong, or indeed as to human nature, which give local disagreements an epic quality yet obscure their substance.

Haya al-Mughni and Mary Ann Tétreault, in Chapter 9, thus question the separation of public and private in the Kuwaiti case, such that women voting or holding seats in parliament might be the natural outcome of their importance generally. (Surveys claiming many have little interest, e.g. *Samrah* May 1996, can be hard to integrate.) The exclusion of women in the case at hand results, however, not from settled ideology, or even settled forms of dominance, runs the argument, but from "an ensemble of antagonistic political interests", not least in the (male) parliament (cf. *al-Wasaṭ* 386, 21 Jun. 1999). Certain female activists themselves petition against political rights; demands for the vote meanwhile provide common ground among others, some "Islamist" and some "liberal". Transnational or even global though the terms may be, this is very much a localised Kuwaiti argument, and all sides in such disputes are prone to invoke a localised, distinctive "culture".

The status of distinctive claims as inseparable or mirror imagery recurs with large issues of identity in a wider, and hostile, world. Islamic claims to moral order by such Saudi figures as Ṣafar al-Ḥawālī and Salmān al-ʻAwdah, for instance, turn consistently on a local nationalism (Fandy 1999: 63, 95, 100–1, 105 and *passim*), though the nation-state may be hard to theorise in strictly Islamic terms. The intemperate rhetoric of Usāmah Bin Lādin – which condemns the Saudi state's conduct yet accepts, it would seem, there might be such a state (Fandy 1999: 186–7, 193, Piscatori 2003) – invokes a wider context and develops its own cosmology. Islamists of quite different kinds thus play the role both of nationalists (Henry and Springborg 2001: 20) and of internationalists. Since Fandy or Henry and Springborg wrote, an attack on New York in September 2001, where Saudi citizens were conspicuous, has brought Usāmah's name to a wider audience.[6] But those who turned to his statements in search of a distinctively Islamic logic were disappointed: give or take pious phrases and a measure of archaic imagery, one could almost be reading the transnational revolutionary tracts of 30 years ago. And in far less dramatic cases, as Fandy reminds us (2000: 393), people change camps with ease.

An appeal to exclusive culture (*thaqāfah*), and to local values or principles (*qiyam*, *mabādī*) such as those of family, is in part an assertion of autonomy in deploying claims and images that, abstracted from immediate context, belong to contradictory fields. High drama is less the issue than a sense of thwarted domesticity. The rulers' claim to uphold both the privilege and the privacy of citizens has a populist appeal here at a local level, which is easy to underestimate. Well-publicised receptions, delegations and formal messages meanwhile locate rulers and their kin in far wider fields of patronage and purchase among the world's countries, where often they act as befits the idea of "globalising monarchy" (Henry and Springborg 2001) and monopolise to some degree exchanges of both wealth and imagery where domestic and foreign interests coincide. Domestic order (*niẓām*) is aligned with a claimed continuity of local values, to be celebrated and defended – hence an imagery of force.

Saudi television, for instance, offers the spectacle even of children's programmes sponsored by the Interior Ministry and the National Guard, where scenes of teddy bears and coloured balloons are prefaced with clips of military parachutists piling out into thin air or of armoured cars parading. The Janādirīyah (a celebratory event named after its site outside Riyad and organised through the Saudi National Guard) is featured endlessly, with rows of male dancers bobbing to and fro with their camel sticks or with bandoliers and swords. Such coverage grows year by year.[7] Nor are the Saudis alone, of course. Omani television on public holidays shows the Sultan's Armed Forces marching up and down for hours on end, in pastiches of British Army uniforms and skirling on bagpipes. "Tradition" is represented equally on these occasions by massed ranks of dancers and singers dressed in pastel shades. The sheer arbitrariness of such cultural projects reflects a claim to identity and difference (cf. Chatterjee 1997) in what many describe as a "globalising" world.

Even browsing the Gulf press suggests how prominent this topic is, and how ill defined (cf. *al-Wasaṭ* 416, 17 Jan. 2000). The unexpected neologism *'awlamah* (globalisation) is supplemented by Islamic *'ālimīyah* (perhaps globalism), and it is often unclear, despite motifs of the United States on book covers, whether globalisation is a general phenomenon or the policy of wealthy powers.[8] The thrust of argument is clear, however: vulnerability in economic and political terms is felt as an assault in cultural terms (al-Mutawwa' 2001), though what the "culture" comprises is hard to specify. The flow of foreign imagery through film, television and the internet is enormous and much debated (see e.g. al-Bāhilī 1990, al-Rumayḥī [1983] 1995: 223ff., Emirates Center for Strategic Research and Studies 1998, Yamani, M. 2000: 15–17, 40–1, 126); the involvement of Gulf societies in flows of wealth and of goods is also plain (see Figure 3). The stress in recent literature (e.g. Fandy 1999, Henry and Springborg 2001) thus falls on such generalised couples as global against local. But the Gulf states' position is specific and so is the outcome of that position. The local is itself distinctive and the issues unusually acute.

Figure 3: Major OECD Trade Balances with the GCC ($m), 2001

	US	Japan*	Germany	UK	France	Italy	South Korea
Saudi Arabia	-7,315	-9,461	2,280	761	-1,042	-396	-6,784
Kuwait	-1,088	-2,787	790	65	-86	313	-2,072
Bahrain	9	23	192	79	-20	52	-82
Qatar	-166	-4,421	347	207	-2,412	577	-2,351
UAE	1,444	696	3,006	1,335	2,428	1,033	-2,464
Oman	-134	-1,196	284	339	193	134	-2,156
GCC	-7,251	-17,146	6,900	2,785	-939	1,713	-15,909

*Figures for Japan are estimates with the exception of Kuwait. Sources: Economist Intelligence Unit; *Middle East Economic Digest*; *Middle East Economic Report*; US Census Bureau, Foreign Trade Division.

A threat to culture is found not only in flows of goods and images but in the number of foreigners who inhabit the Gulf itself (Khalaf 1992, al-Murr 1997). The place of domestic servants has been much written about (Bendiab 1991, Shah 1991, Gamburd 2000); the confinement of foreigners to camps or quarters attracts less attention, yet provides an obvious complement to citizens' exclusivity. The modes of separation and control are effective, and new economic pressures towards free flows of information (like older ones of revenue derived from oil) complement a history of what in fact is growing social isolation.[9] But in several Gulf countries citizens or nationals (*muwāṭinīn*) are minorities in their own homeland. The cities of the Gulf have thus become "towers of Babel" (Bourgey 1991: 73–4); the street life in cities is often predominantly foreign, and the labour-force beyond government offices is almost wholly so, even in countries where citizens are a majority of the population (Kapiszewski 2001: 76). Without the foreign presence neither society nor government would function.

In none of these states can one draw a line between inside and outside worlds, yet discussing how citizen-society works is difficult. Local commentary tends often to the formulaic (see e.g. Yamani, H. 1997), and the language of tradition and modernity sets much of reality itself off-limits to discussion. Rulers both exemplify and enforce certain forms of closure. The deference to rank that recurs so widely in these societies means that only certain persons are expected to speak in a given circumstance (cf. Shryock 1997: 147, 149, 150 and *passim* on Jordan), but the alignment of personal or family privacy with *pudeur* about social forms leads to closure at several levels, such that differences from North Atlantic practice raise inseparable issues of autonomy, privacy and supposed backwardness. To ascribe lack of openness to mere repression (Gause 1994: 11) is not plausible. The opacity of relations with the world economy and with world politics recurs in domestic sociology, not least as a reticence which a novelist encountering the Gulf some 25 years ago identified as "an irrational fear of being misunderstood" (O'Brien 1977: 37). Not only are governments "information shy" (Henry and Springborg 2001: 46-8, 81, 193), but citizens are intensely wary.

The great transformation

Wilkinson (1983: 313) blames European concepts of territory for assigning large oil reserves to populations that could not absorb revenue, and the same idea is expressed by Lienhardt, raising questions of identity and scale: "A view commonly expressed in the larger Arab countries is that this is 'Arab' wealth ...: the few, with their wealth, should be incorporated in the many" (Lienhardt 2001: 11). While Arab Nationalism remained plausible politically – that is, until the end of the 1960s – there were many in the Gulf itself who were ardent Nasirists, Ba'thists or adherents of the MAN (*al-qawmīyīn al-'arab*), attaching their own hopes to the many, as Jill Crystal reminds us for Kuwait in Chapter 7. That moment passed. Wider nationalism became the preserve of intellectuals (more in print than in practice) and the source of a recurrent feeling of helplessness.

The critical date differs slightly from case to case. The importance of shifts both in global concerns and in regional self-definition is hard to ignore, however (cf. Davis, E. 1991). By the time the old imperial power withdrew and the new took a detailed interest in the region, circa 1970, when America replaced Britain on the Gulf littoral, a pattern of family bureaucracy had become entrenched. Such families were identified with the privilege and safety of nationals – newly defined, and in a narrow sense, as Kuwaiti, Bahraini, Qatari – and the appearance of family-run states as having always been there was compelling on many grounds, not least those of self-interest.

As Crystal explains ([1990] 1995: 11-12, 188 and *passim*), such states were in fact quite new. Certain principles of conduct were not, of course. Inequality and arbitrariness were familiar, and Lienhardt (2001: 203) quotes the proverb, "The great is for the great and the middling is for the great and the small is for the great; what is left is for you". Shaykhs or emirs, however, had no bureaucracy. Their reach was limited and if they overstepped themselves, people moved elsewhere (Lienhardt 1975, Crystal [1990] 1995: 4). Gradually free movement of that kind has been reduced and the pattern has emerged of a ruler's kin holding state positions in a wider system defined by states. Citizenship (*mawāṭanah*) becomes a major issue. It is granted by governments whose key public figures are typically related to the ruler and the sum of whose posts equates with legitimate forms of government both locally and internationally (cf. Khuri 1980: 126-7, Gause

1994: 73–4). Such positions did not exist before: "in fact nobody paid any attention to anyone but the Ruler, the Shaykh, and his son, who would help his father ..." (quoted in Graham 1978: 110).[10] The appeal to tradition here is intensely modern.

It is only between the mid-1940s and the 1960s that the great transformation starts, that ruling families acquire "corporate" form (Herb 1999), and the people of the Gulf are swept into intimate involvement with world trade, such that Saudi Arabia's annual income from oil, for instance, reached $300 million already in the 1950s (Al-Rasheed 2002: 107). Even that was eclipsed by the "oil shocks" of the 1970s, when briefly the whole financial world appeared transformed.[11] So too did the local scene. Bahrain and Kuwait may by then have been well established (Khuri 1980, Crystal [1990] 1995) but their place in a post-British world was defined very much by the later oil boom. The UAE was formed only in 1971, and the movement "from rags to riches" (Fahim 1995) was confirmed within years by rising revenue; the "renaissance" of Oman, attendant on Sultan Qābūs taking power in 1970, was made real by new income (Fuccaro 2001: 177). King Fayṣal's management of Saudi affairs was validated also, if retrospectively, as a "renaissance" (Al-Rasheed 2002: 138) and even small regional towns in Najd were transformed in the late 1970s (Altorki and Cole 1989), as indeed was Riyad itself.

The choices made at the time (as early as the 1950s in some states, though validated by the boom or *tufrah*; as late as the 1970s in others) define certain standard themes. The appropriation of land as the rulers' and its allotment to citizens took similar forms in many places, often enriching a small group of leading families; everywhere housing was provided; services were provided by decree; jobs were found or invented, and a huge preponderance among citizens of state employment remains common now (Gause 1994: 58–60, Kapiszewski 2001). Such patterns recur throughout the Gulf. The negative resemblances are important also. Nowhere has the model of a militarised nation – on the Syrian, Iraqi or even Egyptian model – exerted any strong attraction. The sundry shaykhs and princes are scarcely martial figures but rather patrons of a national pageant (cf. Davis and Gavrielides 1991), organised with assistance from foreign retainers and employees.

The Saudi town of Dir'īyah, for instance, outside Riyad, was razed by Ibrāhīm Pāshā's invading forces in 1818 and lay in ruins for a century and a half. It has now been "rebuilt". Its present significance is not only as the base in the 1740s of the pre-eminent religious figure Muḥammad Ibn 'Abd al-Wahhāb, but as the prototype of the current Kingdom, where religious and political authority combined "to embody the rule of God's law on earth" (Facey 1997: 8 and *passim*, cf. Salamandra in Chapter 3). The quarter for "lower income groups" (ibid. 107) has not materialised. But the coffee-table book – produced in London, sponsored by the Chevron Corporation and dedicated to Prince Salmān of Riyad – affirms that Dir'īyah is "the great symbol of Saudi Arabian nationhood" (ibid. 85). As the nearby former Chevron headquarters testifies (built in "traditional" style as offices, now mirrored in reconstructions) it is difficult to discern what the original buildings in Dir'īyah might have looked like in detail or distinguish what was added recently. Reconstructions of this kind are commonplace.[12] They recuperate from dispersed experience a "civic myth" (cf. Crystal [1990] 1995: 161-4) or, as Madawi Al-Rasheed says in Chapter 4, a "national narrative".

The process of state formation sweeps up what resources may have been to hand, and ruling families have surely been central to the process. "In the first quarter of the twentieth century", says al-Azmeh ([1988] 1993: 112), "Wahhabite polity ... becomes strictly Saudi polity". In less dramatic form, with less appeal to scripture, something similar is true of most GCC states. What is Kuwait, for instance, without the Āl Ṣabāḥ? What even is Bahrain, though the name is old, without the Āl Khalīfah? Yet the states themselves are now the basis of much local common sense, and the forms of precedence and exclusion they express are the substance of group identity, to the point where Longva (Chapter 5), for instance, speaks of Kuwait as an ethnocracy. The possibility that so fascinates Western writers, and some intellectuals locally, of ruling families being overthrown is remote (the Āl Sa'ūd are very numerous, after all; the Āl Thānī are a large part of Qatar's whole "local" population) and perhaps is less than fundamental. Would a Republic of Kuwait be so different from the present system? The very forms of inequality derive from the society's position in a wider world.

If monopolies of history and imagery draw the eye of an anthropologist, political science has been drawn to monopolies of wealth and thus to discussion of the "rentier state". The basic idea, one recalls, is that governments with an income from elsewhere, as from oil for instance, have no need of taxes locally and therefore no need to involve their citizens in a political process.[13] The term welfare state (*dawlat al-ra'āyah*) has become well established in Gulf usage (e.g. al-Ḥasan 1997); one hears, even colloquially, of a dependant (*ittikālī*) or rentier "mentality" (al-Sabah 1999: 83, Yamani, M. 2000: 39, 80). More fundamentally, perhaps, governments are conceived as sources or consumers of wealth whose origins are unexplained. The opacity of relations with the world economy that colours Gulf experience is of a kind with that described for nodes of global exchange elsewhere, and what used to be terms of general analysis seem increasingly to describe only special cases.

"Class" for instance, offers little purchase. The strikes and riots of oil history – in Saudi Arabia (1953, 1956) and Qatar (1950-55) most famously; in Bahrain as late as 1965 – took place in classic settings of concentrated labour. The replacement of local labour with migrants removes such possibilities, and the dispersal of citizens anticipates post-industrial economies (Harvey 1989: 153, 171) where fragmented experience means that class in itself fails to gell as for itself. The other components of a class analysis are displaced as well. Constitutional demands – in Kuwait (1938) and Dubai (1938-39), for instance – drew together the *shabāb* (educated or progressive "young men")[14] and merchants, trapped between alternative visions of a future world, to produce what seemed "bourgeois" movements of reform. The merchants since then have arrived at their different accommodations with rulers; the inheritors of the *shabāb*'s position are bureaucrats. Class politics is not prominent (cf. Altorki and Cole 1989: 243), for key relations of class are extra-territorial (Longuenesse 1991), and terms drawn from a simplified view of Western Europe 1750–1950 fail to do the issues justice.

Attempts to connect what is happening with Islamic scholarship are equally problematic. As al-Azmeh notes of the Saudi case (al-Azmeh [1988] 1993: 114, cf. Eickelman and Piscatori 1996: 26), the concept of *maṣlaḥah*, the "general good", short-circuits much detailed argument. Muslim identity is strongly felt, but the history of scholarship and legal practice in many countries is so thin that discussion in Islamic terms evaporates to pure abstraction.[15] Even other confessional groupings, such as Shi'ah or Ibadi, are meanwhile dominated by the style of what some call generic Sunnism (cf. Dresch 2000b: 173): a stress on *'ibādāt* – that is, on such forms of obedience as prayer and dress (Eickelman and Piscatori 1996: 90–1, Al-Rasheed 1996: 21) – displaces *mu'āmalāt*, those actions in the world that include considered statecraft. Powerful criticism of corruption can be lodged at home, or abroad of imperialist power, but insofar as Islam is invoked politically the style is populist.

A certain arbitrariness of interpretation fits easily with "identity politics" in settings as far removed as Western Europe or Southeast Asia, and the homeland is no exception. The equation of Muslims with Arabs, indeed with Gulf Arabs, and of Islam with purely local practice recurs widely (see for instance the quotations in Chapter 6). Debates on marriage and descent (Chapters 4, 5 and 6) are an obvious field for *ad hoc* interpretation; the role of domestic servants (Chapters 5 and 7) provides another, and the ordering of formal politics (Chapter 9) another still. Nativist or localising claims thus align with Islamic imagery; the prescriptions of Western rhetoric on pluralism and democracy, by contrast, are treated – with enthusiasm by some, with disdain by others – as foreign imports. Neither Western nor Islamic generalities give an adequate account of Gulf experience.

The state and its subjects

Mamoun Fandy, in the Saudi case, examines what a polity might be in local terms by glossing the idea of closeness or kinship (*qarābah*) with the tacit neologism *'ā'ilīyah* or "familialism" (Fandy 1999). The account covers much that happens. It is true, for instance, that government does not usually treat its people harshly (foreign residents are a different matter), and that relations with erring dependants are rarely severed by those in power. It is also true that "upholding the good and extirpating what is reprehensible" is interpreted such that citizens' houses are private space. Most importantly the ruling family partake in both formal government and "civil society" (Fandy 1999: 34ff.). Yet bouncing local criticism off global forms (democracy and the fax or internet; Islam and shifting websites), which Fandy explores, suggests domestic tensions that are not well expressed in classic terms of kinship.

Plainly questions need posing, but the terms in which to pose them are unclear. Not only is class not conspicuous, but regionalism is subdued also. This is not to deny local feeling, which is often strong, but there hardly seems an urge to political autonomy. Even Oman is quite tightly integrated. Nor do the differences among Saudi Arabia's great regions translate into obvious politics. And although a third of Saudis in the mid-1980s may have been resident on their tribal territory, as a common estimate then ran, tribes are not a salient issue at national level as they were in certain neighbouring countries even 20 years ago (Dresch 2000b): indeed the greater the folkloric stress on tribes, some would argue (Al-Rasheed 2002: 127, 195–6), the less the substance. The assumptions of "closeness" that tribalism embodies are important, as Gavrielides showed well in the case of Kuwait's elections (Gavrielides 1987, cf. Aarts 1994). Something similar might be found in Bahrain and perhaps Qatar (Bahry 1999: 123). But Kuwait, as three papers in the present volume stress (Chapters 5, 7, 9), shows particularly well how "closeness" now exists within the arbitrary bounds of nationality.

National identity displaces on occasion even confessional identities, often in response to the looming mass of Saudi Arabia. When 'Abd al-'Azīz Bin Bāz (later Muftī of the Saudi realms) in the 1980s denounced Ibadis in Oman, we find even a Shi'ah Omani standing up for the Ibadi Muftī: "The attack on him had nothing to do with sects in Islam. He was attacked as an Omani, and that is how we understood Bin Bāz's words" (quoted in Eickelman 2001: 203). Intellectuals will often stress "Gulf unity" (Gause 1994: 87–8, al-Rumayḥī [1983]

1995, 'Abdullāh (ed.) 1998, Yamani, M. 2000: 36-7), yet Bahrain, for instance, has a memory of rulers recruiting help from the "mainland" (Khuri 1980: 87, 122-3) and in the run-up to elections, in 2002, the suggestion of dual nationality for GCC citizens raised fears not only that privileges such as housing might be compromised but that Shi'ah votes would be overwhelmed (*Ṣawt al-Baḥrayn* 234, Jul. 2002). The argument is pursued in national terms:

> Right! Off you go,
> Go away from our land.
> Bahrain is not your desert ...
> ... Your roots are not here
> But rather <u>our</u> branches and origin.

If a certain emphasis is added in the smaller states by their lying in the Saudi shadow, Saudi Arabia itself has moved beyond the simple equation of territory and ruling family (Fandy 1999: 242-3). Whatever the rulers' efforts, and whatever the perception of shared experience (perhaps quite minor), a feeling of shared position in the world is entirely real in the face of such disparate pressures as the treatment of Palestine, the regional claims of the United States and the attitude of neighbours who are felt to wish the Kingdom ill. Great regions such as Najd and Hijaz, though the practical effect in Hijazi minds is recent, are encompassed in national claims. Hani Yamani's polemic aim "To be a Saudi" (Yamani, H. 1997) seemed eccentric when first published; it now seems less so, and the term *sha'b* or "people" is starting to apply quite naturally to other Gulf populations, running somewhat at odds with family imagery insofar as the *sha'b* is conceived as an undifferentiated mass. As "brothers" and "sisters" in the nation, citizens form a populist body of the kind so evident in support for soccer teams. As "children" or dependants of a ruler they form a more personalised set of the kind made evident in patronage at boat races or camel races.[16] The latter is the image preferred by the state's publicists.

The ideology of "one family" (Fandy 1999: 24, cf. Dresch in Chapter 6, al-Mughni and Tétreault in Chapter 9) remains largely unexplored as yet, and the image of rulers as fathers must remain provisional.[17] Certainly this is "house politics" (Anderson, L. 2000: 58-9, Shryock 2000, 2001). Yet beyond royal households in the literal sense (that is, beyond the *dīwān* or court and the "private department") lie society's other households whose connections with rulers are unspecified by co-residence or genealogy. These households are themselves surely different from the models of 50 years ago: "nuclear families" are everywhere an issue (Graham 1978: 224, al-Easa 1983, al-Thakeb 1985, Altorki and Cole 1989: 211-12), and the term *'ā'ilah* (whence *'ā'ilīyah* or familialism) refers to a replicable unit one suspects was not isolable in Arabia until recently. Now it is. The forms of *qarābah* or "closeness" that govern much state activity arise with the state itself (cf. Eickelman and Piscatori 1996: 82). Although certain principles carry through (Fandy 1999: 23, 30, 246), as they do in the case of rank and wealth, the empirical structures do not and the question remains open of how individuals and small family groups relate to power.

The ideology of familialism runs parallel with that of the *majlis*, the "sitting" or council where decisions are ideally promulgated. Aḥmad al-Ḥaddād, for instance, listing attributes of "the Gulf personality" – honouring one's guest, cleaving steadfastly to Islamic law, diligence in prayer (as usual, much is formulaic) – lists also the acceptance of what he calls "shaykhocracy", for "the policy of the Ruler having an open door is still current through meeting and getting to know the rulers at their *majlis* or *dīwān* … ." (al-Ḥaddād 1998: 86-7). Already near the start of prosperity from oil, however, access had become difficult (Lienhardt 1993: 43-4, 2001: 197-8).[18] In the mid-1990s, the catch-phrase "government by fax" was used, and petitions were indeed submitted that way; technology moves on, and Dubai's lead is followed by Saudi Arabia now in "e-government", which means e-administration, not the chance to supplicate rulers personally.[19] Politically these in some ways are virtual societies (cf. Naciri 1997: 140). The etiquette of the mobile phone is thus revealing. The time spent massaging contacts (*shū lawn-ak? shū al-khabar?*) is impressive and not to have calls returned has a value familiar from tales of Hollywood; access to private numbers is an issue (as indeed is what number you have yourself), and the habit some notables display of gifting their mobiles to retainers means a constant testing of whether one is still in the charmed circle. Where, then, is the state or power?

Fandy touches on issues of this kind in discussing the sons of Salmān, Prince of Riyad, the recipient of Chevron's book on Dir'īyah. Around each young prince is a following of ten or 20 families who depend on that prince for patronage: "the role of the so-called middle class is not to compete with the royal princes but to limit other people's access to them" (Fandy 1999: 15). The implications are profound. Despite a few shaykhs or princes in most Gulf states holding grand levées, limitation of access is a salient feature of the whole region and recurs at every level of bureaucracy, where the hierarchy of offices and outer offices is of a kind with the nested courtyards of palaces. A constant theme in discussion is thus *wāsiṭah*, "mediation", "contacts", the famous "vitamin W" of Arab cartoons and jokes.[20]

The idea of government oscillates between personal concern on the part of notables and a standardised set of rules; but whichever is favoured at the moment, the ideal is not only of prosperity but of fairness and just treatment (Yamani, M. 2000: 46). The reach of such ideals is limited in practice. It is often a shock to remember, for instance, how far from global or transnational issues the badu of Oman still lie (Chatty 1996); much of Saudi Arabia, also, is far off the beaten track, and the modern (or post-modern) architecture of Riyad is supplemented by far broader areas of truck-stops, little restaurants serving *mandī* chicken, and crude cement houses in a wasteland of blowing plastic bags. Land allocation and development is everywhere government controlled, however, and has been so from near the start of state formation; services, too, mean government; education is a vast bureaucracy. The apparatus of control and administration "is no longer merely an adjunct of the country's ruling families but is a central element of political life in its own right" (Lawson 1985: 21, cf. Crystal in Chapter 7). That apparatus, in contemporary style, is everywhere and nowhere.

The state, as Mai Yamani says of the Saudi case (Yamani, M. 2000: 32 cf. Khalaf and Hammoud 1988: 351, Altorki and Cole 1989: 112-13, Al-Rasheed 2002: 125-6 and *passim*), is omnipresent. Yet the Gulf is not conspicuous for what Lewis Mumford (1961) called "Baroque cities".[21] It is conspicuous, as plans for new buildings so often show, for "VIP entrances". If a clue is sought as to forms of politics it may well lie with those of domestic architecture, where the semi-public space of the *majlis* or meeting room disappears within compound walls (Nagy 1998, cf. Naciri 1997: 140, 144-5). Presumably something similar might arise were the present ruling families "constitutionalised" or marginalised, for society exhibits the same basic forms as government. One suspects the general style may prove resilient.

Economics, politics and society

The West still lives with an image of GCC states that dates to the oil boom of 30 years ago. Many citizens of these states live also with an image of "unlimited good" (Khalaf 1992). When oil prices slumped in the 1980s, however, governments came under pressure, and the difficulty of absorbing revenue, from which the story starts, has persisted with results that elsewhere imply violent chaos: thus Saudi income per capita worse than halved in 20 years, from $16,650 in 1981 to $7,230 in 2000 (*The Economist* 22 Apr. 2000, *al-Ahram Weekly* 7 Nov. 2001). The rich and poor have everywhere in the Gulf become more widely separated; distinctions among families have become more pronounced; and within broader family groupings age makes a great difference. A sociologist thus depicts the lot of young Omanis: "Their fathers ... came home to government salaries of $3,000 a month. These guys come out of our own universities, and have to start hunting for work in the private sector, where starting rates now are more like $500" (quoted in *The Economist* 23 Mar. 2002).

What outlasts fluctuations in for instance income figures is the Gulf's exposure to a wider world. Although "the Gulf is not just oil", and some states have only minor income from hydrocarbons,[22] the modern Gulf is marked indelibly by the presence of oil and natural gas (see Figure 4), which inserts the region in others' imaginations and makes the powers of the world central to Gulf concerns. More than this, the Gulf falls in the purview of the world's one hyperpower. The United States draws almost 30 per cent of its petroleum imports from the Middle East at low stated cost, and what costs should be listed elsewhere, to cover "defending" the oil or account for deferred taxation, are hard to guess at.[23] Saudi Arabia alone, meanwhile, controls 25 per cent of the world's proven oil reserves (more importantly, it has low production costs); Qatar controls more natural gas than does North America; and, at least in the short term, the Middle East is looked to by strategists for increased energy production.

Figure 4: Global Comparison of GCC Oil and Gas Reserves, Production and Consumption, End 2000

	Oil			
	Proven Reserves 1000 mill. Barrels	Percentage of Global Reserves	Percentage of Global Production	Percentage of Global Consumption
USA	29.7	2.8	9.8	25.6
Canada/Mexico	34.7	3.3	8.3	4.8
S/Central America	95.2	9.0	9.7	6.2
Europe	19.1	1.9	9.2	21.4
FSU	65.3	6.4	11.0	5.0
Kuwait	96.5	9.2	2.9	0.2
Qatar	13.2	1.3	1.0	n/a
Saudi Arabia	261.7	25.0	12.3	1.8
UAE	97.8	9.3	3.2	0.4
Other ME	577.0	20.5	11.6	3.5
Total ME	1,046.2	65.3	31.0	5.9
Africa	74.8	7.1	10.4	3.3
Asia/Pacific	44.0	4.2	10.6	27.8

Gas				
	Proven Reserves trill. cubic meters	Percentage of Global Reserves	Percentage of Global Production	Percentage of Global Consumption
USA	4.7	3.2	22.9	27.4
Canada/Mexico	2.6	1.7	8.4	4.7
S/Central America	6.9	3.9	3.9	3.8
Europe	5.2	3.5	12.0	19.1
FSU	56.7	37.8	27.8	22.8
Kuwait	1.5	1.0	0.4	0.4
Qatar	11.2	7.4	1.2	0.6
Saudi Arabia	6.1	4.0	1.9	2.0
UAE	6.0	4.0	1.6	1.4
Other ME	27.8	18.6	3.6	0.9
Total ME	52.5	35.0	8.7	5.3
Africa	11.2	7.4	5.3	2.4
Asia/Pacific	10.3	6.8	11.0	12.1

Source: BP *Statistical Review of World Energy, 2001*

Beneath the umbrella of US "security" both governments and people must depend on trade whose forms are highly mythicised, as if they dominated world affairs. Yet local economies are small. Altogether the annual GDP of the Gulf monarchies in recent years, including hydrocarbon activity, has been roughly that of Belgium: their combined national income is about that of Switzerland, whose population is a quarter theirs, and the rulers of the Gulf, each accustomed to enormous deference, are frogs on rather small lily-pads. Nor are Gulf-based institutions large. As elsewhere in the world recently, so in the Middle East, banks have been merging and figures thus become outdated, but as of 2000 the top 40 banks in the GCC by capital were about equivalent to the largest one British bank, HSBC.[24] Trade figures, too, prove sobering, as if everywhere it were natural to trade with distant powers instead of neighbours.[25]

Economists sometimes speak of the ratio of foreign trade to GDP as a measure of "openness". The countries of the GCC, quite unlike for instance Egypt, surpass the nations of Western Europe on this score.[26] If we added overseas investment to the calculation, though nearly all flows outwards, and added to that remittances (expatriate workers in Saudi Arabia sent home almost $19 billion in 1996 alone),[27] then the degree of involvement with a wider world would be still more striking. Gulf citizens themselves have placed their wealth abroad. A sum of $300–500 billion for the GCC as a whole is often mentioned, but such figures have been current for 15 years and more

(Road and Harrison 1985) and whether they were accurate in the first place and whether since then they have increased or decreased is unclear.[28] Foreign direct investment (FDI) inwards is meanwhile extremely low and the region is characterised by through-puts of goods and money which the "thinness" of local economies' means are not translated into relative autonomy, a condition typical of the Third World.

The parallel with poorer states goes further. More than half the "local" inhabitants were not even born in 1975 – the height of the first oil boom – and recent estimates put children less than 15 years old at well over 40 per cent of the total in both Saudi Arabia and Oman, a higher proportion than in India or sub-Saharan Africa (UNDP 2001: 154-7). This demographic shift accentuates a dramatic rupture brought on by "the great transformation", and Clive Holes remarks (Chapter 2, cf. al-Sharhān 1990) how words familiar to people of a certain age are simply unknown to younger relatives.[29] The arbitrariness of the way in which a recent past is depicted by state ritual is not surprising. Injustice, meanwhile, is attributed not to internal developments so much as to the poison of the world economy. Initial prosperity from oil thus produced a small class with vast resources, runs an Emirati argument (al-Badrī 1996: 37), "and a group of non-national merchants have joined themselves to this class, who have come to invest their wealth in a virgin society ...". National merchants and notables themselves, it is feared, "have recourse to dubious (*ghayr salīmah*) ways and means of acquiring wealth" (ibid. 53).

Certain aspects of trade draw specific criticism. A large part of British exports to Saudi Arabia, for instance, was in recent years "defence related" (Hirst 2000); the UAE – national population about 600,000 people – formed agreements in the year 2000 for more foreign arms than any state on earth, much of it from US sources. A sad lack of practicality in the Saudi case was made evident by the Gulf crisis of 1990-91, when Iraq seized Kuwait, and shock at the Kingdom's dependence on foreign powers has never dissipated (Al-Rasheed 2002: 163-84), though American-manufactured fighter aircraft flew above the reviewing stands at the 1999 Janādirīyah to spell out the initials of successive kings. The other conspicuous aspect of expenditure in the age of wealth was, broadly speaking, welfare. This has proved often unsustainable. Saudi Arabia thus raised utility charges in the mid-1980s (ibid. 150), but a decade later faced even worse problems (Yamani, M. 2000: 73). Kuwait, meanwhile, as the first welfare-rentier state, shows every sign of intending to be the last. But none of these countries can sustain the overall level of spending they once did. The ambiguous term "state" needs leaving aside for a moment. Rather, where do governments stand?

The Saudi government at the time of prosperity kept much of its wealth in liquid form and the Kingdom is now in dire straits financially, with a foreign debt of the order of $35 billion and the government owing domestic lenders – note well – the equivalent of the whole annual GDP, something close to $170 billion.[30] The government of Kuwait, having invested abroad for "future generations", is less badly off, though not as wealthy as before the Iraqi invasion of 1990–91. Abu Dhabi, though not the other emirates of the UAE, is extremely wealthy and the government's overseas investment portfolio might well be over $200 billion. Oman and Bahrain have been less fortunate, though the discipline of foreign loans was preferred to the Saudi problem of limitless domestic debt. Qatar, although the figures look comparable to those for certain neighbours (see Figure 5), exemplifies a more profound issue.

Figure 5: Total Debt of Selected GCC States

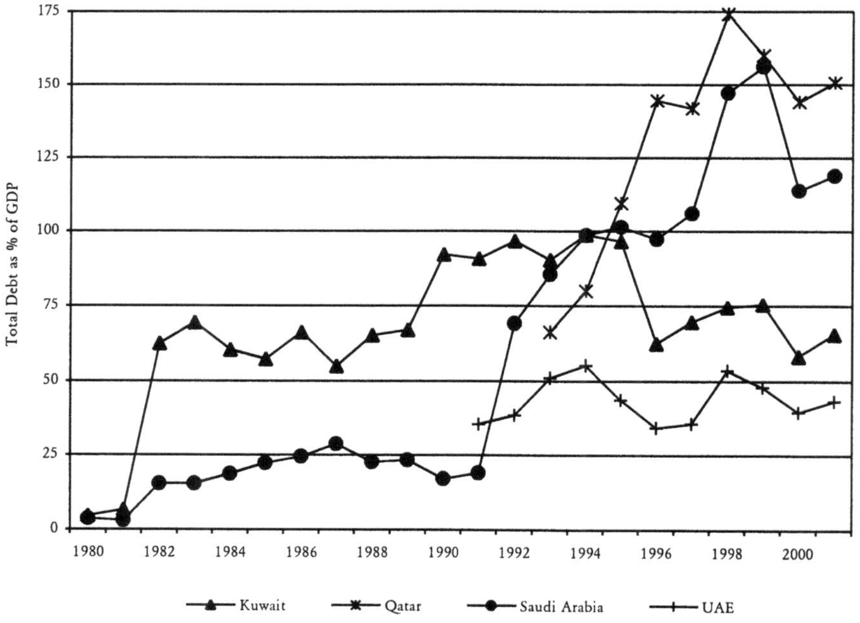

Souce: Economist Intelligence Unit

Twenty years ago Qatar was the very type of a rentier-welfare state, where a "national" population of 100,000 enjoyed, through the ruler, some 300,000 bpd of oil production. By the mid-1990s the country had foreign debts close to $5 billion, and by the end of the decade repayments were in excess of $500 million a year. This was not, however, mere extravagance. Rather, a huge investment was made in developing oil resources and establishing the country as a gas exporter.[31] Presumably arguments about the pace and extent of such investment (present against future prosperity) contributed to the "generational" shift of Shaykh Ḥamad Āl Thānī deposing his father, Shaykh Khalīfah, in June 1995. But Qatar, where the nettle of economic reform has been grasped more firmly than in most Gulf states, is reminiscent now of an ambitiously expansive company, where the levels and the structure of debt are to be assessed against plans to develop markets and against, as it were, a price/earnings ratio.

Governments are not simply rentiers anymore, but managers who must generate wealth, not just control it. They are not in quite the same position as a company, however, despite the prevalence of commercial language. They can establish legal regimes to draw overseas investment, for instance, and they control territory, with implications beyond merely the revenue from hydrocarbons. Whole fortunes in Qatar and Kuwait alike, for example, have rested on land ownership. Riyad, Jiddah and Dubai, even Muscat, are all in their way now global cities (cf. Friedman, J. 1986, Sassen 2001), and the growth of Gulf economies, no matter how uneven, has meant a huge rise in the price of urban land and a vast source of revenue from building rent – a question very much of particular place, not of abstract space and its calculations (Harvey 1989: 295). Access depends entirely on national governments.

In all of these states the huge foreign workforce forms part of what some call "transnational communities" (Portes et al. 1999: 227–8). The question might be asked why local elites did not opt for transnationalism themselves by cutting loose from local concerns entirely. After all, when Shaykh Khalīfah chose exile from Qatar in June 1995, he took with him, so to speak, the cheque book; many Gulf citizens of lesser rank have the means and skills to flourish elsewhere, and the wealthy spend much of the year abroad, where they also invest. But the number of ex-Gulf citizens is vanishingly small. What allows these elites to operate in wider fields is often wealth of precisely the kind so evident in land. Prince Walīd bin Ṭalāl (one of very many nephews of the Saudi King), for instance, is something of a favourite with the Western financial media for investing in high-profile "global" enterprise (Gause 1994: 180, Sakr 2001b: 71–3) from banking through theme parks to television. The basis of his wealth, however, is supposed by some to be land in Riyad, a facsimile of alienable real property held at the King's pleasure (*The Economist* 5 Feb. 99, 5 Sep. 1999, cf. *Middle East Economic Digest* 18 Jun. 1999), the most spectacular example of which is the Kingdom Centre, a skyscraper designed specifically to exceed the

Fayṣalīyah Centre, itself of course linked to the family of the late King Fayṣal.

The importance of territorial control reaches far beyond the case of internationally known figures. Governments each cultivate a local economy that sustains, among other things, the value of urban land, and which nowhere reduces to simple "redistribution". The inequalities that arise are obvious. But they are, so to speak, internalised, such that citizens' options are defined very largely by national boundaries and by national governments controlling localised blocs of population. We live still in a world of nation-states, despite much rhetoric, and governments show no sign of disappearing.[32] They are basic, indeed, to the global system. The World Trade Organisation (WTO), for instance, rests on the premise of geographical sovereignty and supposed autonomy, and much writing on "globalisation", whether pro or con, understates the point that the contracting parties, each of which joins on its own terms through a complex of bilateral negotiations, are national governments. All the Gulf states have joined, except Saudi Arabia, for whom membership is presented as a panacea.[33] In a globalising world the importance of governments is in many ways likely to increase. But the blocs of population who must figure in Gulf calculations are different in kind from those of most of the WTO's signatories.

Wealth and population

The instability of demography in the Arab World and the overdetermination of demographic perceptions by ideology are discussed by Philippe Fargues (2000). The Gulf presents extreme cases. The rate of growth of the Saudi national population, for instance, has recently dropped, or the estimate been revised downward, from more than 3.5 per cent annually a decade ago to around 2.9 per cent annually for the period 1992–99 (*Gulf News* 26 Mar. 2001).[34] That is still high by global standards, but official estimates of growth in GDP per annum have often run at little more than 1 per cent. To plot the lines of population and national wealth is to conjure a vision of disaster (Bonine 1997, Cordesman 1998, 2001: 26). "National" unemployment rates are often of the order of 20 per cent or more (among Saudi males it may be a good deal higher: see Yamani, M. 2000: 77, Henry and Springborg 2001: 179, *Arabies Trends* Oct. 2002) yet much of the workforce consists of foreigners, who in several Gulf states outnumber citizens.

The detailed patterns differ from case to case, and have done so in each state over time, but an overall trend is plain. Where local labour was first replaced by Arab labour, the Arabs in turn have largely been displaced by Asians, even in Kuwait which long showed a preference for Arab migrants (Fargues 1991). In Saudi Arabia there are now 1.25 million Indians alone, and somewhere between 0.25 and 0.50 million Indonesians (for 1997 estimates see Figure 6). None has the prospect of political rights or influence. The status that accrues to citizens or nationals, by contrast with the migrants, is distinctive though not perhaps wholly unprecedented, and Longva draws a parallel with ancient Athens (cf. Salamé 1994: 100, Hicks and al-Najjar 1995). The crucial mode of dominance in the Gulf, however, is *kafālah* or "sponsorship" (Ibrāhīm, S. 1982: 32-4, Beaugé 1986, Longuenesse 1991), which has no obvious precedent except in local common sense about morality and rank. Briefly put, instead of governments simply limiting the overall number of foreign residents and assigning their distribution to the market or to state control, foreign residents are placed directly under the control of specific individuals and local companies who act as the foreigner's *kafīl* or sponsor.

Figure 6: Major Expatriate Communities in Saudi Arabia, 1997

Arabs	thousands	Percentage of total population	Others	thousands	Percentage of total population
Egyptians	1,200	6.4	Indians	1,250	6.4
Yemenis	500	2.6	Pakistanis	800	4.1
Jordanians/ Palestinians	270	1.4	Filipinos	500	2.6
Sudanese	250	1.3	Bangladeshis	450	2.3
Syrians	170	0.9	Indonesians	250	1.3
Kuwaitis	120	0.6	Sri Lankans	150	0.8

Source: A. Kapiszewski, *Nationals and Expatriates*, pp. 39, 65.

The unusual demographic structure of Gulf countries, whereby much of the labour force is "foreign", might stand comparison with the recent North Atlantic pattern of exporting industry to Third World countries. In both cases wealth is generated by enforcing differential access for capital and labour; in both cases local populations may find the logic obscure or indeed objectionable. But the Gulf option gives citizens a seeming precedence at home. One aspect, indeed, is domestic service. Crystal, in Chapter 7, shows how control and surveillance that elsewhere depend on state "policing" devolve on the heads of Kuwaiti households: *kafālah* has profound implications beyond this for the status of nationals socially, as Longva explains in Chapter 5 (cf. Khalaf 1992: 76-7, Longva 1997).[35] But labour is not only household labour, and foreign workers are the source of much minor wealth from retail, manufacturing and trade. *Kafālah* thus had grave implications for the "rentier state" formulations of 15 and 20 years ago. Where many of the national population are themselves minor rentiers, their interests may well be at odds with "national" planning, and these local economies, based on imported labour, have a logic that rentier theory consistently ignored. Philippe Fargues once asked if migration in Kuwait obeyed the "conjuncture" of changing oil revenue, and answered with a qualified no (Fargues 1991). Saudi Arabia deported immigrants in the hard times of the 1980s, and issued fewer visas (Al-Rasheed 2002: 150–2), but the proportion of non-Saudis in the population has continued growing (Kapiszewski 2001: 40). The pattern seems to hold widely (ibid. 72).

Under these pressures and others, the importance of citizenship increases, and the line around the privileged status of "national" or *muwāṭin* is drawn more tightly. Saudi Arabia thus recruited nationals quite extensively until the 1960s (Yamani, M. 2000: 7–8); the UAE did so through the 1970s (see Chapter 6). Neither state does so now, and to "become a citizen" is rare. Kuwait is another case of tightening self-definition (Khalaf 1992: 72, cf. Longva in Chapter 5, Crystal in Chapter 7), and all run counter, as do cases elsewhere in the world, to facile talk among Western-domiciled elites of diasporas, creolisation and transnationalism. Behind the huge stress on citizens' rights and identity in the Gulf case, however, lie specific conceptions of society, encouraged by current circumstance.

Again relations between the sexes provide an instance. Whatever governmental or intellectuals' rhetoric on the importance of females in a national workforce, and the practical importance of women workers in some cases (Seikaly 1997, Chatty 2000), women in many Gulf states are depicted as potential "mothers of the nation" and as responsible for "maintaining the traditional family structure" (al-Mughni and Tétreault in Chapter 9). Many women themselves seem to favour the image of good "social reproducers" (see Chapter 5). Identity, in short, matters more than does economic productivity. The families to which women are depicted as central are ranked among themselves, and exclude or make subordinate their "local" inferiors almost as the national family excludes foreigners: marriage is thus an important theme. So too is descent or origin. Even in formal terms, grades of citizenship exist internally, a phenomenon which some identify with "tribalism" (al-Rumayḥī [1983] 1995, al-Naqīb 1996) and which many Gulf writers (e.g. al-Ḥaddād 1998, al-Muṭawwa' 1998) think at odds with nationalism. The depiction of a "national family" in terms of shared ancestry omits a great deal, as does that of actual families or other groupings.

A parallel between past and present is suggestive here. John Wilkinson reviews concepts of territory in Oman and what was then the Trucial Coast in the period before oil wealth, and touches on the concept of "noble" tribes and their satellites or clients (Wilkinson

1983). In times of scarce grazing these clients would be denied access. The core, meanwhile, typically covered several centres of production, at each of which the population was mixed, comprising members of the core itself, plus clients, strangers and personal dependants (ibid. 309–10) The core was thus a moral category, not an empirical unit. The image of shared genealogy obscures as much as it reveals, for shaykhs would have around them, even in hard times, slaves and retainers who were not kin, while persons with a nominal "closeness" (*qarābah*) were excluded. The logic of *qarābah* itself may turn on differential control of resources beyond the group. Again, perhaps, a principle carries through. Though tribes are not a live issue, rank and access surely are.

There are commonly reckoned three circles of identity in Gulf society beyond that of *muwāṭin* or fellow citizen: *khalījī* or Gulf, then Arab, then *ajnabī* or foreign (Longuenesse 1991: 128, Kapiszewski 2001: 179–80). But the structures of privacy work almost in reverse order. Those outsiders allowed within the core of "family" are those who count for little socially; those who count for more are systematically excluded (cf. Dresch 2000a: 117). As Longva explains in her chapter on Kuwait, Arabs are thus excluded in ways Asian servants, almost chattels, are not. Meanwhile, if one wants to understand the workings of a Gulf company, one does better to befriend the American auditor, the British company secretary or the Indian office manager than the owner's cousins. The constraints of privacy beyond the *maḥram* (the little circle of non-marriageable kin) are everywhere strictest with those closest, and the net effect is a pattern of knowledge and exclusivity quite different from that of, say, European racism.

A second great transformation?

This ambiguous position is now confronted by the (Anglo-Saxon) assumption that economics connects in some simple way with political virtue: global forces encourage transparency and accountability, runs a common argument, which themselves would be conducive to liberty and justice. This is not only a North Atlantic vision. For years it has drawn local modernisers of a broadly "secular" bent (Gause 1994: 53, Yamani, H. 1997: 110–14, 116–17), something like it is current among Islamists (Fandy 1999: 99, Henry and Springborg 2001: 185, 193), and the next stage of the argument among all concerned might well be for a "share-holding democracy". In practice, however, the results of economic change are just as ambiguous as in other countries. In Dubai, for instance, a few large firms run the taxi business, providing an efficient and profitable service, and offering the chance to invest through shares, but the little people (*'āmmat al-nās*) no longer have direct control; in Abu Dhabi a less "rational" system still allows the poorer citizens – and their wives and aunts, conspicuously – to own a taxi, or two or three, each with its Afghan or Pakistani driver to whom the owner acts as *kafīl* or "sponsor". Business more generally, whatever its scale, tends more to the Abu Dhabi model of family or personal control than to that of the publicly quoted company (Henry and Springborg 2001: 85, 97).[36]

Attempts to launch stock markets have encountered problems. The *Sūq al-Manākh* disaster in Kuwait (1982) caused huge discontent as to who was bailed out and who was left to bear the losses (Darwiche 1986, Gavrielides 1987: 170–1, Khalaf 1992: 65, Henry and Springborg 2001: 189). More recently a boom and bust in the shares of a Dubai real-estate company left many Emiratis with appalling debts, having borrowed to join the price-bubble. Oman (see *Middle East Economic Digest* 13 Feb. 1998) is not alone in setting limits now on what banks can lend citizens to buy shares. This "paternal" concern is provoked – in fact demanded on occasion by citizens themselves – precisely by the freedoms that Anglo-Saxon ideology insists are to citizens' advantage. Restrictions are meanwhile placed on foreign ownership, yet visions are pursued of supposed time-gaps between exchanges in Hong Kong and Frankfurt such that the Gulf's location might allow local access to global trading.[37]

In the longer term the choice appears stark to some. One can treat economic matters and the structure of society itself as in effect private and have most of one's population live in poverty, or one can pursue current forms of investment and global trade and be drawn into forms of transparency that have not been usual in the region. The options in fact are not so simple.[38] Family business empires, run in great privacy, thrive in the modern world, and trading states elsewhere at other times have often valued secrecy: Dubai as the Republic of Venice is not a wholly far-fetched image.

The issue, politically, is how to handle changes in the structure of access and of information. Such changes are under way already. Land, for instance, at the start of the great transformation, was appropriated by rulers and distributed in part to citizens, but in most places foreigners were excluded. Dubai is now giving leaseholds, even freeholds, to foreigners. Saudi Arabia has agreed that foreign investors can own real estate (*Arab News* 29 Jan. 2002). More than that, they can sponsor (provide *kafālah* for) their own employees, thus bypassing an essential principle of the social system (*al-Wasaṭ* 405, 1 Nov. 1999), but foreign investment is prohibited in key areas (*Middle East Economic Digest* 23 Feb. 2001). No simple transition is in progress. Bahrain and Oman both allow other GCC nationals to own real estate (*Gulf News* 6 Mar. 2000), but land ownership in Abu Dhabi is entirely by grace and favour, and Saudi Arabia is still "considering" the issue despite the promise of land for foreign companies. How access is defined and controlled remains arbitrary.[39] Information remains at a premium and, just as before, denotes rank and precedence.

In one sense these countries are extremely open. In another they are among the least open societies on earth, and North Atlantic rhetorics of "openness" (where political, economic, even personal virtue are equated loosely) seem often unrealistic. To citizens themselves a whole moral order may seem threatened. Great concern is expressed locally about materialism and consumerism or *istihlākīyah* (e.g. *al-Khalīj* 18 Feb. 2000, cf. Altorki and Cole 1989: 244, Yamani, H. 1997: 35ff.), and the claim that "this does not reflect the culture of the Gulf but Western culture" (al-Badrī 1996: 60) hardly wards off the practical effect; consumption and commoditisation govern young people's lives in Saudi shopping malls just as in Californian malls (Wynn 1997). Levels of domestic or household debts are a constant source of local worry (*Gulf News* 5 Feb. 2000, *al-Bayān* 15 Apr. 2001), while the sight of post-dated or simply uncashed cheques often poses to visitors the question of how personal realities relate to public statistics of finance and economy. In the circumstances a certain nostalgia is to be expected. Once, runs a common theme, we were all of us kin and neighbours, living lives that made sense: now we are mixed in with others and subject to forces we do not control. All that is solid does indeed seem to melt into air. The exceptions are an image of family and the reality of passport holding, where nationality is equated with descent and descent in turn with biology. DNA samples might thus be taken to see who really is Kuwaiti (*Gulf News* 21 Sep. 1998).

If openness has been removed from so fundamental an issue as self-description, we should not expect simple "global" effects in politics, economy or culture, and it may be worth noting these three in sequence. The literature on growing "democratisation", for example, is vast and often seems to imply that some radical change is imminent. In fact, however, Kuwait's National Assembly was elected by something close to universal male suffrage as early as 1971 (Gavrielides 1987: 154), and despite suspensions of the constitution, there is nothing new in Kuwait about votes and parliaments. Similar elections took place in Bahrain in October 2002, and part of the Bahraini package (*al-Wasaṭ* 473, 19 Feb. 2001) was the Ruler's elevation from Shaykh to King. Saudi Arabia has moved more slowly. Kuwaitis, Qataris and Bahrainis may themselves therefore wish to claim civic virtue: "we" are liberalising, progressive and self-confident, "they" are not. But everywhere a certain sobriety and caution are evident, and Kuwait's parliamentary disorders are pointed to by citizens of neighbouring states as an example not to follow. Yet the key to Kuwait, as to all the others, is surely that a calculated "openness" does not extend beyond the circle of state-defined kin or citizens. The political is not as advertised.

Globalisation in its economic aspect may be encountered in several ways. Saudi Arabia, far less open politically than most of the world's governments, can open power generation, for instance, to foreign investment and consider quite seriously freeing areas of oil and gas production. Kuwait, on the other hand, has a high degree of public debate over policy, and it is here that foreign investment meets its greatest blockage (Henry and Springborg 2001: 170, 190). A "national" resource is guarded closely by a national parliament (cf. *al-Wasaṭ* 488, 4 Jun. 2001). The country meanwhile shows "a growing dependence on government to fuel economic growth and provide employment", with the public sector accounting for 75 per cent of the whole economy (*Middle East Economic Digest* 28 Jun. 2002), and the only notable "reform" to date is to levy health insurance on foreign workers, not on Kuwaiti citizens (*Christian Science Monitor* 18 Apr. 2001).

The question of culture (an elusive term, anyway) is at least as ambivalent. The rise of "offshore" media operations in the 1990s (Sakr 2001b) made the Gulf more conspicuous in the Arab and Muslim Worlds, but hardly made the Gulf any better known. The Saudi-funded television company, MBC, was driven by commercial pressures to game-shows and quizzes; the torch of current affairs was taken up by al-Jazeera, funded by Qatar's Ruler, and recently it has found imitators in Dubai and Abu Dhabi, with useful effects in the broader world. Some see this as an element of a "public sphere" expanding through the Gulf itself, and the possibilities even of enlightened despotism can seem important: "Qatar's ruler, Shaykh Ḥamad bin Khalīfah Āl Thānī, takes almost the attitude of Prussia's Frederick the Great (1712–86) in fostering open information and debate ... " (Eickelman 2001: 196). Frederick's celebrated line on the place of his people in this arrangement is not quoted: "They are to say what they please, and I am to do what I please". In fact they are not free to say very much about Shaykh Ḥamad (Fandy 2000: 387, cf. el-Nawawy and Iskandar 2002: 89–90) and coverage of Qatar itself is minimal. Few Qataris, one suspects, would have it otherwise.

The recent migration of Arab print and television operations to Dubai (*Khaleej Times* 28 Apr. 2002) suggests, among other things, an astute political move on Dubai's part. As host to global coverage, Dubai can expect a certain discretion about its own affairs and a fine opportunity to promote its global "brand". But everywhere in the Gulf exclusivity and discretion go hand in hand, turning on local identities that have long since been nationalised and thus made natural. Before the great transformation, political claims of whatever scale ebbed and flowed across a human geography of tribes, trade routes, villages and small towns (cf. Lawless 1986, Fattah 1997). Less and less space is left now for such connections. Even for a Bahraini to become a Saudi or a Saudi to become an Emirati is more difficult than it was some years ago. But funding of transnational media by members of ruling families, then commercial pressures, give a curious illusion of "the Gulf" as the cultural centre of a whole world, with endless depictions of drum-and-string ensembles in the distinctive white robes and head-cloths of a recently constructed Gulf identity.

Connections and identity

A paradox of economic integration nearly everywhere on earth has been the rise of particularity, and every group, of whatever type, now claims a culture. The term offers all the simplicities race once offered, though the new conventions appeal less to blood than to artefacts and heritage. Madawi Al-Rasheed (Chapter 4) shows a typical case in Omani circles, where the culture of Zanzibar takes the form of simply sweets and flour-cakes with perhaps a Swahili band. Christa Salamandra (Chapter 3) finds the other type-form of this phenomenon in a cash-strapped British university, where sensitivity to the culture of Gulf Arabs translates into management of deference: only by cultivating an agreed set of stereotypes can one be sure of extracting money from one's clientele. It is well to remember (see Just 1995: 291–2) that the nearest modern Greek has to offer to "culture" in the current sense is *politismos*. Part I explores how culture and identity are sustained and validated.

Naomi Sakr, in the first of our chapters, examines satellite TV, the great medium by which culture in a trivial and thus penetrating sense is supposed to be spread across national boundaries. Cultural imperialism is an often-heard refrain in the Middle East generally and the Gulf especially. In fact Gulf transnational media have developed programmes sensitive to local interests, but sheer financial imperatives draw them to make compromises. Well-connected owners such as Prince Walīd bin Ṭalāl and Shaykh Walīd al-Ibrāhīm – both part of the extended Saudi royal family – thus serve as intermediaries between Western and local enterprises. The effect has not been straightforward. Regionally owned media, which depict both the Gulf and the Arab World at large, have emerged with quite intimate ties to "the West" and its cultural products, though transmitting in many shades of Arabic.

Clive Holes (Chapter 2) examines self-depiction on local Bahraini television. Through an analysis of *musalsalāt*, or soap operas, he charts the emergence of a standardised local dialect and links linguistic patterns to communal identity. The relatively disadvantaged Baḥārnah, or Shiʿah, are gradually accommodating to the dominant (Sunni) speech-patterns within Bahrain which themselves form part of a larger, regional standard dialect. Television programmes often trade in nostalgia. But over time they reflect and reinforce a style of speech that is becoming increasingly common to the interlocking social, business and political networks of the Gulf. This occurs over longer periods than most "political" change. Its effects are in some ways far more profound, for being Bahraini, or indeed being "of the Gulf" (*min ahl al-khalīj*), acquires the status of deep-rooted common sense.

Christa Salamandra's analysis of Arab London (Chapter 3) reveals another dimension of identity formation, off-site cultural intermediaries. Despite dwindling numbers of Gulf residents and tourists, London-based intermediaries have continued through the 1990s to offer services that formalise Gulf heritage, largely on a national basis, and re-present it to Gulf audiences. Publishing (as of coffee-table photographic collections), art galleries and educational institutions in London have become industries that essentialise and commodify Gulf culture. In the process, they have satisfied Gulf elite expectations of what it means to be "Saudi" or "Kuwaiti", for instance, and perpetuated their own role as "gatekeepers". But even the dependants of elites are accorded a certain status by British institutions keen to take their money, and for a young Gulf student studying abroad the idea of Gulf identity is made real.

Identity is an old enough word in English but gains its current value first in the personal sense, in a world where such a thing as an "identity crisis" became imaginable, and then in a social sense. Arabic *huwīyah* shows a similar trajectory. Where once the obvious usage might have been of personal ID cards, the phrase *huwīyah waṭanīyah* (national identity) now recurs in much Gulf literature in the collective sense: there is something specific, it is claimed, about Kuwaitis, Qataris or Bahrainis, as if people did not simply live in different places but somehow were of different kinds.[40] These essentialising claims are explored in Part II.

Madawi Al-Rasheed (Chapter 4) takes a case that spans the old dispensation of society and the new. Since their return to Oman in the 1970s, "Zanzibaris" have not wholly lost their in-betweenness. Rather, they have used it to function as mediators, first in the oil industry and state security, later in tourism. Elsewhere in the Gulf, people with distant "foreign" connections have often been marginalised: the *ḥwala*, whose families once lived in Iran, are an obvious case (Dessouki 1991). But "Zanzibaris" contribute to, and are used by the government to affirm, a vision of Oman defined both in monolithic terms (as, for instance, in the educational curriculum) and as variegated (in the heritage industry). In practice, marriage with foreigners requires permission; parts of the country remain closed zones;

and research is far from easy. But Oman is depicted as open to the world. The worth of the Zanzibaris' overseas connections depends, meanwhile, precisely on their place in the Omani system.

Anh Nga Longva (Chapter 5) examines the political implications of Kuwaiti identity *in situ.* Terms like autocracy and democracy make little sense of politics: "ethnocracy" is closer to the truth, for a structure of difference allows the reproduction of a seemingly traditional authority that redounds to the benefit of the ruling house at the same time as it marginalises both non-Kuwaiti migrant workers and (to a lesser extent) Kuwaiti women. Differences of nationality, gender and economic power are the key to political and moral order. Loyalty does not follow simply from the logic of rentierism: beneficiaries soon take governmental largesse for granted. But any Kuwaiti is in a sense superior to a non-Kuwaiti, and national endogamy, the clear social preference, engrains over time a sense of citizenship entitlement. Almost regardless of formal politics, something like the existing forms of hierarchy is likely to persist as long as Kuwaitis maintain their marriage pattern.

Paul Dresch (Chapter 6) examines public debates on marriage in the UAE, which reflect and develop wider Gulf debates on nationality and the place of women (*al-Wasaṭ* 383, 31 May 1999). Where culture and privilege alike are felt threatened by a foreign presence, one might almost expect a feminisation of the threat. But the question is scarcely "gendered" in the simplest sense. Part of the constituency supporting state control of marriage is precisely young national women (*muwāṭināt*) whose views are those of certain nationalist older men. Meanwhile older moral norms are quietly turned inside out: what was personal or family business (marriage) becomes a matter of public, state concern. This governmental trend perhaps is spreading. Saudi Arabia set restrictions in the 1970s on men bringing home foreign wives (Al-Rasheed 2002: 128). Libya did the same (Davis J. 1987: 242). But an easy assumption that "the Arab World" specifically is mired in the problems of the old "Eastern bloc" is belied by the theme now recurring among the more primitive polities of Western Europe.[41]

All three of the papers in Part II touch on a phenomenon that easily escapes notice, the shift in kinship (more exactly "closeness") from patrilinearity to bilinearity or cognatic reckoning. That is, the line of descent through men (*nasab*) is not the only image that counts publicly: the mother's line is counted too, or ancestry branching back through both sides of each parental family. On the smallest scale this was always so. It mattered at family level who one's mother was. But the large-scale public invocation of both descent lines means an end to older forms of tolerance and precedence alike. Ethnocracy is substantialised, to follow Longva's formulation: identity racialised, to follow

Dresch. Al-Rasheed can thus write of "impure Omanis". Part III examines how these realities are worked out in practice.

Jill Crystal (Chapter 7) takes the history of Kuwait's police and shows the complement of essentialising definitions. Where the "national" is defined as an in-group, disorder becomes equated with foreignness. But order is coerced, if subtly so, and Crystal suggests a useful distinction between general and specific order. The general order (traffic lights, clean streets, bureaucracy) could be maintained only when the specific order of the state was maintained also. The sponsorship system functioned as a kind of privatised policing, but special security forces were also needed, directed at disturbance one could always depict as a foreign import. Some 40 years after independence, the Kuwaiti state is now everywhere, controlling by its very diffusion throughout society. The spread of bureaucratic control and of standardised practice seems entirely normal, and this affects the usual range of cases: education, uniforms, street signs, forms of all kinds that need filling in. Difference and dissent become hard to formulate.

Mandana Limbert (Chapter 8) takes the key case of education in Oman. Against the backdrop of state bureaucracy, mass education and demands for meaningful employment, young women have begun to organise religious training for themselves. There is a demand for "useful" training, even when it comes to Islam. Religion emerges as a self-consciously separate sphere of activity – including newly defined physical spaces – while exposure to mass educational styles creates a distance from the older religious scholars and uneducated women. The effect is empowerment twice over: the young expect functionally relevant education, and with the acquisition of "new" educational skills, they acquire the voice to interpret traditions for themselves. But this is far from an agenda of "agency". More important is morality and right practice, from which a different form of politics than current affairs might flow.

Haya al-Mughni and Mary Ann Tétreault (Chapter 9) work more with the accepted terms in examining Kuwait, where women are politically influential yet excluded from formal politics. As easily the most open of formal political arrangements in the Gulf, the Kuwaiti case is often the least intelligible. Such terms as "liberal" and "Islamist" need constant explanation. The analysis of parliament's rejection (32 votes to 30) of a bill in 1999 to give women voting rights is thus exemplary. Everyone has their theory of who voted which way and why, as they do of the Emir's initial bid to have women take part in electoral politics – perhaps a distraction from economic issues, perhaps a ploy to inconvenience the liberal deputies, perhaps to favour the Sḥi'ah, to force redistricting or to give ministerial jobs to shaykhly women: "what these changes would accomplish is not clear". What is very clear is that liberals and Islamists alike take Kuwait itself as a political given.[42]

James Piscatori (Chapter 10) takes what in some ways is the extreme case. Transnationalism and global concerns, some would argue, are nothing new in Islam: the great Islamic pilgrimage, the *ḥajj*, is the expression of a global community. The Saudis seek to maximise their position as guardians of the holy places, thus cementing the distinctive quality of the Saudi state. But daily management has often been inefficient; the expansion of the holy places, ostensibly to accommodate growing numbers of pilgrims, has come at the expense of historical sites and thereby confirmed to many an image of "Wahhabi" intolerance; attempts to organise the ritual itself have contradicted well-established tradition or even the teachings of Saudi scholars. A transnational force like the *ḥajj* can call into question the legitimacy of those ruling in its name. As the number of pilgrims grows almost year by year, the complaint is heard that state-controlled access is discriminatory and favours its own citizens. In a globalising world perhaps it cannot be otherwise.

PART I. CULTURE AND CONNECTEDNESS

CHAPTER 1

CHANNELS OF INTERACTION

The Role of Gulf-Owned Media Firms in Globalisation

Naomi Sakr

In December 1998, *New Internationalist* ran a cartoon entitled "D-Day" (Mackay 2000: 61). The "D" clearly stood for "Disney", since the cartoon showed the Disney characters Mickey Mouse, Donald Duck and Pluto in military uniform storming a coastline fringed with palm trees. Using Coca-Cola cans and television sets as missiles, and carrying a flag bearing the Microsoft Windows logo, they were herding the hapless inhabitants out of the picture. Underneath was a two-line quotation from Michael Eisner, the chairman and chief executive of Walt Disney Corporation, which read: "It doesn't matter whether it comes in by cable, telephone lines, computer or satellite. Everyone's going to have to deal with Disney".

This chapter explores questions raised by Eisner's prediction in the context of Arabic-speaking states in the Gulf. It sets out to consider whether Gulf residents do, in fact, "have to deal" with Disney, AOL-Time Warner, News Corporation, Viacom or any other of the handful of Western-based media conglomerates whose myriad subsidiaries have penetrated an ever-increasing proportion of global airwaves over the past decade (Herman and McChesney 1997). There can be little doubt that the concentration of media ownership achieved by these companies in recent years, combined with their geographical spread, represents an important facet of the accelerating process of cross-border interconnectedness summed up in the term "globalisation".

Cultural globalisation or cultural imperialism

Transnational media organisations are optimally placed to overcome time and distance in connecting the local and the global, achieving the "intersection of presence and absence" that, in some definitions (e.g. Giddens 1991: 21), lies at the heart of globalisation. Yet, in the age of globalisation, transnational media are not exclusively Western-owned. The decade that has seen Disney, AOL-Time Warner and others extend their reach has also seen the emergence and proliferation of Arab-owned transnational media empires operating Arabic-language satellite television stations. These stations are based both inside and outside the Arab World and many are carried by more than one satellite to viewers in Europe, North America and Asia, as well as the Middle East.

It is sometimes argued that Gulf-owned transnational media outlets, by advancing a form of cultural globalisation, have the potential to provide the Gulf region with an effective antidote to cultural imperialism on the part of giants like Disney and Viacom. For example, the UAE's Minister of Information, Shaykh 'Abdullāh (bin Zayed) Āl Nahyān, has said that the best way to deal with incoming material that conflicts with traditional Gulf values and beliefs is to ensure that Gulf media output is of such quality that it can provide an attractive alternative (*ArabAd* 8/4, 1998). Thus the paradigm of cultural globalisation can be seen to inform both the act of promoting media flows to counter those from Western sources, and the media theories that explain the resulting multi-directionality of media flows. By the same token, cultural imperialism is the term applied both to a situation in which flows from hegemonic sources dominate the media landscape and to the school of thought that is alert to such dominance, whether it perceives an all-embracing structural dependency or more modest instances of media-related cultural penetration.

As a set of tools for explaining the Gulf media landscape, the theory of cultural imperialism would seem *a priori*, on the basis of contemporary evidence, to belong to the past. By the year 2000, according to data from the Pan-Arab Research Centre in Dubai, access to satellite television among Gulf audiences ranged from an estimated 66 per cent in the UAE, to 73 per cent in Saudi Arabia, 81 per cent in Kuwait and 98 per cent in Oman (Belchi 2002).[1] Viewing figures for 2000 also showed that households were using their satellite access to watch a multiplicity of free-to-air Arabic-language channels, and that all-round broadcasters such as the Saudi-owned Middle East Broadcasting Centre (MBC), or the partly Saudi-owned satellite arm of the Lebanese Broadcasting Corporation (LBC), were among the most popular with Gulf audiences, alongside the news and current affairs channel al-Jazeera, operating from the Qatari capital, Doha. Given this situation it might seem perverse to cling to suspicions that cultural imperialism is at work, were it not for indications to the contrary inherent in the activities of the Western media giants themselves. By pursuing their own global expansion so unashamedly during the 1990s, these conglomerates did a great deal in their own right to keep the cultural imperialism paradigm alive. One has only to listen to Eisner again to get the same sense of invasion portrayed in the *New*

Internationalist cartoon: on the day that Disney took over the ABC television news network in 1996, Eisner spoke of "targeting" 150 countries for politically uncontroversial Disney-owned sports and children's programming (Schechter 1999: 413).

Key questions, therefore, remain about the relative merits of different practical and theoretical approaches to the rise and intensification of transnational media activity in the Gulf, as elsewhere. This was demonstrated most clearly in the aftermath of the suicide attacks in the US on 11 September 2001 as Gulf leaders sought to deploy the media structures they and their associates had built up over the previous decade to communicate their viewpoints at the global level. The Arab Media Summit meeting in Dubai in April 2002 underscored the difficulties. On one hand, participants in the summit were aware they had the technical means and conduits for transnational communication to take place. On the other, they remained sceptical as to whether the content transmitted had the credibility or impact needed to challenge Western misrepresentations of Arab affairs.

Such scepticism echoed a mounting chorus of criticism in the Gulf. A UAE think-tank had blamed the "superficiality" and "monotony" of some Arab satellite programming for driving bored viewers elsewhere in search of "truthfulness" (Markaz Zāyid 2000: 24). Why is it, a Saudi newspaper columnist had asked in 1999, that so many young Saudis are drawn to Western cultural influence (*Gulf News* 26 Dec. 1999)? Why do Saudi boys regard Western rap artists as role-models, when the Western media regard Arabs as the "norm for terrorists, hijackers and other criminals"? Could it be, Hadīl Shaykh asked, because their own media present no alternative role-models, no controversial Arab artists or independent thinkers? In a similar vein was the debunking by 'Abd al-Raḥmān al-Rashīd, editor of the leading Saudi newspaper *al-Sharq al-awsaṭ*, of the notion that an abundance of media outlets equates to media freedom (*Arab News* 26 Aug. 2001). Commentators inside and outside the Gulf media cited timid, sycophantic or non-existent reporting of Gulf news on Arabic-language channels other than al-Jazeera as proof of a lack of freedom. A Bahraini businessman summed up these feelings when he told a gathering of media specialists shortly before the Dubai Media Summit: "The fact that we talk only about al-Jazeera means it's the exception that proves the rule".[2] Observations like these point up the issue of whether Gulf-owned satellite channels are active players in a cultural tug-of-war against Western media dominance, or whether other metaphors, less indicative of resistance, are more apt.

This question in turn poses the dilemma of whether to analyse the available data in the light of cultural globalisation or of cultural imperialism. Shortcomings of the latter approach are well known. For instance, to focus on external media influences is to disregard the renowned "insubordination" of audiences (Golding and Harris 1997: 5). These can not only "zap" from channel to channel at will, but are also liable to interpret media texts from whatever source in unforeseen and idiosyncratic ways. There are also occasions when external influences are benign. It is not unknown for broadcasters based in the West but operating in local languages to stimulate and diversify television output in non-Western countries to a significantly greater extent than those countries' national broadcasters (Sakr 2001a: 157). Examples include CNN's Turkish and Spanish language channels, launched in 1998-99 and received by many other countries besides Turkey and Spain, and News Corporation's expansion into the making of programmes in Indian languages through Star TV (Morley and Robins 1995: 16). Similarly, research has shown that the organisation and content of national media are key variables in the penetration and popularity of foreign programming (Sinclair et al. 1996: 17-18).

Despite the drawbacks, however, it could be risky to discard the idea of cultural imperialism as an analytical tool. An approach that highlights the epiphenomena of cultural globalisation – by stressing, for example, East-West as well as West-East cultural flows, or highlighting the way that media access has been revolutionised in the age of trans-frontier television – may be prone to misreading power relations by downplaying structural concerns about ownership and control. Critical aspects of media decision-making may be more readily exposed by a study alert to signs of cultural imperialism. Such signs include media ownership concentration, whether it is inherited from early bouts of merger mania in the 1980s (Sussman and Lent 1991: 21) or takes the form of "patterns of personal ownership" (Murdock 1990: 6) within multifaceted business empires (McChesney 1998: 33-7) of the kind that one author has described as "private tyrannies" (Wilkin 2001: 121).

This chapter draws on both approaches in attempting to understand the respective roles of Gulf-owned and US-owned media companies in bringing about changes in the cross-border media available in the Gulf. In order to compare like with like, it does not consider the Doha-based al-Jazeera satellite channel, since this limits itself to news and current affairs, is not under private ownership, is not part of a larger conglomerate and is operating according to an institutional formula that is unusual in the Gulf (Sakr 2002: 21). Instead, it takes as a starting point the business empires of four Saudi nationals in the 1990s, working outwards to see whether, and if so how, these individuals' interest in transnational television was translated into resistance to, or collaboration with, the major Western media empires. The rationale for resistance or collaboration is considered in each case, in an effort to determine on whose initiative Western media companies entered the Gulf satellite television market. In conclusion, strengths and weaknesses of cultural imperialism and cultural globalisation theories are compared.

The Saudi ventures in question are reviewed in roughly the order in which they came into being. The first is ARA Group International Holding Company, owned by Walīd al-Ibrāhīm, one of the founders of the Middle East Broadcasting Centre (MBC) in 1991. His original partner in MBC, Ṣāliḥ Kāmil, owner of the Dallah al-Barakah group of companies, left MBC and launched Arab Radio and Television (ART) in 1994. ART became a pay-TV service in 1996. Joining Ṣāliḥ Kāmil in ART was a member of the ruling Āl Saʿūd, Prince Walīd bin Ṭalāl bin ʿAbd al-ʿAzīz, owner of Kingdom Holdings and a high-profile investor in new communication technologies. His media investments are noted as a background to his self-proclaimed role as a "deal-maker" (*International Herald Tribune* 5 Oct. 1999) in the media sector as well as in other fields. Also launched in 1994, in competition with ART, was the Orbit pay-TV network, owned by another member of the Saudi ruling family, Prince Khālid bin ʿAbdullāh bin ʿAbd al-Raḥmān, through his Mawārid Group.

ARA Group

The youthful Shaykh Walīd al-Ibrāhīm, brother of King Fahd's third wife, helped to start MBC in London in 1991, with working capital of $300 million and an annual budget of $60 million (*Time* 22 Jun. 1992). In doing so, he spared no expense in attempting to create a television station that, in its news broadcasts at least, would be the Arabic-language equivalent of Cable News Network (CNN). CNN, created by Ted Turner in 1980 on the back of Turner Advertising, his family firm, had played a dual role for Gulf audiences after Iraq's invasion of Kuwait in August 1990. On the one hand, it had kept them informed of events that Saudi terrestrial television had waited four days to report. On the other, it had introduced them to an unfamiliar style of news reporting, in which the emphasis was on immediacy, spontaneity and encouraging viewers to interpret events for themselves. MBC's early focus on news, and readiness to break with old taboos in news coverage, signalled its management's intention to compete with CNN in the Middle East. A staff member's recollection of being told on recruitment that "we want CNN in Arabic" (Amin and Boyd 1994: 46) is corroborated by the statement of a senior MBC editor, who identified CNN as his chief competition. He said he gained a great deal of satisfaction from scooping CNN, especially on matters of interest to his Arab audience (Alterman 1998: 19).

Despite the cost and the challenge of providing an Arabic alternative to CNN, MBC staff referred to their station as being "news-led" throughout its first seven years.[3] A brochure produced for prospective advertisers, dated July 1997, boasted that the "news and current affairs department compares with some of the best in the world, providing detailed and immediate reporting of world events". But the opening of a news bureau in Jerusalem, the direct reporting of the multilateral Arab-Israeli peace talks in Madrid, and first-hand coverage of potentially sensitive political events, such as an attempted coup in Algeria in January 1992 or the attempted assassination of Hamas's Khālid Mish'al in 1997 (Alterman 1998: 20), were not MBC's only efforts to provide an Arab-owned, Arabic-language counterweight to Western media. Other examples include the first ever television fund-raising event, or telethon, organised by a Middle Eastern television station. MBC's Telethon for Bosnian Relief, held in March 1993, raised $17 million from viewers in Europe, Russia, the United States, the Middle East and Africa (MBC 1997a). It was followed a year later by another for Bosnian children and Palestinian victims of the massacre by an Israeli settler of worshippers in a Hebron mosque. In September 1993, MBC became the first Arab television station ever to interview a US president. In October 1993, it was announced that MBC would supply a package of channels to subscribers in the Arabian Peninsula, one of which would be devoted to news and sport. In 1996, it pioneered an initiative aimed at promoting the exchange of Arab and US views in a programme jointly organised with Voice of America called "Dialogue with the West".

Although MBC was set up in London and installed in a purpose-built $12-million headquarters in Battersea from the beginning of 1995, the parallel US and Saudi strands of Walīd al-Ibrāhīm's business operations should not be overlooked. ARA Group International Holding Company was built up through the acquisition of United Press International (UPI) at a Bankruptcy Court auction in New York in 1992, and the launch, in September 1993, of ANA Radio and Television, distributing Arabic-language news and information from Washington DC (Boyd 1998: 13, MBC 1997a). Shaykh Walīd's company SARAvision, registered in Riyad in 1995, was meanwhile the beneficiary of an exclusive licence to deliver a wireless cable service to Saudi subscribers that would include the package of MBC channels mentioned above. Premises in Dubai were added to the company's portfolio in 2000, as MBC prepared to transfer the bulk of its operations from London to Dubai Media City – a move formally completed in March 2002.

ARA Group financial accounts are not available. Estimates do exist, however, of the financial backing behind it. Indeed, Shaykh Walīd's own wealth, estimated at $9 billion (*Middle East Economic Digest* 15 Aug. 1997), and the family link to his brother-in-law and financial backer, King Fahd (with a personal fortune of some $28 billion[4]), would seem to make his resources at least comparable to those of the magnates heading the leading Western media corporations. Viacom's majority shareholder, Sumner Redstone, had a personal net worth of $12 billion at the end of the 1990s,[5] at which point Viacom owned Paramount film studios, MTV (music television), Nickelodeon, Simon and Schuster publishers, 19 television stations and a large stake in the Blockbuster video rental chain (*Guardian* 8 Sep. 1999). In terms of sales income, by contrast, there is no comparison. Excluding sales from publishing, music and film, Viacom and Disney each earned around $14 billion from television sales in 1998, with Time Warner earning US$10 billion and News Corporation $3.5 billion (Castells 2000: 370). MBC in 1998 was losing money so fast that its owner, fearful that King Fahd's advanced age and failing health would soon cause his subventions to MBC to dry up, decided to take drastic action.

In early 1998, the station's Bahraini managing director, Ḥalā 'Umrān, was replaced by a British national, Ian Ritchie, deemed to have the commercial television know-how to cut costs. Out of a staff of 400 Arab and Western professionals (MBC 1997b), Ritchie made 120 redundant. His evening programming schedules for autumn 1998 demonstrated a clear shift away from news towards films, quizzes and game shows, with the late evening news bulletin made shorter and shown at a later time.[6] After being promoted to chief executive officer, Ian Ritchie appointed British colleagues to senior posts. In January 1999, Philip O'Hara of Mirror Group Newspapers took over as sales and marketing director of MBC, moving up the corporate ladder six weeks later to become chief executive officer of ARA Media Services. October 1999 saw MBC's news and production departments combined under the newly appointed Steve Clark, former head of regional programmes at the UK's Central TV.

Meanwhile, MBC's sources of supply for popular music and game-show programmes also showed a westward shift. The Pepsi Mūzikā chart show, adapted from the worldwide Pepsi Chart programme format, was introduced in June 1999 to provide a teenage diet of Arabic singers and Western pop groups.[7] In a bid to maximise ratings during Ramaḍān of 1998-99, MBC turned to the UK company Action Time to produce Arabic versions of formats that had proved successful with UK audiences, including *Spellbound*, *Wipeout* and *Hilarious Hits*. MBC's link-up with Action Time (a Carlton subsidiary) apparently fitted in well with the latter's aim of extending its game-show licensing and production activities beyond Europe and some Asian countries, including India and Japan (Moran 1998: 32–3).

The new programming trend continued after Ian Ritchie left MBC in 2000. In November that year MBC proudly announced that it had secured the exclusive Arabic rights to another Western game show, *Who Wants To Be a Millionaire?*, from the format's owners, Celador.[8] By this time, the plan for a bouquet of MBC cable channels to be made available in Saudi Arabia had long been scrapped. After repeated delays to the SARAvision cable network, its name change to al-Ruwwād (The Pioneers) and cancellation of the proposed MBC news channel in 1998, the whole project was dropped. As news bulletins on MBC's single general channel continued to cover more international than pan-Arab or local developments (Ayish 1997, 2001), staff noted a sharpened sensitivity among editors regarding Saudi Arabia's relations with the US and US support for Israel. One reporter mentioned in a broadcast that Apache helicopters used by Israel to attack Palestinian towns were made in the US, only to be told afterwards that it was "not MBC policy" to say whether or not armaments were American-made.[9]

Dallah al-Barakah

Over the course of the 1990s, Shaykh Ṣāliḥ Kāmil, the majority owner of ART, regularly intimated in speeches and media interviews that ART's content mattered more to him than the money it cost to produce. It was aimed, he said, at a conservative but silent majority of Muslims who were neither secularists nor so-called "Islamic fundamentalists".[10] "Someone like me", he told an interviewer in 1997, "[who is] not completely to the left or the right – and there are millions like me – wanted to present a more tolerant, middle-of-the-road message to the Arab and other peoples of the world". Married to the Egyptian actress Ṣafā' Abū Sa'ūd, Ṣāliḥ Kāmil backed film and television companies in Egypt and Jordan to the point where, by the mid-1990s, they had reportedly established a bank of some 6,000 hours of programming (*Gulf Marketing Review* May 1997). He also acquired the rights to a library of around 1,000 old Egyptian films (ARTICLE 19 1997: 84). Addressing a workshop on "Media and the Future" at the 1998 Cairo Radio and Television Festival, Kāmil said he believed private channels were better placed than their state-owned counterparts to meet Arab viewers' demands because they could finance viable alternatives to the "dazzling shows that are offered by the West, which do not suit our religion and our traditions" (*TV Dīsh* 56, Aug. 1998). In creating the brand name 1st Net (al-Awā'il) for its package of digital channels, Kāmil's satellite television company ART sought to highlight the fact that each channel was in some way the first of its kind in the Arab World.[11]

ART strove to assert an Arab identity and Islamic values by restricting its Western programming. In the early years this consisted of a single Ted Turner channel, Cartoon Network/TNT. Ṣāliḥ Kāmil told an interviewer in 1998: "We try to introduce content that our viewers will benefit from, and we exercise self-censorship. We are proud of that. If you make a comparison between our film channel and any other Arab film channel, you will see that we are very conservative. The same is true of the music channel".[12] Producers commissioned by ART were required to ensure that no programme criticised religion, political systems or those in authority. Unmarried couples were not to be shown alone together; actors should always be shown fully and modestly clothed; smoking, dancing, consumption of alcohol, female singers, crime scenes and accidents involving blood were not allowed (ARTICLE 19 1997: 84). That these guidelines were strikingly similar to those in force inside Saudi Arabia's own terrestrial television studios (al-Saadon 1990: 110–11) suggested a convenient combination of editorial convictions with a desire to pre-empt any obstacles to expansion of ART within the Kingdom.

As further evidence of its priorities, ART launched a new non-commercial channel in 1998 under the name *Iqrā'* (Read), devoted to religion. Shaykh Ṣāliḥ also demonstrated his commitment to conservative programming when he suddenly halted ART's transmission from the Panamsat 4 satellite in 1997, thereby abandoning the company's shared satellite and decoder arrangements with another pay-TV operator, Showtime. Showtime is jointly owned by a Kuwaiti company and the Western media giant Viacom. ART's move, which caused confusion in the market and puzzled media analysts, was later explained by a company spokesperson as a deliberate attempt to dissociate ART from Showtime's more relaxed and Westernised content.[13]

ART maintained its resistance to non-Islamic styles of programming while simultaneously building up offices and production facilities outside the Muslim world. Ṣāliḥ Kāmil began his business career as a contractor in Saudi Arabia in the 1970s. His Jiddah-based holding company, Dallah al-Barakah, founded in the early 1980s, had manufacturing, trade, shipping, farming and tourism interests in more than 30 countries by 1990 (el-Emary 1996: 258) and total assets of around $7 billion by the end of that decade (*Middle East Economic Digest* 4 Aug. 1995, 23 Jan. 1998). Within five years of its establishment, ART could claim in its publicity brochures that its production and broadcast facilities spanned the globe "from Tennessee to Tunis". Its multiple channels were being beamed by 11 satellites to Europe, the Middle East, America and Latin America, Asia and Australia. It was even accepted by the protectionist French regulatory body, the

Conseil Supérieur de l'Audiovisuel, as one of a very limited number of Arabic-language channels allowed on cable in France (*Arabies* May 1997). Its state-of-the-art production centre at Avezzano in Italy boasted ten digital studios, editing suites and a range of equipment capable of handling more than 50 separate satellite signals simultaneously to broadcasters around the world. However, ART was not an obviously profitable operation. Shaykh Ṣāliḥ had invested in pay-TV precisely because he did not believe that advertising revenues could ever cover the cost of television production of the kind he wanted to see.[14] Yet subscription costs for ART channels were widely deemed too expensive for the non-Westernised target audience, especially given the number of free-to-air Arabic-language channels available. In 1998 the company was said to be losing nearly $170 million per annum (Moody 1999: 6).

In these circumstances, a rethink was needed. Ṣāliḥ Kāmil's pivotal role was such that ART found itself rudderless when he underwent emergency heart treatment in France in the summer of 1998. A year later the possibility of a merger was secretly discussed with the rival Saudi-owned pay-TV network Orbit, also based in Italy.[15] This was ruled out. Instead, a decision was made in 2000 to appoint a Westerner as chief executive of Arab Digital Distribution, charged with managing the distribution of ART. The appointee, John Tydeman, had previously been involved in setting up Showtime, the broadcaster from which ART had briefly distanced itself in 1997. According to Shaykh Ṣāliḥ, Tydeman was hired for his expertise in structuring complex, commercial, technical and legal projects and his skill in motivating and managing diverse teams of professionals (*Middle East Broadcast & Satellite* 7/4, July 2000).

Tydeman set about a repositioning exercise for ART, the results of which were announced in March 2001. Presenting itself as the "total entertainment solution", the revamped ART package offered a choice of 30 channels. The time had come, he told an interviewer, to meet the demand for Western channels and rethink ART's Arabic-only offerings. Whereas ART had previously concentrated on its own production, Tydeman's view was that pay-TV should focus on three things: "quality exclusive events, premium movies and premium sports".[16] Thus ART's new line-up included six sports channels, including Eurosport, Eurosport News and Manchester United TV; four film channels, including Turner Classic Movies and The Film Channel; nine variety channels including Animal Planet and Reality TV; and two channels for children and teenagers, including the Turner Cartoon Network. Of these, Turner Classic Movies and the Cartoon Network were by now part of the world's biggest Western media company, AOL-Time Warner. So was CNN, one of the three news channels added to the ART package. Fox News, another of the three, is owned by Rupert Murdoch's News Corporation. Ṣāliḥ Kāmil had previously stopped ART from producing or broadcasting news in Arabic because of the complications he feared sensitive news items could create in his relations with governments in the many countries where Dallah al-Barakah has business interests.[17]

Kingdom Holdings

When Kāmil created ART in the mid-1990s, he did not do so alone. Sharing his vision was Prince Walīd bin Ṭalāl, holder of 30 per cent of ART's shares. Prince Walīd, ranked by *Forbes* magazine in June 2000 as the sixth richest person in the world (not counting heads of state), had a net worth of $20 billion at the time of that annual ranking exercise. Although smaller than the $60 billion fortune owned by Bill Gates, head of Microsoft, Prince Walīd's personal riches were considerably greater than those of several Western media tycoons (Sakr 2001b: 70). Along with Sumner Redstone of Viacom, these included the Italian owner of Mediaset, Silvio Berlusconi, and Rupert Murdoch of News Corporation (an Australian who had to obtain US nationality in order to buy certain media outlets in the US). It may also be supposed, given the spectacular increase in the Prince's net worth during the late 1990s, that his annual income during this period comfortably exceeded the $575 million annual remuneration received by Disney's Michael Eisner (*Guardian* 18 May 2000, 30 May 2001).

Walīd's investment portfolio in media and telecommunications technology was valued at some $8.2 billion in 2000. Of this only a tiny proportion was accounted for by his stake in ART and, through ART's parent company, Arab Media Corporation, in the Lebanese Broadcasting Corporation's satellite arm, LBC-Sat. The bulk of Prince Walīd's media holdings, built up during the course of the 1990s, was in companies he described as "big giants" of the media world (*Money Magazine* Oct. 1998, cited in *ArabAd* 9/1, Jan. 1999). His first high-profile purchase of a Western media company was part of a rescue package in 1994 for the Disneyland Paris theme park in France. Although Euro Disney had already made refinancing arrangements before the Prince's intervention, the company accepted his offer of help in return for a 23.6 per cent stake (*Financial Times* 2 Jun. 1994). After the restructuring, backed by Walīd, Euro Disney recovered and went on to resurrect plans for a second theme park that had been part of Disney's original agreement with the French government in 1987 (*Guardian* 30 Sep. 1999). Prince Walīd himself went on to acquire a 4.1 per cent share in Mediaset in 1995 and another of 5 per cent in News Corporation in 1997. As a 5 per cent shareholder in the internet browser company Netscape, Walīd became part of the AOL-Time

Warner empire when AOL bought Netscape and later merged with Time Warner in January 2000. By the end of 2000, a web of cross-ownership deals linked Mediaset with the German Kirch group, Kirch with News Corporation and News Corporation with Microsoft, giving added meaning to the declaration Walīd made in 1998: "I have alliances with everybody and I don't have enemies" (*Middle East Economic Digest* 5 Jun. 1998).

Among these alliances were family relationships with the sons of King 'Abd al-'Azīz Āl Sa'ūd, on the Prince's father's side, and with the Lebanese ruling elite on his mother's. As the son of Ṭalāl bin 'Abd al-'Azīz, who campaigned for political reform in Saudi Arabia in the 1950s and 1960s but was later readmitted to the Saudi establishment and given a seat on the 18-member Ruling Family Council in June 2000 (Economist Intelligence Unit 2000: 14), Walīd openly acknowledged that his Saudi heritage and "royal" status gave him an advantage in doing deals (*Middle East Economic Digest* 5 Jun. 1998). He cultivated his Saudi credentials through donations to Saudi charities and mosque construction (*Middle East Economic Digest* 31 Mar. 2000). At the same time, as the son of Munā al-Sulḥ, daughter of Lebanon's first Prime Minister, Riyāḍ al-Sulḥ, he proved his attachment to Lebanon by paying for the reconstruction of Lebanese power stations bombed by Israel in 1999. In 1998, Prince Walīd explained his commitment to ART in terms of both his personal cultural identity as an Arab Muslim and his worldwide travels as a global investor. He said: "I ... adore the fact that ART is present wherever I go ... since ART channels cover the earth, I always feel a little closer to home" (*ArabAd* 9/1, Jan. 1999).

Walīd's direct interest in Arab television found its primary outlet in ART and its affiliates. But even the Prince's extensive investments in non-Arab media and communications were only part of his diverse portfolio of acquisitions, many of which facilitated tie-ups between Western companies he bought into and other investors – both private and public – in the Middle East. For example, Four Seasons Hotels and Resorts and Mövenpick Hotels and Resorts, both part-owned by Walīd, landed important hotel management contracts in the region (*Middle East Economic Digest* 23 Jan.; 30 Jan. 1998). The shareholding in Euro Disney, a subsidiary of the Walt Disney Corporation, should probably also be viewed in this light, given the part played by Walīd in averting a threatened Arab boycott of Disney material and merchandise in 1999.

The UAE information minister, Shaykh 'Abdullāh (bin Zayed), called on the Arab League to consider an official boycott in protest at an Israeli exhibit at Disney's Epcot theme park in Orlando, Florida, because it presented Jerusalem as the capital of Israel. The exhibition, featuring some 35 countries as well as the United Nations and World Bank, was due to open in October 1999 as part of a 15-month celebration of the Christian millennium, with Saudi Arabia and Morocco representing the Arab World. On 23 September, a week before the scheduled opening, Arab foreign ministers meeting on the sidelines of the UN General Assembly in New York decided not to proceed with a boycott. They agreed to accept assurances from Michael Eisner that Disney, being an "entertainment company", had never intended to "offer a political point of view" (Associated Press 24 Sep. 1999). Announcing the ministers' decision, the Arab League's secretary-general, Ismat 'Abd al-Majīd, thanked Prince Walīd for his "active" intervention on the issue. Ten days earlier, an official for Kingdom Holdings in Riyad had told Reuters that Disney's management had personally assured Prince Walīd that Jerusalem would not be depicted as Israel's capital in the exhibition (Reuters 13 Sep. 1999). These assurances were relayed directly by the prince to Ḥanān Ashrāwī, as a member of the Palestinian Legislative Council, who repeated them to the press.[18]

Evidence as to whether the Disney exhibition was significantly altered as a result of this episode is mixed. However, assuming that Disney did take limited action to safeguard its presence in the Middle East market, this would not have been the first or last example of its willingness to reach a political accommodation with governments for the sake of market share. While Rupert Murdoch took steps from 1993 to ensure that News Corporation's broadcasting and publishing output would not offend the Chinese government, Michael Eisner and other Disney representatives held face-to-face meetings with Chinese leaders in late 1998 to try to overcome the damage done to Disney's image in Beijing by its 1996 film *Kundun*, about Tibet.

Compared with the Chinese market, the Arab market is small. Nevertheless, having invested in 1998-99 in developing "entertainment concepts" with international expansion in mind (*Financial Times* 14 Dec. 1998, *Gulf Marketing Review* May 1999), Disney executives would have been loath to jeopardise sales in the Arab World, where an exceptionally high proportion of the population is aged under 15 and seen as a prime market for Disney products. Disney officials estimated in 1999 that the $100 million worth of annual product sales achieved in the Middle East at the end of the decade could be increased more than fivefold, to exceed $500 million a year in the Gulf region alone by 2005 (*Gulf Marketing Review* Oct. 1999). For Prince Walīd, as a stakeholder in Disney's success and a member of the Saudi ruling elite, two sets of loyalties were brought into play by the boycott threat. Like the restructuring remedies adopted by MBC and ART, the Prince's defusing of the Arab League-Disney confrontation may be interpreted as an example of the globalisation process at work.

Mawārid Group

Reflecting the particular interests, tastes and sensibilities of the Middle East region's "distinctive cultures" was said to be a prime objective of the Orbit television network when the Saudi-owned Mawārid Group launched it in 1994. It was to be a "self-regulating, conscientious broadcaster, espousing family values".[19] Orbit's American president and chief executive at the time, Alexander Zilo, explained to *Newsweek* that the company aimed to meet the needs of a niche market of affluent Middle East professionals who watch Western television when they travel but find "nothing" of interest on terrestrial television in their home countries (*Newsweek* 6 Jun. 1994). Declaring itself to be the biggest multi-channel, multilingual pay-TV service in the Arab World, Orbit set out to offer a choice of film, sports and children's channels. In doing so, it sponsored original Arabic material. One of its early moves was to sign a ten-year contract in 1994 for an Arabic television news service to be supplied by the BBC. This arrangement came unstuck less than two years later as a result of Saudi sensitivity to BBC coverage of Saudi affairs.

There were other initiatives, however. For example, in 1996, Orbit started the annual Arab Festival of Song, screened live from a succession of Arab capitals over several days at the end of each Ramaḍān. The network provided a multinational outlet for popular television drama series produced by national Arab companies, such as Syria's *Khān al-ḥarīr* (Silk Bazaar). In January 1996, it became the first Arab satellite station to introduce a local equivalent of CNN's political talk-show, *Larry King Live*. Called *'Alā l-ḥawā* (On the Air), the programme invited controversial guests and encouraged viewers to phone in and ask them questions – apparently freely – without giving their names. Thus Orbit could claim the credit for piloting a format in Arabic that was later famously adopted by al-Jazeera in its stormy talk-shows *al-Ittijāh al-mu'ākis* (The Opposite Direction) and *Akthār min ra'y* (More Than One Opinion). When Orbit covered the World Cup in 1998, it broadcast all 64 games, transmitting live commentary and analysis in Arabic from studios in Egypt's Media Production City.

The decision to hire these studios, despite the fact that Orbit decoders were not licensed for distribution in Egypt, seems to have been based on plans to capitalise on World Cup coverage at a much lower cost than would have been possible from Orbit headquarters in Rome.[20] Similar financial considerations seem to have been behind the company's announcement in January 2000 that it had signed an agreement with the Ministry of Information in Bahrain to establish its head office in tax-free Manama (*Middle East Times* 6 Feb. 2000). Such cost-cutting was in stark contrast to the huge sums Mawārid ploughed into Orbit in its early stages. As one of Saudi Arabia's largest and most diversified private businesses, with interests ranging from petrol stations and fast food chains to banking, manufacturing, construction, municipal services and medical supplies (*International Herald Tribune* 26 Apr. 1995), Mawārid was apparently well placed to invest in broadcasting. Indeed, with an estimated investment of around $1 billion, the Orbit network may well have been one of the most costly direct satellite broadcast efforts anywhere in the world (Boyd 1998: 13–14). Mawārid's owner, Prince Khālid bin 'Abdullāh bin 'Abd al-Raḥmān, a son of one of the younger brothers of King 'Abd al-'Azīz and thus a cousin of King Fahd, entered the latter's close kinship circle through marriage to one of Fahd's four full sisters (Field 1985: 112–13). Before founding Orbit, Prince Khālid had originally expressed an interest in buying Star TV, based in Hong Kong. In the event, Rupert Murdoch bought Star from its first owner, Richard Li, leaving Prince Khālid and his son, Prince Fahd, to headhunt Alexander Zilo, one of Star's founders. A US television executive who had helped to found Star, Zilo was seen as having start-up know-how that could be vital to Orbit's success (Boyd 1998: 13–14). As head of Orbit, he maintained his relationship with Star TV after its purchase by News Corporation.

In time, Orbit obtained a core bouquet of channels from Star TV. The Star Select package of six (later nine) channels, launched exclusively on Orbit in 1997, included Star Movies, Star Sports, CNBC, Sky News and Fox Kids Network. Orbit also negotiated a five-year agreement with Disney, which came into effect in 1997, providing a Disney Channel tailored to an Arab audience (*Middle East Economic Digest* 2 Feb. 1996, *Middle East Satellite Today* Jun. 1997). When the channel was also provided with dubbing in Arabic a year after its launch on Orbit, the service gained the distinction of being the only Disney Channel to be broadcast in two languages in a single market. Scott Hicks, the Disney Channel's Middle East managing director, told an interviewer in 1999 that Disney had chosen Orbit because it was "very strong in Arabic programming" and suitably "quality conscious". Hicks, who marketed Coca-Cola in the region before joining Disney, said there was a "creative ... not a business reason" to dub Disney animation into Arabic, in order to preserve the "subtlety and humour" of the dialogue. But he also admitted that subscriptions had risen after Arabic dubbing was introduced (*Gulf Marketing Review* May 1999). The Orbit–Disney tie-up was reinforced by the inclusion of ESPN Sports in the Orbit package, since Disney owns the ESPN brand.

The major themes

On one level, this chapter set out to track the responses of Gulf-owned media conglomerates to the worldwide expansion of Western-owned media giants. The aim was to assess in particular how active four Saudi media entrepreneurs had been in establishing Arabic-language counterweights and alternatives to Western television programming. In principle, the criteria for judging their activities were resistance to Western encroachment at one end of the scale, and assistance for it at the other, with the option of passive neutrality lying somewhere in between. On another level, by drawing on two theoretical approaches to considering these responses – one predisposed to view the spread of Western media as one-way cultural imperialism, and the other more inclined to draw attention to diversity and multi-directionality in cultural flows – the study sought to establish the relative merits of each approach. In pursuit of both levels of investigation, the analysis focused on distinctive characteristics or programming innovations of the satellite television ventures and their geographical reach, financial strength and evolution in terms of programme content and sources of supply.

The data presented here show that Western media companies, far from facing resistance, had their content adopted by Gulf television broadcasters in the decade following MBC's launch in 1991. At the same time, none of these Western companies needed to mount the kind of invasion, literal or figurative, of which they are sometimes accused. On the contrary, there is strong evidence to suggest that Walīd al-Ibrāhīm and Ṣāliḥ Kāmil were forced by financial difficulties to engage in a process of business restructuring in which they opted to follow a Western business model of cost-cutting and streamlining and, consequently, brought in Western media executives. These individuals naturally turned to the programme suppliers they knew best.

The financial difficulties that affected MBC or ART were not the result of tough competition from Western broadcasters. In MBC's case they were related to uncertainties inherent in the company's particular form of financial backing. For ART, they arose from over-reliance on highly priced subscriptions in a market unused to pay-TV. Orbit, meanwhile, was put in the hands of an American president from the outset; its dealings with News Corporation and Disney began relatively early and came as no surprise. The choice of digital technology, as required for pay-TV, was an important factor in the Western presence in Orbit and, eventually, ART. With digital technology comes an explosion of capacity, as multiple channels need to be filled. Policies conducive to greater output of high-quality local programming might, as indicated by research in other contexts (Sinclair et al. 1996: 17–18), have attracted the audiences and advertising revenues that could have pre-empted the move to Western alternatives. But one Saudi media entrepreneur in particular stood to gain directly from the entry of Disney and News Corporation into Gulf digital television packages. As an entrepreneur with investments straddling both sides of a notional Arab-Western media divide, Prince Walīd apparently enjoyed the deal-making ability bestowed by his stakes in multiple media ventures. His role, as demonstrated in the Disney exhibition saga, was that of intermediary. As such he was in a position to resist or facilitate certain forms of Western media domination. In fact, he seems to have done both.

Gulf-owned media conglomerates thus played an active role in promoting the cross-border interconnectedness captured in the term "globalisation". In doing so, they veered away from their original path that promised innovation and local relevance, whether in film, drama, news or current affairs. Although choices about content were partly based on the need to fill space and protect infrastructural investment, Orbit's broken contract with the BBC and ART's much-vaunted self-censorship demonstrated that choices were also limited by the need to avoid breaking editorial taboos. MBC's shift from news to entertainment was geared to cutting costs and regaining viewers lost to other channels. But, as demonstrated by the obvious success of al-Jazeera, uncensored news about Gulf and Arab affairs could have achieved the aim of boosting audiences equally well. Instead, easily obtainable Western programming offered a potentially less threatening alternative to local material. In these circumstances, Disney's bid for the politically uncontentious ground of sports and cartoons represented an offer that was hard to refuse. With ownership of the most generously funded satellite networks concentrated among members and associates of the Saudi Arabian ruling family, the number of separate links with a potentially more diverse range of foreign suppliers was minimised.

Conclusion

The results of this analysis highlight advantages of viewing the data through twin theoretical frames, one looking for signs of cultural imperialism and the other for signs of cultural globalisation. Relying solely on the first of these would have limited the focus to the marketing and expansion efforts of Disney, Viacom, News Corporation and the rest, without paying due attention to local Gulf dynamics. It would have highlighted the longevity of the ART-Showtime partnership rather than its interruption in 1997–98. It would have remarked on the extent to which Western news, talk-show and game-show formats entered Gulf satellite television schedules, without exploring the reasons why and without giving due emphasis to the nature and volume of original Arabic-language programming. By the same token, an exclusively globalist interpretation would have failed to allow for the fact that Western media empires can still penetrate a media landscape even without invading it through mergers and acquisitions. It would have overlooked the accommodations these corporations are liable to make (as Disney did) for the sake of market share in politically hostile environments. By taking a dual approach, in which the two frames of cultural imperialism and cultural globalisation are positioned so that they overlap, this study has revealed that Gulf-owned media enterprises did experiment with alternatives to "dealing with Disney". But it has also shown that a combination of Gulf-specific political sensitivities and financial difficulties ultimately helped to bring Disney in.

CHAPTER 2

DIALECT AND NATIONAL IDENTITY

The Cultural Politics of Self-Representation in Bahraini *Musalsalāt*

Clive Holes

There has always been a skein of tribal, religious and ethnic threads that have bound the peoples of the Gulf region into supranational communities that do not coincide with political borders. In the not-too-distant past, these deep-rooted bonds were, within individual states, potential sources of political division and civil fragmentation. It is not therefore surprising that a main, if never explicitly stated, aim of all Gulf governments in the years since independence has been to create a sense of national identity and shared history out of the mix of diverse elements in their populations, so that the nationals of these countries no longer think of themselves in the first instance as a member of this or that tribe, community or sect, but as citizens whose first loyalty is to the state in which they live (Davis and Gavrielides eds 1991). This process of nation-building and what might be termed, in the cultural sphere, "identity management" has been most single-mindedly pursued in Saudi Arabia, the biggest and most populous country in the area, and the one with the greatest potential for fragmentation. But, *mutatis mutandis*, it is a problem that all the states of the region face, even the smallest of them – the island state of Bahrain. Because of its finely balanced sectarian and ethnic composition, Bahrain provides a particularly interesting variation on this theme of creating unity out of diversity.

Region and locality

Beyond the borders of individual Gulf states, there has been an attempt to develop a distinctive regional identity. While it could be argued that regional political integration, embodied in the Gulf Co-operation Council (set up in 1981), has been largely superficial, there have been substantial moves to harmonise educational standards across the Gulf, and establish prestige projects like the Arabian Gulf

University (based in Bahrain). Sporting links within the Gulf abound, and since as long ago as the 1970s there has been an annual football tournament for the Arabian Gulf Cup, competed for by the national teams of the area. The physical isolation of the individual Gulf states, one from another, has been completely removed by a network of fast, metalled roads that now allow one to drive from Muscat to Kuwait (something almost unthinkable even 25 years ago) in a matter of hours, and even from mainland Arabia to Bahrain via the causeway opened by King Fahd in 1986. Soon there is to be another bridge linking Bahrain and Qatar, symbolising the new-found friendship between states which until 1999 were bitterly disputing sovereignty over the Ḥawār Islands before the International Court of Justice in The Hague.

In the broadcast media, the advent of home-grown TV production by Gulf nationals for Gulf nationals has coincided with this emergence of the Gulf region as a distinct geopolitical bloc. Plays (known locally as *tamthīlīyāt*) set in local contexts, written by local writers and performed in the local dialect are of course nothing new in the Gulf, and started to be broadcast by local radio stations in the 1960s and 1970s. Up until the 1980s, however, there was little or no local production of TV drama, almost all that was broadcast being imported from culturally dominant Arab countries like Egypt, with scenarios, plots, actors and language to match. Slowly, however, and starting in Kuwait, home-grown production facilities have developed and now exist in every Gulf state. While living in Oman in the mid-1980s, for example, I was surprised to be able to watch imported Kuwaiti soaps on a regular basis, along with the expected Egyptian and Jordanian imports. More recently, at a meeting in 1998 with Khālid al-Dhawwādi, Director of Bahrain Television, I was presented with boxed sets of video-cassettes of two TV *musalsalāt* ("series") which had been shot in Bahrain using Bahraini actors and produced in Kuwait: *Firjān il-Awwal* ("The Neighbourhoods of the Old Days") and *il-Bēt il-ʿŌd* ("The Big House"),[1] each of which ran to 30 episodes. These and other similar series have been widely shown not just in Bahrain but in other Gulf states, and (so the Director told me) have won international television prizes. They have proved very popular with Gulf audiences and have been repeated several times, especially during the prime-time scheduling of Ramaḍān.

Obviously there are several ways in which one can approach these series and their relation to local society. Whatever the approach chosen, however, I think it is worth stressing the importance of language. Not only does linguistic detail allow us to follow and appreciate what is happening in *musalsalāt*, as in the rest of life, but it sometimes reveals patterns of change that are less apparent in "political" events. Indeed, language everywhere shows patterns that are not fully evident to local speakers themselves but that underpin what they do and, in a real sense, who they are. This is not to say, of course, that everyone has equal influence over language development.

In this paper I offer some observations on the kind of language[2] that has typically been used in TV and radio *musalsalāt* and other one-off dramatic productions broadcast in the last couple of decades by Bahrain radio and TV. In Bahrain, as in the rest of the Gulf, the broadcast media are entirely controlled by the state[3] (in fact they are part of the Ministry of Information), and this control extends to "light entertainment" as well as news. The media *musalsal* set in a local milieu and giving a fictional depiction of it in an entertaining, or even informative-didactic, way is fertile ground for investigation by the social anthropologist interested in the self-image that the state wishes to present (cf. Armbrust (ed.) 2000). In particular, as I shall try to show in what follows, the ways in which the local dialects of Arabic have been, and are being, used in such productions give a strong set of clues as to how the state indirectly manages the process of identity formation in a modernising state in which dialect has hitherto been such a potent badge of communal identity.

Meaning of *musalsal*

But first things first. What do we mean by *musalsal* – literally, "series", or sometimes equivalent to "soap opera" – in a Gulf context? From my observations, it seems that there are three broad types:

The first is what we might term the soap as simulacrum of social reality. In a British context, one thinks of the cardboard-cut-out rural squirearchy of *The Archers*, the cosy northern terraces and "Rover's Return" pub of *Coronation Street* and the loveable and not-so-loveable Cockneys and multi-ethnic mix of *EastEnders*. The Gulf version of the genre presents, in a similarly idealised and stereotyped way, an image of everyday life which its audience can recognise and identify with, using the same means – locale, dress, manners and speech – to evoke it. But there are differences in the cultural and political space that the soap opera occupies in the two cases. For one thing, the Gulf *musalsal* genre is really a "series" rather than a "soap opera" in the sense of *Coronation Street* or *EastEnders*. It most often runs for 13 episodes and there is usually a single main plot line and dénouement at the end. Secondly, the plot rarely if ever connects head-on with the kind of contemporary social issues that are the meat and drink of the British soaps. In 2001, the fear of foot-and-mouth disease dominated the lives of the farmers of Borsetshire in *The Archers* just as it did the lives of real farmers in Cumbria and Devon, and how to deal with HIV-positive gays and teenage pregnancy are among the perennial threads in the plot-line of *EastEnders*. But one would search in vain in Gulf television drama for even an oblique allusion to issues like unemployment, marriage breakdown, the problems caused by the influx of foreign workers or drug abuse, all current Gulf social problems. The plot typically revolves around the emotional ups and downs and/or the business problems of a solidly middle-class Gulf family. Sometimes there is a ponderously delivered "moral message" on the importance of correct personal and business conduct, but heavyweight social issues of the day are not addressed. This type of *musalsal* has been cloned directly from a thousand others made in Egypt in the last 30 years and transposed into a Gulf setting, complete with the Louis de Lebanon furniture in the living room and the obligatory Mercedes in the drive.[4] But if the Gulf TV soap is not – or at least not yet – seen as the appropriate public forum for comment on real social problems, that is not to say that a government line on some domestic issues is not occasionally discernible in some kinds of fictive media material, as I shall illustrate later.

A second type of Gulf *musalsal* is a variation on this theme, but with a strong comic element, in which the protagonist is typically faced with some personal problem, and the series recounts his vicissitudes in trying to solve it. An example from Bahrain radio in the 1970s was *al-Dunyā Maṣāliḥ* (roughly, "you scratch my back, I'll scratch yours") in which the anti-hero tries vainly in successive episodes to devise with his bosom buddy, the local gravedigger, ingenious stratagems to kill a nagging wife who has committed the cardinal sin of producing no children. There is no attempt here to reflect any kind of emotional or social "reality": the nagging wife is an international social cliché, as is, in a local context, the barren wife, but the treatment of the subject is farcical, and the whole object is to make the audience laugh.

A third type has nothing to do with the contemporary Gulf at all, but deals in the currently popular currency of nostalgia for a bygone age. This can be dealt with in an up-beat and light-hearted fashion, as in the two prize-winning Bahraini TV series which I mentioned earlier, and which I will have more to say about in a moment. In this kind of soap, a time-unspecified but definitely pre-oil Gulf is the backdrop to the action – in fact, it could be argued the backdrop has the starring role – and is portrayed in a series of all-singing, all-dancing cameos as a place where life may have been hard, but the hardships were bearable because they were shared by all. This is the kind of soap that comes with a free pair of rose-tinted spectacles, and seems designed to provide televisual proof of the kind of statement I frequently heard from older Bahrainis when they were asked to compare the old days with now: *zād il-khēr u-qallat il-anāsa*, "life's materially better now, but it isn't so much fun". On the other hand, the past is sometimes presented from a look-back-in-anger perspective through a dramatisation of the protagonist's life experiences. A good example here is the mid-1970s Bahraini radio *musalsal 'Āshiq fī Hawā z-Zēna*[5] in which the action, concerning an ill-starred love affair frustrated by social convention, is set around the 1940s when the pearl-diving industry was nearing its end.[6]

If future generations were to construct a picture of what late twentieth-century British society was like, basing themselves solely on a half-dozen episodes of *The Archers*, *Coronation Street* and *EastEnders* – and why not, to fill out the regional and social picture, throw in a few of *Crossroads* (Birmingham motel), *Byker Grove* (Newcastle council estate), *Brookside* (suburban Liverpool) and *Goodness Gracious Me* (ethnic minority) – what would it look like? In a word, lurid: late twentieth-century Britons would come across as obsessed with sex, prone to domestic violence and engulfed in a tidal wave of marital breakdown and drug abuse. But budding sociologists among those future generations would also note that British society à la soap had well-defined classes, signalled not just by standard indices such as employment, education and place of residence, but by dress, manner and accent. Moreover, any linguists among them would note that there was a good deal of speech differentiation marking differences of geographical origin: Cockneys telling one another to "leave i' ar'!" in *EastEnders*, Geordie kids "gannin'" to the shops in *Byker Grove*, and Mr Woolly, the Brummie exile of *The Archers*, regaling the regulars at "The Bull" with the latest exploits of his dog Captain in that distinctive nasal whine, which differentiates him on the one hand from the middle-class, middle-England farmers with their received pronunciation, and on the other from the ne'er-do-well farm labourers, the Grundies, with their distinctive West Country burr. In the British soap, accent and dialect (albeit often pastiche) is one of the main devices used to create the illusion of locale and character.

And if future generations were also to look at Gulf *musalsalāt*, and Bahraini ones in particular, what conclusions would they draw there? I have already made the point that the Gulf *musalsal* is not (yet) seen as a means of addressing contemporary social problems. But it is also highly selective in the groups it portrays as typical of Gulf society. This point applies *par excellence* to the kind of Arabic that the writers put into the mouths of the characters. Of course, this is a form of Arabic that viewers recognise and label *al-lahjah al-khalījīyah*, "Gulf Arabic". But as anyone who has done research on the vernaculars of the Gulf will know, "Gulf Arabic" is a cover term which masks wide regional and social differences. To the Gulf listener/viewer, these differences are no less salient, and can be just as suggestive of social and geographical origin and attitude as Geordie, Cockney or "upper-class" accents are in the British case.

In the Bahraini media, the Arabic spoken in *musalsalāt*, as well as in other public and artistic manifestations of dialect use – dialect poetry, song and the speech-bubbles in newspaper cartoons which represent how "typical" Bahrainis are supposed to speak – is certainly "Bahraini" in the sense that a proportion of the indigenous population speak like that. This form of Arabic is the dialect of the Arabic-speaking Bahraini Sunnis, known locally as ʿArab (henceforth "A" for short), so-called because many of them trace their historical origins back to tribes from Najd. On a regional level, this dialect is similar to the main dialects spoken in Kuwait, Qatar and the UAE, and is what people are usually referring to when they talk about Gulf Arabic or a Gulf accent.

But in fact only about half the indigenous Bahraini population actually speak in this fashion. Another indigenous group, the so-called Baḥārnah (henceforth "B" for short), confessionally Ithnaʿashari Shiʿah, and probably in a slight majority,[7] account for the vast majority of the village population and form the biggest single indigenous population group in Manama, the capital. The Baḥārnah speak a dialect of Arabic that in many of its basic phonological and structural aspects is strikingly different from that of the ʿArab or A group. The Bahraini ʿArab themselves routinely use ʿArab as a synonym for "people", as in *mā mish ʿarab il-laylah*, "There aren't many people about tonight". This was said to me by an A resident to describe a deserted street in Muḥarraq along which we were walking. *Al-ḥīn ʿarab drisat u tiṭawwarat*, "these days people have studied and got more sophisticated", was a comment from an A woman about how Bahrain had changed for the better during her lifetime.

On a local regional level, the B dialect is similar to that spoken by the Shiʿah of the neighbouring Eastern Province of Saudi Arabia (Smeaton 1973, Prochazka 1990). With a few interesting exceptions (which will be discussed below), this B dialect has low media visibility, its absence from the *musalsalāt* that depict Bahraini society – whether of the contemporary world or the past – being almost total. From the moment he opens his mouth, the *musalsal* Bahraini speaks like an ʿArab, dresses like one, behaves like one and lives in a community made up of other ʿArab. If one were to review the entire drama output of Bahrain radio and television over the last 25 years, one would hardly guess that a Baḥārnah community existed. Before going further, however, we should consider why differences in dialect have in fact failed to disappear over time, and then briefly review what the major differences are between the two dialects.

ʻArab and Baḥārnah

Nowadays the term ʻArab is loosely used in Bahrain to refer to anyone who is an indigenous Arabic-speaking Sunni, whether or not he has an Arabian tribal pedigree. Strictly speaking, however, the term originally referred only to endogamous groups such as the al-Mannāʻī, Āl Bū ʻAynayn, Āl Bū Rumayḥ, al-Ghatam, al-Dawāsir, al-Zayyānī, etc. who lived in one or other of the tribal settlements referred to below and who had (and still have) genealogical affiliations with the tribes of mainland Arabia. However, there are also long-established communities of non-tribally descended Bahraini Sunnis who live in the overwhelmingly A towns of al-Muḥarraq and al-Ḥidd and the A quarters of Manama, who speak the same type of dialect as their tribally descended ʻArab neighbours, and who in recent decades have to some degree intermarried with them. This non-tribal group also claims that it is originally of Arabian origin, although many of its communities spent decades (even centuries) on the Persian side of the Gulf and have names that suggest this, such as Bastakī, Daylamī, Khunjī, Kūhijī, Kazirūnī.[8] Because they speak essentially the same type of dialect and live in the same areas as the ʻArab, these Ḥwala are also included in the group generically referred to in this article as "A".

The Baḥārnah (group B), as their name suggests, consider themselves Bahrain's original inhabitants. In a manner familiar from elsewhere in Arabia, they were stigmatised, as against those of "tribal" descent, by association with certain occupations and ways of life. Some of these were told to R.B. Serjeant by a Bahraini in 1963 as follows: "it was an ʻayb [shameful act] [sc. for anyone of tribal descent] to open a shop (*dukkān*), to be a tailor (*dirzī*), barber (*muḥassin*), carpenter (*najjār*), butcher (*jazzār*), to engage in agricultural work, or even work in an office, to wear a coat or a sleeveless jacket (*ṣudayrīyah*) over the coat" (Serjeant 1968: 487). I would add that even as late as the 1970s the following trades were still virtually the exclusive preserve of B communities: carpentry, agriculture, animal husbandry, green-grocery, fish selling, butchering and meat selling, bread baking.

In Bahrain until about 25 years ago, there was an almost total residential separation of ʻArab and Baḥārnah. The ʻArab lived exclusively in al-Ḥidd, al-Muḥarraq, Qalālī, Busaytīn, Jaw, ʻAskar, Zallāq, al-Jisrah and Budayyaʻ, all coastal settlements which were once centres of the pearling industry,[9] and in West and East Rifāʻ in the centre of the island, near the Ruler's main palace, where many of them worked as retainers or in the military. Some of the older neighbourhoods of Manama, such as al-Fāḍil (also known as Kānō), al-Dhawāwidah and al-Ḥūrah were also predominantly 'Arab in population and confessionally Sunni. The Baḥārnah were heavily concentrated in most of the older, central quarters of the original settlement of Manama – al-Mukhārgah (lit. "the pearl-borers"), al-Nu'ēm (a community of boat-builders), al-Ḥaṭab ("firewood"), al-Ḥammām ("the public baths") – or in villages close by which over the last century of so have been absorbed by Manama, such as Rās Rummān (well known for its seafarers). The bulk of the B population lived in about 60 scattered villages, several of which were centres for a particular craft such as pottery ('Ālī) or weaving (Abū Ṣaybi' and Banī Jamrah). But in the main, the village economies depended on allotment farming, animal husbandry and palm cultivation until as recently as the 1960s (in the same way as the A communities had depended largely on pearl-diving until the mid-1930s).

Until very recently there was no intermarriage between the A and B communities, and it is still relatively rare, even in the more liberal atmosphere of Manama. Each sect maintains its own mosques, its own religious courts and, in the Baḥārnah case, *mawātim* ("funeral houses"), which serve not only as centres for the recital of Shi'i hagiographies during Muḥarram, but also as places for the Shi'i religious education which is not provided by the government school system. The popular belief of the Baḥārnah is that, as the original inhabitants of Bahrain, their rights were usurped by the incoming 'Arab. Whatever the accuracy of this claim, there is no doubting the lingering sense of historical grievance, especially in the B villages, at the indignities which the Baḥārnah periodically suffered at the hands of the 'Arab until the 1930s.[10]

From that point on, the British Adviserate began to exercise its influence directly on the Ruler in the matter of the relations of his tribal subjects with the Baḥārnah, and the development of the oil industry (the first well produced oil in 1935) offered the Baḥārnah employment and opportunities for self-advancement in a meritocratic environment: the Americans and Europeans who ran the industry were less interested in the sectarian affiliation of those they employed than in their ability to get the job done. This resulted in the hitherto unheard of circumstance of able Baḥārnah being promoted ahead of 'Arab. However, even as recently as 1972, at Bahrain's one and only general election until then, it was clear from the voting returns that in constituencies where the population was predominantly 'Arab, citizens voted overwhelmingly for 'Arab candidates and in Baḥārnah constituencies they voted for Baḥārnah candidates (Nakhleh 1976: 154). In the last 40 years, the building of 'Īsā Town, Ḥamad Town and other new residential areas has had the effect of breaking down the previously almost apartheid-like system of voluntary segregation. Moreover the development of an industrial and trading economy, as traditional neighbourhood- and village-based occupations have been all but wiped out, has brought the two communities closer together, at least publicly, in the work place. However, the 'Arab and the Baḥārnah still remain separate and distinct threads in the warp and weft of Bahraini society and culture.

Dialect and society in Bahrain

One consequence of the separation of the two communities has been the preservation, over more than two centuries, and in an area no bigger than a medium-sized English county, of a major dialectal cleavage that pervades all levels of linguistic analysis: pronunciation, word structure and vocabulary. The historical origins of this split, as is usual in cases of major communal differentiation of this kind, are geographical.[11] The A dialects are indeed a development of the Najdi dialects which the ancestors of today's A communities, prime among them the ruling Āl Khalīfah, brought with them when they began to emigrate to the Gulf coast from the mid-eighteenth century onwards. Dialects similar to them are spoken by tribally descended groups in Kuwait, Qatar and the UAE, who moved into the areas they now occupy over roughly the same period. The B dialects, on the other hand, are so similar in type to those of the agriculturalists of northern Oman, of certain populations of the UAE and of southern Yemen that there is almost certainly an (ancient) historical connection between the populations that speak them. In a nutshell, the A dialects of Bahrain (and other Najdi-descended groups down the Gulf) are historically and typologically "badu" in character, whereas the B dialects of Bahrain (and those of the other areas with which they are similar) are, by the same criteria, "sedentary" and geographically "southern".[12] An important dynamic in the history of the Arabian Peninsula over a very long period has been episodes of migration by badu from the centre to the periphery, where they have gradually achieved, political, cultural and not least linguistic dominance.

Although the social segregation of the last two and a half centuries has maintained the distinctive character of the A and B dialects – such that the speech of uneducated A and B villagers can still reach, or so it is claimed by A speakers, the point of mutual unintelligibility[13] – there has been a good deal of long-term dialectal accommodation in the towns. In Manama, B speech has moved nearer, in certain features, to the A dialect and distanced itself from the rural B dialects from which it originally sprang; and in the B neighbourhood called Firīj al-Ḥayāyīch ("the sail-makers' quarter") of the A-dominated town of Muḥarraq, the B residents speak a dialect that is indistinguishable from that of their A neighbours. In other words, B speakers, long-term, have tended to accommodate to the speech patterns of nearby A communities, but not vice-versa. This pattern of asymmetric shifting is a classic indicator of the relative social prestige of the two dialects,[14] and the process is likely to accelerate in the newly built "mixed" towns.

I have tabulated below some of the most striking differences between the A dialects and the B dialects in "core" areas of the language, noting also certain ways in which the village B dialects differ from the urban B dialects.[15] Educated B speakers, whether from town or village, tend now to avoid many of the stereotypically B features noted (and asterisked) in the table – *f* for *th*, the *-īn* and *-ūn* second person pronouns and suffixes of the past tense verb, and suffixed participial constructions involving the use of an *-inn-* infix, as in *kātbatinnəh*, and *a fortiori* purely "village B" features – whenever speaking in a non-domestic or cross-dialectal context. But there are very many other B-specific features less salient than these stigmatised ones which are less amenable to conscious correction, with the result that it is still fairly easy to distinguish ʻArab and Baḥārnah on the strength of their speech alone.

Classical Arabic (CLA) features	A dialects	B urban dialect	B village dialects[16]	
Phonology				
q	*yigūl*	*yigūl*	*yikūl**	he says
	jirīb	*garīb*	*karīb*	near
q (neologisms)	*taghaddum*	*taqaddum*	*taqaddum*	progress
gh	*yiqanni*	*yighanni*	*yighanni*	he sings
k	*cham*	*cham*	*cham*	how much
	akbar	*akbar*	*achbar**	bigger
j	*iyī*	*ijī*	*ijī*	he comes
ḍ	*ẓābiṭ*	*ḍābiṭ*	*ḍābiṭ*	officer
ẓ	*ẓarf*	*ḍarf*	*ḍarf*	envelope
dh	*hādhi*	*hādi**	*hādi**	this
th	*thalāthah*	*falāfah**	*falāfah**	three

(*continued on p 62.*)

Classical Arabic (CLA) features	A dialects	B urban dialect	B village dialects	
Verb and Noun Morphology				
katabat	*ktibat*	*kitbat/katabat*	*katabat*	she wrote
katabti	*kitabti/ kibabtay*	*kitabtīn**	*kitabtīn**	you (f) wrote
katabtum	*kitabtu/ kitabtaw*	*kitabtūn**	*kitabtūn**	you (pl) wrote
kātibatuhu	*kātbitah*	*kātbatinnəh**	*kātbatinnəh**	she has written it
qahwah	*ghawah*	*gahwah*	*kahwah**	coffee
aḥmar	*ḥamar*	*aḥmar*	*aḥmar*	red
waraqah	*wrigah*	*waragah*	*warakah**	leaf
bintuka	*bintik*	*bintik*	*bintich**	your (m) daughter
bintuki	*bintich*	*bintish*	*bintish*	your (f) daughter
bintukum	*bintkum*	*bintkum*	*bintchim**	your (pl) daughter
Vocabulary				
Interrogatve pronoun	*shinhu*	*waysh*	*waysh, wayshhu, ayshō**	what?
Negative particle	*mu, mub, muhub, hub*	*mu*	*mu* fem *mi**	not
1st person singular pronoun	*āna*	*ana* fem *ani**	*ana* fem *ani**	I
2nd person feminine	*inti/intay*	*intīn**	*intīn(a)**	you (f)
2nd person plural	*intu/intaw*	*intūn**	*intūn(a)**	you (pl)
Question particle		*il-bayt ə*?*	*il-bayt ə*?*	the house?
	rāḥ	*rāḥ*	*ghada**	to go
	ṭagg	*ḍarab*	*ḍarab*	to hit
	ẓahar	*ṭila'*	*ṭila'*	to go out
	tamm	*ḍall*	*ḍall*	to continue, keep on
	gaṭu	*sannūr*	*sannūr*	cat
	mṭawwa'	*m'allim*	*m'allim*	religious teacher

Linguistic "reality" in TV and radio drama

Sociolinguistically speaking, the oddest thing about Bahraini radio and TV drama – whether *musalsalāt* or a one-off *tamthīlīyah* ("play") – is that the only dialect that ever seems to be used is that of the

'Arab. And where an external set has to be created for the action, as in TV nostalgia *musalsalāt* like *il-Bēt il-ʿŌd* and *Firjān il-Awwal*, it resembles nothing so much as the backstreets of Muḥarraq or al-Ḥidd, both A towns, *c.* 1930s. The stated aim of *il-Bēt il-ʿŌd* is:

> to recreate a number of the beautiful images with which Bahrain's and the Gulf's past is filled. It attempts to resurrect the spirit of the old heritage, symbolised in the utensils of the past, with the aim of reviving the memories of the older generation and satisfying their desire and longing for the past. At the same time, it attempts to link subsequent generations to their popular culture, its history, and its customs.[17]

It does this by centring each episode on "old-fashioned utensils which used to be used in people's homes, such as the mortar (*al-hāwin*), the winnow (*al-minsaf*), the broom (*al-ʿasu*), the washing-bowl (*al-ṭasht*), the clothes chest (*ṣandūg il-imbayyat*), the lantern (*al-fanar*), the quern (*al-raḥa*), the brazier (*al-mingalah*), etc." There is a similar aim for *Firjān il-Awwal* except here each of the 30 episodes is built around an old belief or superstition, e.g. "jinxing" someone or something with sterility (*chabs*) and relieving the jinx, avoiding a person afflicted with bad luck (*kishḥān*), cures for "the evil eye" (*il-ʿēn il-ḥasūd*).

In both series the characters dress in traditional A style, and even where characters appear who would, in the reality that the shows purport to represent, have been from the B community and spoken a B dialect – the peripatetic vegetable seller (*baggāl*) with his donkey and cart, or the boat-builder and repairer (*gallāf*) – the actors playing them speak like 'Arab. "Like 'Arab" is perhaps the correct way to describe it. The *musalsal* version of the A dialect is itself a pastiche, with a mixture of traditional address forms, like *yubba* and *yumma* (for "Father" and "Mother") in an apparent attempt to provide local colour, and "educated" words and phrases that jar when put in the mouths of the supposedly uneducated salt-of-the-earth characters depicted.[18]

Although the aim of these highly popular series is thus to conjure up the Bahrain of a rosy but unspecified bygone age – perhaps the early part of the twentieth century (no radio, no TV, old-fashioned banknotes, universally held superstitious beliefs) – there is no attempt to represent the social (still less linguistic) realities of that period, assuming that the script-writers knew what these were. But neither is there any attempt at verisimilitude in other directions. Each show of about 20 minutes is generously sprinkled with songs and dances, performed at the drop of a hat. These take up perhaps half the running time and underline the point of the episode. At the end of the first episode of *Firjān il-Awwal*, for instance, a group of good-for-nothing young men (*lōfarīyah*) who have been caught stealing a fortune-teller's hoard of cash are publicly beaten with a bamboo cane in the open square of the neighbourhood (*il-barāḥa*). But the cane strokes are light, and, as the boys are being beaten, the neighbours, complete with drums, tambourines and choreographed moves, sing an ironic song. One obvious function which these TV *musalsalāt* serve, as the blurb on their box suggests obliquely, is to foster a sense – however ersatz – of a shared past and a continuity of culture across the generations at a time when the pace of change in the real world is disconcertingly rapid. These nostalgia *musalsalāt* seem in fact to be part of the current Gulf heritage industry. In the last few years, one notes the "theme parking" of the pre-oil culture in national museums, with waxwork tableaux of "traditional" scenes and interiors. These are favourite places for family visits. The past is a safe haven, even if it is an artificial, historically inaccurate and rose-tinted fiction.

Below are a couple of extracts that illustrate the kind of sentiment and content that typify the series, and the artificiality of the language. The first, an episode from *il-Bēt il-ʿŌd* which is built around "the water-jar" (*al-yaḥlah*), is concerned with the notion of good-neighbourliness (*ḥusn al-jiwār*). This is the opening scene, in which a well-dressed young woman finds the house water-jar empty and the well in the courtyard of the house dried up. Enter her father:

Father	*Mitkaddira, yā Asma?* Are you upset, Asmā'?
Daughter	(nods)
Father	*Lēsh, yā binti, lēsh?* Why, daughter, why?
Daughter	*Yubba, yubba, il-bīr nishaf māyih … wi z-zarʿ dhiblat awrāgha … wi l-bahāyim byidhbaḥha l-ʿaṭash!* Father, the water in the well has dried up … and the leaves on the crops have withered, and thirst will kill our animals!
Father	*Allāh mawjūd, yā binti, allāh mawjūd!* God watches over us, my daughter, God is there!
Daughter	*Lā ilāha illa llāh u Muḥammad rasūl allāh … bass yubba …* There is no god but God and Muhammad is his messenger! … But father –
Father	*Inti khayfa tmūt min il-ʿaṭash? Lā tkhāfin yā Asma! Dīrat ayāwīd*[19] *ṣidj, flūshum qalīla bass ahalha, ahalha shihām u kirām!* Are you afraid they'll die of thirst? Don't be afraid, Asmā'. This is a town of noble people! True, they haven't got much money but the people who live here are decent and generous!
Daughter	*Shūf, yubba! Idha iḥna aghna ahal il-firīj u hādhi ḥālatna, fa shḥālat il-faqāra?* Look, father! If we are the richest family of the neighbourhood, and this is the state we're in, what about the poor?

Father	*L-imbayyin inha mastūra!* They're respectable, as all can see!
Daughter	*Yubba, āna aqṣud il-māy!* Father, I meant their water supply!
Father	*Min han-nāḥya lā tḥātīn shay! Ahl id-dīrah idha iʿrufaw inna fīh aḥad miḥtāj ʿāyish fī wusuṭhum, tijāsamaw maʿāh illi ʿindahum.* On that subject, don't you worry! If the people of this town know that there's someone living among them who is in need, they share whatever they have with him.
Daughter	*Allāh yihadāk, yubba!* May God put you straight on that point, father!
Father	*Tabbīn tit'akkadīn min hash-shay? Taʿālay maʿāy* You need convincing of that? Come with me ...

The episode that follows this introduction is an object lesson in the benefits of good-neighbourliness. In language (however stilted) and dress, the young woman is clearly from the A community, and relatively well off. Her concern about "crops" and "animals" would be appropriate coming from B villagers in their dialect, but sounds utterly incongruous coming from her.

The second extract is from an episode of *Firjān al-Awwal*, which is concerned with traditional beliefs about how to counteract the "evil eye". Three members of a family each apply a different "cure" to the case of an only son who has fallen inexplicably ill, and each thinks that it was his cure that did the trick when the boy suddenly gets better. Here the grandmother has gone to a *ḥayyām* ("cupper", "quack-doctor"), and receives the following advice:

Yigūlūn in-nās, idha l- əṣbay yinṣāb əb ʿēn tākhidh lih shabbah ... mithil hādhi ... u tifurkīnha bi gāʿat rīlih u chaff yadih u fī yabhatih ... u tāli tibakhrīnih əbha, zēn? ... ʿugub, tākhdhīn sabaʿ bēzāt u tḥuṭṭīnhum fī khirja ḥamra u tiʿigdīnhum sabaʿ ʿigdāt tākhdhīnhum u tigiṭṭīnhum fī l-lēl fī s-sikka ... u yōm ith-thāni, adnāt ādami əbyilga l-khirja u byaylis yibaṭṭil l- əʿgad illi fīha ... u kil ʿigda yibaṭṭilha, l- əṣbay yiṣḥa ... u mā yibaṭṭil sābiʿ l-əʿgad wila l- əṣbay gāyim mithil il-faras!

People say, if a boy is affected by the evil eye, you get him a lump of alum ... Like this ... and you rub it on the sole of his foot and the palm of his hand and his forehead ... and then you waft the smoke over him, right? ... then, you take seven bayzas[20] and put them in a red cloth and tie them up in seven knots and throw them in the street at night. ... The next day, someone or other will find the cloth and will sit and untie the knots in it ... with every knot he unties, the boy will get better ... and no sooner does he untie the seventh knot than the boy will get up, as right as rain![21]

Just as in "nostalgia" *musalsalāt*, the milieu and language in one-off broadcast *tamthīlīyāt* set in modern Bahrain are also always that of the A community. In these short (15-minute-long) plays there is often a clear didactic aim. Typical examples involve thinly veiled criticism of the traditional views of the family matriarch, a powerful figure in Bahraini society whose viewpoint is likely to have been shared by many older female listeners. In one play, an elderly mother rejects her son's attempts to get her treated in hospital for diabetes because she will not be able to eat the kind of food she likes (which is the cause of her diabetes) or have all her friends come and stay all day chatting to her, or be visited by her grandchildren. Cue a homily from the son on the advantages of a healthy balanced diet, the reasons for limiting hospital visits and the ban on young children visiting (which were all apparently government-imposed rules in public hospitals at the time this play was broadcast). In another play, the mother is scandalised to hear from a neighbour of her son's that he has been helping his wife to do the housework! Cue a sermon to the mother from her daughter on how nosy neighbours should mind their own business, and how modern men with working wives ought to lend a hand with the cooking and cleaning; the real scandal was that men of her father's generation had not done likewise.

One sees in both cases the gentle pushing of a government-inspired social agenda. However, compared with the crude pastiche of the nostalgia *musalsal* the words put in the traditional mother's mouth in these plays are a closer approximation to the type of speech I have recorded from real elderly women from the A community – full of traditional address forms, proverbs and other colourful expressions. Characters from the next generation down are made to speak in a more educated-sounding, but still local, A idiom:

Daughter (answering knock at the door)	*Min? yumma? ʿasa mā sharr?*
	Who's that? Mum? I hope nothing's wrong?
Mother	*Ish-sharr əb ʿēni! ʿaṭīni guṭrat māy, babill rīji! Rīji nāshif nashshaf allāh rīj il-ʿadu!*
	Look me in the eye and you'll see the wrong! Give me a drop of water, I need to wet my whistle! My throat is dry – may God dry my enemy's throat!
Daughter	*Māy? inshāllah, inshāllah! … ʿasa mā sharr, yumma, ʿasa mā sharr?*
	Water? OK, OK! … I hope there's nothing wrong, mum, nothing the matter?
Mother	*Yā binti, ana yālsa fī l-bayt mā ʿindi min ish-shayṭān ṭarīj …*

	wila yāyatni waḥdah min ibnayyāt il-firīj u gālat lī kalām, yā binti, farr rāsi farr! I was just sitting at home minding my own business ... when one of the girls from the neighbourhood came to me and told me something that made my head spin!
Daughter	*Shinhu l-kalām, yumma?* What was it she said, mum?
Mother	*Kalām yā binti ibuṭṭ il-chabad! Kalām yikhalli l-ʿājil maynūn* Something that would make an angel swear! Something that would drive a sane person mad!
Daughter	*Shinhu l-kalām, yumma?* What was it she said, mum?
Mother	*Yā binti kalām ʿan akhūch u murtih* About your brother and his wife ...
Daughter	*ʿAsa mā sharr, shfihum?* I hope nothing bad has happened ... what's up with them?
Mother	*Ya binti ila git lich mā tṣadgīnni* If I tell you, you'll never believe it!
Daughter	*Yumma ḥatta ẓẓammīn, shhast? Gūlay shhast, gūlay!* Mum, what is it that you're being so secretive about? Tell me what the matter is, tell me!
Mother	*Yā binti akhūch illi rabbētih ʿala d-dalāl u shiltih bi l-ward u ḥaṭṭētih bi l-yasmīna, ila agūl lich ʿan ḥāltih al-ḥīn, mā tṣadgīn!* Your brother, who I spoilt and pampered and molly-coddled – if I tell you the state he's in now, you won't believe me!

Those familiar with Gulf dialects will spot idioms and expressions that are plainly meant to sound "traditional", and enthusiasts will wish to unpack some of them. *Rījī nāshif*, for instance, in Mother's first line, has a double meaning: not only is she thirsty (her throat is dry), but the phrase means "at the end of one's tether". And "may God dry my enemy's throat" is an imprecation one might well hear from older women in the A community. *Kalām yā bintī ibuṭṭ il-chabad*, translated as "something that would make an angel swear", of course is "words that would make your liver burst". Pampering and molly-coddling the boy, the old lady had "picked him up in roses and put him down in jasmine". It is all quite colourful. But "Bahraini tradition", as presented here, is effectively in an A voice.

Just as it fails to make an appearance in either the nostalgia *musalsal* or the entertaining but often didactic *tamthīlīyāt*, the B dialect is also conspicuous by its absence in children's radio and TV programming (e.g. in stories for pre-school-age children). In short, the default position in all Bahraini media seems to be that whenever local culture and history are represented, whether the purpose is to divert or instruct, and at whatever age group the programmes are aimed, the dialect employed is invariably that of the A community. Or almost. The one exception I have noted is slapstick comedy.

For several years in the 1970s and 1980s, the Bahraini comedy duo Ṣāliḥ al-Madanī and Jāsim Khalaf had a radio *musalsal* called *Aḥmad ibn Aḥmad wa-l-Ḥajjī ibn al-Ḥajjī*. These two (part-time) actors are both educated middle-aged Baḥārnah men from Manama.[22] The characters they play are B archetypes of the generation of their fathers, with urban B accents deliberately exaggerated for comic effect. Al-Ḥajjī is larger than life, uneducated, accident-prone and with a nagging wife. He is an exhaustible source of nuggets of (usually) inappropriate homespun wisdom, who perpetually gets the wrong end of the stick; Aḥmad is the sidekick who feeds him lines. Familiar locales from Manama – the fish-market, a barber's shop, the back streets where the two protagonists live – form the backdrop to the action. There is apparently no script,[23] but an outline plot around which the actors extemporise the dialogue, which, compared with the stilted language of the TV *musalsal*, gives their show a sense of humour and linguistic spontaneity that rings true.[24] A certain amount of gentle fun is poked at the government on issues that concern ordinary people – crooked merchants in the bazaar, the price of goods during Ramaḍān or the chaos of public services – as in the following in which al-Ḥajjī is telling Aḥmad about an accident he has had in the fish-market:

al-Ḥajjī	*Adiyya! wallah adiyya! rjūli hēkhi maksūra!* It's a calamity! God, what a calamity! Just look at my foot, it's broken!
Aḥmad	*Wēsh fiha rjūlik?* What's the matter with your foot?
al-Ḥajjī	*Ana, allāh yisallimk riḥt sūg is-samach* Went off to the fish-market, see –
Aḥmad	*Ē* Uhuh.
al-Ḥajjī	*Min iṣ-ṣubḥ* In the morning –
Aḥmad	*Ē* Uhuh.
al-Ḥajjī	*Riḥna, is-samach mā jābōh, mit'akhkhur ... wugafna ... jaw u ṣārat ilamma rakaḍat in-nās!* We all went, but they hadn't brought the fish, it was late ... so we stood around waiting ... then they came, and people started running ...
Aḥmad	*U rakaḍt iyyāhum* And you ran with them?
al-Ḥajjī	*Wiyyāhum! Allāh yisallimk wi t-tawāfig, u anzalik chidiha wa ṭāyiḥ fi rjūli at'awwar!*

	I did! And then – I hope it never happens to you! – I goes and slips like this, falls on me foot, and hurts myself!
Aḥmad	*Ē, kisāfah u rṭūbah hnāk wājid!*
	Yes! There's loads of muck and moisture over there!
al-Ḥajjī	*Khamag ila hni! Māy ila hni!*
	Clag up to here! Water up to here!

Any Bahraini would immediately recognise the language of this exchange as typical of the urban B dialect. A few examples: phonologically, the use of *d* for *dh* in words like *adiyya*, "calamity", and of *j* rather than *y* in such core vocabulary items as *jābōh*, "they brought it", *jaw*, "they came", *wājid*, "a lot" (the A dialect has *yābōh*, *yaw* and *wāyid* respectively) marks the speakers as from the B community. Lexically, *rjūl* for "foot" is a purely B form (the A dialect has *rīl*), as is *wēsh* for "what?" (the A dialect has *shinhu*) and *chidiha*, "like this" (the A dialect has *chidhi*). Morphologically, forms like *yisallimk*, "(May God) save you", with a final consonant cluster are purely B; the A dialect has *yisalmik* without the cluster (and consequently with a different stress pattern). No example of a word containing the shibboleth *th*, which uneducated B speakers pronounce as *f*, as in *falāfa*, "three", appears in this extract, but *f* for *th* is a stock-in-trade of these comedians' stage performance (though in a "serious" Bahrain Radio interview about his early life that I recorded in the late 1970s, Jāsim Khalaf avoided use of this stereotypical marker of B speech).

Linguistic sociology

The dominance of the A dialect in broadcast drama, and the performing arts more generally, is partly the result of the dominance of the members of the A community in the dramatic arts, the A community having tended historically to adopt a less conservative and censorious attitude to such activities than the B. But that by itself does not explain the glaring lack of "community realism" in the vast majority of *musalsalāt*, in which there is no attempt to represent the B community that makes up half the population. The absence of representations of the B community and its dialect is partly also a question of respecting delicate sensibilities. The common perception among members of the A community has been that the Baḥārnah, particularly those from the villages, are socially backward and superstitious, and their speech incomprehensible.[25] The Baḥārnah are of course aware of these beliefs. It may be that the mimicking of B dialectal characteristics in *musalsalāt* for the sake of verisimilitude, in programmes whose main function is to entertain, is avoided on the grounds that it might seem insensitive or patronising. It is, in other words, fine for B comedians like Jāsim Khalaf and Ṣāliḥ al-Madanī to poke fun at B mannerisms and speech, and for everyone to laugh, but not, perhaps, for A script-writers and actors to represent typical B speakers for fear their efforts might be interpreted as mockery.

Certainly, the observable tendency, in public contexts, of educated A speakers to maintain stereotypically A linguistic features, set against the avoidance by educated B speakers of stereotypically B features in similar circumstances is a clear indication of each community's relative degree of "linguistic security".[26] Even in the cases where B dialect features correspond with those of Modern Standard Arabic (for example the *j* realisation of CLA *jīm*) – that is, with the external and universally accepted yardstick of linguistic "correctness" – my own research shows that the educated B speakers show a slight but unmistakable tendency to switch to the A-dialect features which are, by this criterion "incorrect", but locally more prestigious.[27] There is no doubt that members of the B community are broadly aware of the way their communities, in speech, dress and way of life, are starting to accommodate to those of the A community which dominate both Bahraini and Gulf public life. It was no doubt this that lay behind the comments from village B speakers I occasionally encountered when doing fieldwork in the 1970s, such as (in reference to how weddings were starting to be celebrated in B villages): *mā ista'rab il-awādim illa l-ḥīn*, "It's only now that people have started to 'get Sunnified'."[28]

But there are other reasons for the dominance of the A dialect in Bahraini *musalsalāt* which have to do with the increasing importance of regional factors and their homogenising effects. As already noted, the dialects of the dominant political and economic groups in all the Gulf states were not all that different from one another to begin with because of their common central Najdi origin, reaching back no more than 250 years. But in the last 20 years or so, the Bahraini A dialect and its analogue in other Gulf states (in a suitably educated form) has gradually assumed the status of a kind of "regional dialectal standard" from Kuwait to the UAE as a by-product of the increasingly tightly knit pan-Gulf social, economic and political networks that have been emerging. To the extent that the speakers of the same type of dialectal Arabic dominate media representations of ordinary life on TV and over the airwaves, the social and political hegemony is being translated into a linguistic one.

The process is hastened everywhere by the rapidity of change in recent decades, one aspect of which is language. Just how fast the linguistic change has been was brought home to me by an undergraduate research project I supervised a few years ago. A student of mine from the UAE constructed a test that involved the testee picking a picture to match a word which was read to him. The 20 words were among those commonly used in Abu Dhabi in the late 1950s, as evidenced by T.M. Johnstone's fieldwork at that time, e.g. *khāshūgah*, "spoon", *maywah*, "fruit", *ālu*, "potato", which he put to two groups of 20 adults, one aged over 50, and the other under 20. The under-20s had almost no idea what most of the words meant, while the over-50s scored virtually 100 per cent. Something similar might be found in many Gulf states. The dialects spoken by younger people are meanwhile not just related historically but exposed to all the current interactions that I sketched at the start of the chapter, symbolised by roads and bridges. Inventing a specific past linguistically, as we see being done in Bahraini *musalsalāt*, tends to produce a set of related pasts, each of them expressed in something like an A dialect – a "Gulf dialect" – such that the real complexity of local society, in Bahrain or Qatar or Abu Dhabi only a few decades ago, is lost to view.

What seems to be happening now at local level is the repetition of a process that has been observed elsewhere in the Arab World over the last century, whereby the dialects of large cities, usually the capitals, become locally prestigious within the borders of one country: Cairo in Egypt, Damascus in Syria, Baghdad in Iraq (Holes 1995). Incomers who do not speak this dominant dialect (e.g. southern Egyptians emigrating to Cairo), or others already resident but from non-dominant social groups (e.g. Christians in Baghdad) accommodate, at least publicly, to it, and what begins as a temporary accommodation becomes permanent in succeeding generations. The novelty of the situation in the Gulf is that there is not one, but several regional centres in which the same general dialect-type has assumed the position of prestige dialect. What we see in the language of the Bahraini *musalsalāt*, and in other media representations of local speech, is both an expression of this regional dominance and a public artistic reinforcement of it: a two-way flow.

Conclusion

Media drama in the Gulf is not a mirror of the society that produced it, still less of that society's past, but presents a part of the image that those who control it wish to project to the outside world. What it includes and what it omits is not merely, I would argue, a matter of chance or individual artistic whim, but the result of constellations of power and conscious decision. Much the same can be said about the choice of what is included and excluded in the national museums that are springing up all over the Gulf. A visitor to the Bahraini museum would never guess that a mainstay of the island's economy until no more than 40 years ago was agriculture – but then that was the exclusive preserve of the village Baḥārnah. Would it be taking things too far to see in the unconsidered trifle of the Bahraini nostalgia *musalsal* another part – a small one – of the attempt to rewrite Bahraini social history? If so, it is, like all such revisions, a biased one. In offering the viewing public a romanticised past to which all can apparently sign up, it sedulously excludes the inconvenient bits of the story.

CHAPTER 3

CULTURAL CONSTRUCTION, THE GULF AND ARAB LONDON[1]

Christa Salamandra

Over the past 25 years, London has been a major site – arguably the international centre – of GCC-funded financial dealing, cultural production and Arabic-language media. London forms a central node in the transnational flow of ideas and wealth to and from the Gulf. Yet little scholarly attention has been focused on this dramatic instance of global interconnectedness. The present chapter examines one aspect of the Arab London phenomenon: the role of a global city in the construction and commodification of Gulf Arab imagery and local knowledge. As a centre of cultural scholarship and commerce, London has become a primary locus for the creation of Gulf heritage and of part of the Gulf's own national and regional "culture". Literature on heritage industries and national culture-construction assumes usually that these processes occur within national boundaries (Handler 1985, Lowenthal 1989, 1996). In the case of the Arab Gulf, however, national culture-construction not only takes place within a context of increasing globalisation but is itself a transnational process.

Globalisation, transnationalism and Arab London

Since the rise of oil wealth in the mid-1970s, London has served as a second home, tourist destination and offshore investment site of choice for GCC states and nationals. Several factors contributed to London's attractiveness: historical links between the Gulf and Britain and the resultant English-language familiarity; the perception of the city as more Arab- and Muslim-friendly than other European capitals; a comfortable climate and geographical position midway between Europe and the United States; the presence of British ex-army and ex-civil service personnel once stationed in the Gulf; and periodic influxes of Arab and Middle Eastern migrants following episodes of political upheaval in the region.[2] Populations of British and Middle Easterners familiar with the Gulf form a culturally sensitised and often bilingual workforce of mediators.

Close and mutually legitimising imperial connections underpin the contemporary affinity between the GCC and British elites. Britain's informal empire in the Arab Gulf during the nineteenth and early twentieth centuries depended on collaboration with local merchant and ruling families (Onley 2001), and historians of empire, writing on other areas, emphasise the importance of alliance and co-optation to the success of imperial projects generally (Robinson 1972). In stressing local resistance to Western dominance, anthropologists and others have tended to ignore collusion, co-operation and shared interests (Jacobs 1996: 15). Cannadine, however, notes that shared notions of aristocratic rule, expressed through a royal culture of costume, title and ritual, often reinforced both the British monarchy and its local clients (Cannadine 2001). In contemporary London, a (post)imperial symbiosis of elites lives on in an industry of Arabian heritage.

Today these joint rituals of dominance, of which the Gulf heritage industry forms a significant component, often serve as public-relations exercises embellishing the transnational flow of money and weaponry. Heritage production operates against a backdrop of multi-million-pound transactions, chiefly arms sales,[3] such that London-based multinationals and their Gulf clients co-produce and consume the cultural veneer of a defence industry that absorbs much of the GCC's oil wealth (Aburish 1997: 87–94). Such practices do not proceed uncontested, as London is also home to numerous opposition Arab and Islamic organisations, presses and publications.[4] Yet much of this dissent is expressed in simple political terms; the realm of Gulf culture is largely left to ruling elites and multinational corporate sponsors and their London-based transnational mediators.

Over the past ten years, a series of general or theoretical volumes has attempted to define and describe transnationalism and globalisation, and to suggest useful approaches to its study (Robertson 1992, Morely and Robins 1995, Featherstone 1990, 1995, Appadurai 1996, Hannerz 1996). However, much of this material consists of intertextual literature reviews, with original contributions often limited to speculative arguments and programmatic suggestions, and little ethnographic evidence given. Robertson, writing in the early days of the trend, saw the problem as a lack of true engagement with the globalisation process (Robertson 1990: 15–16). As Ong and Nonini note (1997: 13), globalisation and transnationalism are still commonly treated as "a set of abstracted, dematerialized cultural flows, giving scant attention either to the concrete, everyday changes in people's lives or to the structural reconfigurations that accompany global capitalism". Notable exceptions to this generalising tendency depict London as a major nexus of transnational interaction (King 1990, Eade 1997, 2000c, Sassen 2001).

One useful formulation for understanding Gulf Arab London is the concept of "third cultures", which Featherstone (1990: 1) describes as "conduits for ... diverse cultural flows which cannot be merely understood as the product of bi-national exchanges between nation-states". Skills of cultural mediation are increasingly crucial in a context of growing interconnectedness, as globalisation "renders different local cultures more immediate and the need to make them practicably intelligible more pressing" (Featherstone 1995: 93). Arab London intermediaries are third-culture bearers. Transnationalism is very much about third-culture occupations involving contacts and mobility across state boundaries (Hannerz 1996: 242), and competence in third cultures is itself commodified: a new category of professional interculturalists now trains the marketplace in cultural sensitivity and awareness (Dalén 1997). While explicitly engaged in facilitating exchange, intermediaries have become, perhaps unwittingly, cultural gatekeepers with vested interests in maintaining reified notions of difference – most obvious perhaps in art and publishing.

The Islamic art market

The buying and selling of Islamic art and antiquities in London predate the influx of Arab oil money. Historically, the city has served as a global centre for the buying and selling of all types of art, and the United Kingdom's colonial links with the Middle East and South Asia rendered London a logical site for the collection and sale of Islamic material. Marcus Fraser, director of Islamic and Indian art at Sotheby's, points to three reasons for London's prominence: a strong tradition of upper-class patronage; its geographical position midway between Europe and the New World; and "grand tour" travel collections of continental art and antiquities. Those who work in London also claim a greater degree of transparency and accountability than competitors such as those in Paris have.[5]

The first auction of Islamic material, a collection of Arabic manuscripts from a British estate, was held in 1755 at Sotheby's. Sotheby's was at this time primarily a bookseller, and its early association with Islam introduced Islamic art to London in manuscript form. But a true market for Islamic art in the West did not develop until the 1920s and 1930s, and in Paris and New York rather than London. During the early part of the twentieth century the popularity of Islamic pieces formed part of a wider fashion for Orientalia and exotica (Clifford 1988, Errington 1998), and a series of major exhibitions –

Munich in 1910, London in 1931, New York in 1940 – introduced Islamic art to Western collectors.

Iranian oil wealth in the 1960s fuelled a generation of art dealers from "an established cultural elite", as Fraser puts it, who, led by the then Empress of Iran, created a boom in Persian miniatures in London. No restrictions were placed on the export of antiquities from the Middle East until 1973, and copious material flowed westward. New oil wealth from the Arab Gulf was, however, first used to showcase Islamic art in Britain with the World of Islam Festival of 1975. An official publicity brochure noted that the festival involved "no formal government sponsorship" but was nonetheless "only made possible by support from the governments concerned and by the generosity of many institutions both in the lending countries and in the UK" (World of Islam Festival Trust 1983: 2). Although underwritten by a British Treasury bond, most of the festival's funding came in fact from the UAE government, which contributed 80 per cent of the total £2,250,000 cost. After the festival, donations from Saudi Arabia, Jordan, Oman, the Islamic Solidarity Fund and the Arab Bank supported the Festival Trust's continuance.

Emphatically apolitical, the Festival's expressed aim, according to its own publicity material, was to educate and to promote tolerance (Duncan 1976). Yet the status of participants and the tone of Festival reports reflect the conservative, elite proclivity common to much British mediation:

> Distinguished and important people attended the inauguration of the Festival by Her Majesty Queen Elizabeth; ... the opening exhibition of "Science and Technology in Islam", at the Science Museum, by Her Imperial Majesty the Empress of Iran added to the regal elegance of the opening ceremonies and represented the role played in the Festival by those countries outside the Arab world whose influence and culture have contributed to and enhanced the synthesis and development of world-wide Islamic civilisation (Duncan 1976: 3).

The Festival also involved the participation of a wide range of scholars and institutions around the world. Half a million visitors were estimated to have attended its various exhibitions, including the Haywood Gallery's "Arts of Islam" and the Science Museum's "Science and Technology in Islam". A further million viewed the six-part World of Islam documentary television series. Over 150 public lectures were delivered at more than 800 British educational institutions, and the Trust sponsored more than 20 scholarly publications.[6]

The World of Islam Festival proved a watershed for the Islamic art trade. The Islamic market in London is now bigger than its Chinese, Japanese and Indian counterparts, all of which have shifted largely to

New York, and Britain is home to the world's strongest community of Islamic art scholars. The Islamic art world is relatively small, closely knit and informal. As Fraser puts it, "a conference will include 90 per cent of the major players in one lecture hall". Links among museum curators, university experts and art-sellers are strong, and wild fluctuations prompted by the vast, periodic ebbs and flows of Gulf money have created a skewed and insecure market for Islamic art, perhaps accentuated by these close ties. According to Michael Spink, "the market has become extremely erratic; the traditional notion of value has been abandoned. Something that should make £5,000 goes for £50,000".

Iranian and, to a lesser extent, Turkish dealers continue to dominate the market numerically, but in terms of buying power, a handful of Gulf collectors now reign supreme. Robinson estimates that there are between 50 and 60 big buyers, ten of whom are from the Gulf, and two of these ten collectors are "the keenest buyers of all, whose presence or absence can make or break a sale". Recent buoyancy has forced less wealthy collectors into niche buying and has limited museums to "study piece" acquisitions. But according to a long-time Lebanese observer, a single big buyer has nearly always driven the Islamic market: "when a big buyer appears on the scene, auction houses spot them and tailor-make themes". The first major Gulf collectors, Kuwaiti Shaykh Nāṣir al-Ṣabāḥ and his wife Shaykhah Ḥussā, amassed an impressive collection during the 1980s and donated part of their collection to form the Kuwaiti National Museum.

The current boom, under way since 1997, has been fuelled by the emergence of Shaykh Sa'ūd Āl Thānī and the Qatari state museum project planned for Doha. In addition to buying, the cataloguing and administration of the collection take place in London, through Qatar's Islamic Art Society in Mayfair. While those in the art business discreetly conceal his name, the dynamic presence they speak of as the force driving present prosperity is undoubtedly the 30-something Qatari shaykh:

> The Islamic art market's current liveliness is due to one buyer, who has come in with an enthusiasm and buying power that I suspect has never been seen before in any market. Even when David Khalili[7] was buying, and Shaykh Nāṣir forming his collection in the early 1980s, they were more restrained.

Shaykh Sa'ūd bears the title President of the National Council for Culture, Arts and Heritage of Qatar. A flamboyant dresser – an informant recalled his lime-green snake-skin boots – with a fine collection of art deco furniture, Sa'ūd is said to have a good eye and to have acquired quickly a wide-ranging knowledge of Islamic art. In addition to his art-collecting duties, he accompanies the Emir on visits to Britain. His flat in central London buzzes constantly with art dealers, decorators and other visitors. The Shaykh himself is "always in another room", as one informant puts it.

Shaykh Sa'ūd's unpredictable purchasing practices serve to finance a small but well-paid cadre of art professionals. A Lebanese dealer who has worked with him describes the co-operation of auction houses, dealers and advisers involved with the lucrative Qatari project:

> Some material his advisers know he wants, so the advisers go to dealers, who then put the material into sales, where it will be sold with an official invoice with a respectable auction house name on it, like Christie's or Sotheby's. So it won't be questioned. The piece may then fetch 25 times its original price, and everyone involved gets a cut. There's big money and a lot of people involved. He bids against himself, to thwart criticism of the high prices he pays, and creates an illusion of interest.

As this example shows, a network of highly skilled British and resident Arab experts draws Gulf consumptive capacities to London. Once acquired, and validated, the art is taken to the Gulf. Cultural and economic capital converge, as Islamic material culture is appropriated by Gulf elites and set up as part of "national" heritage. London serves as the construction site for the production of a local heritage from a globally circulating body of antiquities.

Varieties of Arab art

London also provides a focal point for the sale of contemporary Arab art to GCC buyers. Housed in an elegant gallery in Chelsea Manor studios – a well-known artists' space – the Egee Art Consultancy was the leading seller of modern Arab and Islamic art to the GCC countries. Over 23 years Dale Egee became a major presence in London's art circles and helped raised the profile of modern Arab art. She founded Egee Art Consultancy in 1978 with a single commission – from the Dubai Hyatt Regency Hotel. Her company grew to serve a long list of GCC corporations, banks and hotels, in addition to individual clients, and Gulf buyers, particularly Emiratis, formed the bulk of her customer base. In 2001, she sold her consultancy and gallery to ArRum, an upscale Muslim private club and leisure centre designed for a well-heeled British Asian clientele.

While she dealt in antiquities and European Orientalism, Egee's speciality was contemporary Middle Eastern art, loosely defined. "We call ourselves *fann al-'ālim al-'arabī* [art of the Arab World] but sometimes stretch this to fit in Pakistan". The consultancy also dealt in Western artists, but only those whose work refers to the Middle East. "Our Gulf clients love Orientalist works; they remind them of what they've lost". With Orientalist art "our rule of thumb is no odalisques, no cutesy-pie study pieces; they have to be genuine". Middle Eastern artists dealt with may have depicted any subject matter, or may have been abstract, and although the consultancy sold sculpture, ceramics and tapestry, it specialised in works on paper that could be transported easily during the several three-week trips Egee and her partner Evonne Eklund made separately to the Gulf each year. They also held regular exhibits in both London and the Gulf; a calligraphy exhibition travelled to Kuwait, Dubai, Abu Dhabi and Oman.

Egee chose to base her company in London for a number of reasons. The city serves as home in exile for many contemporary Arab artists. London's relationship with the GCC was also a factor, as was its relative geographic proximity to the Gulf. Egee pointed to an "international spirit" that makes the city attractive to an art dealer. "We have thought about setting up shop in Dubai, but Gulfies tell me London is the place". "They don't trust buying expensive things in their own countries", added Eklund. In addition to the city's cachet, it is also less expensive than the Arab World, where "local art is beyond belief in terms of price. Here there's more competition". Pricing is a key factor: "most Gulf clients are not keen on spending a lot on art". Someone else, less committed to the project's aims, added, "because they don't understand it. There is a market in the Gulf, they like artwork, but they don't know what it's all about. They can't tell the difference between a painting worth £300 and one worth £3,000". This of course raises basic questions about how, if at all, cost relates to value in the case of "art". All we can say here is that Gulf buyers have been drawn into a world where sophistication is judged by knowing what it is that other sophisticates value.

Tastes have thus changed through the years, with abstract art becoming more popular among young collectors. Until recently, the social capital of art was so low that "gold frames were more important than the art, as with Victorian Americans". Younger buyers, however, are becoming more discriminating: "our last client wants really modern art in plain wooden frames", noted Eklund. Collections are becoming more eclectic. Egee described the London residence of an Abu Dhabi shaykh: "There's Arab abstract art in the foyer, Orientalism in the *majlis*, religious in the mother's room and Western contemporary abstract in the sitting room".

Western Orientalism is popular with collectors from the Arab Gulf, and during the years of oil wealth, London galleries conducted a brisk business in romanticised Western images of the Arab World (cf. MacKenzie 1995: 45). Here an imagined East recreated in the West holds fascination. Much of the voluminous literature criticising Western aesthetic representations of the Middle East ignores the uncomfortable fact that these images attract Arab buyers, and writing on Orientalism as a "politics of representation" focuses instead (indeed, almost exclusively) on Western constructions of an essentialised East and the relationship of these constructs to colonial and imperial projects (Said 1978, Alloula 1987, Kabbani 1994, MacKenzie 1995). In ignoring the varied Arab responses to Orientalism, these writers are ultimately restricted by the same Eurocentric perspective they claim to criticise. An examination of the politics of consumption reveals a much more complex picture in which Arabs themselves often accept Orientalist essentialisms (al-Azm 1981) and embrace Orientalism's romantic aesthetic (Sharafuddin 1994).

The Mathaf Gallery, located in the elegant diplomatic district of Belgravia, is London's – and the world's – leading seller of nineteenth-century Orientalist paintings. This elegant showroom features top-of-the-market works from artists such as Gérômes and Ernst. Heavy gilt frames incorporate designs from the paintings themselves or patterns from the Umayyad Mosque in Damascus. Proprietor Brian MacDermot became acquainted with the Arab World as an officer in the Irish Guards in Egypt during the 1950s but his strong connection with the Middle East dates to the late 1960s and early 1970s when, as a stockbroker with Panmure and Gordon, "he got to know quite a lot of important Arabs".[8] MacDermot opened the Mathaf in conjunction with the World of Islam Festival in 1975. Its initial aim was to promote contemporary Arab painting. Arab embassies each chose one artist, whom the gallery then supported. "It was not a great commercial success", says MacDermot, "but it created interest". He later shifted to dealing primarily in nineteenth-century European Orientalists "from Delacroix to Matisse".

MacDermot found it difficult to estimate the proportion of his custom that comes from the GCC. He guesses that in volume about 75 per cent of the gallery's paintings are sold to the Arab World, and the GCC states form a major component of this block, though in terms of value the United States buys more. Nineteenth-century European collectors may have been drawn to exotic images of places never visited, but not so the recent Arab buyer:

> Colour, light, depictions of the desert. Something with which you can associate. In other words, it's not much good showing them a picture of the English countryside with a few cows grazing on the grass. It doesn't really – unless they live in England or have a house there – mean much ... But a lady lounging on a balcony – a typical scene – carpet sellers, the *sūq*, all of these things have some relevance.

These two essentialising visions – an England of countryside and grazing livestock, an Arabia of carpet sellers and balconies – might in other contexts be considered stereotypes. Yet the same images that Gulf Arabs sometimes find demeaning and inaccurate are in this case embraced, even purchased, as cultural authenticity. As Herzfeld notes, stereotypes may embarrass before an outside world; yet within a space of cultural intimacy they also provide insiders with a sense of commonality (Herzfeld 1997: 3). Such stereotypes are cultural operators, tropes with constitutive, world-building powers (Chock 1987: 348). Images framed as "tradition" often have little to do with contemporary everyday life, and remain, as Just notes in the case of Greece, "both iconographic and prescriptive" (Just 1995: 293).

Painting and patronage

Although London has never again matched the spurt of Arab cultural activity that took place in the mid-1970s during the World of Islam Festival, occasional exhibits continue to promote GCC art, culture and heritage. Many of these are sponsored by British or Gulf corporations and reflect the deep financial linkages between the Gulf and Britain. In June 2000, the Banqueting House in Whitehall hosted one such show, designed to underscore UK–Saudi relations.

Supported by BAE Systems (formerly British Aerospace) and Shell, "Painting and Patronage" juxtaposed stylised landscape paintings by the Prince of Wales with the vibrant folkloric canvases of Saudi Prince Khālid al-Fayṣal Āl Sa'ūd. A poster-board featured photographs of British royals alongside their Saudi counterparts through the years: a young Queen Elizabeth and Duke of Edinburgh with King Fayṣal at Buckingham Palace in 1967; Prince Charles, Prince Fayṣal, Prince Khālid and falcon in 'Asīr; Khālid giving Charles a present; Prince (now Crown Prince) 'Abdullāh riding in a carriage with Queen Elizabeth on the first day of Ascot in 1988; King Fahd receiving the Freedom of the City of London in 1987. Quotations recounted a history of co-operation and mutual affection: "that which binds our two worlds together is so much more than that which divides us" (Prince Charles); "our talks have had a positive effect in promoting the strong ties of friendship between our two countries and our peoples" (Crown Prince 'Abdullāh); "Saudi Arabia is an anchor of stability in the Middle East and a long-standing ally of Britain" (Prime Minister Blair).

This exhibit coincided with Prince Khālid's visit to Britain to publicise his development of the 'Asīr region in southern Saudi Arabia.[9] The basement of the Banqueting House was devoted to a display of 'Asīrī folklore. The cavernous vaulted space was decorated as a tent interior, with seating areas set up to offer visitors tea and dates, while handicrafts and other items of 'Asīrī material culture were displayed in alcoves along the walls. Designed to promote tourism, the exhibit also featured large colour photographs of Japanese tourists smiling and waving from bus windows. Folklore exhibit designer Dhafir al-Hamsan used material brought from the replica village he had constructed in ʻAsīr. A former Saudi Airforce radar technician, Hamsan is working to preserve and reconstruct local material culture for his country's budding tourist industry.

A rather different exhibition the year before, at the Mall Gallery, had shown another aspect of "tradition". Julian Friers's "Gifts from the Desert" featured 32 wildlife paintings, mainly of endangered species. The accompanying book, calf-bound and displayed in a glass case, formed the exhibition's centre-piece and was available in a limited edition at £3,000 per copy. Each copy's outer cover was decorated in gold leaf, and its inner cover with a gold-embossed Friers watercolour, both covers being lined with green silk; the pages of course were stitched and gold-edged, and the volume, presented in a green silk box, weighed 11kg. A further "royal edition" of 15 copies was produced, which presumably was even more elaborate. This extraordinary book – "Published to acknowledge the efforts of HRH Prince Sultan in protecting the desert and its wildlife" – appeared at the Mall Gallery under the sponsorship, again, of British Aerospace/BAE. Sulṭān bin ʻAbd al-ʻAzīz Āl Saʻūd (Minister of Defence, Minister of Aviation and Inspector General) is not himself an artist, but "artistic" depictions of wildlife, landscapes, heritage and folklore are judged suitable gifts for princes.

The Prince of Wales, for his part, not only attempts Saudi landscapes but favours on occasion a Gulf aesthetic. Visitors to his residence at Highgrove are thus entertained, reportedly, in something like a *majlis* with a tented roof (fabric is suspended somehow from the ceiling), where such curios as Aladdin lamps and boxes with cascades of pearls adorn both side-tables and the dining table.[10] Entering this personal space of royal hospitality, or leaving to visit the Prince's "Islamic" garden, dignitaries are liable to be ushered through the Highgrove gift-shop. Here the Prince's own biscuits and jams are on offer beside pencils and erasers emblazoned with his motif of feathers, and more expensive "gifts" such as signed landscapes. This transitional space features also a great many picture books on royalty, gardens and comparable "English" themes. Though Gulf elites do not stoop to gift-shops at the entrance of *dīwān* or *majlis*, they do favour similar publications.

Books: Stacey International

The largest London-based publisher of what might be termed "coffee-table books" about the Gulf and of popular histories of the region is Stacey International. Tom Stacey, a *Times* foreign correspondent to the Gulf during the 1960s, founded the business in 1974, at the beginning of the oil boom: "I perceived a gap, a publishing need, in countries which were going to become quite prominent in economic and other terms, and without the skills to present themselves to the outside world". Using contacts forged during his years as a journalist, such as the Saudi Deputy Minister of Information, Stacey entered into collaborations that became books. Now run from Stacey's Victoriana-filled house in Notting Hill, the company has produced dozens of volumes, many of which remain in print and are periodically revised and reissued. The initial motivation for the move into publishing was largely financial:

> To be honest, I came into the business to make enough to pay school fees. We publish what we can to turn an honest dollar. But our initial vision remains the same – to present to the world at large as full a picture as possible of these countries and cultures. We do a lot now, in all sorts of ways. The skills are here.

Despite the fact that the "world at large" is the intended audience, the Gulf itself remains Stacey's primary market. His first buyers were English-speaking expatriates seeking to learn about the countries they found themselves working in. Gulf government ministries and other public institutions formed another important market. More recently, Gulf Arabs themselves began buying his books "to give to foreign friends and have sitting around their own houses". Some were produced in Arabic translations to fulfil this demand, but many Arabs prefer the English versions. Publicity, in the form of book-launches, advertising and reviews in the local press, takes place in the Gulf.

Stacey usually solicits assured sales before publishing, and sometimes sponsorship is secured from governments or from corporate sources such as British Petroleum. Countries and subjects little studied are targeted: "for example, we think a new book on Saudi crafts is needed. But there's no huge market. So we put the book together, then shop for sponsorship from BP or Mobil. But sometimes we can't wait, and we just publish". Stacey, who has no academic specialisation in the Middle East but read history at Oxford, describes himself as "neither an Arabophile nor an Arabophobe – the Foreign Office-style Arabophile is out of fashion now". He has written three gripping and poignant novels set in the Gulf, all published outside Stacey International. *Deadline* (Stacey 1998), set in a fictionalised Bahrain, was made into a BBC television drama starring John Hurt and Imogene Stubbs. In his fiction Stacey explores the roots of mutual misunderstanding between Arabs and Western expatriates:

> The novels probably tell more about the failures and mutual ignorance than anything else. If not for censorship, they would be known [in the

> Gulf]. You have to take care, though, because you can quite easily confuse simple people. In one novel, written under a pseudonym, characters had lots of irreverence for the "cloth heads" for whom they were working. I tried to paint a picture of mutual cultural incomprehension. It was an extraordinary period. People lived at a subsistence level, then suddenly this vast wasteland had an astonishing amount of money. I sought to explore the unresolved, unrecognisable differences between traditional and Western ways of life.

This is not, of course, what the company's own publications do. Negative stereotypes of Arabs among Westerners are one problem. On the other hand, Stacey points to a closedness, a cultural gatekeeping, in the Gulf itself and the corresponding GCC state censorship as a root cause of misunderstanding. Religious issues are particularly sensitive:

> Should a Westerner be involved in religious concerns, we scaffold our religious faith with a great deal of reason and argument, and we will talk to sceptics. People in the Gulf will always say, "become a Muslim, then you will understand; I can't explain it". This is unwelcoming. Islam, through its attitude, shows huge insecurity. ... There is a sense that the West should not know Islam except in its purest form. The slightest theological glitch, alternative view, or wrinkle that might cause offence results in months of debate by censors. We could not conceivably write a Westerner's guide to Islam with anything more than a few superficial descriptions of rituals.

Much the same might be said of politics and economics.

One author published by Stacey's firm is Sir Donald Hawley, a retired diplomat and Britain's first ambassador to Oman (1971-75), who wrote the first pictorial history of Oman (Hawley 1977, 1995). We met at the Institute of Directors in Pall Mall, where we drank tea under vast portraits of generals, and Sir Donald described the impetus behind his Oman book:

> When I was first asked, I was ambassador in Muscat. A friend of mine had a publisher friend. I had some material left over from my book on the Trucial States – when you research the Trucial States you inevitably find a lot about Oman – and my friend said, "I think my friend would publish it". That turned out to be Tom Stacey. He wrote out the skeleton of the book, and I filled it in.

Stacey International issued a revised edition of *Oman and its Renaissance* in 1995 to mark the 25th anniversary of Sultan Qābūs's takeover. It has been translated into Arabic "under the Sultan's direction" and distributed in Omani schools and universities.[11]

Hawley's memoir, *Desert Wind and Tropic Storm*, meanwhile reflects a particular era of the British Arabist and diplomat. The first chapter establishes the author's own pedigree, beginning with anecdotes about his fifteenth-century ancestors and moving on to tales of his prepatory and public-school days, the backgrounds of his teachers and the eventual prominent careers of classmates. Subsequent chapters recount years spent in Oman and the UAE, as well as Nigeria, Egypt, Iraq and Malaysia. Largely a series of ceremonies and diplomatic comings and goings, the book describes relationships of trust, affection and sentiment built over the years with local royalty, officials and elites, as well as household servants and fellow diplomats, where it is sometimes unclear quite who is custodian of which tradition:

> Sayyid Shabib, who had been brought up abroad, called on me one day shortly after his arrival in the country, impeccably dressed in spotlessly white Omani costume and wearing his curved *khanjar* at his waist. Hamdan, our Omani butler, offered him coffee, tea and *halwa* in the Omani tradition and, when Shabib came to take his leave, incense was produced, followed by rose-water, which was sprinkled with the liberality which his rank merited. Shabib looked highly astonished at his drenching and later confessed that it was not till he came to the British Embassy that he had experienced the full effect of old Omani customs! (Hawley 2000: 167)

Sir Donald wrote about the Gulf at the very beginnings of a cultural and heritage industry, produced largely by Westerners and used in various ways by Gulf elites. He expresses disquiet over the way this industry has developed:

> I know my book [*Oman and its Renaissance*] is used as a gift, but that is not why I wrote it. That is what has happened in the industry, and it slightly bothers me. I wonder if I have been sufficiently objective, in that they like it so much. I'm not one of those who believe you have to insult everyone in order to be good, but I sometimes wonder if there were more things I should have brought in.

Missing from the memoir (as, indeed, in large part from the history) is any hint of intrigue, discord or dissonance, as well-intentioned senior British civil servants guide grateful locals into the second half of the twentieth century. A sense of decorum regarding the messier aspects of informal empire and its legacy in fact unites former diplomats and Gulf rulers, resulting in aestheticised, even folklorised accounts of interaction, which extend beyond the world of books. One can agree with Sir Donald that a book does not "have to insult everyone" to be good. But an odd impression is left by many works on the Stacey list of distance and formality, and of the Gulf itself as a series of decorous tableaux.

The London Centre of Arab Studies

William Facey, author of a prolific number of Gulf histories, represents a younger generation of Stacey International authors. Like Tom

Stacey, with whose firm he sometimes publishes, Facey's involvement in the Gulf reflects the ways in which opportunities arise through chance, personal contacts and information networks:

> I was not particularly fascinated with the Arab World; it happened by accident, and I made a career out of it. My own personal proclivity is to produce material that is historically and academically sound ... my mission in life is to make books sell out there, nice books, books that are good for people.

In addition to historical writing, Facey has wide experience in the presentation of Arabian material culture. After completing a degree in classics at Oxford, he took a job as a museum consultant in Qatar in 1974. Since then he has worked on numerous Gulf heritage projects, helping construct archaeology, history and natural history museums and exhibitions.[12]

In 1994 Facey set up his own organisation, the London Centre of Arab Studies (LCAS), which conducts a range of activities and services, including publishing, research, museum consultancy and translation, and employs a staff of three core personnel. "We started from nothing, with no backing at all", he says; "we just make it work from project to project". Operating from an office near Edgware Road, LCAS maintains arrangements with Stacey International and holds rights to Arabic editions of several of the Stacey books. Facey agrees that expatriate communities form the major market for his English-language books, but points out that his *Saudi Arabia by the First Photographers* (1996) sells better in Arabic than it does in English. Commercial concerns are paramount, and LCAS draws on a pool of well-known authors, rejecting almost all unsolicited manuscripts ("We get masses of archaeology, but it is not commercial").

> We accept quasi-government projects to keep the place going. An extreme form of government commissioning would be a book of old photographs of Saudi Arabia – the Saudis bought the lot. They wanted to show the contrast between old and new. This book was completely sponsored, and will not be in bookstores.

Even where the intention is primarily public sales, LCAS never prints more than 4,000 copies and usually attempts to line up approximately 1,000 pre-orders. Most LCAS publications receive some extent of sponsorship. Some reflect more subtle collaborations:

> Prince Sulṭān bin Salmān – who is interested in traditional architecture – built himself a mud-brick house which raised questions about the interface between traditional and modern forms. He approached me to see if there was a book in it, and I wrote it. His project was his input, and he read several versions of my manuscript. He wrote the introduction, but did not change the text at all. He is interested in handicrafts, and puts his money

> where his mouth is. We distribute the book in the West for him. It is wholly sponsored, but it sells in bookstores, and is selling well, with good reviews in the architectural press. ... Prince Sulṭān's Heritage Foundation markets books for us in Saudi Arabia, and we market their books in the UK.

Facey downplays the interference of censors in what he publishes: "My policy is to write what I think is good, but not to try to second-guess the censors. When they want something changed, we can talk about it". When the Saudis banned his *Riyadh: the old city* (Facey 1992), the then Saudi ambassador Ghāzī al-Quṣaybī called him in, told him he saw nothing wrong with the book and somehow had the ban lifted.

Intercultural trainers

While the intermediaries profiled above produce and promote an aestheticised high culture of heritage and history, others exploit a market niche for the nuts and bolts of Arab mores. Offering books and seminars on "how to behave in the Gulf", these consultants form part of a wider industry in cross-cultural training. Unnoticed by most anthropologists, an international sector of cultural consultants has developed since the 1960s. Purporting to teach intercultural sensitivity to business people and others who work with foreigners, these professionals market an essentialist notion of culture and cultural difference rather alien to present-day academics but not so far removed perhaps from the world of books and paintings.

This phenomenon, which Hannerz calls the "culture shock-prevention industry" (Hannerz 1996: 251), is examined in Dalén's 1997 ethnography, *Among the Interculturalists*. Dalén describes how a profession of intercultural training grew from the establishment of foreign student advisers in a handful of American universities into a lucrative business complete with professional teacher-training degrees, lines of teaching products and international organisations such as the Society for Intercultural Education, Training and Research. Saudi Arabia, he notes, is one of the most frequently depicted areas in intercultural teaching materials (Dalén 1997: 98).

Dalén based his study on fieldwork conducted in Sweden and the United States. Intercultural training organisations exist in Britain as well, such as Cedant International of London and the Centre for Intercultural Briefing, in Farnham, but these tend to employ on a freelance basis individuals with practical experience in the Gulf rather than trained interculturalists. There is a small network of people who often hold seminars together. Foremost among them is Jeremy Williams and his one-man company, Handshaikh, offering tailor-made coaching sessions for around £1,250 per day. The Arab-British Chamber of Commerce recommends Williams's book *Don't They Know It's*

Friday (Williams 1998) as a cultural guide for Westerners living and/or doing business in Saudi Arabia or the Gulf. He has produced several instructional videos and has become part of Emirates Airline's pre-landing orientation programme – his interview with British television personality Gloria Hunniford is shown to passengers about to disembark in the Gulf. Williams sees his own role, modestly, as the "interface between suits and Arabs".

Although familiar with some of the intercultural literature, Williams emphasises that he does not see himself as an interculturalist in the sense Dalén describes, but rather as a specialist offering practical experience of the Gulf: "I am amused at the industry of cross-culturalism. I don't think its prominence is justified. There is no need. Live with them, talk to them, limit your own arrogance and certainties. That's all that's needed". Like Stacey and Facey, ex-army officer Williams had no academic training in area-related subjects. Nor did he have any particular interest in the Arab World before serving in the Gulf: "I just happened to know the area. I didn't choose it; I'm not enthralled with the Arabs. I discovered an employment opportunity for myself, post-army. I found a niche, something I can do forever".

Williams's experience of the Gulf began in 1972 in the Dubai Defence Force, Ṣalāḥ al-Dīn Armoured Car Squadron. "Shaykh Rāshid asked the British Army to lend British officers to command their forces. ... I – we – would watch how the Arabs behaved. We would ape them". After years of working in the Gulf (not least as a defence attaché in Abu Dhabi and Bahrain), Williams was inspired to correct the "stupid mistakes" he saw made by his fellow Westerners. "The most basic information, even half a crack of the door, is an enormous advantage for a Westerner". To help with this, Williams often enlists former diplomats – usually ambassadors – as seminar speakers because "they know the political scene". Given that British diplomats generally work their way up through embassy ranks, they know well the countries they have worked in; they are usually accomplished speakers and comfortable in public. In Dubai, an Arab colleague joins in and Williams tries to invite a few Arabs to attend "so it doesn't look like a closed shop. We're teaching communication. Usually people realise it's a family atmosphere – that's what I try to create".

The seminar

Williams's seminars reflect a carefully choreographed informality. Where possible, he set-dresses the meeting room the day before with Arab coffee pots and textiles. For small groups, seating is arranged in a semi-circle. A slide-projector flashes the word "patience" in bold capital letters on to a sidewall. An overhead projector is draped with an Arab head-dress. Williams notes that he begins the day with his suit-jacket on in order to take it off shortly after the first session begins, reinforcing the casual atmosphere he works to create. Friendliness and informality are intended to hold participants' interest and ward off any sense of threat or intimidation.

The Handshaikh seminar I attended in July 2000 was commissioned by the technology faculty of a minor British university. Over the past few years, Gulf Arab students had lodged complaints with their embassies and home funding bodies, accusing tutors and administrators of rudeness and cultural insensitivity. The faculty dean's opening address stressed the financial consequences: while the faculty was the only one at the university generating a financial surplus – with 20 per cent of its funding coming from overseas students – "we have made mistakes". The dean, although he did not use these terms, emphasised in effect the increasing commoditisation of university teaching. "We tend to operate on the belief that everyone must conform to our bureaucracy", he argued, "but the customer is out there, and we must conform to what the customer wants"; the department was "getting it wrong" he said, "not because of the quality of our courses but because of our behaviour".

Williams began the first presentation, entitled "Why Bother About Arabs?", by teaching the audience the Arabic greeting "*al-salām 'alaykum/ wa-'alaykum al-salām*" and some basics of Arabic pronunciation. He then showed a map of the region, and provided some essential geographic facts and definitions of terms such as "GCC", "the Arab World" and "the Middle East", before moving on to a series of statistics illustrating the economic importance of the Arab Gulf to Britain. He noted that 50 per cent of the Gulf population is under the age of 15, and pointed to the implications of this demography for future student populations. He stressed the general economic power of the Gulf countries, which have purchased from the UK more than £60 billion in defence materials, and suggested their possible generosity towards British universities. The academic audience was offered the encouraging thought that "one or two tricks with rich young Arab students can have an enormous effect".

Williams then suggested two questions to ascertain the sensitivity of a particular situation: "Do you know who you're dealing with? Is the person in question from a significant Gulf family?" At this point the dean added that on a recent visit to Dubai he received a "severe dressing down" over the faculty's behaviour towards Emirati students. Williams in turn added that briefs on various students' backgrounds were available from their embassies. Then, using overhead visuals, he presented material drawn from cross-cultural training literature, notably Fons Trompanaars's *Riding the Waves of Culture*. He ended the session with a question, originally devised by sociologists Stouffer and

Toby (1951: 404) and often used in intercultural training to promote cultural relativity (Trompanaars 1997: 33–4, Dalén 1997: 162–4):

> You are riding in a car driven by a close friend. He hits a pedestrian. You know he was going at least 35 miles per hour in a 20 miles per hour speed zone. There are no other witnesses. His lawyer says that if you testify under oath that he was only driving 20 miles per hour, it might save him from serious consequences. What right has your friend to expect you to protect him?

Williams did not call for participants to answer, as is the practice in most cross-cultural seminars. Instead, he left them to ponder the dilemma, and moved on to the next session.

Mu'āwiyah Derhalli, a Palestinian with long experience of cross-cultural training, gave the next presentation, "How Young Gulf Arabs See You". To make the point that English is not the only language, he began in Arabic, waiting for protests from the audience before switching to English. Derhalli pointed out that before starting their courses, Gulf Arabs may know the Britain of Harrods, Marks and Spencer and Selfridges, but they do not know the "real Britain". For them, "British" equals "English", and "England" equals "London". Gulf students often arrive with high expectations, Derhalli said, and are then confronted with a reality that fails to meet these. He offered a list of positive and negative stereotypes Gulf Arabs hold of the British. On the positive side, the British are deemed:

1. well-mannered, always say "sorry" and "excuse me";
2. truthful, can be taken at their word, frank and direct;
3. punctual, keep commitments;
4. meticulous in applying rules, show no favouritism;
5. conscientious, active and concerned with human rights;
6. tolerant, flexible;
7. orderly, stand in queues, wait their turn;
8. technologically advanced.

On the negative side, they are perceived as:

1. ignorant of Arab culture and of Islam as a noble religion. Still think of us in terms of camels and tents;
2. looking down on us, treating us as inferiors;
3. inhospitable, "hospitable in their own way" – don't serve enough food;
4. lax in the upbringing of teenagers, particularly of girls, whose dress and behaviour reflect on their fathers' lack of honour [sic];
5. having loose family ties;

6. treating their elderly badly by putting them into homes;
7. aloof and lacking in warmth;
8. arrogant;
9. unconcerned with Arab political problems, like the Palestinian cause.

Derhalli noted that it is "the small things that offend", and suggested that the effort should be made to learn and use full first names, not abridge them to, for instance, "Abū". Sensitivity should be shown towards fasting practices during Ramaḍān, with any parties or entertaining held after rather than before sunset. Gulf Arab students are often shy and uncertain, said Derhalli, and need guidance. But they should never be shouted at, called names or disciplined in public. Gulf Arabs, he said, hold not the sophisticated mores of urban Arabs, but rather "Bedouin" values, including a strong concern with honour and a quickness to anger. The stereotypes urban Arabs often have of their rural neighbours (or Palestinians have of the Gulf, for that matter) were thus added to the stereotypes Gulf Arab students have of the English and vice-versa, but the aim was not "deconstruction". The practicalities, indeed, require a certain shared essentialism.

Following Derhalli, I gave a brief talk on transculturalism under a heading that Williams chose: "We're Not Foreigners, We're Normal". In order to justify my presence at the seminar, I had been asked to present a brief talk, from an anthropologist's point of view, on the importance of recognising and respecting cultural difference. Lunch followed, a stand-up buffet designed to encourage mingling between participants and presenters. After lunch, Derhalli led a session on Islam, taking the audience through the steps involved in prayer, explaining dietary practices and stressing the special needs that arise during Ramaḍān. He also gave a brief history of Islam, emphasising its affinity with Christianity and Judaism.

Next came a role-play session, "I Must Have the Day Off", presented in a set arranged earlier at the back of the room. The skit was drawn from actual incidents reported to the dean over the years. The dean played an "eminent professor", complete with academic gown, a strangely archaic touch for a modern British university; a woman administrator took the role of Arab student. The student knocks on an imaginary door and is greeted with a brusque "go away". The student insists, and the professor again refuses. After a third plea, he grudgingly admits her and asks her to close the door. He offers her a bite of the dried pork sausage he is munching on. She declines and asks for a day off lectures for a Muslim holiday. The professor refuses and adds that since she is already performing poorly, he will fail her if she neglects to turn up. The distraught student bursts into tears, at which point the professor agrees to the day off and puts his arm around her to comfort her. Another imaginary knock, and the professor tells Williams – playing another lecturer – to come in, as he is only advising a student that her performance is poor and she had better shape up. The dean then asked the audience to "spot the mistakes".

Obvious errors like the offering of pork were easily identified, while others, like humiliating the student in front of another lecturer, had to be pointed out. This exercise initiated a general discussion period, entitled "How We See Gulf Arab Students", offering participants an opportunity to air their own grievances and ask questions. Williams began with an explanation for the Arab students' difficulty in adapting to the university's system, not least that they may have grown up with rote learning and that "self-motivation" may not be well ingrained. To encourage frank discussion, he then read a list of complaints from the administrator of the university's Language Centre, who prefaced her own remarks with a suggestion: "Their general lack of knowledge of the culture they are coming to makes life unnecessarily difficult for them and us". Cultural briefing in their own country before they leave might help. The complaints that staff and teachers made consistently, she said, came roughly in this order:

1. Poor time keeping – the importance of keeping appointments in general and class times in particular.
2. Exhaustion, lethargy and hangovers when they are in class, caused by their being free to stay out late and drink for the first time in their lives! (This is usually translated as "I am sick today".)
3. Apparent lack of respect for students from other cultures who are studying with them – especially quiet female students. Asians have the greatest difficulty sharing a class with these boys. Young Arab students often refuse to work with anyone apart from other Arabs and their noise in class (when in a group) is intimidating to many. (We have had several student withdrawals due to this.)
4. Their treatment of host families. They tend to think that if their hosts are being paid for their services they can be treated as servants and their homes as hotels, which can result in great (two-way) resentment.
5. Telling teachers exactly what they want to hear, and then doing exactly the opposite.
6. Expecting their wishes and expectations to be attended to immediately while appearing to ignore everything which is reasonably asked of them in return.

I could go on!

Participants agreed with the administrator's list, but were reluctant to add to it, perhaps embarrassed in the presence of the dean to air what might be perceived, after a day of "sensitivity training", as prejudiced views. One asked if they weren't losing money from other groups because of the Gulf Arabs' behaviour, but the dean replied that those who had withdrawn were enrolled in short language-courses, while the Gulf Arab students undertake longer – and therefore more lucrative – technical degrees. The few other questions asked included how to turn down gifts graciously.[13] At the very end of the question period, one lecturer expressed distaste at the sense, imparted throughout the day, that "we should do all this just for the money".

Culture and sociology

The seminar foregrounds issues that inform the cases even of art and books. As students of museum-ethnography know, removing the sociology from "culture" leaves texts and objects either meaningless or open to false interpretation. On the British side of these exchanges the sociology is interesting. The prominence of royalty in exchanges between states is supplemented by a supporting staff, in both publishing and the art world (not to add intercultural training), drawn from what the British consider the upper middle class, a surprising number of whom are ex-army officers. Lower down the pyramid are the lecturers in a minor university. It is they who are required to undergo intercultural training, to learn respect for cultures whose reality is attested by the coffee-table books and the works of art.

Intercultural training is somewhat of a misnomer. What is being taught is not so much a Gulf Arab culture, facilitating dialogue and interaction, as a political strategy indicating the appropriate level and tone of obsequiousness. The effect is a lopsided and disingenuous degree of deference on the part of the British, an elaborate pantomime of servitude and preferential treatment performed "all for the money". Without the sociology it makes little sense even of Gulf society. Hawley's bilingual collection of etiquette phrases, *Courtesies in the Gulf Area* (1998), and Williams's highly practical guide, *Don't They Know It's Friday* (1998), along with its various commercial rivals,[14] place considerable stress on deference and rank. An unwary reader might deduce from Gulf "culture" a society in which, impossibly, everyone is superior to everyone else.

The courtesy and deference in Hawley's *Courtesies* must often be reciprocal, such that an Omani may honour as guest a fellow Omani who will act as host on the next occasion. In Gulf society, of course, permanent asymmetries of status are expressed as asymmetry in visiting patterns. Where this is not so, equality and mutual respect depend on separation such that everyone has their own space in which (at least potentially) to act as host.[15] As we see from the university administrator's comments, above, not following the rule leads to resentment with British "host families". But the British recipients of sensitivity training (the academic proletariat, as it were; not the government ministers or the Prince of Wales) are told they can never act as host on their own territory.

Moral symmetry is not, of course, a feature of life in the Gulf states themselves, at least for foreigners, as another practical guide warns readers. Thus a local employer who tells an expatriate worker "Respect yourself!" (meaning behave yourself), receives the answer, "You should respect yourself!", and the expatriate worker, judged guilty of "verbal assault", is dismissed, his contract voided.[16] In other circumstances, "most matters are forever negotiable"; but as Williams carefully warns his readers:

> it would be the height of folly for the Westerner to assume that this friendly 'jam tomorrow' approach works in both directions: Western contractual failure to provide goods or services on time usually means that the Arab organisation concerned will quickly invoke the relevant contract penalty clauses (Williams 1998: 77).

Gulf populations, for their part, feel exploited in broader terms of imperialism or global dominance, and feel that strategically they are anything but equal partners.

Extracting "culture" from a context like this is notoriously difficult, and often self-contradictory. If one of the positive attributes of the stereotyped British, for instance, is that they "show no favouritism", then the advice to "know who you're dealing with" and to check whether students are from eminent Gulf families is likely to produce dissonance. Politeness tends towards dishonesty. In the absence of any more spontaneous relationship, or indeed of irony (Chock 1987), rules and values come into conflict.[17] The standard question, posed earlier, about the traffic accident presents the problem in acute form. Set out in black and white on paper, it presents a choice between perjury and insensitivity. To conclude that another "culture" favours deceit and lying will scarcely be acceptable to either party. Better, perhaps, to stay with the formalities of incense and rose-water, dates and coffee, which Sir Donald Hawley describes so well.[18]

This is very much the role of both coffee-table books and fine art. A pictorial world of mud houses and skyscrapers, of falconry and shopping malls, depicts the acceptable values of "tradition" and "modernity" seen as natural complements. Fine art depicts the former, be it wildlife, landscape or imagined *sūqs*, and the best such depictions, validated as important by London auction-rooms, are the province of Gulf elites. The past, in a sense, is theirs. Together with the contrived, commercial deference accorded the elite's dependants, these exchanges define in large part who people are – as Arabs, as "Gulfies", and as Saudis, Kuwaitis or Emiratis.

Conclusion

This study has examined a particular instance of globalisation – the role of an offshore centre of Arab Gulf cultural production and consumption. The historical relationship between the oil-rich GCC states and Britain, the availability of expert mediating personnel, and the UK's fairly user-friendly legal system, climate and geographical position all contribute to London's centrality. Strong affinities between members of Britain's conservative diplomatic, financial and cultural establishment(s), wealthy London-based Middle Easterners and the ruling families and elites of the Arab Gulf buttress Arab London's culture industries. The results, however, are not symmetrical. The London-based industry, paid for with Gulf money, does more to define the Gulf for its own citizens than any Gulf-based enterprise can do to define what Britain is. "Cultural" links between the Gulf and London are largely one-way. Indeed without the art, books and artefacts, the polities of the region seem often ill defined. Paradoxically, the construction of strong notions of place, of local culture, requires transnational processes drawing on an offshore and alien metropolis.

PART II. LOCAL IDENTITIES: THE IMPORTANCE OF NATION-STATES

CHAPTER 4

TRANSNATIONAL CONNECTIONS AND NATIONAL IDENTITY

Zanzibari Omanis in Muscat

Madawi Al-Rasheed

> From antiquity the monsoon winds which blow southwards and northwards with unfailing regularity have made the East African Coast and the Middle East practically one (al-Barwani 1997: 275).

If transnationalism is the multiple links, connections and movements which people and institutions maintain in the world, then Oman is an ancient master of the art. Omanis were pioneers in establishing links beyond the country itself, the most important of which were with East Africa. These links made Omani society one of the most "transnational" in the Arab Gulf. This paper traces the roots and experiences of Omani Zanzibaris, a community of recently settled immigrants who returned to Muscat from Zanzibar and East Africa in the 1970s. Using life histories, I focus on the tension between notions of Omani descent or ancestry and life experiences grounded in Africa. In doing so, I highlight the transnational connections of a Muscat elite.

Oman and Zanzibar in the nineteenth century

Omanis from both the interior and the coastal areas travelled to and settled on the coast of East Africa, not least in Zanzibar, for centuries.[1] These links were well established before Zanzibar became the seat of an Omani Empire in 1832 when Sultan Sa'īd bin Sulṭān (1804-56) moved his court to the island.[2] Several Omani tribes from the Sharqīyah region, such as al-Ḥirth, were involved in the slave trade as early as the tenth century (Le Cour Grandmaison, C. 1989: 176). The establishment of an imperial base in Zanzibar was an attempt to save what remained of Oman's commercial interests in East Africa. It was also a response to pressures imposed on Oman by the Āl Sa'ūd of Najd.[3]

With the death of Sa'īd bin Sulṭān in 1856, Zanzibar gradually detached itself from Muscat as his two sons, Mājid and Thuwaynī, under the influence of Britain, divided their father's patrimony between them. Thuwaynī secured his rule in Muscat while Mājid consolidated his control over Zanzibar. Throughout the nineteenth century the Sultanate of Muscat remained nominally independent, but Zanzibar eventually became a British protectorate and Britain ensured that Mājid, the Sultan of Zanzibar, continued to pay a subsidy of £40,000 per annum to Muscat (Le Cour Grandmaison, C. 1998: 58). In the second half of the nineteenth century, Muscat and Zanzibar were separate political domains, but the flow of trade and people continued. It followed the cycle of the monsoons, the winds that since ancient times have allowed Omani *dhows* to sail back and forth from Ṣuḥār, Muscat and Ṣūr to ports in East Africa and India.

The movement of people and trade made the population of Zanzibar one of the most heterogeneous in East Africa. Indigenous Africans from the mainland coexisted with Indian, Persian, Omani and Hadrami merchants (Bhacker 1992, Sheriff 1987). At the top of this cosmopolitan world stood the Omani ruling elite, a branch of the Āl Bū Sa'īd family, rulers of Oman since the eighteenth century. The Āl Bū Sa'īd, together with sections of Oman's tribal nobility and religious scholars, controlled the political, religious and economic affairs of the island, assisted by Hindu and Muslim Indian merchants (Allen 1981). The Omani population of the Sultanate of Zanzibar, known locally as *manga/wamanga*, included merchants from Muscat (both Omani Arabs and Indians) and sections of important tribal groups that had their roots in different regions of Oman itself. The commercial interests of the Muscat merchant community were seriously affected in the late nineteenth century by the abolition of slavery and the control of arms traffic, both imposed by the British.[4] The migration of Omanis to Zanzibar continued, however, as some chose to join their compatriots, already settled in Africa since at least the expansionist era of the Ya'āribah in the mid-seventeenth century (Bhacker 1992: 68). While some Muscat merchants chose to settle permanently in Zanzibar, others were "seasonal residents", travelling back and forth between Zanzibar and Muscat or Oman.

While the majority of Omani migrants came from the Sharqīyah and travelled through the port of Ṣūr (Le Cour Grandmaison, C. 1989), recent research shows that Omanis as far inland as Buraimi were involved in wide-scale migration (Bhacker 1992: 85). In Zanzibar, Omanis became a commercial and political elite, occupying high government positions as judges, ministers, governors and ambassadors

(Le Cour Grandmaison, C. 1998: 54). Descriptions of the Omani inhabitants of Zanzibar at the time paint a picture of "handsome men, with a certain grace, courtesy, and beautiful manners, hospitable and generous. They were often seen during Friday prayers with wonderful turbans, their silver daggers and camel-hair burnouses ornamented with gold thread and accompanied by their kin and retainers" (Godfery [1920] 1969: 23).

Omani settlers and seasonal residents were descendants of tribal groups of Ḥirth, Mazāra'ah, Marḥūbī, Barāwinah, Nabāhinah and Manādhirah among others. Names such as al-Mālikī, Banī Riyām, Banī Ruwāḥah and al-'Abrī attest to roots deep in the interior of Oman. These immigrant communities continued to function within the familiar Omani tribal structure, retaining tribal ancestry and their Ibadi and Sunni faiths. Most had practised agriculture in Oman, and in Zanzibar they owned plantations, which were worked by slaves. In 1948 the Arabs in Zanzibar were estimated at 16.9 per cent of the island's population. They were not, however, undifferentiated among themselves or isolated from the African majority of the island's people. They included "an 'aristocracy', the urban bourgeoisie and the planter class. ... Racially they were greatly assimilated and were generally referred to as 'local Arabs' in English" (Lodhi 1986: 405).

In addition to using African slaves on plantations which they owned in Zanzibar, Omani migrants established kinship relations with the indigenous population, taking African wives and concubines. This seems a common strategy used by diaspora groups, such as overseas Yemenis and Hadramis.[5] According to one source on Zanzibar, "there was so much intermarriage between Omanis and Africans during the nineteenth century that nobody could tell the difference between an Arab and a Zinji negro" (Bhacker 1992: 68). It was common for "young Omani men to arrive in Zanzibar having left behind a first wife, often a first cousin. They were accompanied by sons, brothers, uncles and cousins. As some prolonged their stay in the island, they took African wives" (Le Cour Grandmaison, C. 1998: 41). Early settlers, who had been in Africa before the nineteenth century, were completely "Swahilised". A small minority acquired Arabic for religious purposes, but with the exception of learned members of society, the majority could not write a simple letter in Arabic (Bhacker 1992: 68).

The twentieth century

Omanis continued to migrate to Zanzibar and the east coast of Africa during the first half of the twentieth century. Driven out of Oman by the autocratic rule of Sultan Sa'īd bin Taymūr (1932-70), they joined the early settlers. People from the interior of Oman, Sharqīyah and

Baṭinah, together with merchants from Maṭraḥ and Muscat, fled economic hardship and political oppression, while those who were too old to travel sent their children to Zanzibar and other destinations in search of wealth and education, both of which were in short supply in Oman at the time.[6] During the Second World War, migration was "a standard feature of every male career of the most senior generation in Oman" (Barth 1983: 22). Many Omanis sold their property and land in Oman to enter the clove and cocoa plantation economy in Zanzibar.

The economic situation in Muscat and Oman deteriorated with political conflict between the Imamate of the interior (1913-55) and the Muscat Sultanate (Peterson 1976, Eickelman 1987, Wilkinson 1987). Tribal rivalries in the interior, together with worsening economic conditions and oppression on the coast, reduced Oman's population to a state of poverty. The triumph of the Sultan of Muscat over the Imamate in 1955 and the crushing of tribal rebellion in the interior did little to improve the situation, however. In fact the consolidation of the Sultan's rule had negative immediate consequences as far as the population of the interior was concerned and many were now driven into exile in neighbouring Saudi Arabia and other Gulf countries. Between 1957 and 1959, approximately 400 dissidents fled Oman. Some returned in 1963 under a guarantee of amnesty by the Sultan (Kelly 1972: 133). At about the same period, however, hundreds of Omanis still sought employment in neighbouring Gulf states where oil had already been discovered, for example in Kuwait, Qatar, Saudi Arabia and the United Arab Emirates. Indeed, Zanzibar had its share of this mid-twentieth-century flux of Omani migrants and exiles. Omanis who already had relatives in Zanzibar tried to establish contacts with them, hoping they would welcome them on arrival.

Upheaval in Zanzibar and the Zanzibari returnees

The migration of Omanis to Zanzibar stopped in 1964. The old Omani settlers themselves were expelled by an African nationalist government (Prunier 1998: 98), and the last Omani Sultan of Zanzibar, Sayyid Jamshīd bin 'Abdullāh bin Khalīfah bin Ḥārib (1963-64), fled to Britain. The political crisis in Zanzibar led to the slaughter of hundreds of Omanis and the deportation of thousands of old settlers, considered a foreign elite by the African majority. About 2,200 were detained and their property was confiscated, with African workers claiming ownership of the plantations; in the end about 5,000 Omanis fled or were forcibly expelled (Prunier 1998: 104-5). The Zanzibar revolution ended the rule of Omani sultans there, which had lasted for more than 130 years, and the pre-eminence in Zanzibar of the Omani minority.

In 1964, Omanis in Zanzibar were told to go home. However, the idea of "home" was ambiguous, for most had been settled in Zanzibar for decades. While some male immigrants had travelled backwards and forwards to Oman, the majority had established households, businesses and plantations in Zanzibar. A Zanzibari Omani resident in Muscat commented on the ambiguity: "Which home? In 1964, they had no home to claim because the then prevailing regime in Oman did not want them, hence they became refugees and were scattered everywhere in the Gulf states" (al-Maamiry 1988: 75). Thousands of Omanis have nevertheless returned to Muscat, where today they constitute one of the most prosperous elite groups in the capital.

The returnees had Omani ancestry and as such are defined by the state as Omani nationals. Since the 1970s Omani nationality law has considered children of Omani nationals born abroad to be full Omani citizens. In 1999 the latest modification of the law defined Omanis as (1) those born in or outside Oman of Omani fathers, (2) those born in or outside Oman of an Omani mother and an unknown father or a father who has lost his Omani nationality, (3) those born in Oman of unknown parents, and (4) those born in Oman, and who became resident there, of fathers themselves born in Oman but without Omani nationality (*al-Jarīdah al-rasmīyah* 661, 15 Dec. 1999).

Zanzibari returnees do not feature as a separate sub-category in Omani official population statistics and census data. There is nothing in the most recent *Omani Statistical Year Book* (Oman 1999), for instance, that would give an indication of the size of the Zanzibari community or any other "Omani" group, such as Baluchis and Lutis.[7] Only data on the new expatriate population, the majority of whom arrived in Oman with the oil wealth of the 1970s, include sub-categories relating to place of origin (Winckler 2001). According to one source, however, between 8,000 and 10,000 Zanzibari Omanis had settled in Oman by 1975 (Townsend 1977: 55). Members of the community today claim there are 300,000.

While official statistics do not categorise the returnees as a separate group, they are often referred to colloquially as *ʿumānīyīn min zinjibār* (Omanis from Zanzibar) or simply *zinjibārīyīn* (Zanzibaris). A Zanzibari Omani thus claims that whereas the indigenous African population of Zanzibar have become Tanzanian, those who were considered foreign in Zanzibar and were forced to leave have retained their identity as Zanzibaris (al-Maamiry 1988). One famous case is that of Saʿīd bin ʿAlī al-Maghīrī, a literary figure and author *of Juhaynāt al-akhbār fī tārīkh zinjibār* (1995). He was described upon his return to Oman in the 1960s as "Zanzibari" although his ancestors were originally from Oman and had migrated to East Africa during the Yaʿāribah period (Bhacker 1992: 68). Al-Maghīrī was born in Oman in the late nineteenth century and was sent to East Africa by his grandfather. He became a member of the Executive Council in Zanzibar and accompanied Sultan Khalīfah bin Ḥārib (1911-60) during his visit to London to attend the coronation of King George VI in 1936 (al-Maghīrī 1985). Al-Maghīrī's case illustrates that, in spite of genealogy and scholarly status, certain Omani personalities continued to be defined as Zanzibari upon their return to what was said to be their "native" country.

Zanzibaris distinguish themselves from other Omanis, such as Lutis, Dhofaris and Baluchis. These other Omanis use the term "Zanzibari" of Omani returnees from Africa generally, as do the returnees themselves. In addition to Omanis from Zanzibar, the term thus refers to those who came from Kenya, Tanzania and other parts of East and Central Africa. This generic name invokes a common experience but does not override internal distinctions, and Zanzibaris in Muscat have their own hierarchies derived from tribe, profession and their history of settlement in Africa.[8] Among the elite in Muscat, however, education and professional status override minor differences of dialect, and tribal origin seems not to play a major part in marriage choices. With respect to other Omanis, however, the obvious marker was, to start with, language.

In the 1970s one of the first obstacles facing the returnees was their poor Arabic. They were fluent in Swahili, and those who were educated spoke good English, a function of the availability of schools in Zanzibar. They were immediately seen by others in Oman as an economically and socially advanced group that would soon monopolise key positions. The returnees, in fact, were not easily integrated. They combined their Omani ancestry with an obvious African heritage: their Swahili language, and in the case of some Zanzibaris physical features of mixed African-Arab parentage, added to the complexity of a newly unified country with its own social and political divisions.

Among the Zanzibaris who returned to Muscat in the early 1970s were descendants of the tribes of the interior and the coast of Oman. Some of the returnees were born in either Oman or Zanzibar and were brought to Muscat as young children.[9] Others returned to Oman in their early 20s after a sojourn in Arab countries, mainly the United Arab Emirates, Saudi Arabia and Egypt. Yet a third group arrived in Oman after an interval in Britain or in other European countries as far off as the Soviet Union. Whatever their precise history, the complex political loyalties of the returnees, some of whom were high-ranking officials in the Zanzibar government before the revolution, influenced the prospects and timing of their return to Oman. Al-Maghīrī, mentioned earlier, was one such person. Another factor was that the political crisis in Zanzibar in 1964 followed closely the military confrontation within Oman between the Imamate and the Sultan of Muscat. Then, after the Imamate's collapse, Oman faced a second rebellion in Dhofar in the late 1960s (Kelly 1976, Peterson 1977). Both crises made the return of Zanzibaris a complicated matter for the government in Muscat.

While it was not possible for Zanzibaris to return to Oman *en masse* during the reign of Sa'īd bin Taymūr (1932-70), hundreds of Zanzibaris were welcomed after Q̱ābūs bin Sa'īd overthrew his father in July 1970. Many who had settled in the United Arab Emirates, Saudi Arabia, Egypt and other Arab and European countries after their brutal expulsion from Zanzibar began returning, and Sultan Q̱ābūs invited them to contribute to modernising the country at a time when Oman lacked substantial human resources. According to Oman's state narrative, this was part of a national reconciliation initiated by Q̱ābūs himself. Both official publications and oral narratives depict the coup of 1970 as the time when it became possible for the Omani diaspora to come home at last. An Omani commented that in 1970 Oman "opened the doors for its sons to return and build a country, shut off from the outside world by instability, tribal warfare and poverty". Educated Omani men and women returned to fill posts newly created by government modernisation plans (Chatty 2000: 243).

The expertise of Zanzibaris was much in demand, but there were other reasons behind Oman's open-door policy. Members of the Zanzibari community claimed tribal links with important sections of Omani society yet were considered to be relatively far removed from Oman's internal conflicts. A substantial majority had mixed Omani-African descent, which automatically placed them outside the straightforward tribal categories. They were thus seen as potential supporters of the regime: insiders in Oman by virtue of their ancestry, but outsiders to the tribal alliances and rivalries of recent times by virtue of their early migration. Zanzibaris, for their part, demonstrated allegiance to the new regime by accepting the invitation to return. They were well positioned to contribute to the modernisation of Oman in the early 1970s as they brought with them high levels of education, expertise and skills still in short supply. They immediately established a niche for themselves in the Muscat area. Since then, a flourishing community benefiting from oil wealth and the expansion of government bureaucracy has been growing.[10]

Muscat suited Zanzibari merchants, some of whom settled in Maṭraḥ, the old commercial centre and port of Muscat. Muscat was also the centre of government employment, and Zanzibaris took advantage of expanding bureaucracies and ministries. In the early 1970s they were concentrated in the Ministry of Defence, the security apparatus and police force, the only well-developed state institutions at the time (Eickelman and Dennison 1994). Zanzibaris were also the first to be employed in the oil industry. Petroleum Development-Oman (PDO) employed hundreds of Zanzibaris whose proficiency in English proved to be an advantage over native Omanis.

More recently, Zanzibaris have been the first to respond to economic opportunities made available in the early 1990s by the government's decision to open the country to tourism. Educated Zanzibari men and women are employed in hotels as managers, receptionists and guides. Less educated members of the community perform menial jobs which the Omani government is eager to transfer from expatriates to citizens. Omanis comment that employment in the tourist industry, where regular contact with foreigners is an essential dimension of the sector, is easier for Zanzibari women than native Omanis. According to a Zanzibari owner of a Muscat-based tourism agency, Zanzibari women have a longer history of employment than the majority of native Omani women. Their families are well travelled and are less likely to object to their employment in hotels and other sites where they come into contact with foreigners, considered by definition as ignorant of "Omani" traditions.

Such comments reflect a general understanding that the Zanzibari community is more open and relatively less *muta'aṣṣib* (strict in a religious and moral sense) than mainstream Omani society, especially that of the interior. It was early women returnees from Africa who "first appeared in the workforce – in offices, in radio, in television, and in business" (Chatty 2000: 244). Some Zanzibari entrepreneurs have established travel agencies in Muscat specialising in tours to the forts of the interior, setting up desert camps and "bedouin" villages, and organising lavish dinners on the decks of restored *dhows* for tourists in search of the Sindbad experience. Zanzibaris also capitalise on their African connection and mobilise their knowledge and experience of Africa to win entertainment contracts from five-star international hotels. "Zanzibari Nights", designed at grand hotels for tourists who enjoy Swahili music, dance and food, have become quite regular events.

The Zanzibari community is distinguished from other Omanis by its recent settlement in Oman and its high educational achievement. However, the most open marker of difference between Zanzibaris and other Omanis remains the use of Swahili. Zanzibaris who congregate in departments within government ministries continue to communicate among themselves in Swahili (it is not uncommon to find whole ministries dominated by closely knit groups of Zanzibaris), and Zanzibaris above the age of 30 speak Swahili among themselves in all social settings. Their children may understand Swahili but are more fluent in Arabic, itself a function of enrolment in state schools where

Arabic is the language of instruction. While for a period in the early 1970s, Swahili may have seemed briefly out of place in Oman, today with the increasing cosmopolitanism of the capital, it is simply yet another language spoken by a substantial section of the indigenous population, distinguishing Zanzibaris from the Arabic-speaking majority on some occasions, but not on all (Le Cour Grandmaison, B. 2000: 31).

Like other Arab Gulf cities, Muscat is characterised by cultural, linguistic and ethnic pluralism, whereby the cities and ports have evolved into veritable "towers of Babel" (Bourgey 1991: 73, Valensi 1986). But Omani diversity predates the oil boom of the 1970s. Sunni Baluchis from Iran and Pakistan (Barth 1983), Shi'ite Persians, Hyderabadi Lutis, Ismailis, Khojas and Hindu Indians (Allen 1981) were already intermingled with the Arab population, a testimony to the ancient transnational connections and the imperial expansion of Oman. These old settlers have been "Omanis" for generations. Established Indian merchants and high-ranking Baluchis in the army had this status before 1970. In Muscat the Omani sultans relied on Indian merchants, and in Zanzibar the Topans and Sewjis (great Indian trading families) had controlled customs duties (Le Cour Grandmaison, C. 1998: 54). In present-day Muscat the financial empire of Khimji Ramdas holds several international franchises, and the Indian Khoja community in Maṭraḥ is among the richest in Oman. Historically such Indian groups were often British subjects, and with the establishment of the modern state, several important families were granted Omani citizenship. By contrast, the new arrivals from the Indian subcontinent form a quite separate category of "expatriates". As elsewhere in the Gulf, citizens and expatriates constitute different moral and statistical universes, and while official statistics document the diversity of the new immigrants, ethnic and religious differences among citizens do not count officially and are hardly mentioned.

One marker of difference in practice is the mixed Omani-African ancestry of some but not all Zanzibaris. As mentioned earlier, many Omani tribesmen who settled in East Africa took African wives and concubines. In Zanzibar descendants of mixed Omani-African couples were defined as Omanis. Their descendants fall into the colloquial category of "mixed" ancestry, while in Oman the same type of mixed marriage is popularly reckoned to produce "impure" Omanis. As is well documented, Oman itself had a large population of descendants of African slaves, historically known as *mawlā/mawālī* or *'abīd* (Barth 1983). Marriages within that group produced *'abīd* in turn, while inter-marriage with other groups produced "impure" Omanis, although all are now citizens or *muwāṭinīn*. These people do not speak

Swahili and as such they are a separate category, socially though not officially, from the mixed Omani Zanzibaris.

The Omani heritage

Both old and recent settlers in Zanzibar returned to Oman with a strong sense of Omani identity. The majority of returnees had kinship relations and tribal connections with the Omani interior, but the claims to "Omani heritage" were solely dependent on genealogy and descent. A long period of settlement in Africa did little to weaken this: in fact most of the returnees capitalised on identity by descent (and thus by history) as a way to enforce their right of return. But real connections were less obvious. Zanzibaris claim often that their *kunyah* (surname) is a symbol of their Omani roots.[11] Other Omanis may refer to the "foreignness" of Zanzibaris,[12] distinguishing them from mainstream society, itself highly pluralistic; but the tribal roots of hundreds of Zanzibaris stretch deep into the interior of Oman, believed by many to be the cultural and religious heartland of the country.

In the 1970s, the majority of Zanzibaris did not return to the interior, the most isolated and underdeveloped region at the time. They preferred the comfortable life of Muscat, where the beginning of the modernisation process was taking place. At that time the interior was still under strict supervision and surveillance, and even today the Jabal Akhdar is inaccessible without special government permission. The relationship between Zanzibaris and the interior thus remains ambiguous, as the biography of Zahrah illustrates.[13]

Celebrating one's attachment to a location that one has never seen or intended to settle in even when the opportunity arises is common not only among diaspora communities but also among well-established national entities.[14] Zahrah herself was thus born in Zanzibar and resides in Muscat, but her ancestors had lived in the heart of Jabal Akhdar for centuries and she boasts about the purity of her Omani descent: "When my relatives migrated to Zanzibar, they brought with them their Omani wives. They never married African women. This is why our blood is pure. We do not have African features, like those Omanis who married black women". Although not directly related to the last Imām of the interior, Zahrah's ancestors were associated with important supporters of the twentieth-century Imamate. Cautiously, she refers to important historical personalities who challenged the Sultanate and whose names, even now, remain controversial: "If you read the history of Oman, you will find that my tribal name is mentioned. If you visit Jabal Akhdar, you will find schools named after my ancestors. Our presence was strong there".

Zahrah's father had left Oman in the early 1950s and established a flourishing trade in Zanzibar, where he was part of the tribal nobility surrounding the Sultan of Zanzibar. In 1964 the family was forced to leave. Two of Zahrah's uncles were slaughtered in their own houses. This is remembered as the moment of tragedy and dispersal: "it was horrible. My mother told us stories about massacres by Africans. I do not want to talk about it. It hurts". The household in which Zahrah was born in the early 1960s consisted of an extended family of aunts, uncles and cousins, but the sudden political crisis in Zanzibar meant that each male member of the household had to find a way of getting his particular dependants off the island. One major obstacle was lack of travel documents. Through personal contacts and tribal connections, Zahrah's father secured an Omani passport issued by the government of the Imamate in exile, at that time based in Dammam, Saudi Arabia. He thus travelled with his wife and children to Dammam, where he joined a small exiled community from the interior of Oman, and Zahrah spent her early childhood in Saudi Arabia. Together with her sisters, she was later sent to boarding school in Baghdad: "I was very young to be sent to a boarding school. We did not have a choice. My elder sisters spoke English and could not follow the Saudi Arabic school curriculum. It was decided that we should go to school in Iraq".

In the late 1960s, Zahrah's father moved to Abu Dhabi where he tried to rebuild his trading business. Zahrah and her sisters were brought from Baghdad to Abu Dhabi where she finished her schooling. In the early 1980s, her father moved to Maṭraḥ in Oman where his trading company was now based. He secured his right of return to his native country after several years in limbo, and after settling in Maṭraḥ he married a second wife while keeping his first spouse in Abu Dhabi. Zahrah remained with her mother, but continued to visit her father regularly during school holidays: "I really did not like to visit Oman in the summer. I preferred to stay with my mother in Abu Dhabi, but my father insisted".

Zahrah's father secured an Omani scholarship to send Zahrah and her sisters to university. As Oman did not then have its own university (the only university in Oman, Sultan Qābūs University, opened its doors in 1986), Zahrah belonged to the first generation of Omanis sent abroad for higher education. She spent five years in Britain studying computer science and was able to renew contacts with an aunt who had settled in England in 1964. "My family is scattered all over the world and I can find relatives almost everywhere. I did not feel lonely in England because I had relatives in Southampton and Portsmouth".[15] Zahrah regularly visited her mother in Abu Dhabi and her father in Maṭraḥ. She graduated in 1986 and returned to Muscat to find a job, easily establishing herself in one of the prestigious ministries where 17 years later she is still an employee. Until her return to Oman, Zahrah described her life as a series of uprootings.

Zahrah's Omani heritage was based on ancestral links. She identified with Oman as the land of her ancestors, but her personal experiences reflected transnational connections stretching beyond Oman, let alone the interior. Apart from "ancestry", the interior of Oman has little relevance to her present life. She is part of the urban educated elite of Muscat. I was surprised to find that Zahrah had never so much as visited Jabal Akhdar where her tribal group once had prestige and influence, but as far as she is concerned, the tribal past belongs to a remote era. She is not interested in exploring its intricacies. The landscape of the interior is, in her words, "dotted with reminders of her roots" (*judhūrī mutanāthirah fī arḍ al-jabal*); but practical life goes on elsewhere, and collective memory refers to somewhere else again.

The African heritage

Zahrah's Omani ancestry and vague identification with the interior coexist with an important African heritage. As mentioned earlier, Zahrah claims "pure" Omani ancestry. But, although she left Zanzibar at a very early age, she grew up in a household where Swahili was the usual language. She claims she was lucky to learn Arabic in Saudi Arabia, Iraq and the United Arab Emirates. Several of her older sisters missed the opportunity to study Arabic at an early age, and one claimed she had only learned it in her early 20s at the American University in Cairo. Her Arabic remains limited. This does not seem to affect her employment in Oman as she is currently working for Petroleum Development-Oman, where English is dominant. In social gatherings, the language used is always Swahili, now inter-cut by English and Arabic phrases especially among Zahrah's generation that has benefited from higher education in Western universities. Interaction with the old generation is predominantly in Swahili, larded with phrases such as *al-ḥamdu li-llāh* (praise God) and *in sha' allāh* (God willing).

A sense of nostalgia permeates the memory of Zanzibar. Recollections of that past, not fully experienced by Zahrah herself because of the young age at which she had to leave, always include references to the lush island, the land of plenty, affluence, servants, coconuts and banana plantations. Such recitations conclude with bitterness and with horror stories about expulsion, massacres and violence. The loss of home is particularly lamented by a previous generation, that is, Zahrah's parent's generation. Given the trauma associated with the expulsion from Africa, it is not surprising that I have come across only one case where a person has recently returned to Zanzibar. He has begun to restore his family's home, abandoned since 1964, and envisages using the house for future holidays. He remains an exception. Several Zanzibaris refused to go back after political conditions improved. They argued that it would be too painful to return even for a short visit.

Zahrah's memory of Zanzibar is almost entirely based on stories she heard from her parents and older relatives. She describes the community in Zanzibar as closely knit, a function of living in great proximity. She contrasts this imagined past with present-day Muscat, where Zanzibaris are scattered over a large area, and comments on how it has become difficult for Zanzibaris to maintain the intense visiting and socialising patterns that the community enjoyed and encouraged prior to arrival in Oman.[16] She hardly has time, she says, to visit her sisters or other relatives, given that most women in the community are in full-time employment. However, in present-day Muscat, intense socialising takes place within the networks of extended family. Zanzibaris maintain regular contacts with relatives. While men meet in the neighbourhood mosque, elite Zanzibari women organise lavish dinner parties where a predominant Zanzibari majority is obvious. Among the professional elite, hospitality ensures contacts among similar individuals whose employment networks stretch beyond a single economic niche. According to Zanzibaris, most socialising is with members of the community, who share kinship relations, language and experience. It is only recently that their social events would include non-Zanzibaris. At one occasion that I attended, a Luti Shiʿah woman married to a Zanzibari (rare but possible in present-day Muscat) was the only non-Zanzibari in a group of over 30 guests.

In the 1970s, Zanzibaris were seen as a community with a "family orientation", though their social standing in Muscat was mostly defined by professional position and economic achievement (Scholz 1997: 154). Now financial means determine in large part where people live. Omanis with an annual income above $1,500 tend to live in new neighbourhoods in the mountains around Muscat, while the poor, with incomes of less than $400 per annum, are in Maṭraḥ al-Rūwī. Those with average incomes, between the two extremes, live in various places, mixed in with other groups (ibid. 157). Zanzibaris are no exception to the general pattern, and collective identity is not expressed by spatial segregation, though prosperous Zanzibaris tend to cluster in elite neighbourhoods such as al-Qurm and Madīnat Qābūs.

It is at wedding ceremonies that most Zanzibaris seem to express their identity most obviously. Weddings are the context for maintaining contacts with other members of the community and exchanging news, but above all the wedding ceremony has become the arena where a distinctive Zanzibari identity is imagined and experienced. Although elite weddings in Muscat and elsewhere in the Arab World tend to be very similar,[17] Zanzibaris insist that theirs are different. They claim that their weddings are distinguished by their music and dancing.

It is common for members of the Zanzibari elite to hold weddings in one of Muscat's international luxury hotels, a pattern observed in other parts of the Arab World among groups of similar socio-economic standing.[18] There is nothing in the surroundings, such as the decoration of the wedding hall or the food offered, that would distinguish a Zanzibari wedding in such a context from other weddings. A mixture of international and Lebanese food is offered, together with the white Western wedding cake. Photographers and video cameramen intermingle with the guests, sometimes over 500 women. While women attend such celebrations wearing the finest and latest fashions, some remain veiled even in an all-female context. On such occasions, the veil consists of a large colourful scarf, or *lasu*, covering the hair. At some weddings female guests request that the band, often consisting of several men, should be separated from the dance hall by a screen so that women can dance unseen by males. It is also common for the hotel management to provide waitresses, usually Filipino women, to serve food and look after guests, all of which is fairly standard practice. But according to Zanzibaris, music and dancing make their weddings different from others in Muscat's international hotels. Swahili music and songs are requested from the band, often hired in advance for the occasion.

While other Arab popular songs are sung, Swahili music seems to be appreciated and enjoyed by the guests. Wealthy members of the community import famous Swahili bands to Oman for the wedding ceremony; others are content with local bands who can sing Swahili popular songs. Women wait for such songs to perform an African dance where they form a series of outer and inner circles while swinging their upper and lower bodies to the rhythm. They hold each other's waists to keep the circles closed, and the bride, in white Western wedding dress, is expected to join in the middle of the circle, surrounded by other dancers, especially members of her own family such as her mother and sisters. The wedding ceremony, where all this goes on, is similar to other Zanzibari social gatherings in the way that the language of communication is predominantly Swahili, especially among women above the age of 30. Zanzibaris claim their African heritage is also expressed in their food. Women refer to special dishes, for example *mandazi*, a kind of fried flour cakes, together with sweets prepared using coconuts and bananas, as distinctively Zanzibari. They continue to prepare them regularly and introduce their children to the culinary traditions of Zanzibar.

Visiting patterns and weddings are organised primarily on the basis of strong kinship connections. There is a preference among Zanzibaris for marriage within the community, and here the "community" proves still to be anything but local. There are even cases of Zanzibari men having "imported" brides from East Africa. One such case is Noha, a young educated woman of "Omani" descent from Burundi.[19] Noha spoke Swahili and French, a function of an education in a French lycée. Luckily she learned English at university in Britain and this became her language of communication with non-Zanzibaris in Oman. Even after more than a decade in Muscat, Noha cannot speak Arabic. In Zanzibari social contexts this is not a problem, and she clearly counts as Zanzibari.

Zanzibaris defend the bringing of wives from East Africa on the basis that in the absence of suitable Zanzibari candidates in Oman, one is better off "importing" one from East Africa. Real or quasi kinship relations are often a pretext for the practice. According to the community, Zanzibari women are ideal wives, clean, good housekeepers and educated. Their *mahr*, or dowry, is also cheaper. Marriages with such women not only cement community relations, but also overcome the problem of residence permits and citizenship. Men who seek African wives (indeed foreign wives more generally) must obtain permission from the Ministry of Interior.[20] When disputes over defintion arise, however, the government seems quite tolerant in the Zanzibaris' case.

If one is to consider marriage, language and food as markers of a Zanzibari identity, language is definitely an aspect of the past that is difficult to maintain in present-day Oman, where Arabic is the dominant language in schools, ministries and official circles. Zanzibaris of the old generation, whose Arabic was virtually non-existent, were not assimilated immediately when they arrived in Oman. Today teachers express concern when young Zanzibari children join schools with little Arabic, if the child's parents still converse in Swahili at home.[21] Second-generation Zanzibaris, who were born in Oman after the 1970s, are far more fluent in Arabic. For them Swahili remains the language of their older relatives, a set of familiar sounds and utterances.

Oman's national narrative and Zanzibaris

Oman has had a sense of its own identity and national character since before the establishment of the Ibadi sect in the eighth century, but the modern state and nation-building are recent. A unified Oman came into being only in the 1950s and the modern state was born with Sultan Qābūs's coup in 1970. The old pre-modern Omani identity remained rooted in the interior, the land of tribes and the Imamate. The coast was an amalgam of people with diverse languages, religions and origins. While descent and tribal origin divided the people of the interior, language and ethnicity marked differences on the coast. In present-day Oman, the indigenous population is an amalgam of the tribal interior and groups of the coastal areas.

Faced with the reality of pluralism, one is tempted to ask whether the Omani national narrative, itself a product of recent oil wealth, can accommodate the diverse heritage of the people of Oman. A national narrative is potentially a powerful tool, a form of representation concerned with expressing coherence and order through time. Such narratives transform fragmentation, contingency and randomness into a meaningful sequence of events. The objective of the Omani narrative is thus to establish *al-waḥdah al-waṭanīyah*, or "national unity", which itself requires *ṣahr*, a melting of difference among various sections of society (al-ʿAnsī 1991: 37). However, a close examination of the content of this narrative reveals the official emphasis on past pluralism. It is fair to describe Oman's national narrative in summary as based on the ethos of reconciliation.

The national narrative, embedded in museums and official publications, also emphasises Oman's openness to the outside world and its long tradition of social and religious tolerance. Since the 1970s, there has been a deliberate attempt to promote Oman's transnational connections as part of the identity of the country. In present-day Oman, museums celebrate the nation's maritime heritage, travel and exploration by the early Omanis, who feature as pioneers in a long history of overseas connections. In the 1970s, a book produced by a London-based research centre for the Omani government with the title *Oman: a seafaring nation* (Facey 1979; cf. Salamandra in the present volume) became an icon of identity purchased by tourists or offered to distinguished government guests. The book is displayed on coffee tables in the homes of the educated Muscat elite together with Omani daggers, dates, incense burners and chains of pearls.

The emphasis on Oman's openness to the outside world was exemplified in one of the most unexpected places in Muscat, the Sultan's Armed Forces Museum, Bayt al-Falaj.[22] The museum documents Oman's military history from pre-Islamic times to the era of Sultan Qābūs. It highlights Oman's independence from foreign powers – for example the Persians, Portuguese and Ottomans – throughout its history. More importantly, the museum glorifies the success of Sultan Qābūs in suppressing rebellions and insurgency. The museum is meant to:

> retell the forthcoming generations the story of the progressive development that the Sultan's armed forces has achieved by the powerful hands and sacrifices of the Omanis during the renaissance era under the leadership of

> HM Sultan Qabus bin Said, the reviver of the glories of Oman and the leader of its blessed renaissance.[23]

In the exhibition hall marking the imperial expansion of Oman in the nineteenth century, a Baluchi guide in military uniform points out to visitors two versions of a famous book, one entitled *Mudhakkarāt amīrah 'arabīyah* (Sulṭān 1993) and the other entitled *Memoirs of an Arabian Princess from Zanzibar* (Ruete 1998). These are displayed together with portraits of Sultan Sa'īd bin Sulṭān and Aḥmad al-Nu'mānī, Oman's nineteenth-century envoy to the United States. While the story of Princess Sālmah's marriage to a German, her elopement, conversion to Christianity and later disputes with her brothers over inheritance rights are well known inside and outside Oman,[24] the guide's comments on the book were revealing:

> In Oman we are open. Princess Sālmah married a German. Yes of course her family wasn't happy about it but these things happen. Do you know that Oman had an empire in Africa? Lots of Omanis lived abroad and it was natural for them to fall in love with non-Omanis. We do not want to hide these things and we are not ashamed of her story. Today in Oman, when people marry foreigners, we encourage them to bring their spouses to the country. We cannot afford to lose our children. We are an open country unlike yours [Saudi Arabia] across the border. Our Sultan is very understanding of the modern world. Thanks to his efforts, we are able to display the books. People will read them even if we do not allow them in the country. So why ban them? It is better to have them in the museum. Foreigners visiting us can also see them.

My guide was no doubt aware of the requirement these days to obtain permission from the Ministry of Interior before marrying a foreigner. Family jealousy and honour, however, are displaced by state decrees, and the state is free to elaborate its history as it wishes. The value of boundaries perhaps has changed.

It seems that some localities are able successfully to switch themselves into global networks, while others remain unconnected. Fortunately, in an age of dwindling oil revenues, Oman is easily capitalising on its transnational connections and seafaring heritage,[25] slowly attracting a small number of Western tourists to its past treasures. The Omanis responsible for developing these present transnational contacts are the ones who had themselves been part of Oman's "seafaring heritage", namely Zanzibaris. The story of Princess Sālmah becomes acceptable in a tourist site whose main *raison d'être* is to glorify the power of the state.

Besides its overseas connections, an important dimension of the Omani national narrative is the celebration of regional differences manifested in folklore, dress, customs and traditions. Several exhibitions in the Omani National Museum are dedicated to highlighting the traditions of Dhofar, Baṭinah, Dhahirah (al-Ẓāhirah), Sharqīyah and other regions. The agricultural heritage of the oases coexists with that of nomads and fishermen. The state-controlled television, meanwhile, has several series dedicated to Oman's cultural diversity (one such programme, for instance, was concerned with the diversity of wedding ceremonies and dress in different regions), and while Zanzibaris do not feature as a group in such displays, the emphasis on Oman's links overseas and the glorification of Sultan Sa'īd bin Sulṭān's expansion draws visitors' attention to Oman's connections with Africa. Zanzibaris indirectly fit in with this version of the past. They are part of Oman's seafaring rhetoric and heritage. In fact, they are a living testimony of Oman's glorious past and imperial expansion.

Since the 1970s, Zanzibaris have successfully become mediators between Omanis and the outside world. Their early employment in the Ministry of Defence and the oil industry, heavily under foreign influence in the pre-Omanisation period, attests to their ability to position themselves as key players in politics and the economy. Their ancestry anchors them in Oman while their settlement and experience in Africa substantiate the national narrative by adding a rich dimension to an already complex and heterogeneous social setting. Their welcome in Oman in the 1970s was a decision based on expediency. Those among them who had grand genealogies were excluded for obvious political reasons;[26] the rest were accepted because they represented an intermediary group between a newly established political authority (that of Qābūs in 1970) and a society torn by decades of tribal warfare and rebellion. Bounded by kinship, language and the African connection, Zanzibaris are a truly transnational community whose identity is anchored in multiple localities.

CHAPTER 5

NEITHER AUTOCRACY NOR DEMOCRACY BUT ETHNOCRACY

Citizens, Expatriates and the Socio-Political System in Kuwait

Anh Nga Longva

Compared to the rest of the Middle East, the Gulf countries, with the occasional exception of Bahrain, are not associated with overt social turmoil and political upheavals. In spite of substantial material transformations over the past half-century, the power structure – both political and social – appears to have changed little since pre-oil days. Rather than being positively assessed as stability, this state of affairs is generally seen as a sign of immobility, the combined result of oil-based prosperity and lack of political and social freedom. Gulf societies are considered among the most conservative in the world, and Gulf rulers are frequently referred to in Western media and literature as "autocrats".

This view, while not ungrounded, begs some interesting questions, not least concerning the use of "autocracy" and "democracy" in the Gulf context. It also tends to gloss over intra-regional variations. For example, while Bahrainis in the first half of the 1990s lived in fear that their most innocent statements might be construed as criticism of the regime and, as a result, always preferred to discuss society and politics within the four walls of their homes, Kuwaitis openly criticised their government in public places and never worried much about being heard and seen doing so. How then are we to describe the regime in Kuwait? Neither autocracy nor democracy is an adequate description. A third alternative arises from the conjuncture of traditional Kuwaiti socio-political organisation, the advent of the oil economy and the presence since independence in 1961 of a population of foreign workers (locally known as "expatriates") whose number since the 1970s has consistently been greater than that of the native population.[1] This article focuses mainly on the last factor, which, it will be argued, allows us to describe Kuwait as an ethnocracy.

Autocracy and democracy

At first sight, Kuwait shares many of the features that prompt foreign observers to describe the region as autocratic. Like its neighbours, it has a hereditary monarchy with a dynasty, the Āl Ṣabāḥ, who concentrate considerable power in their hands, so much so that terms like "the state", "government" and "executive power" are all understood as referring to the ruling family. But unlike elsewhere in the region, Kuwait has developed legal means to ensure a degree of accountability. Much has been written about the Kuwaiti constitution and the institution of an elected National Assembly, which make Kuwait stand apart from its neighbours. The general tendency, however, is to dismiss the country's political system, which excludes women from participation[2] and does not allow political parties, as a poor imitation of democracy. One could argue, nevertheless, that the existence of a written document guaranteeing a separation of powers and setting in place mechanisms of check and balance has had a valuable impact on the relationship between rulers and the ruled. Unlike the *majlis al-shūrā* (consultative council) in Bahrain, Oman, Qatar or Saudi Arabia, the Kuwaiti legislature is not (either partly or wholly) appointed by the Ruler but is elected in its entirety through secret ballot. Evidently, elections can be rigged and votes can be bought. There have also been two unconstitutional dissolutions of the National Assembly.[3] And, even when the legislative body is in being, there is more than one way in which the ruling family can get deputies to comply with its will. This does not mean, however, that the National Assembly is a docile institution, and the reason for this is to be found in popular perceptions of its function.

To Kuwaitis, the *raison d'être* of the National Assembly is not so much to legislate as to oppose the ruling family, which means, in practice, to watch over the government and prevent it from abusing its power (according to critics of the regime) or from carrying out its tasks effectively (according to regime supporters). In the Kuwaiti context, the term "opposition" does not refer to a political group or groups that have been defeated in an election and are waiting in the wings for their turn to regain executive power. Rather, it refers to deputies who seek to introduce change within a political system where the constellation of power has in principle been defined once and for all, where the ruling family *always* rule, and the people can choose either to support or to oppose them. The task of forming the Cabinet belongs by law to the Crown Prince, whose complete title is "Crown Prince and Prime Minister".[4] The choice of ministers is entirely at the Crown Prince's discretion.[5] Politicians outside the family can never accede to executive power unless they are vetted by the Crown Prince, and no individuals or groups are free from Āl Ṣabāḥ interference.

Against this backdrop, the perception of the elected National Assembly as intrinsically oppositional makes sense. One illustration of the popular perception is the way pro-government deputies are disparagingly referred to as *nawāb al-khidamāt* (service deputies) as opposed to the *nawāb al-mawāqif* (deputies with a stance, or principled deputies). The former see their task as simply looking after the material interests and well being of their constituents, leaving the government free to run the country, while the latter have a political programme that disagrees, at least partly, with that of the government and which they seek to implement. Deputies described as "principled" invariably belong to anti-governmental, "opposition" factions – liberal[6] as well as Islamist. It is generally agreed that service deputies are useful to have, but that principled deputies are those who deserve respect, whether one likes their ideas or not. It seems that a deputy who is not oppositional somehow does not quite fulfill his duty, and a National Assembly that co-operates with the government is looked upon as toothless. Political opposition in Kuwait has therefore a clear moral dimension.

Common to all opposition deputies, but particularly the secular "liberals", is the view that the government must be watched closely, not least because of its tendency to appropriate oil resources which rightfully belong to Kuwait's people. Over the years, some deputies have not hesitated to call the government – meaning the ruling family – "thieves" and "looters of public funds".[7] Whether the criticism, protests and objections of the opposition deputies are always justified and whether they lead to genuine changes is another question.[8] Still, although Kuwait's rulers make use of political privileges that to most Westerners seem unacceptable, they are not in a position to disregard the *vox populi.* The present-day regime in Kuwait may be flawed in several ways, but it cannot be described as a conventional autocracy, and the government is known to have bowed to the majority's decision.[9]

If Kuwait is not a typical autocracy, nor is it a democracy – and certainly not a modern one. The prime instance of pre-modern democracy, of course, is Athens in the fifth century BC. This was direct democracy in which only a certain class of Athenian citizens – all of them male – could take part, and several groups were excluded, among them women, slaves and the *metics* or non-citizen residents (Finley 1973). As is well known, the exclusion of women and the poor also characterised European countries and the United States not long ago. We find similar features in Kuwait today, and in the case of women, many of the same justifications for exclusion are used, e.g. that women are too "emotional" or "irrational" and not educated enough to be entrusted with decisions affecting the life of the country.

"Modern" democracy, by contrast, emphasises universality of political rights. Such rights are everywhere *acquired* rights and are subject to clear conditions: they are not granted before a certain age, and can be withdrawn (for example as a sanction against criminal behaviour) or forfeited (through migration, change of citizenship or as a result of the fulfilment of certain functions in society).[10] Political rights are "universal" in the sense that they are held by all adult citizens of the state regardless of gender, race, class and cultural background, and not in the sense of being birthrights for all human beings. The necessary, though not sufficient, requirement is citizenship. Almost everywhere, non-citizens are lawfully denied political rights on the principle that the exercise of such rights is indissolubly associated with the nation-state, which constitutes the natural frame for their practice.[11]

The national principle has important implications for the status of non-citizens, all the more so when these find themselves at the bottom of the socio-economic structure. Unable to exercise political rights in a state of expatriation, non-citizens everywhere are vulnerable. They depend for their protection on the goodwill of the host country and on the ability and readiness of the authorities of their native countries to intervene in their favour. Such intervention, however, is not guaranteed in an international legal order founded on the principle of non-interference in states' internal affairs. When the nationals in need of assistance are, in addition, humble migrant workers whose remittances represent a major source of income for the cash-strapped home economies, as is the case with most labour-sending countries and the Arab Gulf, their governments' reluctance to intervene is even greater. Similarly, should the host country violate their rights, this is likely to go unnoticed or unsanctioned.[12]

Lack of security, legal and otherwise, is a problem common to working-class expatriates all over the world and is not specific to Kuwait or the Gulf region. However, in Kuwait, non-citizens' lack of security takes on a particular significance because of their sheer number: the demographic imbalance between Kuwaitis and expatriates has consequences for the place the latter occupy in the former's social imagination. It also provides the rationale for the system of migrant control devised by the Kuwaitis. The resulting asymmetry in the structural and human relations between the two populations cannot fail to leave its imprint on the country's political regime. More than oil prosperity *per se*, it is the presence of non-Kuwaiti workers and their legal, social and political subjection to Kuwaiti citizens that allows for (1) the reproduction of a political structure with quasi-autocratic features, and (2) the continued marginalisation of Kuwaiti women from productive work, their willing confinement within the role of biological reproducers and their formal absence from political life.

The political exclusion of women and that of migrant workers differ in terms of international legitimacy. The political exclusion of women violates the principle of non-discrimination on the basis of gender, enshrined in a series of international bills of rights.[13] Hence this form of discrimination is the object of general condemnation, and Kuwaitis who campaign for women's political rights enjoy international support. The exclusion of foreign workers, on the other hand, is entirely in line with the equally widely accepted principle that political rights are a function of national citizenship. Originally, this exclusion is grounded in the foreigners being exempted from such basic rights as real property ownership and such basic duties as tax payment (if they are short-term residents) or military service. The linkage between ownership, taxation and representation is essential for understanding the logic of political entitlements: when long-term foreign residents in northern European countries, for instance, are allowed to take part in municipal (not parliamentary) elections, it is precisely because of their contributions to the municipalities' coffers.[14] In Kuwait, neither nationals nor expatriates pay personal income tax, but the right of ownership of real estate belongs exclusively to the former. Expatriates here own neither land nor means of production. Furthermore, although they work *in* Kuwait and *for* the Kuwaitis, they are a non-national underclass towards whom the Kuwaiti nation-state does not wish to have commitments.

From the perspective of capitalist and national logic, the political exclusion of expatriates rests on a double rationale which is widely and unquestioningly accepted. Very few analysts react to the total absence of linkage between studies of Kuwaiti politics and studies of Kuwaiti labour relations. In particular, writers on democratisation (Farah 1989, Ghabra 1994, Meyer et al. 1998, Alnajjar 2000, Tétreault 2001) fail to appreciate the social, psychological and political impact that a majority population of rightless migrant workers, imported for the sole purpose of serving the native minority, can have on the way this privileged minority conceptualise and practise political rights among themselves. Most analyses leave out the one social variable on which the native minority population depends for its identity as well as its material well being.

The concept of ethnocracy

The term ethnocracy was coined in the 1970s by Ali Mazrui to describe the situation in Uganda under Idi Amin, but has since been applied to a wide array of societies, ranging from Africa (Young, J. 1996) to Latin America (Stavenhagen 1989), to Eastern Europe (Juska 1999) and Israel (Yiftachel 1997). Mazrui (1975) defines ethnocracy as "a political system based on kinship, real or presumed". In its more recent use, however, the term describes the tendency for an elite to posit their own physical characteristics and cultural norms as the essence of the nation over which they rule, thus narrowing its definition and excluding all those within the polity who do not exhibit the same characteristics or embrace the same norms. In this sense, ethnocracy as a socio-political regime is the outcome of ethno-nationalism, that brand of nationalism that views the nation as a "natural" and ethnically "pure" community, as opposed to its liberal conceptualisation as a community based on equal rights and duties.

In practical terms, ethnocracy is government by an ethnic group. Ethnicity, however, is a notoriously vague concept and there are various ways in which groups identify themselves. In the case of South Africa prior to the dismantling of apartheid, race was the critical feature for the definition of dominant and dominated: South African ethnocracy could thus be described as a racial ethnocracy. This is also the case in Bolivia and Guatemala, where whites and mestizos rule over Indians (Stavenhagen 1989). Besides race, any other iconic item, most notably language and religion, can be used as the defining criterion. In Israel, for example, the ruling ethnic group defines itself in terms of Judaism. In Kuwait and the rest of the Gulf, the defining feature is not race, language or religion but citizenship conceived in terms of shared descent. All expatriates, being non-Kuwaiti citizens, are excluded from the ruling ethnie, even if they are Arabs or Muslims or both; the few Christian Kuwaitis, on the other hand, are part of it. Since citizenship is the major diacritical feature, I choose to describe this as "civic" ethnocracy.

While all ethnocracies can be described as domination through exclusion, some criteria for exclusion are seen internationally as more acceptable than others. For example, following the official demise of the notion of race in international discourse in the wake of the Second World War, exclusion on racial grounds provokes immediate negative reactions: as a result, racial ethnocracies attract attention and condemnation. Civic ethnocracy on the other hand, where exclusion is practised on the basis of citizenship, strikes most observers as a "normal" state of affairs: as suggested earlier, it appears rational and justifiable in our world of nation-states. Unless it is accompanied by gross power asymmetry and human rights abuses, it is not the object of general condemnation; nor does it attract much scholarly attention.

Kuwait's civic ethnocracy

Ethnocracy develops in societies that are heterogeneous, and with a pronounced degree of perceived cultural variation. In Kuwait such variation is striking. Kuwait has a population of 1.9 million with 800,000 Kuwaitis, the remaining 1.1 million being non-Kuwaitis of different kinds. Eighty-three per cent of the labour force are expatriate workers (Kuwait 2000: 87). While 92 per cent of those Kuwaitis who work are concentrated in the public sector, the private sector employs almost exclusively non-Kuwaitis (ibid.). The expatriates consist of Arab and non-Arab elements. Arabs come from all over the Middle East, the largest group being Egyptians.[15] Non-Arabs are mainly from the Asian subcontinent (India, Pakistan, Bangladesh and Sri Lanka), Southeast Asia (mostly Filipinos, but also Indonesians and Thais), and from Iran. Among the non-Arabs is also a minority of Westerners – Europeans, Americans and Australians.

As to the Kuwaiti population proper, variation runs along two main axes: Sunni–Shi'ah and urban–tribal. These internal differences are of major importance and represent specific forms of ethnocracy of their own that could be described as sectarian (the dominance of Sunnis over Shi'ah) and cultural-historical (the dominance until now of urban over tribal elements; see Longva n.d.). The presence of a significant population of stateless – the so-called *bidūn* – further adds to the complexity (Longva 1997). In the larger context, however, these internal structures of domination must be viewed as *de facto* stratifications which do not rest on any legal basis, are challenged by the non-elite and decried by official state discourse. Most relevant for our present purpose, they are overshadowed by the rule of Kuwaiti citizens – male as well as female, urban as well as tribal, Sunni as well as Shi'ah – over non-Kuwaitis. In light of this overarching ethnocracy, sectarian and other internal power asymmetries are subject to negotiation and are strategically overlooked by Kuwaitis when it suits them. The opposite possibility (namely that the Kuwaiti/non-Kuwaiti divide be disregarded in the face of, say, the sectarian divide) is more unusual.

The category "non-Kuwaiti" – or more specifically "expatriate" – includes both Arabs and non-Arabs, with a whole range of nationalities. The dominated group in this ethnocratic state is thus not a single ethnie. Expatriates are a miscellaneous category, and whatever common characteristics they may exhibit result mainly from the social status they are ascribed by Kuwaitis rather than from self-ascription. "Expatriate" and "non-Kuwaiti" are, in other words, designations applied by local bureaucrats and statisticians to groups that have little in common except their status in Kuwait as migrant workers. Nor is mobility between the subordinate and dominant categories permitted.

We should reserve the term "ethnocracy" to describe situations where the acquisition of the defining feature of the ruling ethnie lies beyond the reach of the dominated groups. Mechanisms are devised by ethnocrats to bar access. Thus "ethnocracy" should not be used of societies where the defining feature is a spoken language or a way of life: in such cases, one can hardly speak of restricted membership, as anyone can learn a language given adequate opportunity, and espouse a way of life given the necessary material and social facilities. Stavenhagen's (1989) description of France as an ethnocracy based on linguistic domination and the United States as an ethnocracy based on WASP culture is therefore problematic. A Breton willing to adopt French as her mother tongue does become part of the French nation.[16] The same argument obtains with regard to the United States, for if embracing WASP culture is the main condition for crossing over from the dominated to the dominant ethnie, it is difficult to see how a consistently ethnocratic regime can be maintained. Discrimination against non-white minorities, most particularly African-Americans, even when they submit to WASP culture, clearly indicates that where the US shows ethnocratic features, these in fact are founded on the specific criterion of colour – difficult to transcend, hence "closed membership" – and not on culture. Domination founded on culture gives rise to hegemonic, not ethnocratic, systems. For the dominated ethnie in a true ethnocratic regime, being willing to pay the price of assimilation will not help: membership is priceless; it cannot be bought, only bestowed.

In Kuwait, the cornerstone of the ethnocratic regime is the 1959 Nationality Law. Who is genuinely Kuwaiti has been the object of endless debate among Kuwaitis themselves for the past 40 years. Until recently, the authorities operated with an official ranking of citizens to distinguish between "original" Kuwaitis (*bi-l-aṣl*) and "Kuwaitis by naturalisation" (*bi-l-tajannus*). The latter category was in turn finely differentiated. According to the 1959 law, the category "originally Kuwaiti" includes descendants of those settled in Kuwait since 1920. Whereas for a short while prior to 1959, children of Arab or Muslim fathers born in Kuwait could acquire Kuwaiti citizenship (Crystal 1992), this is no longer allowed: from *jus soli* (nationality based on territory), the 1959 law shifted back to *jus sanguinis* (nationality based on parentage) – the latter principle being a characteristic feature of ethnocratic regimes. Furthermore, it is *jus sanguinis* with a patriarchal twist, as only sons of Kuwaiti fathers can claim Kuwaiti citizenship. Within less than 30 years, the law was amended seven times, each time for the purpose of further restricting access to membership: in 1960 an amendment set a ceiling of 50 to the number of naturalisations allowed each year,[17] and the 1981 amendment restricted the granting of Kuwaiti citizenship to Muslim candidates only.

It is worth noting that while there is much disagreement about who is genuinely Kuwaiti, practically all Kuwaitis agree that access to citizenship should remain closely restricted. The intensive campaign of naturalisation of the badu, which went on in the first two decades after independence and was viewed with misgiving by "original" Kuwaitis, was brought to an end in 1980. Since then, very few cases of naturalisation have been registered, and the only people from outside the Gulf region to acquire Kuwaiti citizenship nowadays are foreign women married to Kuwaiti men.[18] Although Kuwaitis are aware that a larger and more productive population would increase the country's viability, demographic growth through naturalisation is an option that seems to have been discarded.

A sense of external threat

As a minority in their own country, Kuwaitis live with the feeling of being permanently under siege. It is not that they fear the competition of foreigners in business, political power or social prestige: citizens know very well that, given the existing legislation, expatriates cannot compete with them on these counts. What they worry about could be summed up under the vague term "cultural integrity". Not surprisingly for a society where the natives are in a minority and which undergoes rapid and extensive material changes, there is much talk in Kuwait about the need to preserve Kuwaiti identity (*huwīyah*), along with social "values and principles" (*qiyam wa-mabādī*), and over the years the public discourse on cultural threats from the outside world conveys an increasing note of urgency. Conventional wisdom has it that "Kuwaiti traditions" and "the Kuwaiti way of life" are under threat and that expatriates are the major source of this menace. Two kinds of general knowledge inform this conviction: the stark, formal arithmetics of demography (1.1 million others versus 800,000 Kuwaitis) and the fact that foreigners are not only highly visible in every aspect of Kuwaiti social life, but fulfill critical functions in it.

In the eyes of many Kuwaitis, all expatriates, regardless of ethnic background, are disturbing elements within the local context. Yet the cultural damage commonly attributed to Arabs differs from that wrought by non-Arabs, in that the former is of a clearly political character while the latter is more of a moral nature. The perception of an "Arab political threat" is grounded in several factors: Arab expatriates enjoy a special position in Kuwaiti society. They are not seen by nationals as "foreigners" (*ajānib*), but simply "non-Kuwaitis" (*ghayr kuwaytīyīn*). They share with Kuwaitis the Arabic language and the majority adhere to the same religion, Islam.[19] Arab expatriates come from all walks of life, so some hold prestigious jobs (judges, medical doctors, university professors, business executives) while others are semi-skilled or unskilled workers. They are numerous in education (as teachers), the media (as journalists) and religious institutions (as preachers). All this makes it difficult to describe the Arab expatriate population in Kuwait in general terms, but compared to non-Arabs, they have a unique opportunity to meet and spread their ideas among a wide Kuwaiti audience. The Arab impact on Kuwaiti nationals at the intellectual, cultural and political level is extensive. In addition to a common medium of expression, Arab expatriates and Kuwaitis share many common concerns and interests.[20] Arabs who come to work in Kuwait bring with them their political opinions and ideologies, which has always worried the Kuwaiti authorities. The political alignments and conflicts that take place in the expatriates' homelands are often reproduced in Kuwait, boosted by the flow in the opposite direction of Kuwaiti students, businessmen and other visitors to these countries, and by the wide distribution of Arab radio and TV programmes as well as press articles and literature.

More threatening than the narrowly political effect of Arab expatriates on Kuwait is their potential impact on the native citizens' hearts and minds. For example, during the early decades of Kuwait's development – the 1960s and 1970s – practically all the teachers in Kuwaiti schools were Arab expatriates, many of them Palestinians (Brand 1988). Although a number were replaced by Kuwaiti teachers from the 1980s onwards, the Kuwaitisation of school staffs remains limited to central neighbourhoods inhabited mainly by urban middle-class Kuwaitis. In the outlying areas with a heavily "tribal" (badu) population, most teachers still are Arab expatriates. This means that despite the close monitoring of courses and syllabuses by the Ministry of Education, several generations of young Kuwaitis have been in effect taught and influenced by non-Kuwaitis whose scholarship and worldviews were developed elsewhere and whose loyalty, the Kuwaitis fear, also lies elsewhere.

That the political development of Kuwait over the years (most notably the move from Arab Nationalism in the 1960s and 1970s to Islamism from the 1980s onwards) reflects political developments elsewhere in the Arab World, particularly in Egypt, is not only due to the Middle East being a cultural or political unit. It is also because, through their physical presence and the central functions some of them fulfill in Kuwait, Arab migrant workers create, in a literal sense, a replica of the world from which they originate, and this replica finds substantial resonance among Kuwaitis. Thus Arab expatriates' ideas and trends make profound inroads in Kuwaitis' lives in spite of the vast scepticism Kuwaitis harbour towards outsiders. Last but not least, a small but steady number of Kuwaitis marry non-Kuwaitis.

The place and role of non-Arab expatriates in Kuwait differs substantially from that of Arabs. Cut off from the Kuwaiti population by language and other cultural barriers, they are seldom employed in positions of authority. Not only their lowly social rank but also their visible alienness deprives them of a voice in Kuwaiti society. Yet because they have the monopoly of employment in the so-called domestic sector, Asian expatriates have a unique access to Kuwaitis' private worlds and, paradoxically, develop an intimate knowledge of this aspect of citizens' lives, which remains little known to Arab expatriates. Despite, but also because of, cultural familiarity with their Kuwaiti hosts, relations between the Kuwaitis and Arab migrants are hedged with caution and characterised by social distance (Longva 1997). Few Arabs are ever invited to Kuwaiti homes, and few Kuwaiti families would consider having an Arab maid. On the other hand, low-skilled Asian domestic servants are ubiquitous and identified by Kuwaitis as the prime source of moral threats mainly because of the kind of low-status jobs they perform in Kuwaiti homes. Agents of supposed immorality can thus be defined in terms of both ethnicity and class. "Moral threats" consist in violations of Kuwaiti behavioural norms and regulations. Prominent among them are use of alcohol and sexual offences (prostitution and adultery). Reviewing information gathered by the Ministry of the Interior and published daily in the local press, one is struck by the rather large involvement of Asian expatriates in "sexual" offences. While prostitution, organised and driven mainly by South Asians, is a recent phenomenon in Kuwait, adultery can be said to have been a constant theme in the Kuwaiti perception of non-Arab expatriates.

There are several reasons why Arabs are less frequently associated with sexual crimes than Asians, in particular Indians and Sri Lankans. First of all, the majority of Arab migrants are men, while at least 50 per cent of the Asians are women, many of them unaccompanied (Kuwait 2000: 89). Most female Arabs who live in Kuwait come as dependants of their husbands, fathers, sons or brothers. If they work at all, it is usually in skilled, "respectable" jobs. No Arab woman ever works as a domestic servant. Secondly, Arab women are familiar with Kuwaiti sexual ethics, while the same is not true of Asian women, especially those employed in the domestic sector, whose level of education tends to be low and who are ignorant of both the local culture and the local language.

The consequences of this lack of cultural familiarity are most serious in the case of adultery. While in most of the societies that expatriates come from "adultery" is understood as voluntary sexual intercourse with a person to whom one is not married, in Kuwait the term has a much wider definition. It includes any sexual relations outside marriage, regardless of the civil status of the partners involved. Furthermore, in the case of domestic servants, it is common for employers to define as adulterous the mere fact that the employee is alone behind closed doors with a person of the opposite sex. Their structural position at the bottom of the social hierarchy, combined with their status as unaccompanied women,[21] and the inevitable cultural and linguistic miscommunication render foreign maids vulnerable to all sorts of accusations against which they are incapable of defending themselves. For reasons I have detailed elsewhere (Longva 1997), the domestic sector is burdened with conflicts and human exploitation. Workers in this sector are submitted to the employers' round-the-clock surveillance and have practically no lives of their own.

The danger emanating from Asian maids is considered all the greater as their influence is in many ways unobtrusive. Domestic servants do not share a common language with their employers, their social status is far below that of a teacher, journalist or preacher, and they are undoubtedly the most vulnerable of all categories of expatriates. But because they are part of the household, they partake of the private world of their employers, which is also the locus for the reproduction of the most important part of the society's moral system, namely family relations and relations between men and women. The introduction of a total stranger with an alien cultural background into this most intimate sphere of the employers' lives challenges many of the latter's norms and categories. Central taboos are violated, which vividly heightens the Kuwaitis' sense that their customs are being imperilled. The foreign servant placed at the heart of the Kuwaiti family often has, through no fault of hers, an upsetting effect on the organisation of routines and even relations within the family. She thus epitomises the moral danger that emanates from the large expatriate presence and is said to threaten the cultural fabric of Kuwaiti society.

Besieged empowerment

Most studies on labour migration to Kuwait (e.g. Alessa 1981, Russell 1989a, 1989b, Longva 1997, Shah and Menon 1997) point to the power asymmetry between Kuwaiti employers and migrant employees, and stress the weak legal position of the latter at the hands of the former. Most Kuwaitis, however, do not see the situation in this light. Their perception of expatriates is not of victims, and Kuwaiti employers, in their own estimation, far from wielding arbitrary power, merely exercise their right to self-protection. On this view, the numerous foreign residents represent a threat to the country's internal security and stability.[22] Furthermore, they are in Kuwait for one single purpose, to make money, and unless they are held in check, they may resort to any means to achieve that end. Kuwait provides them with much needed jobs and income that ensure not only their own livelihood but also that of their dependants. In fact, entire regions in Asia and the Middle East owe their economic survival, if not prosperity, to remittances from Kuwait and the other Gulf countries (Heyzer et al. 1994).

This mutual dependence, it is claimed by Kuwaitis, means that the relationship between Kuwaitis and expatriates is ultimately symmetrical, with each part exerting pressure on the other. But, it is also claimed, the Kuwaiti population, being at the same time numerically smaller and wealthier, is the one more in need of protection. It is important to be aware of this perception, because herein lies the rationale of the *kafālah* or sponsorship system, the source of Kuwaitis' tremendous power over migrant workers. The efficacy of *kafālah* is proportional to its simplicity: in order for a migrant worker to enter and reside in Kuwait he/she must be sponsored by a public or private Kuwaiti institution or a Kuwaiti citizen. Expatriate workers cannot leave their sponsors/employers before one year has elapsed;[23] their residence permit hinges on remaining in their sponsor's employment, which again depends on the sponsor being satisfied with the worker.[24]

The power of the *kafīl* or sponsor over his[25] employees is much more extensive than one might expect. Sponsorship is not a labour-contract through which an agreed amount of labour is performed and an agreed salary is paid. It is in essence a moral contract in which the written clauses are less important than the unwritten expectations. Because of the impending threat of sponsorship-withdrawal, expatriate employees will more often than not feel obliged to perform more than the tasks required by a formal job description. In the case of domestic workers, the power of the *kafīl* is practically limitless, the only real constraints being those that sponsors set upon themselves. Actual treatment of servants varies from case to case, and not all sponsors take advantage of their power over employees. But there is a disturbing pattern of exploitation and mistreatment.

Ethnocratic regimes draw their *raison d'être* from a peculiar state of mind, widespread among the ruling ethnie, in which a vivid awareness of being under threat combines with an equally vivid experience of empowerment derived from control over subordinate groups. The perception of vulnerability and the experience of empowerment critically underlie the will to maintain and reproduce the ethnocratic structure. The view of domestic servants as the epitome of external threat is shared by most Kuwaitis because practically every household has at least one maid, and every citizen knows what this means in practical terms for his or her daily life. Although, as already mentioned, foreign workers are present in all sectors of social life, not every Kuwaiti has daily encounters with Palestinian journalists, Lebanese bankers or Egyptian schoolteachers and judges. On the other hand everyone meets and deals with their maids, cooks, nannies or drivers on a daily basis. If we wish to ascertain the qualitative nature of the relationship between citizens and expatriates, and understand the former's experience of empowerment and control over the latter, we should turn our attention to this level of everyday life where control and empowerment are most vividly experienced by citizens. All the more so as this daily face-to-face interaction, unfolding as it does within the narrow space of the employer's home, has a deep impact on the way each participant in the interaction defines self, other and their mutual relationship.

The persistence of pre-oil stratification

A common principle in the dynamics of group relations is that of fission and fusion. As a rule, most communities, when confronted with an external threat, disregard their internal divisions and close ranks, but when the perception of danger recedes then internal divisions reassert themselves. In an ethnocratic system, especially one where the privileged ethnie is in a minority, the perception of external threat is constant. There is a feeling that internal fissions should not to be allowed to divert the community's attention from the main threat. Conflicts within the group tend therefore to be underemphasised and their treatment postponed. External threats, in other words, ensure group solidarity. It has been said often enough that the pervasive presence of foreign workers is a problem, even a scourge, for Kuwait; yet this "scourge" plays a critical role in displacing the social tensions that inevitably arise when a traditional society is faced with rapid transformations, as is the case in the Gulf region. Even under the best circumstances, such as when change entails considerable improvement of living conditions, it inevitably upsets the traditional way of life and causes people to question the old power structure. Yet in Kuwait, and elsewhere in the Gulf, it seems that change has had the opposite effect: instead of being challenged, the pre-oil order emerges from the process if not strengthened, at least stabilised. This is most clearly expressed in the way the pattern of social stratification and the dominance of men over women are being reproduced.

It has become banal to say that under the impact of the oil economy the Arabian Peninsula has undergone extensive transformations since the end of the Second World War. But behind the banality of the observation lies a story of change that is all but ordinary. While much of the Third World struggles at every step on the road towards development, in Kuwait the process has been painless and effortless for the local population, since financial means were plentiful and the labour required was entirely performed by foreign workers. Within one generation, Kuwait went from being one of the world's poorest countries to being one of the richest. In the process, many basic features of the society were transformed (Zahlan 1989, al-Naqeeb 1990, Crystal 1992) and others have disappeared: sea trade with the Indian Ocean, caravan trade with central Arabia, and nomadism are no longer practised. Sailors, pearl-divers and nomadic shepherds have turned into state employees working in offices and living in air-conditioned houses distributed by the government. The advent of oil also put an end to the Āl Ṣabāḥ's dependence on the merchants, and today it is the merchants who depend on the ruling family's willingness to create and maintain conditions favourable to their businesses (Crystal 1992). Several decades of free education are now producing a growing population of women and men trained in local and foreign universities whose parents or grandparents could not read and write.

Welfare and education have upset the pattern of kinship relationships. Most Kuwaitis today no longer live with their extended families, grouped in quarters divided along sectarian and tribal lines. The fact that government houses have, over the past decades, been distributed indifferently to married couples on a first-come-first-served basis has resulted in the coexistence within the same residential neighbourhoods of people whom traditional *'aṣabīyah* ("group feeling") would have kept spatially and socially apart. Furthermore, the architectural design of government houses, built for a couple and their children, has in practice meant a redefinition of the notion of the household: the basic social unit in Kuwait today is the nuclear, two-generation family.[26]

Because the majority of Kuwaitis are now state-employees whose main source of livelihood is the monthly salary paid by the government, and because old people are supported by the state, the household's budget is planned with the needs of the nuclear family rather than the extended family in mind. An incipient but fast-growing process of individualisation in daily life is taking place that would have been unthinkable earlier, when brothers and their wives, children and grandchildren lived together in family compounds run on the basis of common resources. Not only the housing system but also compulsory education contributes to weakening previous barriers between families, sects and communities. At government schools, Kuwaiti youths are told that sectarian and tribal allegiances are things of the past, and they are taught to think of themselves as Kuwaitis, whose only loyalty is to the nation-state. The pattern is further strengthened when they attend university and training colleges in which Kuwaitis of all backgrounds are thrown together. What we see here are both a *de facto* weakening of old loyalties and attempts at realising some degree of equal opportunity in the areas of education and housing.

Against this backdrop of change, it is surprising that the stratification that characterised Kuwait in pre-oil days is practically the same today as on the eve of independence in 1961. The Āl Ṣabāḥ still have the monopoly of political power, while the same prominent merchant families – Āl Ghānim, Āl Bahār, Āl Qatāmī, Āl Ṣaqr – retain the monopoly of big business.[27] Although a few newcomers have appeared recently and successfully carved out for themselves a place, the social prestige that surrounds the old merchant families has remained unchanged and mostly unchallenged since the days when their ships sailed the Gulf and the Indian Ocean. Like the Āl Ṣabāḥ, this mercantile aristocracy practise class endogamy (Rush 1987). With the ruling family and the big merchants controlling access to political and economic power respectively, the rest of the population is kept in the role of clients to these patrons, and Kuwaitis talk with considerable insight and self-irony about their predicament, especially the need for the average person to have an extended network of *wāsiṭah* (contacts). Yet, surprisingly few are ready to question seriously the continued reproduction of the pre-oil power structure.[28] Several factors need to be considered here.

First of all, better education and other social improvements have not led to social mobility in the sense the phrase is conventionally understood, where each individual has the opportunity to work their way upward, moving freely across class boundaries and thus undermining them. Upward mobility has indeed taken place in Kuwait, but in a collective fashion, with the Kuwaiti class structure as a whole being lifted upward through the introduction at the bottom of the hierarchy of a new underclass, the foreign workers.[29] Especially for the Kuwaiti working class – that is, for most of Kuwait's people – this has meant an overnight promotion which did not result from being integrated into the middle classes or from the social division between the classes being in any way reduced. The relationship between classes remains as it has always been, except that the working class now has an ethnic underclass beneath it and the whole Kuwaiti citizenry enjoys a higher collective status.

This leads to the second explanation: whatever sense of unease and powerlessness is engendered by social change is to a certain degree counteracted by the unique sense of empowerment derived from domination over the migrant underclass. Oil prosperity has indeed brought Kuwaitis material comfort and the welfare state. But if the citizens had had to build up this welfare state with their own hands – if they had erected their own houses, built their own highways and personally manned the desalination plants that ensure the daily supply of water or the electrical plants that keep homes and offices cool in the sweltering summer heat – in brief, if the welfare state had been the result of Kuwaiti sweat and toil – demands for greater social equality among citizens would undoubtedly have been louder and more persistent. The 1.1 million non-Kuwaitis in the country not only relieve nationals from the burden of physical nation-building: in a system organised by ethnocratic principles, they ensure that each Kuwaiti citizen enjoys a measure of middle-class status and a feeling of empowerment. When combined with the vivid perception of being a minority under siege, this gratifying experience helps convince Kuwaitis that there is more to gain in accepting the *status quo* than in trying to challenge it.

The persistence of patriarchy

Just as the presence of migrant workers at the bottom of the social hierarchy has allowed the persistence of the pre-oil class structure, it has also allowed for reproduction of pre-oil patterns of gender relations, despite vast changes in the life of Kuwaiti women.[30] I have argued elsewhere (Longva 1993) that ethnic stratification and the devaluation of work – an activity associated with expatriates – lead Kuwaiti women to opt out of the labour market unless they can have a "Kuwaiti" job (i.e. mostly symbolic and in the public sector). Here, I wish to pursue a different but complementary line of argument by examining the discourse of women's protection that pervades Kuwait.

In presenting the state of their socio-economic development, most societies nowadays like to emphasise their real or wishful efforts at improving and increasing the contribution of women to the national economy. In contrast to this discourse of female participation, one finds in Kuwait and the Gulf generally a discourse of female protection. The idea is that women should be protected from all that is bad in life, including activities considered arduous, dangerous or degrading. Kuwaiti labour legislation recommends, for example, that women should not be required to work night shifts. A law adopted in 1996 reduced the minimum requirement for female citizens' retirement with full benefits from 20 to 15 years. A male informant, who had visited China in an official capacity, told of his shocked reaction at seeing Chinese women carry basket-loads of stones on a construction site under the glaring sun: "In Kuwait", he assured me, "this would never happen: we protect our women from this kind of hardship and indignity". In the public arena, meanwhile, Kuwaiti women are usually the object of thoughtful consideration. In a queue, they would commonly be allowed to go first; when in need of assistance, they are usually treated with sympathy – a reaction that often extends to non-Kuwaiti women as well, especially if they are from a middle-class background. For instance, women – both Kuwaiti and non-Kuwaiti – are not expected to have to stand by the road and signal for help if their cars break down: assistance is promptly offered by other motorists. Even in self-service petrol stations, they remain seated at the wheel of their cars while a station attendant fills the tank for them.

At least as far as national women are concerned, and whatever goes on behind closed doors, one gets the feeling from observing interactions in public places that their safety and well being are matters of some importance for Kuwait's society. Although the presence of a large, male-dominated migrant population may partly account for the perceived need to protect women, it is not the major reason. In this ethnocratic society, "protection" is stretched to mean privileged treatment. Thus when a national woman works in an environment that includes Kuwaitis and non-Kuwaitis, she is usually given the better job – better not only in terms of salary (Kuwaitis are better paid than expatriates by law, anyway) but in terms of less demanding work performance. The very few Kuwaiti women I know who have tried being stewardesses on the national airline have automatically been assigned to the first-class section, regardless of experience and qualifications. Female Kuwaiti doctors never work night shifts, unlike expatriate female doctors and nurses. In ethnically mixed work places in the public sector, a major concern of the management seems to be sheltering national women from heavy work by shifting this on to non-Kuwaitis.[31]

Privileged treatment in all areas of life, including work, is granted to and expected by both male and female citizens. But whereas privileged treatment contributes to enhancing Kuwaiti men's social power, it has a more ambivalent effect on the status of Kuwaiti women because of their position between expatriates and Kuwaiti men. By not working night shifts, for instance, Kuwaiti women confirm their superior status as privileged citizens vis-à-vis expatriates. By the same token, however, they confirm the male prejudices underlying Kuwaiti patriarchal ideology, namely that women are weak and defenceless creatures who tire quickly, can be assaulted if out on their own after dark and so on. Therefore they are in need of protection and special treatment. Each privilege Kuwaiti women enjoy in society in relation to non-Kuwaitis is a tacit admission of their weakness in relation to Kuwaiti men. They have to juggle constantly the privileges they enjoy through ethnic stratification and the negative implications this has for their relations to Kuwaiti men.

The intricate relation between citizenship, ethnicity and gender as three important ways of defining self and others, and of organising the power structure in which people meet and interact, is clearly illustrated in the Kuwaiti context. Analyses of gender politics in

Kuwait often overlook the implications of ethnic stratification, while analyses of Kuwaiti-expatriate relations treat Kuwaitis as a homogeneous category and fail to problematise the gender aspect of Kuwaiti social life. A more holistic approach in which the mutual workings of ethnicity and gender are carefully investigated is required if we are to achieve a better understanding of the social dynamics of ethnocracy and patriarchy.

The local discourse of protection throws into relief two aspects of Kuwaiti women's identity. They are protected because they are "vulnerable", hence "weak"; but they are also protected because they are "valuable". While the former reason is usually cited by men, the latter is more often than not invoked by women. According to this view, women's value lies in their being Kuwaiti citizens responsible for the production of new citizens. This assertion, however, seems to beg the question when we know that the Nationality Law, which disqualifies practically all potential male candidates, allows the naturalisation of foreign women married to Kuwaiti men. Thus Kuwaiti women can, in principle, be easily replaced, at least as biological reproducers. As mentioned earlier, mixed marriages between Kuwaitis and non-Kuwaitis occur, although not on a substantial scale. Among the non-Kuwaitis who enter such marriage contracts, Arabs are the preferred ethnic group, and most of the time, it is Kuwaiti men marrying non-Kuwaiti Arab women.[32] There are no statistical indications of the national origins of non-Kuwaiti Arab spouses. According to my own observations, however, the majority are citizens from other GCC countries, especially in the case of mixed marriages where the woman is Kuwaiti. GCC nationals are not classified as "Arab expatriates" in the Kuwaiti statistical and social vocabulary.

The relatively rare occurrence of marriages with Arabs from outside the Gulf region is interesting. Ethnic endogamy, whatever the reasons, does seem to confirm that Kuwaiti men value being married to Kuwaiti women, and that their choice is not dictated only by legal constraints upon citizenship.[33] Instead families "of good stock" (*aṣīl*) pride themselves on fetching their brides from backgrounds similar to their own. Many people, men as well as women, agree that foreign women make bad social reproducers, as they will never instil in their children true love for Kuwait. Also "ordinary" Kuwaitis (known in earlier days as *baysarī* – the opposite of *aṣīl*) tend to find wives among their own. And although the state carries on an active campaign enlightening the population on the health dangers of marrying close relatives, most marriages still take place between kin, albeit more distant ones than previously (el-Najjar 1996, Longva n.d), which means in practice that the incidence of female hypergamy is relatively small.

In light of this marriage practice, the argument that Kuwaiti women are valued as biological reproducers is not far from reality.

There is a clear presumption that Kuwaiti men who marry foreigners do so as a way of solving the problem of the *mahr* or brideprice, which tends to be much higher when the bride is Kuwaiti. Many cannot afford such high amounts, even with the support of the state, which gives a KD2,000 grant to male citizens who marry Kuwaiti women for their first marriage. To lower the brideprice is not seen as a viable solution, at least by women, for the brideprice conveys a clear message about the bride's status and her social worth. As a young woman put it, "if they [Kuwaiti men] want good, decent, respectable wives who will bring up their sons to be loyal Kuwaitis, they simply have to pay for it. Quality comes at a price". There are indications, however, that the emphasis on the woman's genealogical pedigree as such is becoming less prominent. Thus I have been told by young male informants that what matters for them in a prospective bride is the girl's "personal character". Another frequently cited quality is her being Kuwaiti. One's impression is not that concern with genealogical pedigree is waning, but that it is being recast as concern with citizenship.

Under present circumstances in Kuwait, the only way the ethnocratic system can be weakened is through Kuwaiti men marrying non-Kuwaitis. To limit such marriages is therefore a task of critical importance. Here, Kuwaiti women and Kuwaiti society at large are in agreement, a fact borne out by the findings of the Kuwaiti sociologist Fahed al-Naser (1995): most Kuwaitis of either sex condemn mixed marriages. Of 1,763 Kuwaiti adults surveyed in 1995, 62 per cent supported the passing of laws banning Kuwaitis from marrying non-Kuwaitis, 40-50 per cent believed punitive measures, e.g. disallowance of marriage loans, rent subsidies and government housing allotments, should be devised,[34] and 75 per cent were of the opinion that better education and better information would work as deterrents against mixed marriages. If these findings indeed reflect popular views of mixed marriages, then the continued viability of the discourse of female protection, and thus the reproduction of patriarchy, are directly dependent on Kuwait remaining a civic ethnocracy.

Conclusion

Political and social life in Kuwait is a combination of innovation and tradition, of freedom and constraint. An interesting question is why rapid change has not had a destabilising effect and why the pre-oil power structure has not been more vigorously challenged. Several analysts have examined this puzzle and offered their explanations. Two trends run through the literature. On the one hand we have the "cultural and functional" explanation, whereby stability in the Gulf is due to the political regime being a faithful reflection of local tradition (Hudson 1977) or at least providing citizens with a national narrative to which they can agree (Anderson, L. 2000). In the case of Kuwait, this critically includes the social contract between rulers and merchants. According to the other, "economic and geo-political", explanation, stability is paid for by oil money, notably through the establishment of a generous welfare state (the trinity of free health-housing-education, plus guaranteed jobs); and in addition, oil wealth secures for local regimes the support of powerful Western allies (Gause 2000). These explanations, which do not necessarily contradict each other, can hardly be disputed. Yet they are what I would call "views from afar" (cf. Levi Strauss 1985), of the kind that see only big historical events and large structures. They are not interested in how these events and structures are understood and experienced by Gulf men and women in their daily life.

By failing to pose such humble questions, the economic explanation in particular, which strikes most outside observers as particularly to the point, may exaggerate the role of oil money at the expense of human reactions. For example it overlooks the fact that once basic welfare goods and services are acquired and become a matter of routine, they tend to become taken for granted and lose their potential as a means of political co-optation.[35] The emphasis on material inducements as a sufficient condition for guaranteeing stability betrays, in fact, a dismissive attitude towards Kuwaiti society by excepting it from the ordinary dynamics of social tensions and conflicts. That the rulers buy off potential opponents through the distribution of oil money is a proposition that may, indeed does, make sense. But why should Kuwaiti society remain impervious to tensions when it is confronted with the weakening of important old loyalties (to tribes or sects, for instance) and deep transformations of family structure and kinship relationships? Or why should the younger Kuwaiti generations living on state salaries remain unaffected at the sight of wealthy merchant families blocking entrance to the lucrative agency business? Does the welfare trinity or gratitude to the Emir really blind them to this inequity? It is not part of Kuwaiti culture to bow meekly to differential treatment, so why is not discontent more vocal? These down-to-earth questions, which direct the focus of the research away from the political establishment towards ordinary men and women, are seldom asked.

Views from afar could be criticised as symptoms of an elitist scholarship, one that deals only with power-holding groups and ignores the marginal and the powerless. In the Gulf, this neglect is glaring as far as the role of expatriates is concerned. In failing to see the connection between the presence of millions of rightless migrant workers and the way Gulf citizens imagine their nations, construct their national identities and organise their class and gender relations, the research community has carried out a great deal of its analyses solely on the premises of the power-holders. That migrant workers are rightless, powerless and voiceless in Gulf societies does not mean that they are sociologically insignificant. Somehow this simple truth seems to have escaped the attention of many writers.

CHAPTER 6

DEBATES ON MARRIAGE AND NATIONALITY IN THE UNITED ARAB EMIRATES[1]

Paul Dresch

Kinship and marriage interest anthropologists. Geographers and political scientists deal more usually with nationality and migration, while nationalism commands a literature spanning several disciplines. Yet nationality, kinship and marriage are interlinked. Even where citizenship is given by place of birth it is then inherited by the accident of birth, transmitted as arbitrarily as membership of a clan or an Aboriginal marriage class. Certain patterns of group ascription seem arbitrary in a stronger sense. Notoriously, German citizenship has been granted on a large scale to people of German "blood" who speak scarcely a word of German, while the children of guest-workers who speak nothing else and have lived in the country all their lives cannot be citizens.

In the Arab World weight is often attached to the Islamic precept that "the child belongs to the [father's] bed" (*al-walad li-l-farāsh*): group membership is transmitted usually patrilineally. The question then arises of where women fit. There was never in Arab kinship a formal "marriage rule", either of endogamy or of exogamy, but women were always treated as a locus of men's honour, far more so than the contrary is true, and in the Gulf states this colours problems of defining nations. Meanwhile older notions of marriage (perhaps rather male-centred notions) run counter to newly perceived "national" interests. While all states define a link of some kind between kinship and nationality, the governments of Saudi Arabia, Qatar and Oman thus have laws, distinct from those of citizenship and published some decades later, which govern marriage with foreigners. The United Arab Emirates do not as yet, but debates on the issue have gained momentum in recent years and these debates are examined here.[2]

Population and self-definition

The smaller states of the Arab Gulf face particular pressures of self-definition. Their indigenous populations are small in any case, quite prosperous and highly mobile (with all that implies for recruitment to the population by marriage or birth elsewhere) and at home are surrounded, if not outnumbered, by foreign migrants. The Emirates are in some ways an extreme case (Kapiszewski 2001: 39-40, 64, 163). But marriage raises issues of personal and family status as well as of national boundaries, and it touches on basic feelings. Everywhere in the region female hypogamy is frowned on, that is, girls must not marry down (Bonte 1994). Among families, themselves defined publicly through male descent, this idea can take the practical form of a claim to superiority in that we can marry your girls but you cannot marry ours, as evidenced sometimes by ruling groups (Herb 1999: 37). The Āl Ṣabāḥ of Kuwait are a well-documented case (Rush 1987): they claim, doubtless rightly, that their women have not married out in more than two centuries but their men routinely took wives from the tribes around them. In recent times, however, there seems to have been something of a shift from female hypergamy (that is, from women marrying up or not marrying) to endogamy, so the boys now "marry in" as well as the girls, and the same looks to have happened with the Āl Khalīfah of Bahrain (Khuri 1980: 238).[3]

Such phenomena overlap with a long-established value that attaches, if the context is right, to marriage among close agnates. A citizen of one of the major emirates thus remarked to me of his own country's ruling family that if they married with others "they would be less brilliant", meaning less special, perhaps less magical; but more than that, certain members of the family are "real" shaykhs because they, unlike their brothers, are shaykhs on the mother's side as well as on the father's (*baṭn wa-ẓahr*, or "belly and back", as the saying goes). At less elevated levels, close marriage may increase as one is forced to deal more with the outside world: when all else becomes a source of risk, one consolidates close-range kin-links, much as globalisation encourages ethnic or national exclusivity.[4] The group may thus be defined out from others, at whatever level, and within the group ranking may be at issue, perhaps expressed through close-range marriage. But for an individual man, would-be master in his own house, there is reason to marry outside the local system altogether and avoid the complex domination of affines who are also kin.

In the middle range, among families known to oneself but not clearly ranked, one is dealing with prestige and thus usually competition. To take an obvious aspect, bridewealth and marriage expenses, despite efforts from governments of all sorts,[5] rise rapidly when cash is available, and in the Emirates in the 1990s, where a young national graduate might earn Dh9,000 per month, marriage expenses of Dh200-500,000 (say $100,000) were not unusual. Much local commentary, meanwhile, turns on the status-concerns of close kin, and women correspondents to papers and magazines often mention the obstacles to marriage presented by the caution or ambition of their fathers, who never think a suitor good enough: "he isn't from our level ... he's from a different tribe ... ."[6] Among Emirati tribes, not least those of the Banī Yās, who are associated particularly with Abu Dhabi but are found in several emirates, one hears it said that the Muhayrīs won't marry the Rumaythīs, or the Mazrū'īs the Qubaysīs, for instance – which is not true empirically but expresses this same concern for status provoked by nominal equality.[7] The formal weighting of the sexes, moreover, is far from equal. For men to marry out is at worst a misadventure to be dealt with by selective recall of genealogy; for women to marry out is to have the whole family give hostages to fortune.

Marriage involves prestige or honour, which is spoken of in a metaphor of "covering": it is said of a family whose girls have married in that "their bread is in their own basket" (*khubz-hum fī muchabbat-hum*), the *muchabbah* or *mukabbah* being the woven conical lid one traditionally placed over dates or bread. One of the striking features of the GCC states is the way such issues have persisted or been re-established (in some ways, indeed, they have been much strengthened; see Doumato 1992, Longva 1993) despite women controlling independent wealth. Extended family connections remain important, perhaps particularly to women, and the nuclear family is not always central to people's lives, although it seems to be tacitly a model for many now of what a family is at the same time as they claim "traditional" values are under threat – which surely they are and have been for some decades.[8]

Everywhere in the Gulf strange things happened when major wealth spread. Before oil, a combination of occasional polygamy, high rates of serial marriage (brought on in part by high death rates) and a tendency to marry close produced patterns which were not those of middle-class Europe. European women who have married into Gulf families even in recent times thus mention how odd it seemed to be pregnant at the same time as one's mother-in-law, and how odd at first to have aunts much younger or nephews much older than oneself. With oil wealth, however, the distinct fields of male and female sociability often peeled apart. The men have shown a tendency in their travels abroad to collect foreign wives (the issue of quasi-wives will be left aside here) and to evade at least some of the complexities of marriage at home, while in several Gulf states whole cohorts of local women are left to marry late or never marry at all. Spinsterhood (*'anūsah*) is an issue, and what used to be a hazard for women of prominent families afflicts women of many sorts.[9]

The Emirates

Briefly, the United Arab Emirates (UAE) came into existence in 1971. The seven emirates differ greatly among themselves, but Abu Dhabi, whose people were desperately poor and once marginal to the affairs of Sharjah or Dubai or further north, commands 2 million barrels per day of oil wealth and enormous gas reserves.[10] As by far the richest emirate and now officially the Federation's capital, Abu Dhabi not only supports much of the Federal government and offers help on occasion to other emirates but looks after its own people handsomely. In recent years, men of "original" Abu Dhabi families have been entitled to separate gifts from their emirate's government of residential land, agricultural land and commercial property, plus a grant at marriage of Dh900,000 towards a house. Dubai's aid to citizens recently has been Dh500,000 in the form of a free loan, Sharjah's Dh200,000. The details must be examined elsewhere (Dresch 2001), but citizenship involves material benefits and it confers a legal status quite different from that of foreigners.

With oil wealth came foreign workers, and with the boom of the 1970s their numbers rose exponentially. The 1995 census, although the results were never released in full, recorded close to 600,000 Emirati nationals in a total population of about 2.4 million: in other words, nationals were a quarter of the country's inhabitants. Sixty per cent of the total were South Asians, the biggest groups being Indian and Pakistani; non-Gulf Arabs made up 12 per cent, and Europeans about 2 per cent.[11] In the usual manner of Gulf states, foreign residents must each have a "sponsor" (*kafīl*), placing much of the national population in the position of minor rentiers (cf. Beaugé 1986, Longva 1997, 1999). Patterns of housing, income and sociability all differ along these lines, and a great deal at every level of experience depends on the distinction between "locals" or "nationals" (i.e. citizens, *muwāṭinīn*) and "migrants" (*wāfidīn*), whose overall numbers keep rising as citizens seek personal prosperity or comfort.

Dubai, although in fact it has the most non-Emiratis per head, is not the most striking case on a day-to-day basis, but a character in one of Muḥammad al-Murr's short-stories, describes it this way:

> It's an amazing country. The guy who bakes your bread there's Iranian, the person running the restaurant is Indian, and the carpenter's Punjabi. The man who irons your clothes is from Madras, the taxi-driver's Pathan, the electrician's Pakistani, the salesperson's Indian and the nurse who gives you an injection is from Ceylon. We're like ornamental fish or birds: they

> feed us, clean out our pools and cages, and like looking at us. In this country we're just something to look at (al-Murr 1992: 384).

Frustrated though the character is with the state of things, there is something in what he says, and al-Murr later struck a chord with local readers in a set of essays which begin with a vignette (al-Murr 1997: 7). Arguing with an Asian shopkeeper (in Urdu, note well) about where to park his car, the local complains, "Brother, this is my country". "Shove off", replies the Indian, "this isn't your country, it's international property!" (*Jāo, yeh tumhāra mulk nahī, yeh internashyanāl mulk hay*). Emiratis complain in the manner of France for instance, that their "culture" is being swamped. Only rarely do authors from within the region (e.g. al-Sayar, *Khaleej Times* 7 Jan. 1986, al-Ḥamad, *Gulf News* 10 Nov. 1996) suggest that the rhetoric may be misplaced.

Such concerns occupy the local press by waves. But fears of "demographic imbalance" have recurred for decades (see e.g. Sakr 1986, Bū Kalāh 1998), and a threat to local culture is found at home as well as on the streets. Huge numbers of domestic servants are employed. A survey in 1995 suggested an average of two foreign servants per national family, and four years later a further survey lamented that a third of national families were "totally dependent" on Asian housemaids for child rearing (*Gulf News* 2 Nov. 1999). Among Emiratis as well as foreigners, a salient "urban myth" (it may well have a strong basis in fact, of course) is of local children growing up speaking Malayalam, Tagalog or Tamil, not Arabic, and the question of foreign maids recurs frequently in the local press.[12] The question of foreign wives aligns with this. However Emirati society may be defined, save by mere outlines of male genealogy, it seems to face a flood of cultural foreignness that nobody can stem.

A dramatic campaign against illegal residents was mounted in 1996 (the same date as many articles on cultural invasion; the same date, as we shall see, as a wave of hostile comment against external marriage) and some thousands of foreign workers, mainly Asians, were shipped home. By the decade's end, however, there were at least as many foreigners as there had been to start with, and probably more. In early 2000 officials were saying informally that citizens were outnumbered not three to one, as previously, but four to one.[13] Crudely put, if everyone wants to be a chief, one needs a great many Indians, and the question arises of how one defines the nation.

Descent and marriage

Nationality is a fairly new concept in the world; that curse of modernity, the obligatory passport, is newer still. In the Gulf the first state to have laws on the subject seems to have been Bahrain (1937), still then very much under British influence – to the point where foreigners born in Bahrain who wanted Bahraini citizenship could register, within a year of their 18th birthday, at "Government House". The Saudi nationality law of 1956 appealed in part (perhaps surprisingly) to the Kingdom's status as successor to the Ottomans. Kuwait, by contrast, which has led the way in so much of Gulf affairs, defined nationality independently of empires, and the Kuwaiti model was widely followed.[14] An Emiri decree of 1959 defined Kuwaitis as "basically those resident in (or indigenous to, *mutawaṭṭinīn fī*) Kuwait before the year 1920 who have maintained their normal residence there until the date when this law was issued". The decree goes on to say that one could be "normally resident" although living elsewhere if at least one "intended" to return, but in practice a line was drawn at an arbitrary date around an arbitrary grouping. Notoriously, one of the by-products in Kuwait has been a population of *bidūn*, people with no formal nationality but nowhere else to go.

Emirati provisions for defining citizenship begin with a "nationality and passports" law in 1972. Nationality may accrue by law (*bi-l-qānūn*), by dependence (*bi-l-tabī'ah*, as of wives on husbands) or be granted (*bi-l-tajannus*). The first of these categories is defined rather on the Kuwaiti model, such that anyone usually resident in one of the emirates from 1925 is reckoned Emirati. So is anyone born henceforth, whether at home or abroad, to an Emirati father. The provisions for gaining nationality (*tajannus*: what in English would be called naturalisation) distinguish among categories, so Omanis, Qataris and Bahrainis resident in one of the emirates for three years are eligible;[15] other Arabs must show ten year's residence, at least five of which must fall after the date when the law was issued; others again are eligible if they have been continuously resident in one of the emirates since 1940, with a proper means of livelihood and good Arabic, or for 30 years of which 20 must fall after the law comes into force. Lastly, nationality may be granted to persons giving noteworthy service to the state.

Establishing the state involved at least two very different views of nationality. Shaykh Rāshid of Dubai is supposed to have said, "Those who were with us when we were poor should be with us now we are rich", implying that shared experience carried weight. Shaykh Zayed of Abu Dhabi, by contrast, looked more to *nasab*, "genealogy" of the kind claimed by Arab tribes; for his own family, the Āl Nahyān, are hereditary chiefs of note among the Banī Yās (for the difference between Dubai and Abu Dhabi see Herb 1999: 55). In Abu Dhabi a number of "Iranian" families had a claim to consideration also, often having been traders there in the days of poverty. Many of these, who have married their daughters to established Abu Dhabi families, have in most people's eyes become thoroughly assimilated. Certain other families, of Najdi or Omani origin, were close to Shaykh Zayed in the early days. They too attract little comment. But "Yemeni" families are another matter.

At the time the Federation was formed, Abu Dhabi was short of people (generously defined, the "indigenous" population of the whole emirate may have been about 20,000), and citizenship was widely granted among tribes long connected with the Banī Yās. The Manāhīl, whose range extended to Hadramawt, are an obvious case. As the UAE took form, however, the immediate post-colonial order in South Yemen was collapsing (Dresch 2000b) and people from such Yemeni tribes as Yāfiʿ and ʿAwlaqī, who had no shared history with Abu Dhabi, were recruited also. One finds men in government service, holding Emirates nationality, who originally are from little tribes such as al-Masʿabayn, near Bayḥān; even some Adenis became Emiratis. A certain distrust is expressed about all these people, who figure heavily in, for instance, the armed forces. In other emirates the worries may be reversed, so in Dubai, for instance, "Yemenis" are not an issue but "Iranians" are. In Dubai, however, though certain of the ruling family seem obsessed on occasion with Iranian connections, so many people have Iranian mothers or grandmothers that a sense of threat is hard to inculcate.

Recent though it is, the formation of the UAE fell within very old forms of political demography. Certain families of Omani tribes, for instance, had left Oman when the Imamate's resistance to the Sultan collapsed in about 1957; some spent years in Saudi Arabia before Abu Dhabi welcomed them (see Al-Rasheed in the present volume), and some have since been invited back by Oman's new Sultan, with mixed results. More recently, sections of the Shammar, despairing of their prospects in a failing Saudi economy, have sought and acquired Emirati passports. If members of "foreign" tribes were sometimes recruited to particular emirates, so were elements of local tribes, who switched their allegiance among rulers. The most famous case are those Zaʿabīs who decamped from Ra's al-Khaimah just before the UAE was formed and are now an established part of Abu Dhabi life (Heard-Bey 1996: 75).

The complexity can be imagined. Not only are different tribes and origins involved, but under a tribal name may lie people whose families were in some sense adopted by the tribe (there are people, of course, of slave origin) or people whose mothers were not as "noble" (*aṣīl*) as their fathers. Male genealogy provides the public image, but it matters who one's mother is (cf. Lienhardt 2001: 73, 79). In the old days, when the number of wives from outside the system was small in any case, much detail would have been reworked through the generations and old alliances and origins assimilated to the structure of male genealogy; a foreign mother or grandmother might even have provided a certain cachet. Nowadays it is not so easy. Several Emirati authors mention the prejudice encountered by the children of Indian mothers, whose fathers perhaps are of no great standing, and much older history may also be locked in place by appeal to matrilateral ties. A great deal is thus omitted in the public use of male-derived tribal surnames.[16] If one asks, one is told that all the detail is known to the *dīwān* (the shaykhly court); but given that initial complexity has been compounded by rapid population growth, it would be hard for anyone to keep track of exactly who is who and thus entitled to what.[17]

To read off from male descent, or even from descent on both sides, to political and economic status would be misleading, for "access" (mediation, *wāsiṭah*) is enormously important and often shaykhs are surrounded by advisers rather than close kin. An Emirati of the blood thus complains of a naturalised Bahraini with an Indian wife gaining wealth and privilege; what seems an entitlement by birth meanwhile eludes a man of impeccable descent on both sides from, for instance, Līwā. But foreigners boast particularly of "access" and their compatriots put them down by explaining that the person their rival knows is not a "real" local, but actually half-Iranian, half-Omani or half-Yemeni. Nationals do just the same. Given that even the Banī Yās are a "compound tribe", authenticity of descent recedes indefinitely towards the Ruler's judgement, and Emiratis and foreigners alike will often simplify to say there are three strata: Abu Dhabi citizens, the citizens of other emirates and citizens by naturalisation (*mutajannasīn*).

Naturalised citizens may in law have their status revoked if they threaten state security or are judged habitual criminals. They are, so to speak, Emiratis on sufferance. One noteworthy feature of the 1972 legislation (clause 10) as interpreted in practice is that the legal distinction between real and naturalised citizens is itself transmitted: not only are wives of a naturalised citizen (*muwāṭin bi-l-tajannus*) themselves naturalised citizens unless Emirati by male descent, but the children of a naturalised citizen are naturalised citizens (*mutajanassīn*) in turn, and so on, presumably, through the generations.[18] They never become fully Emirati. Nationality, meanwhile, of whatever grade, is assumed to be transmitted through men, and although national women have explicitly the option of retaining Emirati citizenship if they marry a non-Emirati, wives in the normal way of things acquire the citizenship of husbands.

A Federal law of 1975 clarified or amended the provisions somewhat. Those entitled to citizenship by law were now defined as "Arabs" resident at the critical date (previously there was vaguer reference to "Arab culture"), and the earlier reference to Omanis, Qataris and

Bahrainis was reinforced with mention of "members of the Arab tribes who migrated from countries neighbouring the State" (clause 5): the Abu Dhabi view, one might think, was winning out. Citizenship through a national mother is also mentioned for the first time. Not only does one have national status by "right of blood" through the father but also through an Emirati mother if either one's attachment to the father was not confirmed by law (*lam yuthbat nasab-hu li-abīhi qānūnan*)[19] or the father is unknown or has no nationality. Presumably Emirati women with non-Emirati husbands had come to notice. On the other hand, the law relating to foreign wives was rephrased, perhaps replacing their prescriptive right to citizenship with an administrative process.[20] Whatever the legal details, at that date foreign wives were impinging on local consciousness as Emirati men brought brides home from overseas.

The phases of out-marriage by local men are part of Emirati folklore, and a widely accepted version would go like this. Down through the early 1970s older men with cash to spare would go to India (typically Bombay) and acquire young Indian wives to enliven their dotage: supposedly death and divorce have left many "national" wives and children who speak Arabic poorly, if at all, and who now figure disproportionately in crime statistics or on the rolls of social services (for such rhetoric see *al-Khalīj* 22 Apr. 1999, *Gulf News* 4 Feb. 2000). The original numbers would not have been large, however. The oil-price rises that followed the Arab-Israeli war of 1973 transformed everything. Emirati men began to travel widely and to acquire wives from Egypt, for instance, or in far smaller numbers from studying in Europe and America, and the dodderers on flights to Bombay and Hyderabad were supplemented by men their sons' age. As al-Murr puts it (1997: 105), the numbers went from tens to hundreds, and in the 1980s to thousands. A connection with Morocco has become important also, as it has for men from many GCC states; more recently, women from what used to be the USSR have been conspicuous. "It's become a business", says one Emirati official angrily, "and these Indians and Sri Lankans, they just try to have children here as fast as they can".

Village ethnography in many parts of the world suggests status among the husband's relatives can accrue from producing children. If the same applies among highways and skyscrapers as among mud houses it should not surprise us.[21] But such concerns are accentuated by state policy. A woman from Egypt, let us say, who finds herself divorced (as well she may do, for divorce rates are said to have risen sharply) has access as a divorcee to social security as long as she is resident, but has no automatic right of residence. She needs a *kafīl* or "sponsor", and one readily encounters cases where women, now divorced or widowed, are "sponsored" by their own children: an Ethiopian sponsored by her seven-year-old son, for instance, a Somali by a child in diapers. More important than the passport, even, is *khulāṣat al-qayd*, perhaps literally a "summary of kin-links", a family book of the kind issued by some European states, which has proved increasingly hard to gain or to gain a place in. The book begins with the male head of family (*rabb al-usrah*).

Although the law has not changed since 1975, practice has. One can readily find cases of foreign wives who are comparable in all formal respects (country of origin, educational level, status of paternal family) but whose success with nationality differs greatly according to when they married: a lady who married 20 years ago, for instance, and secured all the benefits of nationality not only for herself but for her ageing mother (granny too is recorded in *khulāṣat al-qayd*), and another married less than ten years ago who secured nothing. By the mid-1980s, the ability to get along individually in local society, in some sense just to fit in, was being swamped by numbers.

Of a little over the 800 marriage contracts recorded by Abu Dhabi courts in 1989, some 47 per cent were between nationals, 17 per cent were of national women to foreign men and an enormous 36 per cent were of national men to foreign women (Muḥammad 1999: 31). Some versions of the figures are still more extreme (Kapiszewski 2001: 163), and the fact that men can marry abroad means that local figures may record just a fraction of something larger. From a "national" viewpoint, the problem was obviously the men, and certain local stereotypes were played out statistically. We are told, for instance, that of the national men who married foreign women 36.7 per cent were 40 years old or more, and 45.8 per cent of this ageing sub-set had married Asians (Muḥammad 1999: 31). The Bombay syndrome. But the majority of cases now involved younger men (supposedly often the less well educated and the less well off), and the number of different countries involved was larger than it had been, which itself worried local commentators. The male genealogy, which from outside seems often to describe society, was in danger of becoming a hollow shell. How many "foreign" marriages were in fact with relatives is meanwhile not examined, for genealogy is cross-cut by national self-definition, and redefinition, as we saw, has been extensive.

Of the national women who seemed to "marry out", a good number married kin. One constantly encounters cases where a Yemeni or Omani man became an Emirati citizen (most often an Abu Dhabi citizen) and his brothers did not, so when his (Emirati) daughter then comes of age even the "classical" marriage between brothers' children is a marriage across national boundaries. Statistics tell one little here.[22] But the impression the figures are meant to give of men being more the problem than are women recurs in more fundamental ways. If property is at issue, for instance, then in Islamic law a husband has no claim on his wife's wealth: the foreign husband of an Emirati woman could easily be written out of property transactions by the state, the municipality or the family if need arose. The foreign wife of an Emirati man, by contrast, does have legal claims. If the marriage should last that long, then by Islamic law she has claims as a widow. Her children, with national passports, of course have claims, and these may be entangled with the wishes of foreign relatives over whom the agnatic kin have little influence. The depth of feeling produced by this in a society organised quite largely by reference to families and inheritance needs little stressing.

Surveys in search of causes, before and since the late 1980s, refer often to rising brideprice and wedding expenses (Kapiszewski 2001: 166), which must surely be important.[23] But it also seems an easy answer if faced with a questionnaire. Brideprice itself forms part of a wider set of status-worries which appear in both female and male accounts of first-hand experience, the female accounts being often phrased in standardised terms of social and educational "level" (*mustawā*), the male accounts being various and sometimes odd. One male interviewee, married to a foreigner, complains that Emirati women always want trips abroad, expensive cars and the latest clothes, to the point where "one starts to think of something else". Another complains that they are too much concerned with differences of status, not least of age. A third complains they will not do what their husbands tell them, and then says, most oddly, that anyway people want to learn English (sic) and are interested in other cultures.[24]

What is clear is the asymmetry between the sexes. Women on the whole still marry close, but in the early days – and perhaps still now – they often refused to countenance a second (maybe foreign) wife, thus adding themselves to the lists of unmarried women; not all men by any means made second marriages, let alone to foreigners (and the rate of marriage *only* to foreigners is never listed) but enough did so for the phenomenon to be linked rhetorically with that of spinsterhood. Yet the idea of keeping one's bread in the family basket turned out to be more immediately compelling than attempts to constrain Emirati males. As debates unfolded, so the last of these concerns structured what was made public and what was dealt with quietly. It was as if the whole society were being treated as one large family, with the ruler as *pater familias*.

In search of a marriage law

As early as 1986 the Supreme Federal Council decreed that work should start on a law controlling marriage specifically to foreign women. By 1996 nothing concrete had resulted but the press began discussing a draft law (it seemed, indeed, that a final draft was imminent),[25] and suddenly there was widespread gossip that, even before such a law was promulgated, Emirati women who married foreigners, though comparatively there were few of them, would lose their passports. This last was somewhat shrouded in mystery. In March 2000, indeed, the middle-aged male anthropologist taking tea with a young lady from a famous family, educated abroad and just the person one expected to know the details, was asked by her what the rules were. It was widely known that something had happened in 1986 and something again in 1996, but quite what it was remained obscure to most people.

Between these dates, in 1992, Federal law established the Marriage Fund (*Ṣundūq al-Zawāj*), an organisation directed towards: (1) encouraging marriage among citizens; (2) providing financial help with marriage expenses; (3) curbing marriage by Emirati men to foreign women; (4) helping promote the stability of family life.[26] The last of these topics was the first addressed at conferences. Survey work was put in hand on divorce and its causes, while a vast range of talks and meetings was promoted, not least in colleges and schools. Young women were lectured on the dangers of dependence on foreign maids, young men on the dangers of foreign marriage, the campaign as a whole being phrased in terms of "Emirati society" (*al-mujtama' al-imārātī*), a unit whose stability and coherence were important to its members and depended, it seems, on stable family life.

From the outset the project was closely identified with the Ruler (formally the President of the Federation, and always much more than just the ruler of Abu Dhabi), Shaykh Zayed. In May 1993 he met with the Fund's council, who "tendered to his highness, the President of the State, sincere thanks and appreciation for the profound interest and complete care he shows for his sons the young men of the Emirates", and he urged young men to live within their means, to live as his generation had done, without maids, cooks and drivers; he urged Emirati mothers, for their part, to run up their daughters' clothes on a sewing machine, as used to be common practice, and show the daughters how to do it for themselves. Two days later he attended a meeting on the island of Sīr Banī Yās:

> During the fatherly dialogue which his highness, the President of the State, held with his sons, those citizens approaching marriage, the young people greeted sincerely the step his highness had taken in setting up the Marriage Fund (Ṣundūq al-Zawāj 1995: 12).

In the Emirates one often encounters the image of a ruler as father (it is not only state rhetoric), and to use it of Shaykh Zayed, at this point over 80 years old, would be thought quite natural. To depict society as one large family, with the ruler in some sense at its head, however, is to ask that constituent families cease competing for prestige, and Shaykh Zayed was quoted at the outset to the effect that the honour of daughters does not lie in vast bridewealth (*karāmat al-bint laysat bi-ghalā' il-muhūr*). A string of tribal pledges was gathered, undertaking to support this idea in "an exchange of trust and love" between themselves and their "leader and father". Funds were made available at once to construct wedding halls and to help pay young people's marriage expenses, Dh435 million being paid in the first three years.

The Marriage Fund's most conspicuous activity has been the sponsoring of mass weddings. Various local funds to help with wedding expenses had existed since at least the mid-1980s, and Sharjah had promoted a communal wedding as early as 1990 (Muḥammad 1999: 38), but the Fund now organised such events on a large scale. The scale of the events themselves has also grown. In one of the more recent (March 2000), in Dubai, 376 young grooms were married off at once in an enormous televised ceremony, where questions of status among families were displaced by eulogies to Dubai's crown prince and to the Federation's leader, Shaykh Zayed of Abu Dhabi (*al-Ittiḥād* 26 Mar. 2000).

By the end of 1997 some Dh950 million had been spent (over Dh500 million of this would have been in grants), and by the decade's end perhaps Dh1.5 billion.[27] The Fund represents a massive attempt at social engineering. Nor is it just "top-down". At local level, in the cities and countryside, it does a remarkable job not just of organising talks and seminars but of intervening as a social service and mobilising other services to solve family problems. The *point d'appui*, as it were, has been a grant of Dh70,000 (this was increased recently to Dh120,000) for each young Emirati man who marries an Emirati woman. Latterly the Fund has become involved in provision of housing for newly formed couples (*al-Ittiḥād* 10 Mar. 2000), and it recurs now in a wide range of official contexts. The rhetoric throughout is of stability and security (*istimrār*, *istiqrār*) of national families.

In passing one might note that second marriages are not supported. Indeed, the literature encouraging "stable families" treats polygamy as a cause of disruption, which deserves noting because not long ago it was certainly an option and perhaps an ideal for some men, if scarcely a common fact statistically (Shaykh Zayed, the very paragon of the senior generation, married at least eight times). Nor are different forms of "marriage" discussed.[28] The symbol of the Marriage Fund itself, meanwhile, is an isolated couple – he in blue, she in pink – with a child between, and the ideal families depicted in the Fund's literature are very much those in women's magazines or in commercial advertising: mother and father and two children. Had there been a public symbol of the family 40 years ago, it might well have been a string of paper dolls reaching out indefinitely among the relatives of bride and groom. The image now is of small individual households whose integrity should be preserved from disruption by foreign elements, such as Asian co-wives. By the turn of 1996–97, newspapers were making reference to Qatar and Oman as models for legislation.

The Qatari law (No. 21) of 1989 banned certain categories of state employees from marrying foreigners at all: ministers and deputy ministers, members of the diplomatic service, officers of the armed forces, the police or intelligence service, and students on overseas study-missions. Others needed permission from the Minister of the Interior. Male citizens wanting to marry foreigners had to show "social causes" (*asbāb ijtimāʿīyah*) and sufficient funds to support a family. A prospective husband had also to show that there was no more than 15 years' difference between him and his prospective spouse, that there was not more than one wife in his household already (again, note here the distrust of polygamy) and that he had not divorced more than one wife previously. None of this applied if the proposed new wife were a GCC citizen, had a Qatari mother or was related to the would-be Qatari husband "by a kinship relation in the fourth degree" (*bi-sillah qurbā ilā l-darajah al-rābiʿah*). Qatari women wanting to marry out needed permission of the Minister and of their legal guardian. No rules or conditions were specified.

Oman's provisions took the form of a Sultani decree and a string of ministerial decrees, the substance being given in the annexe to Interior Ministry decree 92 of November 1993. The rules (clauses 1 and 2) were clear. There should be social or health reasons for extranational marriage (what the "health" reasons to get married might be we are not told). If an Omani man were to marry a non-Omani woman, he had to show adequate financial means and that he was not already married to an Omani, and in any case "social research" (*baḥth ijtimāʿī*) would be done in each instance before papers were passed to the Ministry. Regardless of sex, if a candidate for transnational marriage was from the GCC the rules did not apply, or if they had been born in Oman to an Omani mother and usually resided there for 18 years (clause 3); a widow or divorcee with Omani children could also act as she saw fit. Everyone else had to have permission. There is a certain irony in the fact that all the important male relatives of Oman's Sultan (himself, of course, not married or ever likely to be so) had married foreigners. But one can see why a line might need drawing. Not only is Oman involved in marriage transactions whose effects extend systematically beyond Zanzibar, but with its singular maritime history, even the male genealogy that might define who Omanis are extends from Africa to India. The Qatari case and the Emirati are in that respect a little easier, although historically of course as arbitrary (cf. Crystal [1990] 1995: 162–3, Lienhardt 2001: 11–12).

If we return to the beginning of Emirati debates, we find the initiative came from the Ruler of Ra's al-Khaimah. This is the northernmost of the emirates, and one of the poorest; it joined the Federation a little later than the other six and, whether expressed in quasi-Nasirist or Islamic terms, Ra's al-Khaimah retains an air of independence. By 1986, Shaykh Ṣaqr felt its social fabric was under strain:

> Whoever looks carefully at our social affairs (*aḥwāl*, conditions) finds that many citizens are marrying foreign women and introducing into their homes strange breeds of people (*'anāṣir gharībah*) who have not by any means acquired our customs and traditions. The result is that the children grow up in an unsuitable environment (*bī'ah ghayr ṣāliḥah*) divided against itself and disputed by different cultures. This is one aspect. Another is that marrying foreign women denies our daughters their right to marry and bring up children within a happy and blameless family. This state of affairs cannot be pleasing to one who cares for the welfare of his country and people.[29]

Shaykh Zayed of Abu Dhabi, in his capacity as President of the Federation, decreed in October that year that a law be drafted. So far as one can gather, little happened until the appearance of the Fund six years later.

All the main themes to be developed by the Marriage Fund were apparent from the date of its inception in 1992 – the concern with social cohesion, not least, and the relation of marriage abroad to the domestic threat of "demographic imbalance".[30] From an early date the influence of the Women's Union (under Shaykhah Fāṭimah, favourite wife of Shaykh Zayed) was apparent also, particularly in connection with questions of divorce and spinsterhood. Through the early 1990s the press reported widely on the perils posed by marriage to foreign women. But until 1996 there was little sign of progress towards a law.

Emiratis explain much that happens by appeal to the wishes (be these real or imagined) of the Ruler. It is said that urgency was given to the marriage issue by Shaykh Zayed having had brought to his attention on a trip abroad some 300 young men in Cairo, apparently the product of the first large wave of overseas travel 20 years before, now all attaining their majority, most with no clear national status and many in trouble with the Egyptian authorities. Typically enough, it is said, he gathered them up as Emiratis, brought them back to the Emirates and vowed they should be looked after. No matrilateral equivalent existed (by definition: children of foreign men are foreigners), but reportedly cases of female misadventure were brought to the Shaykh's attention also. Care for the welfare of young women might lead one to suggest that the country, like a family, keep "its bread in its own basket", and it seems a young national woman from al-'Ain formed some misalliance with a Lebanese. From this date, while constraints on Emirati men made little progress, there was talk of Emirati women being stopped from marrying outside the national circle.

Though no law or decree could be found in the Official Gazette, there were indeed orders issued. The first, dated 19 December 1996, was from the Presidential *dīwān* to the Ministry of Justice: this forbade female citizens marrying foreigners, "but if she wishes to marry then she loses her citizenship".[31] Though not retrospective, that was surely a change from the 1972 and 1975 policies, yet it seemed to go unremarked at first, and discussions of a new survey, launched by Shaykhah Fāṭimah, of Emirati wives with foreign husbands went on as if marriage to foreigners remained a live option.[32] A second order, from the Ministry of Justice to judges, dated 25 January 1997, explained that by "foreigners" the President did not intend GCC citizens. Neither document, so far as I know, was published. In Dubai the orders seem to have been quietly ignored for some years, at least for those with passports issued in Dubai, while elsewhere sundry forms of politeness and indeterminacy make it difficult to know what policy, if any, was applied to whom. But there were certainly instances where endogamy of some kind was enforced. A girl from a well-known Abu Dhabi tribe, whose mother was Indian, for instance, decided after her father's death to marry her maternal cousin (*ibn khāl*). Her paternal uncles objected fiercely. The couple fled to Bahrain but were forcibly retrieved and obliged to dissolve their marriage.

Well aware of the note from the Ministry of Justice, a lawyer in Dubai still said in early 2000 that the whole issue was *ḥadīth majālis*, just "gossip". Even an official of the Abu Dhabi Marriage Fund, who perhaps might have been expected to support such a ban, declined to take the order seriously: "There are people around the Shaykh all the time. Some are serious, some are not. He listens to them. But he has never made an official decision". Plainly someone had. Until a formal law or presidential decree appeared in the Official Gazette, however, people involved with the issue seemed to feel there was room for manoeuvre, as doubtless there always would be.

Private vice and public virtue

From February 1999 the Marriage Fund began a quarterly family magazine, *al-Mawaddah* ("friendship", "love"). The title was decorated with a pair of hearts, the graphics inside much given to floral designs in pastel colours. The first issue was largely taken up with family questions of children and schooling, but later issues recapitulated many of the themes we touched on earlier, citing survey work on marriage, divorce and, not least, the disruptive effects of foreign wives. Volume 2 gave extensive coverage to the Third Colloquium on the Family, held in Ra's al-Khaimah in April 1999, which dealt precisely with "the problem of marriage to foreign women" and was widely reported in the press.

What press reports of the seminar did not dwell on was the presence of very vocal young Emirati women – about 60 or 70, according to people who were there. When it became apparent that the draft ignored them but that they were forbidden (if tacitly) to marry foreigners, they demanded to know what was meant by "foreigner". The GCC did not count. What about fellow Arabs from elsewhere? Are we somehow no longer Arabs ourselves? Here there was a real problem, for in the richest emirates about half the boys drop out before they finish high school, and at the Emirates University, al-'Ain, not only do the girls on average work harder than the boys but there are far more of them.[33] Eligible young men, by the standards of young women's magazines, are scarce. Young women with these sort of preferences in Kuwait and Bahrain, to take a pair of obvious cases, have often solved their problem by marrying age-mates (if not kin, perhaps friends of the family; occasionally boys simply met at college) from, for instance, old Iraqi families or the Arab Levant. If a line is drawn around the nation by administrative order, that option is removed. Though admission of GCC citizens doubtless covers the bulk of immediately likely cases in the Emirates, young women with foreign in-laws face particular problems and what issues may be faced in future by their nieces and younger sisters are hard to guess at.

A divergence of interest between male and female is evident, not least for younger people. Doubtless differences of view might be found, in some form, between generations or even among different emirates. But most interesting of all is the contrast between the common sense of the present and that of only a few decades back. Collection of wives from elsewhere, which once would have been a token of success and status (we can marry your girls but you cannot marry ours), is now judged a social problem; the autonomy of families, or of family heads, is meanwhile subordinate morally to collective needs. By late 1999 these concerns had been generalised in the public media. There are several ways one might argue the rights and wrongs.

National women married to foreigners had stressed two years earlier that Islamic law allows marriage to any suitable Muslim man they choose (*Gulf News* 24 Jan 1997). Men, with a still wider choice of legitimate marriage partners in *sharī'ah*, might well plead in parallel terms on their own behalf. But the "general good" (*al-maṣlaḥah al-*

ʿāmmah) carries huge weight in public rhetoric. Al-Murr, for instance, having argued that a problem has developed almost unobserved and that legislation by the state is needed, says, "Everyone knows that God constrains through authority what He does not constrain through the Qur'ān" (al-Murr 1997: 113): in other words the ruler may legitimately act (indeed, often he should act) without precise scriptural warrant. The Marriage Fund, for its part, invoked "brotherhood" in explaining state intervention, particularly in the contentious area of marriage payments: "the pious life is not one where the person lives alone, nor is the believer isolated from other people ...; the Muslim is he who works together with his brothers in this society ... (*fī hādha l-mujtamaʿ*)" and the needs of society must be respected.

The needs of society or the nation are thus seen as binding on Muslims, and to separate out a scriptural view is often to misrepresent the course of argument. Indeed in Gulf societies an equation of Muslim with Arab slips in. Dr ʿAbdullāh al-ʿUbayd, the (Saudi) Secretary General of the Muslim World League, while agreeing in principle that marriage with strangers is allowed by Islam, thus argues that in the Emirates and elsewhere "everything has become mixed up" (*ikhtalaṭ al-ḥābil bi-l-nābil*) by the presence of so many foreigners:

> if we sons of the Arabs, ... we sons of the Muslims [that is], bring these people into our houses and beget children by them, they will come to rule over our affairs. Affairs will fall into their hands. And we see clearly that marriage with foreign women – with non-Arabs to be precise – tinges and affects our Arab households.[34]

The state has not only a right but a duty to deal with this, he argues, and "as is well known, the Muslim is obliged to conduct himself in accordance with what God permits or forbids, and certain provisions and arrangements are governed by the good of the community". These apparently have the force of law, whatever God's word in scripture.

Emirati arguments turn equally on the public good. "Foreign wives" are associated in such public claims with divorce, cultural disruption, the failure of children at school and burdens on social services, all of which are state concerns. The rhetoric, of course, lumps together cases which are very different and in some sense opposites: roughly, it is comparable to assertions in Britain or America about "unmarried mothers", where lost 16-year-olds with no job prospects are equated with prosperous career women. In the Emirati case it is not hard to find parallels to the first group. If many disastrous marriages involve Asian wives it would be no surprise, simply on account of economic patterns. On the other hand, one can easily think of prominent Emirati men married for decades (and most successfully so far as one can see) to women from Asia, the Arab World, Europe or

America. One suspects, indeed, that this may be one reason why progress on a marriage law has been so slow.[35] It does not, however, constrain public rhetoric.

By 1999 the rhetoric had become intense. The cover of the third issue of *Mawaddah* featured a desert with a dead, dried-out tree stump and the caption, "this is the offshoot (*ghirs*) of the foreign woman"; inside, an illustration of the foreign woman, caught loosening her *'abāyah* to try on a formal hat, used not a model but the real thing.[36] Western women and children are conspicuous in the graphics; statistically the bulk of foreign wives are Eastern. To attempt to decipher the symbolism may attribute more coherence to what was happening than in fact it had, but the campaign against foreign marriage touched on wider concerns, and in a society so attentive to propriety the very fact of the campaign was striking. The private concerns of family life were made the subject of appeals to generalised morality and public order.

An interview in 1999 with the Director General of Nationality and Residence discussed sundry "nominal" marriages, not least "transit marriage" (*al-Mawaddah* Aug. 1999; miscopied later, *al-Bayān* 8 Aug. 1999, as "internet marriage", another source of popular concern). Russian women, in particular, we were told, would arrive on a tourist visa, then marry some local for cash to acquire right of residence. On the Asian front, the President of the Marriage Fund, Jamāl al-Baḥ, went so far as to speak in an interview with the Abu Dhabi newspaper *al-Ittiḥād* of "marriage brokers":

> Certain weak-minded and unpatriotic citizens wrongfully take advantage of the legal privileges accorded them, such as issuing and withdrawing visas, to conduct something resembling a white-slave trade (*tijārat al-raqīq al-abyaḍ*). They collect foreign wives, then dissolve their marriage contracts abroad while inside the country looking out for husbands for them in return for 10–15,000 dirhams. ... When he has found a husband for her, the broker divorces his wife and marries her off to the citizen who has snapped her up (*al-Ittiḥād* 23 Mar. 2000).

In some cities, he said, up to 20 of these characters, were "knocking at the doors of young men unable to marry national women and of old men" to marry off foreign women "obtained at cheap rates". As if this were not bad enough, such brokers used their homes as offices and some thus had houses "stuffed with young Arab and Asian girls" (*taktaẓẓ bi-fatāyāt 'arabīyāt wa-asyāwīyāt*).

At the conference in Ra's al-Khaimah in April 1999, the logic facing "Emirates society" had been spelled out:

> We find that the states of the world without exception, whatever the orientation of their thought and beliefs or their political systems, have introduced legislation intended to protect their social structure, particu-

> larly as regards demographic composition, with the aim of preserving their social, cultural and religious roots. This is so even to the point that some of the communist states, quite lacking religious manifestations and social relations [sic], issued legislation banning their citizens, whether male or female, from marrying foreigners.[37]

Citing the godless communist states shows how desperate the situation is, and how any state surely has rights of self-protection. But governments in the Gulf, it is claimed, have something specific to protect:

> As is well known, every society has distinctive peculiarities which make it different from other societies even if they resemble each other in religious belief or language. Among these peculiarities which distinguish some societies, such as that of the Emirates, one of the most important is relationships of kinship and descent (*al-qurbā wa-l-nasab*) among families within the state. This connects with authentic (*aṣlī*, original, noble) Arab customs and manners which originate from [the society's] Islamic belief and from ethical values inherited from [our] ancestors.

One can sympathise with the ideal, perhaps; to distinguish specifically Arab from Islamic beliefs in the region would, meanwhile, be work for scholars. The proponents of a law on foreign marriage, however, saw a political need which perhaps states of other kinds do not face (cf. Fargues 2000: 89). Again the draft agenda for the conference on the family spells out the issue, explaining that kinship

> leads, on the one hand, to strong relationships, continuity and mutual co-operation among the peoples of the region (*shu'ūb al-minṭaqah*) and on the other, to their connections and co-operation with their rulers, to whom they are linked by bonds of love and respect. This is what makes society close-knit, strong and keen to protect itself, whether politically, economically or socially.

In the circumstances, if private vice is not to corrupt public virtue, legislation seems unavoidable.

The proposed draft law (*al-Ittiḥād* 24 Apr. 1999) followed closely the Qatari example. Students on study-missions abroad and certain state functionaries would both be forbidden to marry foreigners at all, the grammar of the draft assuming that Emirati men are the ones who marry out (Emirati women are not mentioned). The rules would not apply if the foreign wife were a GCC passport holder or some other Arab national related to the prospective spouse "in the fourth degree", or had an Emirati mother and was resident in the Emirates, or herself was widowed or divorced from an Emirati and had Emirati children. Men not in the restricted categories of employment who wished to marry non-nationals would have to seek permision from the Marriage Fund, and certain conditions applied here. The man would have to be 35 years old or more and not married to an Emirati woman; he would have to show means to support a family; he would have to be no more than 15 years older than the proposed wife. Like the Omani law but unlike the Qatari, the draft Emirati law says the requisite "social causes" might be replaced by "health causes" (*asbāb ṣiḥḥīyah*, again frustratingly unexplained: might infertility be the issue?). Unlike the case in either Qatar or Oman, the foreign wife must not have been convicted of crimes touching on "honour or security" and would anyway need to be "of Arab Muslim nationality".

The national interest

In the smaller Gulf states, such as the Emirates, there is genuinely a fear among some people that national society might evaporate. The idea of "society" perhaps is new, and the way it is conceived has changed over recent decades, invoking the kinds of (bilateral) identity through kinship that the West might associate with race and that everywhere are expressed now in terms of "culture". Al-Murr forces home the implications (al-Murr 1997: 23ff.). An issue of *Newsweek*, he says, had raised the problem of German "national identity" (*huwīyah waṭanīyah*) and suggested that a crisis set in as the percentage of foreign workers in the population grew from 2 per cent to 8-9 per cent. If we carry on as we are doing, says al-Murr, the proportion of foreigners to locals in the Emirates will be the other way around: "we" will be a tiny minority, perhaps tending towards 2 per cent. Somehow by privileging individual wishes over national interests (out-marriage is the prime example) we have ended up in danger of not knowing who we are. Such appeals to the common good, to protection of the state and of the nation, now dominate all discussion of the subject in public settings.

Privately opinion remains divided, not always as outsiders might expect. A female academic, very much the secular modernist, argued for close state restrictions on marriage for both sexes and dismissed concern with individual liberties as disguise for creeping "Westernisation": the resolutions of UN conferences on women, even, she saw as an imperialist plot directed at the Arab World. On the other hand, a male journalist, well on in middle age and not personally engaged in the problem (his children were married), stated firmly that restrictions of this kind were "contrary to humanity and the spirit of the age". It was a woman lawyer, much involved with family practice and fluent in the modernist issues of women's rights, who argued to me most strongly that state restrictions on marriage were at odds with *sharī'ah*: her feelings and scholarship alike spilled out in distinctively Islamic terms. A more common view, in discussion at least, is probably that the "general good" (*maṣlaḥah 'āmmah*) overrides the niceties of jurisprudence.

It was Durkheim's sound principle that social facts such as marriage rates (let us add for ourselves local discussions about marriage rates) could not be explained by appeal to individual psychology. Nor can historical facts be reduced to single causes. The context is plain in the case at hand (call it "globalisation" if one wants a catch-word) but the constituencies, so to speak, are complex, so for instance a common view among younger women runs parallel with that of older men who dominate national policy. What is unfolding is precisely a social fact. One can point to its forms at least: to the prominence of such ideas as society and social structure; a certain wariness of solutions that directly impinge on existing family matters (divorce law, marriage contracts, maintenance);[38] a striking distrust of polygamy, which within living memory had the status of common sense; the changed ideal, therefore, of the family; and the new idea of a national family in which the ruler acts as *pater familias*. Perhaps most interesting of all is what happens when marriage, the archetypical case of family self-definition, is submitted to legislation and the issues thus stated in general form.

Early in the year 2000 Muḥammad al-Rukn, a Dubai lawyer who headed the Emirati Jurists' Association, argued in his weekly newspaper column (*al-Khalīj* 24 Jan. 2000) that it was time to rethink laws on nationality. The *ex tempore* provisions of the early 1970s may have worked when drafted, but building a sense of national identity, as government and intellectuals alike both wish to do, is difficult when many citizens are defined as forever only semi-national. In the space of three decades the problems facing state and people have changed out of recognition. The position on personal status is now problematic also: as al-Rukn points out, one of the paradoxes of legislation from the 1970s is that the illegitimate child of an Emirati woman is better placed in law than her legitimate child by a foreign husband, which cannot have been the drafters' aim. The paradoxes of banning "marriage with foreigners", if or when it should happen, may prove every bit as odd.

PART III. PRACTICAL AND MORAL ORDER

CHAPTER 7

PUBLIC ORDER AND AUTHORITY

Policing Kuwait

Jill Crystal

All rulers, even the most benign, use force to maintain order. When rulers rely on force or its threat in routine, systematic ways, they police. Although all governments police, they vary tremendously in the nature and size of the forces retained to do this and in their willingness to use them. This paper argues that the relatively benign (by both global and Gulf standards) policing that exists in Kuwait is the result of two factors: the particular police institutions that emerged prior to independence, and the transnational nature of the opposition the police faced during their formative post-independence period. Choices made by the British as they departed and by independent leaders as they took over did not create inevitabilities, but they did create path-dependencies, making certain outcomes substantially more likely, others less so. These origins are important because, once established, police institutions, as Bayley and others have argued (e.g. Bayley 1985: 43), remain remarkably stable over time.

The legacy of the colonial period is important, but institutions are not established in their initial form for eternity. They must be sustained. Particular patterns of policing, structured by earlier political arrangements, were reinforced by independent rulers as they tried to control opposition. In Kuwait, the first major post-independence policing problem was a transnational problem: policing expatriates. This was handled in two ways. For daily control, the government came to rely on ordinary Kuwaiti citizens. The government drew a line (previously faint) between expatriates and nationals, then turned the policing of the former over to the latter in an effort to reinforce this distinction. Some foreigners, however, were also dissidents, and their policing could not be left to the public, for in the era of Arab Nationalism, expatriates and nationals often engaged in serious political exchanges. To handle this threat, specialised security forces concerned primarily with dissent, with the particular rather than the public order, were employed. Through these two techniques, privatising daily policing and adding specialised security forces, the rulers contained expatriate dissent. They took away from the experience the lesson that threats to the political order could most effectively be handled when defined as external.

Origins of public order: learning to police

Although policing is as old as the Middle East – indeed, the world's first civilian police forces emerged in Egypt and Mesopotamia (Adamson 1991) – policing as it exists today is a relatively recent historical development (Bayley and Liang 1992). Policing through separate, community-based forces first emerged in Europe in the nineteenth century in response to the social dislocations and concomitant unrest accompanying the emergence of an industrial economy. Gradually European states shifted from their historical reliance on the military (which had a tendency to excess force) and on irregular militias (which tended to be politically unreliable) towards new, public police designed primarily for handling domestic disorder. Unlike the military, garrisoned and episodically mobilised, these police lived in small units within the community they controlled. They functioned continually and maintained order on a routine basis. Relying on regular sources of information and to an extent on community support, they were more able to anticipate and sometimes avert opposition and so required less force. While politicised in the broad sense, they were, to paraphrase Bayley (1985: 45), less transparently partisan than militias.

These European transformations affected policing in the Middle East as well. Contemporary policing begins with nineteenth-century Tanẓīmat efforts to reform the Ottoman police and restructure it on a European model (Ralston 1990, Swanson 1975). By the late nineteenth century, Ottoman reforms had made the police a separate non-military force in Istanbul, paralleling contemporaneous developments in European policing. In the Gulf, however, largely beyond the reach of Ottoman reforms, policing was shaped more by direct British intervention and the particular constellation of opposition each ruler faced as the police emerged.

Although Britain worked from similar police templates in its colonies, its goals differed markedly from one colony to another. How the colony fitted into the larger imperial picture was one important factor shaping public order. Bahrain, for instance, developed a larger and more forceful police than its neighbours, in part because it played a more central administrative role for Britain. Kuwait, more peripheral and peaceful, required less direct policing. Qatar lay in between. By the end of the 1950s, there was already surprising variation in policing that carried into independence and continued through the following decades. Bahrain had a very forceful police, Qatar's was intermittently so, Kuwait's was far less violent. When Arab Nationalist demonstrations swept the Gulf in 1956, Qatar consequently called out the police; in Bahrain a state of emergency was declared and tribal levies recruited into a special riot squad, while in Kuwait the police chief resigned rather than fire on Kuwaitis. Even the election of consultative bodies that appeared so similar at the time had different driving forces and different effects on policing. In Kuwait, the goal was to strike a balance between the ruling family and the opposition and to create an institution where the Emir could cultivate new allies. In Bahrain, the goal was to get the opposition out in the open so it could be arrested. One reason for the later differences between Kuwait and Bahrain is that Kuwait never really had a colonial police while Bahrain retained one long after independence. All began from similar positions.

At the beginning of the twentieth century, Kuwait's rulers, like other Gulf rulers, relied on a small standing force of slave and badu bodyguards and, in a crisis, on a modest urban levy and tribal allies.[1] In the 1930s, Kuwait's merchants began to challenge the ruling family, beginning with the establishment in 1930 of a Municipality, based loosely on Bahrain's (al-Jāsim 1980). This Municipality was financially independent of the Ruler, raising revenues through business and import taxes and rents. While chaired by a shaykh (in other words, a member of the ruling family), its members were all merchants and its decision-making authority rested with its merchant-elected board of directors. The Municipality focused initially on supervising and cleaning the markets but also took on policing economic activities: monitoring professions and the market. Within a few years, most of its expenses were guards' salaries.[2]

In the 1930s, today's conventional distinction between police, courts and correction did not yet exist. The police were the criminal justice system: they investigated, convicted and sanctioned.[3] While some courts existed (largely for civil matters, e.g. pearl-diving courts), clear lines between police, courts and correction did not. In the past, the Emir had often administered justice directly (Lorimer 1908–15: ii, 1074–5); in the 1930s, his badu guards continued to handle disputes among the badu and tribal retainers (Freeth and Winstone 1972: 121). Some cases went before the head of the Municipality police, first Shaykh Du'ayj Jābir, then his son Ṣabāḥ.[4] Known as "Ṣabāḥ al-sūq", he and his force of roughly 80 men (mostly badu, with Persian Baluchi night guards) patrolled the city, investigating and adjudicating. *Sharī'ah* corporal punishments were rarely imposed, although a secular beating often was. Prison was rarely used for either dissidents or deviants. Until the 1938 Majlis Movement, Kuwait had no formal prison, only a place in the palace that rarely held more than one prisoner (al-Fahed 1989: 115). The preferred sanction was a fine.

In 1938, growing merchant dissent over the distribution of political power coalesced into the Majlis Movement, culminating in a merchant-elected legislature. During its short tenure, this body set in motion several changes that institutionalised policing. In July 1938, the Majlis promulgated a body of laws, including some on justice, public security and emergencies. Concerned at corruption in the existing forces of public order, the Majlis set up a new police force, gave its members special badges and built the first police station to house it. This force was run by two leading merchant dissidents, Ghānim Saqr al-Ghānim and Muḥammad al-Qaṭāmī, under two important shaykhs, Ṣabāḥ Sālim (who headed the force until 1959) assisted by his nephew Sa'd 'Abdullāh. The police had some 60 men and included both townsmen (unarmed and largely older recruits, favoured to gain public trust) and badu from the Ruler's bodyguard (al-Fahed 1989: 108). The organisation was modeled loosely on the Iraqi police system favoured by the Kuwaiti opposition (some of whom had studied law in Iraq) and was initially administered by an Iraqi instructor (ibid. 113–19). Policing was not yet involved with national identity.

The Ruler retained his bodyguards and tribal allies. When conflict with the merchants came to a crisis in December 1938, he used this older force to put down the rebellion and dissolve the Majlis. The precipitant was the return from Iraq of a Kuwaiti dissident, Muḥammad al-Munāyis, who handed out leaflets calling on Kuwaitis to overthrow the Emir and assuring them of the Iraqi Army's imminent arrival (relations with Iraq were rather different then).[5] When al-Munāyis was arrested, two supporters, Yūsuf al-Marzūq and Muḥammad al-Qaṭāmī, tried to release him and a fight ensued. In the struggle, al-Qaṭāmī fired on the police, but missed; they returned fire, killing him and wounding al-Marzūq and a nearby shopkeeper. The Emir duly gathered his guards and tribal supporters. He had al-Munāyis executed, then had his badu supporters arrest those Majlis members who had not fled to Iraq. After failing to persuade India or Bahrain to take the dissidents, he built a prison for them.[6] Policing was becoming a domestic responsibility.

The 1938 movement formalised policing; its defeat placed a new institution in the hands of the ruling family. The question raised by the Majlis Movement – whether the police were answerable to the Majlis or the ruling family – was answered clearly by the dissolution of the Majlis. Indeed, this event catalysed the more thoroughgoing centralisation of political power in the hands of the ruling family that came to characterise Kuwaiti politics. The Political Agent summarised this change in a letter to the Political Resident in early 1939:

> You will remember, as you often remarked to me, that the Ruling Family here, unlike those of other Arab states, were allowed to take no part whatever in Administrative affairs. ... Since the 18th of December the Subah family have taken up superior posts in all departments of the Government, including security, sea and shore police, the control of the arms reserve, the city police etc.[7]

The rebellion brought home to the rulers the need for routinised domestic policing. Through his relatives, the Emir held on to the new force, which was itself, of course, a new form of controlling society.

Dissent continued, but was now expressed through and to a degree contained within the ruling family. Two competing police forces emerged, mirroring a larger family struggle. When the Majlis Movement was defeated, Shaykh Ṣabāḥ Sālim and his nephew, Shaykh Sa'd 'Abdullāh, held on to the old Municipality police, building it up by incorporating badu from the Ruler's bodyguard. This constituted one force. The other was controlled by Shaykh 'Abdullāh Mubārak, the youngest and last living son of Mubārak the Great. In the 1940s and 1950s 'Abdullāh Mubārak served as deputy Ruler and was a leading contender for the succession (Crystal [1990] 1995: 68). At the end of 1938 he took over a small force that Shaykh 'Alī Khalīfah had established to police the port and began to build this unit into a competing police force (Ingleton 1979: 107). As policing became the focus of the power struggle between 'Abdullāh Mubārak and Ṣabāḥ Sālim, both forces grew. If Ṣabāḥ built a police station, 'Abdullāh built a station nearby; when Ṣabāḥ demanded new armoured cars, 'Abdullāh blocked it and Ṣabāḥ threatened to resign. The Kuwait Democratic Party, one of the mildly dissident merchant groups emerging in this period, even submitted a letter to the Ruler complaining about the schism between the public security and police departments (al-Fahed 1989: 125).

Emir Aḥmad and after him 'Abdullāh Sālim (who succeeded Aḥmad in 1950) tried to contain 'Abdullāh Mubārak, much as they tried to contain other ruling family dissidents. One strategy was to bring in British advisers and British-trained Palestinian officers, sometimes over 'Abdullāh Mubārak's objection. They trained the force, and placed it, via the British presence, under the Ruler's control. This was the same technique 'Abdullāh Sālim used with eventual success against Fahd Sālim, another major dissident shaykh, who found himself hemmed in by British financial administrators (Crystal 1995: 66–73).

Meanwhile, as oil operations got under way (oil had been discovered in commercial quantities in 1938), the oil company developed its own security force, hiring local guards. This created other tensions. Shaykh Aḥmad occasionally sent *ad hoc* forces to the villages in trucks the oil company provided, but he wanted more direct control. In 1949, he created a new police post in Aḥmadī, the growing city at the site of the oil operations, under his son Jābir. The oil company acquiesced reluctantly. According to Joyce,

> the Political Agency told oil company executives to advise employees to deal courteously with the police and when asked by a policeman to accompany him to a police post, to do so. Since most regular policemen were illiterate and the station officers were literate and often bilingual, it was in the best interest of foreigners to go to the station. However, if a Kuwaiti policeman attempted to detain an oil company employee, impose a fine or hold a vehicle, the employee was directed to call one of the Special Police Officers, who were authorised to deal with those under British jurisdiction (Joyce 1998: 59).

Arab Nationalism in the 1950s brought heightened political tension and forced the Emir to confront the question of what sort of a police force he wanted. In 1954, he placed Jāsim al-Qaṭāmī, a graduate of the Egyptian police academy, in daily charge. Al-Qaṭāmī had high hopes, and he aimed to improve police-community relations under the slogan, "the police in the service of the public" (al-Fahed 1989: 127). But as Arab Nationalism, of which al-Qaṭāmī was himself an ardent supporter, swept the Gulf this posed problems of its own. In 1956, when demonstrations erupted, the Emir ordered al-Qaṭāmī to use force to put down the dissent. He refused and was told to resign. In February 1959, demonstrations again erupted with local Arab Nationalist support, and there were fiery speeches from (today veteran dissident) Aḥmad al-Khaṭīb and former police chief Jāsim al-Qaṭāmī (who was placed under house arrest). The ruling family argued about how to respond, with some advocating force (Joyce 1998: 54). Ṣabāḥ Sālim chose a more tempered response, detaining some of the organisers and closing the political clubs and papers, but forgoing violent confrontation. Perhaps he was constrained by personal inclination, perhaps by concern that his police were as much with the crowd as with him, perhaps by concern that internal dissent and division meant his family was not fully behind him. But the decisions of the late 1950s set a direction in policing.

The concern with ruling family divisions was certainly on the Ruler's mind. The year 1959, in addition to demonstrations, also brought the death of rival shaykh Fahd Sālim. With Fahd out of the way, the Emir now felt freer to move against 'Abdullāh Mubārak and gain more direct control of the police. In 1957, he had tried to consolidate some of 'Abdullāh Mubārak's forces into Ṣabāḥ Sālim's police, but backed down when 'Abdullāh Mubārak resisted. This time he was successful. In 1959, he merged the two police departments into one domestic force, the Directorate of Police and Security Forces, under 'Abdullāh's longstanding rival, Shaykh Ṣabāḥ Sālim. Today's Public Security Department in the Interior Ministry is the descendant of this unified force created in 1959. Ṣabāḥ Sālim then stepped down (formally, in 1961) as head of police, handing the force to his deputy commander, Sa'd 'Abdullāh, who had meanwhile received police training in England and who had managed the city police since 1945. Sa'd now took over the unified police and went on in the coming years to serve as Interior Minister (1962-78) and (from 1964) Defence Minister as well, then Crown Prince and Prime Minister. 'Abdullāh Mubārak was placed nominally in charge of external security, but when he tried to develop a separate force, the Emir would not allow it. In 1961, a showdown between them led to 'Abdullāh Mubārak's exile.

The Ruler's control of family dissidents left him, at independence, positioned to develop a now unified police force much more his own. Having brought in British advisers to build this force and marginalise his opponents, he could now dispense with the advisers but keep the police, though under the control of the ruling family. Both the military crisis associated with the Iraqi threat (1961) and the administrative requirements of independent statehood enabled the Emir to institutionalise the police further. During the Iraqi crisis, he established a Supreme Defence Council and formed several thousand badu into a National Guard. In 1962, Emiri decrees established several ministries including Interior. This ministry, built on the now unified police, came in the following years to comprise a number of General Departments. Most were concerned with public order – traffic, communications and emergencies, public relations. But among them was also the General Department for State Security. Housed in Interior, but functionally autonomous, this force was concerned with internal security, with the particular order of the state. In 1968, when the first official reference to the police's basic organisational structure appeared (Emiri Decree 23), State Security was a General Department (al-Ebrahīm 1992: 218). The work of this Department, as with its counterparts everywhere, remained shrouded in mystery (even the 1968 decree was confidential and its reproduction forbidden, al-Fahed 1985: 241).[8] As the regular police became ever more visible, this force became less so.

Creating a new order

Most of the General Departments comprising the unified police were entrusted with protecting public order: the police in the service of the public. To do this, they themselves were made orderly, with badges, uniforms and ranks. In the 1950s and 1960s, the police also introduced training geared to emerging international norms, and began to articulate professional standards and a goal of recruitment and advancement by merit. Kuwaitis were sent to Egypt's police academy for training, later to Britain. In 1956, Kuwait opened its own Police School, where instruction ranged from basic literacy through criminal procedure to military training. A special civil defence force was created from the ranks of the police and given training in guerrilla warfare and civil defence. In 1969, a two-year course of training for officers began and, with this, students were no longer sent abroad. The programme was gradually extended to four years, giving students a college degree.[9]

New technology also arrived, initially as a by-product of the struggle between the two shaykhs over the police. Both forces in the 1950s had fought hard for new technology, such as armoured cars, even as they resisted the advisory control that typically accompanied it. Technology followed the money. As a Ministry of Guidance and Information publication of the day proudly noted, "The Criminal Investigation Department is equipped with the latest machines in crime detection. One of these is a lie detector, made in Indiana, U.S.A., which has been used and found effective in several cases. Electrodes are attached to one finger on each of the suspect's hands, while a detective watches the swing of a needle against a dial as he asks questions" (Kuwait 1963: 64). Laboratories with microscopes and "an electric machine to gauge forged coins' components", breathalysers and other technology all followed. A Police Identification Bureau opened in 1956 with then cutting-edge technology, and promptly began collecting the fingerprints and photographs of those who came in contact with the police (the vast majority expatriates). The same bureau also began keeping records on all government employees. As the state emerged as the country's largest employer, these records gave the Emir another form of control with an improved ability to monitor the population.

Professionalism was still an aspiration, however, and one limited largely to the top of the force. At the bottom, there were no admissions qualifications, and indeed most of the students were illiterate.[10] An expatriate doctor wrote in the early 1960s that "for Kuwaitis who come from the poorer classes, jobs are invented or overstaffed. For instance, there are ten guards for the grounds at the mental hospital who are paid \$150 to \$175 per month when in point of fact no guards are needed. Similar occupations, such as the municipal policemen ... are quite frequent, and the town is liberally sprinkled with such individuals who really do nothing but walk around in their uniforms and lean against the buildings" (Kline 1963: 766–7). Like US airports relying for security on people who could not keep a job at McDonalds, public order relied on specialists, but ones who were not terribly special.

One challenge the police faced in protecting the general order was that no such order yet existed. Before the police could maintain public order, this order, too, had to be created. The order of the past was far more localised and transient, consisting of multiple, overlapping hierarchies that were maintained in multiple, overlapping ways: neighbourhoods organised around mosques, family elders watching youngsters, merchants monitoring markets, ship captains monitoring divers. For the most part, previous rulers were indifferent to these processes unless the system broke down badly, whereupon they would send in their badu supporters to restore order and then leave again.

The arrival of the police signalled the emergence of something very different: permanent public order. General order was now imposed on the city. The old walls were demolished in 1957 and British town planners were brought in to convert "the old seaport into a modern city with broad thoroughfares and traffic roundabouts, new markets to replace the congested covered shops, new Government Offices and public buildings" (Kuwait Oil Company Limited 1959: 65). Maps, aerial photographs and architects carefully bounded the city, employing "major traffic surgery" to solve, for example, the congestion problems of the inappropriately pear-shaped Safat Square, the centre of the old city (Shiber 1964: 410). Outside the old walls, self-contained neighbourhoods were carefully laid out, each with their own schools, shops, clinic, mosque, post office and, of course, police station. Streets were built and marked, neighbourhoods were identified and designated for certain populations. Visible order appeared as the state created divisions that had not previously existed – bounded spaces where traffic flowed and designated populations dwelled. The police presence was important in visibly marking these new boundaries: "Police stations, or posts, are dotted all over Kuwait, each responsible for a section of the town or country" (Kuwait 1963: 64). Police were deployed in such a way as to define these spaces. Uniformed officers tamed the traffic, and police stations typically sat at a new neighbourhood centre, aside the local co-operative, shops, post office and fast food establishment.

Above the clean streets grew tall government buildings housing new ministries with uniformed guards looking as sharp as they could. The process of creating and maintaining order mobilised the whole apparatus of state. Inside those buildings, administrative consolidation and control continued through the 1960s and the state expanded its reach. With the new public schools, hospitals, housing and jobs came the eyes of the state, now everywhere and nowhere. The gaze it cast was less a controlling gaze than an ordering one. The technology of surveillance, while helpful to the police in defining themselves as specialists, and hence professionals, was less helpful in detecting threats to the public order. As even the FBI knows, data do not organise themselves. The emerging state was thus not Orwellian, nor meant to be, but more a Foucaultian (1977) panopticonic state, with widely dispersed, largely invisible power controlling the population. The state was apparent everywhere: in the new streets and houses as well as the ministries. Sets of very ordinary rules and norms came to order all aspects of life. Constant but diffuse scrutiny, not fear, kept people in line.

A host of institutions contributed to the process: not the factories of Foucault perhaps, but certainly the hospitals and schools, and especially the welfare state. To get married (and receive housing), to have children (and receive money), to get an education, a job or a prescription filled, to walk down the street, you went through the state. Non-conformity could be monitored and sanctioned by a variety of state agencies: state employment (in many sectors, the only option available), education or health-care abroad, housing, loans. All these could be denied. The panoptic surveillance was not lodged solely in the government but diffused throughout the population. Thus the new physical spaces also created new cognitive spaces. This more diffuse, internalised self-monitoring and correcting behaviour was especially important in creating Kuwaitis, who now began wearing identifying uniforms like the *dishdashah* with greater consistency and exclusivity. In this process, the police played not just the formal role of surveillance but the informal one of signalling the norms of order. An aggressively neutral, impersonal police emerged, ensuring public safety through public order, with everyone and everything in its sights.

But beneath this general order lay a very specific order, a system of privilege and dominance. Kuwait was no sovereign-less panopticon. The sovereign was quite real, as were his enemies. When maintaining a particular order (one centred on a ruler or a structure of government), the regular police are typically backed by an array of often shadowy security forces with more explicitly political functions, forces for whom regime maintenance is their primary task. Whether these are special military or police units, they are organisationally separate, their communication with the regular police typically one-way. These security forces – in Kuwait, State Security – protect the regime from its enemies. They rely, often heavily, on force or threat. They have a broader mandate, fewer checks and a greater propensity for violence. Kuwait's Emirs thus continued to handle their opponents in well-established ways: controlling one group by recruiting from another (badu policing urban Arab Nationalists) and keeping their retainers, now institutionalised in State Security, available for a crisis. The problem, however, was that the logic of these two systems of policing conflicted. The problem of policing expatriates clarified the contradictions.

Policing expatriates

The panopticonic state, made authoritative through a discourse of Kuwaiti nationalism, worked for Kuwaitis, but not for foreigners. It kept Kuwaitis in place: a Kuwaiti could not disappear into the population, and would hardly want to; a Goan maid could and in fact did. As in every Gulf state, so many regularly absconded that they had to be amnestied every few years. For foreigners, the government devised two very different systems of policing. One was formal police surveillance, often very high-tech and dependent on contracted expatriate expertise. In the early 1960s, the government proudly noted that its Police Bureau had "records, fingerprints and photographs of 48,000 people who have come in touch with the law at one point or another in the last seven years. It is not irrelevant to add that 45,000 of them are not Kuwaiti. The bureau also keeps a full record of all government employees" (Kuwait 1963: 64). The other system was low-tech and rested on private Kuwaitis.

In the 1960s, the mass influx of foreigners into Kuwait made expatriates the government's primary policing concern. Among the most important decisions made in the 1960s was to privatise their control and surveillance. Privatisation was achieved through the sponsorship (*kafālah*) system, which delegated daily control of foreigners to individual households and employers. The government no longer relied on paid professional police personnel to perform this task; instead, they authorised unpaid volunteers to do it. At first, this seems a surprising choice. Most governments guard jealously their monopoly on force. Moreover, there is a widespread belief among Kuwaitis that expatriates have a higher propensity to commit crime; certainly their chances of being apprehended are higher (al-Ajmi 1985). But as the above discussion of diffuse policing suggests, the public/private division typically employed when discussing European or US police never existed in Kuwait (nor perhaps in the West, really). In any event, this decision was an administrative necessity. The sheer number of expatriates made direct policing too large a task for the new force to handle. This population was immune to a panopticonic state designed to shape Kuwaitis, and its active policing was far beyond the bureaucratic capacity of government. Fortunately (for the state, if not the expatriates) there was sufficient harmony of interest between the rulers and ordinary Kuwaitis to rest daily control with private citizens. As in earlier days, only when the system broke down visibly, as it did with the occasional labour riot, did rulers intervene, using their new retainers, State Security. And as in the past, having restored order, they left.

If the government and the population granted policing authority share basically similar interests, private policing can work. Force or its threat does not have to be lodged in the state to be effective. As Longva argues in this volume (Chapter 5), residency laws in Kuwait, not labour laws, came to constrain foreign labour, and application of these laws was left largely to the private sponsorship system and the Kuwaiti sponsor. That the state did not relinquish this policing without ambivalence is suggested by the recurring shifts in immigration control. Before 1965 immigration was handled by Social Affairs and Labour, from 1965 to 1974 by Interior, after 1974 by Social Affairs and Labour again (Russell and al-Ramadhan 1994), and from 1990 by Interior.

A precedent existed in Kuwait for this kind of private policing. Longva (1997: 105–5) traces the practice to the pearling industry, built on debt bondage and indentured labour, where, historically, a diver in debt needed his captain's release to work for another or face arrest for absconding. In both cases, the labour market was regulated by freezing the labourer in his relationship to one employer, who in turn provided for his needs. Private policing of women has also occurred. The police and the courts reinforce this privatisation, generally resolving family disputes informally. They refer serious cases not to the criminal justice system, but to the Health Ministry's psychiatric department, whose goal is to return the problem to the private sector, assisting the family's efforts to solve matters domestically. But this private policing historically also had private checks, typically in the form of interlinking family relationships. Where these were absent, as with expatriates, private policing could be very rough. Problems were particularly acute for expatriate women. Most police complaints of domestic violence involve non-national women (USDS 1998: 2). Female employees, particular those working as domestic labour, were especially at risk,[11] and the problem was so acute that the government in the early 1990s designated a special police station in al-Dasmah to investigate complaints from absconded maids.[12]

This system of private policing most probably deterred some criminal behaviour among expatriates, but it also facilitated criminality among sponsors. Here the expatriate had little recourse. Despite some highly publicised trials, charges of assault or rape against an employer rarely went to court. What more typically occurred, as Brown argues (1997: 215), was a stand-off mediated by the police. The worker would level a criminal charge against the employer (without this, she would have little to bargain with). The sponsor would counter-claim that the employee had absconded (a violation of immigration and labour law) or level a criminal counter-charge. And then the two would bargain. If necessary, the police would mediate an informal solution.

Private policing did not entirely replace public policing, even of expatriates. Behind private control lay, of course, the official threat of deportation – a threat so effective that it was rarely used. Fear of deportation was universal. As Longva notes, "as a mechanism of control, the importance of deportation resided less in its actual implementation as a legal sanction against crimes and violations than in its pervasive presence as a *threat* and in the unclear contours of its modalities: what may trigger deportation, who may take the decision, and under what circumstances" (Longva 1997: 100). Another, but far less important, mechanism for controlling expatriate labour was labour law, which also appeared in the 1960s. The irrelevance of these laws to the essential nature of control, however, is evidenced both in their fairly benign nature (as Longva argues, the 1964 Labour Law is on the face of it a liberal showpiece) and in the fact that when expatriates go to court, they often win. However, since exercising this right typically prompts retaliation through the residence laws, most do not go to court.

These solutions worked. Sponsors, with police support, kept labour in check by holding their passports. This became standard practice and, although not required by law, was explicitly recommended by the Interior Ministry, which regularly issued statements reminding both employers and employees to follow this practice. Even when a crime occurred, the police were often not informed. The expatriates feared deportation if the matter went to the police and, as Brown points out (1997: 215), the employer's bargaining position was so strong that he did not need the police. The police themselves encouraged this private policing. If they arrested an expatriate, they contacted his sponsor first. As Longva notes, the police would wait for the sponsor to appear personally before dealing with the charge. "Even if the arrest turned out to be a mistake, the expatriate was not set free before this formality had taken place" (Longva 1997: 111).

The effect of private policing on public order was to privatise the uglier aspects of control, leaving the ordinary police to engage in public order: handling traffic, investigating burglaries, guarding important buildings. The government was willing to use force, but since the system for controlling expatriates largely worked, it rarely needed to. By the 1970s, the expatriate problem, as a police problem, was under control, largely because of the decision to leave much of it to the private sector. But by then the government had new problems.

The Shi'ah and the Sunnis

The Iranian revolution focused the government's attention on the Shi'ah. Although long the object of discrimination in Kuwait, the Shi'ah had not been politically very active in the past. Perhaps, as Mamoun Fandy argues in the Saudi case (Fandy 1999: 5), because the Shi'ah are a minority, they do not threaten the dominant order unless linked to external forces. As in Saudi Arabia, because the larger opposition in Kuwait is Sunni, the Shi'ah may prefer working with the existing regime, the ruling family, to working with an unwelcoming Sunni opposition. Historically some prominent Shi'ah families (e.g. Baḥbahānī) were even linked closely in commercial matters to the ruling family in Kuwait. As with expatriates, however, there were few interlocking family connections to temper the regime's use of force.[13]

With the Iranian revolution, the government redefined the Shi'ah as an extension of an external threat. Some Shi'ah dissidents certainly were tied to Iran, notably through the Islamic Call Party (*Ḥizb al-Da'wah al-Islāmīyah*), a transnational Shi'ah organisation involved in several car bombings in 1983, but there is no evidence that the Shi'ah community as a whole was less than loyal. Nonetheless, the government defined the Shi'ah as hostile and treated them as such, and they responded in kind. The concerted attack on the Shi'ah unified historical divisions within the community (social class, period of settlement in Kuwait, ties to Iraqi or Iranian religious authority). Policing of the Shi'ah community grew harsher. Force replaced more benign methods of control. Arguably the worst period of state violence now began, lasting until the Iraqi invasion of 1990. Kuwait State Security took over primary responsibility, arresting and torturing dozens who they asserted were linked to Iran (Alnajjar 2000: 256).

To facilitate the crackdown on the Shi'ah, the government took several measures. First, it purged the police. As it would later do with the *bidūn* (those locals "without" Kuwait nationality), the government began eliminating Shi'ah from sensitive security and military positions. In late 1979, 26 high-ranking police officers took early retirement (Assiri 1990: 68). Control would again be achieved through manipulating the composition of the force rather than professionalising its lower ranks. As one officer noted: "The issues of concern were and remain: literacy and loyalty ... " (al-Ebrahim 1992: 247). In 1986, the Emir also dissolved the National Assembly, suspending constitutional clauses relating to civil and political rights, and ruled by decree. When the Shi'ah were contained, the police turned their attention to the mainstream Sunni opposition.

The 1986 Assembly dissolution created a new opposition movement, organised around *dīwānīyah*s. Historically, these were weekly meetings held in a special area of the house where friends and relatives met to discuss politics and business. They now became the basis for huge anti-government rallies, coalescing into a movement known locally as the *dīwānīyah* movement. In 1989, thousands of Kuwaitis began attending weekly *dīwānīyah*s sponsored by former Assembly members, calling on the government to reinstate the body. This opposition was led by secularist liberal Sunnis. The Sunni Islamists, discussed below, still largely supported the government, and the government's initial response to the movement was restrained. With the first outbreak, the government arrested several, but detained them for only a few days and did not torture them (Alnajjar 2000: 256). In December 1989, when people attending a prominent opposition *dīwānīyah* pushed through police barricades, the police did not stop them (Lawyers Committee 1990: 5). As the opposition continued, however, the government turned control increasingly over to the regular police and then to Kuwait State Security, which began responding with dogs, stun grenades and tear gas. Assembly members loudly protested against the unprecedented *dīwānīyah* closures and the government's use of force.

This use of force, however, was unsettling for the ruling family in a way that force against the Shi'ah had not been. Sunnis of standing led the *dīwānīyah* movement. The liberal pro-democratic opposition in Kuwait, the older among them being the old Arab Nationalists, had long been the loyal opposition. Even when they were Arab Nationalist, they were still merchants' sons from the *aṣīl* ("original") families. These were as Kuwaiti as Kuwaitis got: it was hard to argue that this was in any way an external problem. In February 1990, the government opened negotiations with the opposition, but vacillated on its position. It was not ready to tolerate an opposition movement it saw as a direct challenge to its authority, but neither did it have the political will to respond with the same level of force it willingly used against the Shi'ah. In April 1990, the Emir offered a non-violent but far less democratic compromise: a new National Council to be partly elected and partly appointed. The mainstream Sunni-liberal opposition largely rejected this. Before the government could decide whether it was willing to police this opposition with the same ferocity as it used against other groups, external forces really did intervene.

The Iraqi invasion and its aftermath

On 2 August 1990, Ṣaddām Ḥusayn invaded Kuwait, annexing it days later. Iraq policed Kuwait, as occupiers in the initial pacification phase typically do, with military units and force, targeting those communities most likely to harbour opposition. Some 22,000 Kuwaitis were detained at various points during the occupation. Many were tortured, hundreds killed, hundreds more simply disappeared.[14] In February 1991, US and allied forces ousted the Iraqis. From February 1991, following the withdrawal of the Iraqi forces, to June 1991, Kuwait was governed by martial law. This latter period was characterised by another wave of violence as the re-emerging state engaged in or tolerated torture, disappearances and extra-judicial killings of members of those communities that had co-operated with the Iraqis or had been accused of doing so.[15]

Police and armed civilians, in collaboration with government forces, turned on nationals of governments that had supported Iraq (Palestinians, Yemenis, Sudanese) and on *bidūn* (discussed below). Armed vigilantes tortured and murdered suspected collaborators. Some vigilantes were believed to belong to the security services; others were linked to members of the ruling family. The Interior Ministry, thought responsible for many of these violations, was left to investigate itself. According to critics, State Security members, subject to neither legal constraints nor the Interior Ministry, responded to direct orders from the ruling family.[16] The government also turned over to State Security the job of handling residency visas from states supporting Iraq during the war, leading to a rapid increase in renewal denials (USDS 2001: 10). As one human rights group noted, "the coercive pressure of the State Security apparatus has been one of the most effective tools deployed by the authorities to persuade tens of thousands of unwanted non-Kuwaitis to leave the country" (Lawyers Committee 1993: 24-5).

The government also established martial-law courts, which, while grounded in the constitution, were unprecedented historically. Without due process, representation or, frequently, evidence but amidst allegations of widespread torture, suspected collaborators were summarily convicted. In 1994, their work done, these courts were abolished, although in 2002 Amnesty International could still report that "more than 40 political prisoners, including prisoners of conscience, continued to be held; they had been convicted in manifestly unfair trials since 1991. The fate of more than 70 people who disappeared in custody in 1991 remained unknown" (Amnesty International 2002: 1).

Once the private sector had completed the nastiest part of policing, the state slowly retook control. Martial law and accompanying limitations on public freedoms were lifted and elections were announced for 1992. In May 1991, Crown Prince and former Interior Minister Shaykh Sa'd announced to senior Interior officers that even ruling family members, if implicated in vigilantism, must be arrested. While not a realistic directive, it set the tone. Police and prison guards were immediately made aware of the speech. A shake-up at the top of the

Interior Ministry took place in early June (Ross 1996: 91). But the Emir also made it clear that this did not mean an end to political policing, just an end to widespread private policing. Ignoring a petition from senior military officers calling for the dismissal of the former Defence and Interior Ministers, the Emir promoted Shaykh Sālim Āl Ṣabāḥ, the former Interior Minister largely responsible for the crackdowns on the pro-democracy movement, to Foreign Minister (*Middle East Economic Digest* 17 May 1991). In 1992, the government hired the former Egyptian Minister of Interior, General Zakī Badr, as a security consultant. As Interior Minister in Egypt, he had intensified the use of force against state security prisoners in the anti-Islamist campaign of the late 1980s. Egyptian advisers were sent to aid State Security.

Meanwhile the police as a whole had new problems. The invasion had left psychological scars. General crime increased, drug-use rose and juvenile crime increased dramatically. Also too many people were armed: Iraqi forces left large numbers of weapons when they were ousted from Kuwait. The government, after offering an amnesty for return of weapons, made possession punishable by fines and imprisonment. Even the traffic police had problems, as road fatalities increased in the post-war period because so many traffic lights and signs had been destroyed (Ross 1996: 91). At the same time, much of the police infrastructure was gone. The Iraqis had gutted nearly every police station: equipment, vehicles, records were taken or destroyed. The government moved quickly to rebuild the police, relying heavily on American contractors. Even before the electricity was back, the Interior Ministry had awarded a $1.3 million contract to the US Computer Sciences Corporation to develop a new information technology infrastructure to handle internal security (*Middle East Economic Digest* 22 Mar. 1991).[17] The police force had also dwindled owing to the war, and a year of recruits had been missed. A team from the US Army's 352nd Civil Affairs Unit of Riverdale, Maryland, advised Kuwaiti law enforcement officials on reconstructing their force, down to 2,000 from the previous 6,000 (*USA Today* 12 Mar. 1991). To recruit enough police, they were forced to lower their standards.[18] To add to the challenges, the government instructed the police that as far as possible they were to hire only full Kuwaiti citizens. This was a more difficult problem.

The *bidūn*

At the centre of police efforts to reorganise was the problem of the *bidūn*. This group, an umbrella category of stateless people in Kuwait, includes badu who, having settled in and around Kuwait decades before, had nonetheless not registered with the authorities under the

1959 Nationality Law. The category includes those who probably could have received citizenship but failed to register; it also includes those who were unable to prove continuous residence after 1920 (the critical retrospective date), people who migrated to Kuwait and became stateless, people with Kuwaiti mothers but non-Kuwaiti fathers and the children of all these people. The category is thus a messy one: it is not unusual for someone "without" clear status to have close family members with Kuwaiti nationality. This is a definitional problem that the National Assembly has regularly revisited. It is also an emotional issue because it taps into the question of Kuwaiti identity.[19]

The *bidūn* posed a particular problem for the police because many worked for the police. Before independence, rulers relied on badu as guards. When the police were regularised, these guards were incorporated into the new forces. As al-Taher writes, "the high-ranking officers ... had originally been soldiers employed to guard the Sheikhs 20 or 25 years before. When the Police Department was established, they became its original employees, and those in authority subsequently favoured them with promotion because they knew them personally and were assured of their loyalty" (al-Taher 1995: 257). As Kuwait grew, and with it the need for more policing, the problem of staffing the force grew. A degree of Kuwaitisation occurred as foreigners were replaced by nationals. In the 1950s, for example, Kuwaitis took over the Baluchi watchmen's duties (al-Fahed 1989: 52). The government offered incentives: Kuwaitis entered at higher rank, with higher pay and received more promotions and educational opportunities (ibid. 90). But few Kuwaitis were interested in joining except at the highest levels, and not always then. In the police, as with the rest of the bureaucracy, the 1960s and 1970s were years of massive hiring, and police recruiting had a hard time competing with other public-sector jobs available to Kuwaitis. Even the Kuwaiti officers were said to be sons who could not find success in other ventures (ibid. 280). But for the *bidūn*, without Kuwaiti nationality, the job offered obvious advantages.

Many *bidūn* were badu, belonging especially to the Shammar and 'Anayzah tribes. In the late 1950s, many began settling outside the old city wall in large numbers, with the Emir's encouragement. A 1959 aliens residence law formally exempted tribal members from residency rules governing other foreigners but did not grant them citizenship. Urban Kuwaitis did well in these years; the *bidūn* – poorer, uneducated, disenfranchised – had fewer choices. Lacking citizenship, they could not legally own businesses. While educated *bidūn* entered the professions, others went into the police and military. Their incorporation seemed a natural extension of their historical role as the Emir's guards, and disinterest in the ideological concerns of the era (mainly

Arab Nationalism) provided a certain distance between them and the groups they would be called on to control. This ethnic policing is not unusual in the Middle East (or indeed in the Third World) nor is reliance on badu, who form, for example, the historical core of Jordan's police (Enloe 1980). Many *bidūn* saw this work as their best chance for full citizenship; in the meantime, the job gave them access to the free housing and other services otherwise available only to Kuwaitis. But citizenship proved to be a moving target. In the following years, even as leaders held out vague hope of citizenship, the government repeatedly amended its citizenship laws, making it increasingly difficult for *bidūn* to qualify.

In 1968, with the restructuring of the Interior Ministry, a law was passed requiring that police be citizens (al-Fahed 1989: 230). At first, the law was applied loosely. Birth certificate holders – that is, *bidūn* without passports but allowed to live in Kuwait – retained their jobs, but with heightened uncertainty (ibid. 89). In 1974, after the government established a new police college, it officially stopped accepting *bidūn*. The problem, however, lay in replacing them. A 1983 decree, issued at the height of concern over the Shi‘ah, reorganised the Interior Ministry, adding several new General Departments. However, "in order to staff these departments more men were needed. There were fewer native Kuwaitis available so there was an extensive recruitment of Bedouins" (al-Ebrahim 1992: 245–6). And so the practice continued, but on a case-by-case basis – if men seemed loyal, had a long history of service or were married to a Kuwaiti.[20]

Still, the noose was tightening. A 1981 law had reopened registration for *bidūn* for a second time, but cases were heard by secret internal bodies of the Interior Ministry without appeal (Human Rights Watch 1995: 13–14). Few received citizenship. In 1985, the government, which for years had issued vague promises of citizenship while simultaneously tightening the requirements, changed its official policy virtually overnight. *Bidūn* were now declared illegal residents, subject to deportation. Different forces drove this policy shift. The first was the culmination of efforts to create a Kuwaiti national identity over the previous two decades. This identity had emerged in large measure in response to a fear of being overwhelmed by expatriates. But to be Kuwaiti required non-Kuwaitis. The grey area had to go. Second, the government, largely as a result of its crackdown on the Shi‘ah, had learned that it could use a degree of force, as long as it did not use it against every group at once. Third, the Interior Minister must have believed that the *bidūn* could do little in response (which was true) and that the police could do without them. That was less clear.

In 1985, the government began applying the 1959 Residence Law to the *bidūn*, stripping them of most of their previous benefits and rights. The government stopped enlisting them as officers.[21] In July 1986, the Interior Minister announced to the National Assembly that he had received 63,211 applications (not counting dependants) for citizenship from *bidūn* who believed they qualified. He told the Assembly that he believed that 90 per cent of them were lying (Human Rights Watch 1995: 13). In 1986, the government restricted eligibility for travel documents used by *bidūn*, then announced that all public and private employees lacking valid passports risked losing their jobs. Between 1987 and 1990, thousands of *bidūn* were fired for failure to produce passports. For those who remained, life became increasingly uncomfortable. The Interior Ministry denied them renewal of drivers' licences. It banned them from public schools and instructed private schools not to enrol children without proper residency papers; universities had to do the same. The many professional and cultural associations were instructed to dismiss them, and most did. Again, however, people serving in the army and police were usually allowed to keep their jobs as well as travel, drive and send their children to state schools. On the eve of the Iraqi invasion, the overwhelming majority of the rank and file of all branches of the police were still *bidūn*.

The Iraqi invasion of 1990 accelerated the crackdown. Two days after the invasion, Ṣaddām Ḥusayn created the Provisional Free Kuwait Government, made up entirely of *bidūn*, Kuwaitis having refused to work with the puppet government (Aarts 1994: 20). In September 1990, Iraq ordered all non-nationals in Kuwait to join the Popular Army under penalty of death. Those who could not produce evidence of military registration were imprisoned. Many *bidūn* joined, some voluntarily, some not (Human Rights Watch 1995: 23), and this registration became the basis for collaboration charges later.

Things worsened for the *bidūn* after the occupation ended. The Shammar and ʻAnayzah tribes, to which many belong, extend over parts of Iraq (as well as Syria and Saudi Arabia). Their association with Iraq now made them part of an "external" problem. Kuwaitis treated them as a generally suspect class. All the *bidūn* who worked for government were dismissed *en masse*, retrospectively from 2 August 1990, though a few were then re-hired. Those who had fled were not allowed to return; others (by one estimate, 10,000) were deported (Lawyers Committee 1993: 31). The courts issued some deportation orders, but most were administrative orders from the Interior Ministry with no appeal (ibid.). Those remaining in Kuwait faced increasingly difficult circumstances. Their uncertain status left them vulnerable to exploitation. In the years leading up to the invasion, *bidūn* areas, among the poorest, were already subjected to frequent security sweeps, detentions and summary expulsions (typically by leaving the *bidūn* at the Iraqi border). After liberation, security service surveillance increased (Human Rights Watch 1995: 12). Some efforts were made in the following years to sort out these people's status. The Assembly amended the citizenship law clarifying which *bidūn* were eligible for Kuwaiti nationality and the steps necessary to regularise their status. In 2000, the Assembly passed a law requiring them to register with the government, but of the estimated 110,000 *bidūn* (down from 220,000 before the Gulf war) only 8,000 did so.

The police and military moved, but more slowly, to limit the *bidūn*. In 1993, the government had banned them from the military and begun replacing those serving (USDS 2001: 10). By May 1995, the government said that 25 per cent of the 20,000 soldiers were *bidūn*, down from a pre-war level of nearly 80 per cent (Human Rights Watch 1995: 30). Police policy ran parallel. The Interior Ministry created an Executive Committee to examine the issue, but continued to find it difficult to recruit qualified Kuwaitis. So, again, many *bidūn* remained in the police but in a state of uncertainty. In 2000, the Director General of Police Affairs even announced that *bidūn* police officers need not worry about dismissals (*Kuwait Times* 11 Mar. 2000). Meanwhile, new job opportunities opened at the bottom as the government pressured them to join the state security forces as informers (Human Rights Watch 1995: 31).

The *bidūn* issue placed the police as an institution in a curious position, requiring them to police most heavily the very community from which they had long recruited. The *bidūn* in the police could not have welcomed this task, yet they were unable to resist or subvert it, so tight was the Emir's control over policing. They were now defined as external enemies, even if they were in the police (where they were also blamed for the post-invasion increase in police crimes).[22] Labelled foreign, but for the most part with nowhere to go, tainted by association with Iraq, the *bidūn* were in a precarious position.

The Islamists

Islamist groups in Kuwait had been growing steadily since the 1970s when the government encouraged and often subsidised their organisations. As Ghabra argues, when the government closed the National Assembly in 1976 "it reached out to those who were not critical of their decision. This marked the beginning of an informal, undocumented government alliance with the then passive, non-radical, and non-political Islamic forces in Kuwait. The government rewarded the Islamic Social Reform Society (*Jamā'at al-Iṣlāḥ al-Ijtimā'ī*), which had not condemned the dissolution of Parliament, by appointing its chairman, Yūsuf al-Ḥajjī, to the position of Minister of Awqāf" (Ghabra 1997a: 60). In the following years, Islamists expanded their networks in mosques, neighbourhood organisations, the government bureaucracy, Islamic banks, charitable organisations and the university and professional associations. In the 1980s, they shifted their recruitment efforts away from disaffected members of the old urban elite and towards urban families outside the merchant class and towards the settled badu concentrated in the outer suburbs (outside the wall). Once compliant, the Islamists now began publicly articulating positions at odds with the Emir, calling for full application of the *sharī'ah* (in Kuwait restricted largely to personal-status law, i.e. family and probate law), segregation of sexes at Kuwait University and other changes. By the 1990s, they fell into roughly three camps: the Islamic Constitutional Movement (*al-Ḥarakah al-Dustūrīyah al-Islāmīyah*) associated with the Muslim Brotherhood (*Ikhwān al-Muslimīn*); the Salafīs (with two wings, the Islamic Salafī Group, *al-Tajammu' al-Islāmī al-Salafī*, and the Salafī Movement, *al-Ḥarakah al-Salafīyah*); and a third looser grouping of independent Islamists, mostly badu. Often joining with Shi'ah Islamists, the Sunni Islamists now openly opposed the government in the National Assembly.

The Islamists were a clear political threat, but the Emir did not want to attack them in a way that made him appear insufficiently pious. He also faced the same dilemma with the Sunni liberals: treating as foreign an opposition group that was clearly Kuwaiti. Stressing the groups' ties to transnational Islamic organisations was complicated by the strains that had emerged during the invasion between Kuwaiti and other Islamist groups. So the government moved against them, but hesitantly. In the 1999 election, it cracked down on tribal primaries and sacked several *imāms* who had protested the Emir's May 1999 decree (later reversed by the Assembly) granting women suffrage (see the al-Mughni and Tétreault chapter in this volume).

The events of 11 September 2001 gave the government the opening it needed to do what it had learned to do in the past – define the opposition as foreign. A number of Kuwaitis with ties to local Islamist groups belonged to al-Qā'idah, some fighting in Afghanistan (a few ending up at Guantanamo Bay). The government, insisting that those involved in al-Qā'idah were "not Kuwaitis", denationalised them if necessary: when al-Qā'idah's spokesman, .Sulaymān Abū Ghayth, a Kuwaiti national, appeared on al-Jazeera, the government stripped him of his citizenship. State security reportedly detained dozens of Kuwaiti nationals (in addition to non-nationals) suspected of links to al-Qā'idah, holding them incommunicado and without charge (Amnesty International 2002). It began listening more closely to Friday sermons. It also began scrutinising and closing dozens of unlicensed Islamic charities, to the delight of liberals who had long called for this, removing the many collection boxes from public areas (*Financial Times* 25 Nov. 2001, *Le Monde Diplomatique* Jun. 2002).

The Emir now had an arsenal of working responses to deal with dissent. To keep the opposition at bay, he relied on a Kuwaiti nationalist discourse that defined anyone disloyal as foreign. Dissent, whether Shi'i, Islamist or *bidūn*, was externalised and recast as a job for State Security. Threats to public order more generally would remain the concern of the regular police. The result was a dual system of policing: harsh for expatriates and those political opponents defined as part of a foreign problem, more benign and orderly for those defined as loyal. The police entrusted with the latter task were intended to seem neutral: they could not appear to be defending a particular order (when the Social Reform Society called for establishing a religious police to patrol every neighbourhood, the government proposed allowing women to become regular police officers). Behind the police was the vast power of the state, surveying and shaping in even more apparently neutral and innocuous ways: through provision of welfare and social services, health and education.

Conclusion

Policing at its core consists of two very different functions: maintaining general order and maintaining a particular order. Maintaining general order is the visible and primary task of police everywhere. The daily work of Gulf police, like any other, consists largely in the mundane tasks of public safety. The police thus control traffic, mediate disputes, prevent and investigate crimes and apprehend criminals. Their job is to maintain general public order and this is largely what they do. What is striking about the police in Kuwait, compared to other states, is the degree to which the regular police actually spend their time in tasks related to maintaining general order. They are not found plotting coups, as in Qatar, enforcing dress codes, as in Saudi Arabia, or using excessive force, as in so many states, to protect the regime.

This outcome occurred, first, because Kuwait's police did not emerge originally to handle regime-threatening internal dissent. As a result, it never developed the ability or inclination to rely heavily on force. The dissent that accompanied its birth came from ruling family members and merchants: two groups with whom the rulers were able to form and institutionalise accommodations. Because the result was stable, and because Kuwait was not a central administrative concern for Britain, Britain was content with this situation and did not intervene more directly, as it did in Bahrain. The relatively benign public policing was sustained by the transnational nature of the opposition the police faced in their formative post-independence period: the influx of large numbers of expatriates. For the few dissident expatriates, specialised security forces were employed, but for everyday control of foreigners, the government relied not on its new public police force but on private Kuwaiti citizens. The *kafālah* system gave daily control of foreigners to individual households and employers.

Thus for foreigners, two very different systems of policing emerged: one informal and low-tech, the other formal and often very high-tech. State Security forces acted only when the system broke down visibly (as with the occasional labour riot) and then, having restored order, left. When serious dissent appeared among Kuwaitis, the problem, however indigenous (Shi'i, Islamist), would be recast as foreign and assigned to State Security. Either way, the regular police were left free to handle public order. Consequently, Kuwait's police officer corps were able to remain committed to professionalism through a fiction it shared with the regime, that all of Kuwait's important internal problems were really external problems. The rhetoric of foreignness helped the government to police general order.

This rhetoric of professional public policing protected not only the visible general order but also the specific order, the regime in power and the interests and values of those supporting it. This kind of policing, protecting the regime from its enemies, is a normally invisible task, but occasionally becomes visible simply because when something goes wrong, the police are usually the first on the scene. When a cache of arms is discovered that could belong to smugglers or to dissidents, the regular police investigate; when a sudden strike occurs, a crowd turns angry, or a bomb goes off, it is the regular police who arrive first. But for the most part this political purpose is hidden behind the visibly neutral job of keeping the traffic moving and the buildings guarded.

The police protect the particular order not so much by use of force but as part of the panopticonic state, the general order that masks the particular, which they played an important role in creating. Indeed, the arrival of the police signalled the emergence of permanent public order, a radical departure from past practice. While the police, with their uniforms and cars, were a very visible symbol of this order, they could not maintain it alone. To maintain continuous order required the energy of the entire state. Behind them, monitoring and maintaining general order invisibly is the vast modern apparatus of bureaucracy. Where rulers once policed nothing with regularity, they now police everything. The State Security forces are the new badu retainers: they arrive, set things right and leave. But the expansive state and the concomitant permanent public order remain.

CHAPTER 8

GENDER, RELIGIOUS KNOWLEDGE AND EDUCATION IN OMAN

Mandana E. Limbert

This chapter examines two intersecting processes in the activities of a young women's summer study group in Bahlā, a town in the interior (*dākhilīyah*) region of the Sultanate of Oman.[1] First, it illustrates how teachers defined and invoked different forms of education in the construction of a shifting religiosity. Criticising new state schools and invoking both local practices and the well-known history of study circles among Ibadis (the branch of Islam prevalent in Bahlā), teachers and students articulated their admiration for religious authority and knowledge. Arguing that the new schools had purposely worked to produce secular citizens, the young women insisted that religious knowledge must be pursued independently – and through "traditional" education – lest they "forget" or not even learn what it means to be good Muslims.

Second, the women's study groups in Bahlā reveal the ways that these women and girls struggled with how to speak of themselves as specifically gendered and sexual beings. The recognition that particular kinds of religious practices and religious knowledge would help them become "good women" ultimately worked towards self-definition. The authority vested in these young women from their own education and their deference to the continuation of a religious tradition does not translate, however, into what many feminists might recognise as "liberatory" discourse or practice. Although the women felt that they were entitled to demand space outside their homes for their classes, for example, much of the discourse within the study groups revolved around limiting their own and other women's movements. I explore this tension between entitlement and limits, focusing on the ways it emerges in discussions about appropriate womanly modesty and intellectual respect as well as bodily categorisations and rules.

Modern mass education

It is no surprise that education has become the focus of debates about the socialisation of proper religiosity, womanhood and the changes in Oman over the last 30 years. Official Omani publications and foreign commentators continue to herald the dramatic increase in "modern" (non-Qur'ānic) schools since the 1970 *coup d'état* when Sultan Qābūs bin Sa'īd ousted his father, Sultan Sa'īd bin Taymūr, as one of the most important developments in the last three decades.[2] Histories and newspaper articles about Oman rarely leave out proud references to the increase in schools.[3] On a local level too, men and women often mention the construction of schools as one of the primary changes in Oman. While many young people acknowledge the importance of this change, they also question the implications of this kind of schooling. They are proud of their training and abilities. At the same time, however, they are confronted with tensions surrounding their status in the social hierarchy as well as with challenges of maintaining the values of "traditional" knowledge and practice.

Anthropological research on education in the Middle East has tended to focus on the specifics of traditional teaching and learning in Qur'ānic schools and more advanced seminaries (e.g. Eickelman 1978, 1985, Fischer 1980, Wagner 1982) or, inspired by Foucault (1977), on "methods of ordering" in schools in British and Ottoman colonial contexts (Mitchell 1988, Messick 1993). For the most part, these scholars focus on one system or the other. Some, however, note how in particular contexts, schooling systems have changed and, sometimes, how they influence each other. Messick, for example, notes the internal transformations of traditional schooling in Yemen (Messick 1993: 102), and Spratt and Wagner (1986) have discussed the transformations of Qur'ānic schools in Morocco with the introduction of modern education at the beginning of this century and the formation of the national education system after 1968.

Focusing on policies and philosophies of Islamist movements, Roald (1994) outlines the different ways Islamist intellectuals in Jordan and Malaysia have discussed education. While these intellectuals insist that Islamic learning and teaching comprise both everyday experience and particular schooling practices, their policies centre on formal schooling, where most demand the "integration" of different schooling styles such that all fields of a "modern" school would be "approached from an Islamic point of view" (Roald 1994: 59, 94–5). Although those running the women's study groups in Bahlā also considered it essential that modern schools conform to "Islamic points of view", they were, unlike the groups that Roald describes, much less opposed to what they saw as traditional schooling. While the educational philosophies of the movements that Roald examines argue for modern schooling, which would teach and be based on religious principles, in Bahlā the young women were much more inclined to praise what they considered to be traditional education.

In fact, these young women expressed respect for the older generation, at least older men, when it came to religious knowledge. Unlike in countries where independence movements of the 1950s and 1960s were tied to secular nationalist languages and ideologies, the older generation in this part of Oman was generally seen as religiously righteous, supportive of a theocratic state and opposed to the British-supported Sultan in the Jabal Akhdar war of the 1950s. This admiration, however, was complicated by gender dynamics. While many older men were respected for their devoutness, older women were often castigated for their "ignorance". Nevertheless, and despite this respect for older men, younger men and women, with their access to mass state schooling, have not only gained access to cultural capital that distinguishes them from the older generation, but are also asking different kinds of questions about themselves and their religiosity.

Education provides a source of authority and cultural capital, and it helps, as Messick (1993), Mitchell (1988) and others have illustrated, to produce notions of personhood. Eickelman (1992), in particular, has reflected on the implications of the introduction of modern mass education for religion in the Middle East and has suggested that this change is related to the emergence of new forms of religiosity and shifts in communal identity: a shift from experiencing religion through local symbols to identifying with particular, shared statements about belief and practice. Drawing from Eickelman, other anthropologists have analysed how the new institutions of schooling transferred religious socialisation from private to public worlds resulting in the formation of public religious discourse – public pronouncements of individual and collective religiosity (Fahy 1998, Starrett 1998). Although much religious socialisation has moved to "publicly" recognised sites of learning in Oman also, it has involved less a general move of religious discourse from private to public than the emergence of a certain *style* of religious discourse. In fact, what might be considered to be public discourse itself has changed in Oman. Focusing on the absolute limits of required and prohibited acts has taken priority over positions on inclusion and exclusion or corruption and righteousness.

Speaking of the construction of gendered subjectivities in religious education, Torab (1996) and Mahmood (2001) have argued that agency and resistance to patriarchy are not coterminous. My concern here is specifically with how, at an everyday level, mass education was related to the ways young women understood and expressed what it meant to be Muslim women, a question which extends from how they responded to state schools and their ways of seeing their responsibilities for upholding the integrity of a good home, to the necessity of studying and the ways they spoke of their bodies and sexuality. Their responsibilities, bodies and sexualities all became objects of scrutiny in the state schools, and the study group became a place where they criticised the new schools. At the same time, it became evident that these young women were struggling with a tension between the desire to be respected as politically active "public intellectual figures" and their responsibilities as "good women", bound to spatial and bodily restrictions. The tensions they faced were in part related to a growing sense that they needed to participate *in* religion, thus confirming the idea that religion is a distinct category of life and one that requires participation. There was equally a growing sense that they needed to draw the line between what constitutes "gendered participation" and "religion".

From father to daughter

It was no coincidence that 'Ā'ishah, a young woman from Bahlā, would be organising a summer study class. She was training to be a teacher at the Teacher Training College in Rustāq, a town on the eastern side of the Jabal Akhdar mountains, and was home for the summer holidays. I met 'Ā'ishah through her elder sister and her elder sister's husband, Hilāl, an English teacher in Bahlā as well as the co-owner of an agricultural supplies store. 'Ā'ishah's father, Jamāl, is the shaykh of their neighbourhood and an Islamic studies teacher in one of the Bahlā boys' schools. He had been a teacher before the introduction of mass schooling in the 1970s and continued to work in the new system. He had also been a teacher at the now-closed state-run alternative religious elementary school in Bahlā.[4] Teaching ran in 'Ā'ishah's family: from her father to herself and to her elder sister's husband.

Although many people saw teaching as a good job, several young men I spoke to complained about how it was no longer a desirable profession for them: there was neither enough money nor prestige in teaching. Hilāl, like many others, had a second profession in business. Male teachers at the new state schools did not command the same respect that Qur'ānic teachers and scholars once had. Young women, however, saw teaching as one of the most desirable professions, since they could gain money independently in a job where they did not have to worry about "mixing" with men. While scholarship and the pursuit of knowledge in general had not lost prestige in Bahlā, for men, teaching in the state school was simply another "job" that paid less than one might gain in business. For women, however, teaching provided a source of income in a respectable profession where their schooling could be put to good use. The main drawback for many young women was that they might not work in their home towns. If they came from a town with enough teachers, it was likely that they would be sent elsewhere. 'Ā'ishah was well on her way to entering the job market, but it was unclear where she would be teaching. The family tradition of scholarship and teaching, then, was being taken up not so much by the other men as by the young women.

This shift to young women meant, however, that 'Ā'ishah and her colleagues were also being challenged with the prospect of negotiating a role for themselves in the changing and gendered world of authoritative religious knowledge. For 'Ā'ishah, taking up this role meant demanding the same respect that had been accorded to her father and her brother-in-law; it especially meant being entitled to the access they enjoyed to places to teach and study.

A question of place

'Ā'ishah held her classes in her neighbourhood *siblah* or meeting room. Her neighbourhood, like most in Bahlā, was walled with close, mud houses, narrow alleys and neighbourhood gates, now always open. This *siblah* was a cement room next to the new town library in the courtyard just outside the entrance of one of the neighbourhood gates. The courtyard stood at the edge of the neighbourhood: it was not quite part of it, yet clearly attached. It hinted at a separation between a space of more "official" gatherings and the daily activities of the area, including social gatherings of men and women. The new library and the meeting room were two neighbourhood institutions distinct from other daily activities. They were also separate from the mosque. Some of the mosques in Bahlā used to have small libraries and schools either in or next to them. Until the early 1980s, most of Bahlā's Qur'ānic schools were set in rooms attached to mosques or held within mosques.[5] At the beginning of the 1980s, the Ministry of Islamic Affairs and Religious Endowments began building Qur'ānic schools in separate buildings on religious endowment property, corresponding to an approach to education as an activity distinct from prayer and parallel to "secular" schools outside the town walls.[6]

Siblahs are usually used for men's gatherings such as mourning ceremonies or speeches. The government also uses them for distributing monthly payments to widows, the disabled and the poor. 'Ā'ishah told me that she did not want to hold the gatherings in someone's house and, she said, as long as no one died, the girls could use the neighbourhood meeting room. She had tried to get permission to hold the classes at one of the schools, but this request had been denied. A male official from the Ministry of Islamic Affairs and several other town citizens held summer classes for elementary and high-school boys in one of the schools, but for some reason the men organising those classes had been granted permission and she had not. Why, she asked with a shrug of her shoulders. 'Ā'ishah's holding of classes, although in line with a general emphasis on the pursuit of knowledge in Oman, raised an institutional question of who would be willing to take responsibility for the "safety" of the girls and women and, more likely, for the content of their discussions.

'Ā'ishah's determination to hold the classes in a formal setting, ideally in the school building and by necessity in the *siblah*, and her refusal to host them in someone's house, was an indication of her self-conscious intention to break with the social roles and places usually reserved for unmarried, local young women and girls. 'Ā'ishah and her colleagues also assumed that if they held their classes in their homes, people, including the girls themselves, would not take their intellectual goals seriously, not to mention that they might be interrupted by young siblings, parents, grandparents or neighbours. The conceptualisation of a separate space for their intellectual endeavours suggested an idea of institutional education as necessary to learning. As part of a "complex" next to the library, the meeting room seemed a good place to hold the classes.

A struggle for space was not limited to the class. Six months earlier the town library next to the neighbourhood *siblah* opened. Besides private collections and the school libraries, it was the only library in town. It was more convenient than the school libraries because it was set within the town walls and open to everyone. It was a tiny room lined with bookshelves and filled with the usual list of Omani history books published by the Ministry of National Heritage, collections of *ḥadīth*, law manuals (*fiqh*), biographies of the Prophet and his Companions (*sīrah*s), dictionaries, literature and poetry, children's books, school textbooks and some magazines, as well as cassettes and video tapes of sermons. There were also folders with legal opinions (*fatwā*s) of Shaykh Aḥmad al-Khalīlī, the leading religious scholar (nationally sanctioned through his position as Grand Muftī) and research projects by local students on Bahlāwī scholars and Omani history. In the middle of the room was a plastic table and chairs that visitors to the library could use to write and read as they did at school.

The library was open for women three hours a week on Friday mornings, which, 'Ā'ishah said, was not enough time for all the women and girls who wanted to use it. Sometimes the tiny library got so full on Friday mornings that everyone had to stand, holding books up in front of them. 'Ā'ishah explained that she had written a letter to the organisers asking that they provide additional hours for women, but this request was also denied. On this occasion, her demand that more time be set aside for women to use the library was not really a question of who would take responsibility for the girls, but of transgressing boundaries expected of young women.[7]

The meetings

'Ā'ishah explained that she would hold her classes three times a week: Saturdays for Qur'ān, Mondays for *ḥadīth* and Wednesdays for Ibadi history from 8 to 10 or 10:30 am. Each Saturday, Monday and Wednesday for two months the group of approximately 25 girls met in front of the metal *siblah* door. Each morning, we shook hands and waited for 'Ā'ishah's younger sister to arrive with the key. I knew two of the girls from lower Bahlā, the other side of town where I lived, and recognised most of the others from the library: 'Ā'ishah told me they were from her neighbourhood. About 15 of the girls wore black *'abāyāt* (cloaks) over their dresses and black scarves covering their hair.[8] The other ten girls wore colourfully patterned dresses and scarves. Five of the 15 in black *'abāyāt* also wore black socks, but no one's face was covered. The different styles of covering marked not only modesty, but also the way in which the *siblah*'s place in town and the girls' activities there were perceived. Some of the girls wore *'abāyāt* any time they left their houses, others when they went to school or beyond the boundaries of their neighbourhoods; yet others wore *'abāyāt* when going to particular places such as the meeting room for a talk or class. The ways in which the women related to the spaces they were passing and going to partially dictated their mode of dress.

'Abāyāt come in many different styles, from the fashionable to the simple. All the young women and girls who wore *'abāyāt* to the class wore plain styles without sequins or sharp angles. Young women also wore overcoats to school in either black or muted tones, signalling a kind of professionalisation that older women did not evince. None of the girls wore these overcoats to the summer class, indicating that this was not *really* school. Although some of the girls wore colourfully patterned dresses and headscarves, none wore the shorter knee-length dresses and colourful trousers that are seen as "traditional" dress. 'Ā'ishah and her sister both wore the black *'abāyāt*, headscarves and socks. The socks are particularly important for identifying the degree of covering that a woman might consider religiously recommended (not to mention their unwillingness to engage in agricultural work). Changes in approach to dress and dress codes in Bahlā could be read as part of a generational shift in religious discourse more generally: whereas older women necessarily wore headscarves, younger women instead wore particular emblems to indicate their religiosity.[9] In addition to the differences in styles of religiosity, there was a mix of former servant and free families as well as girls from different economic backgrounds.

When 'Ā'ishah's sister arrived with the key, she would open the metal door and we would enter, following 'Ā'ishah and her colleague, Mawzah, to the one corner of the room where there were plastic mats. The *siblah* was a large room with a wall-to-wall carpet. There were two air-conditioners and several ceiling fans. 'Ā'ishah would put down the tape-recorder that she would sometimes bring, close the windows and turn on the fans and air-conditioners. The girls would sit in a circle with their backs to the long wall of the rectangular room and the low dividing wall that runs down the middle of the room. 'Ā'ishah and Mawzah would sit along the wall at the end of the room and I would usually sit on the other side of the circle, farthest away from the two teachers. Occasionally, I would sit closer to 'Ā'ishah and Mawzah because my tape-recorder would not always pick up their voices above the hum and whir of the air-conditioners and fans. Although the teachers did not assign a seating arrangement, the girls tended to sit in the same place at every class, usually next to the girls with whom they had arrived.

At the library the Friday before the classes began, I had seen 'Ā'ishah ask some of the girls whether they were going to attend. Her questioning had an air of pressure and it is possible that some of the girls attended the class as a result of this. In addition, 'Ā'ishah would say that the girls could improve their grades at school through summer study. In either case, because of an ethic of furthering their religious knowledge for its own sake or because they wanted to improve their grades at school, the girls would not be wasting their summer vacation if they attended. While 'Ā'ishah put some pressure on the girls, I doubt whether parents pressured their daughters to attend. I knew that the girls from lower Bahlā were responsible for watching their younger siblings and I suspect that this was the case with most of the other students. Parents tended to discourage their daughters from being away from home in the mornings when they did not have to be at school, especially since that was the time their mothers visited neighbours. The combination of self-motivation and peer pressure was evident in the girls' attitude towards and conduct in the class. Although by the end of the two hours, the girls would fidget and chat, they were, for the most part, very attentive and serious.

Instead of devoting the entire two hours to one of the three topics (Qur'ān, *ḥadīth* and Ibadi history) as they had planned, 'Ā'ishah and Mawzah usually spent the first hour on one of these and the second hour listening to taped lectures, watching videos, playing quiz games or simply giving lectures. Sometimes, however, they would discuss two of the main topics in one class and then spend the next class on a video or a lecture. There was not much general discussion, although occasionally 'Ā'ishah and Mawzah would ask questions about a particular issue that had come up. These were certainly "classes" in which students learned from teachers who lectured and controlled the stream of discussion and who sat at one end of the circle against the wall at the end of the room. The students were not expected to read on their own or arrive with questions in mind. These summer classes were thus similar to the state-run classes during the school year. Discussion was divided among the three topics like the religious studies classes in the schools, and the style of teaching – lectures, established questions and answers and memorised responses to well-known debates – all marked the teachers and students as participating in the new pedagogic style.

On the other hand, 'Ā'ishah, her colleagues and the students were also aware that they were in some ways pursuing a "traditional" education. The similarity between their basic practice of sitting in a circle, as opposed to the straight lines of the classrooms, and the oft-invoked representations of traditional scholarship were not lost on the girls. The fact that they were discussing religious issues, no matter the style of teaching or the particular issues raised, also connected these summer study groups to a particular past, when education necessarily meant religious education. As these young women and girls negotiated their relationships with different styles of schooling, they were also participating in the formation of a new religiosity in relation to their mothers and grandmothers as well as a new understanding of what it meant to be women in a world where they, as well as men, had the authority to interpret religious doctrine and demand respect for their interpretations.

Commenting on state schools

While the women were drawing, in practice, from different styles of education, it was clear that the teachers, at least, firmly believed that there were problems with the new state schools. On 14 July 1997, for example, 'Ā'ishah gave a 20-minute lecture on the history and dangers of the schools introduced in Egypt after the British occupation. Her lecture revolved around distrust of the Euro-American and, by extension, Egyptian education systems and respect for "traditional" religious knowledge. Her main argument was that the introduction of this "new" education was a colonial plan to diminish the role of religion and religious education. 'Ā'ishah began the lecture after the students had listened to a tape of another lecture by a Saudi man on the dangers of Western calls for "liberating" women in the Middle East. The connection between the new schools and the demands for women's liberation was clear, yet 'Ā'ishah pointed them out again in her own talk. Such demands for liberation, 'Ā'ishah noted, would cause the demise and weakening of the Middle East.

'Ā'ishah began by explaining how Egypt was the first Arab country to submit to the British and where the British installed "education" (*ta'līm*):

> In Egypt, at the beginning, the education was like ours: the system was of *makātib*, that is Qur'ānic schools (*madāris al-qur'ān*). With this system, the students would study everything. Then, there was also the glorious university of al-Azhar where those who graduated (*kharīj*) would become *imāms*, teachers or judges. If a family had a graduate from this university or mosque, his house would be well considered. The British government in Egypt had a minister who was responsible for education and who introduced government schools (*madāris ḥukūmīyah*). At first they didn't have schools like ours now. The name of the minister was Dunlop and he wanted to change education so that education wasn't only religious education; he was not open to Islamic education. He made education like ours is now.

Although 'Ā'ishah focused on Egypt, she compared the Egyptian system with the system in Oman. Moving from the past in Egypt, both before and after the introduction of the new schools, to the present in Oman, which she used as a point of reference to explain the types of schools she was describing, she suggested connections between the two places. While discussing Egypt, 'Ā'ishah marked a linear trajectory from Qur'ānic to "new" schools. In reference to Oman she at first seemed to imply that the two systems co-existed. As the lecture continued, however, it became clear that 'Ā'ishah was arguing that while there might be Qur'ānic schools in Oman, religious knowledge and practice were in danger of decreasing, just as had happened in Egypt. The education system was, in fact, too similar to Egypt's to be reassuring.

By referring to the British in Egypt, 'Ā'ishah was also commenting on how colonial governments had worked to make religious knowledge less important in the Middle East, by both rendering religious education tangential to education and tying the question of development to women's rights. With the British colonial government in Egypt, 'Ā'ishah stated that, as graduates from new schools received higher salaries than al-Azhar graduates, religious studies became an elective and the Egyptian dialect (*lughah miṣrīyah*) rather than "true" Arabic (*'arabīyah ṣaḥīḥah*) became the language of schools. It soon became evident, however, that she was not restricting this discussion of the decline of religious knowledge to Egypt. 'Ā'ishah made the point about ignorance in Oman directly. She said that if she asked any of the girls present in the room a historical, religious or cultural question, none of them would be able to answer because of their inadequate education. In other words, although some of the issues that she raised about the Egyptian education system might not apply to Oman, there were still problems with what students in Oman were learning.

The focus on Egypt pointed to the possibility that Oman was colonised not only by Euro-American powers, but also by Egypt. Many of the teachers and doctors in Bahlā and throughout Oman were and continue to be Egyptian. Irrespective of a shared religion and language, and, at times, a shared politics, 'Ā'ishah's condemnation of Egyptian education spoke directly to the presence of Egyptians in Oman's schooling system. Animosity between Omanis and Egyptians in Bahlā was hardly hidden: many women openly stated that they would much rather go to an Indian doctor than an Egyptian, be taught by a Sri Lankan than an Egyptian and be neighbours of a Bengali worker than an Egyptian. Later in this lecture, however, 'Ā'ishah also recognised that many of the shopkeepers in the Bahlā market were Indian, which led her to comment on how they have different and un-Islamic morals and how women should stay away from the market where these shopkeepers work. The un-Islamic morals of Indians could be similar to the un-Islamic morals of Egyptians.

'Ā'ishah's distrust of the new school system and the literature, religious or otherwise, that students read, was reflected also in the books that she had the students bring to class and the ones that she relied on to teach. When 'Ā'ishah mentioned the text she was going to use for the *ḥadīth* class, I asked if it was something that she had learned from school. 'Ā'ishah answered with an emphatic "no"; the text was from her father's library. The knowledge she was going to be passing on to the young students was something that belonged to the "traditional" world of her father's generation, the generation of religious knowledge unmediated by state interference. Even though her father had become a teacher in the state religious schools that were now closed and in the regular state schools, he represented for her and for the rest of the community the religious knowledge and education of a previous age. 'Ā'ishah was continuing the respect for these that she saw as pervasive in the local practices of her father's youth. But more was also in play: the respect and authority that her father was accorded would now presumably be accorded her.

'Ā'ishah's relationship to the new schools was, of course, ambiguous. Despite her criticisms, she was studying at the Teacher Training College and, furthermore, the students in her summer class were all students at the new schools during the September to June academic year. Ā'ishah's insistence on using the school to teach this class and her maintenance of the pedagogic methods of the new schools complicated her criticism of the new state system. 'Ā'ishah employed the methods of teaching that she had learned there. She was neither denouncing the system outright, nor chastising the students in the class for attending state schools. Rather, she was warning the girls about the possible future of religion in Oman as well as suggesting how the girls could maintain their religious integrity through their further self-education. Becoming good Muslim women demanded that they be aware of the dangers of the educational system and of their responsibilities as inherently powerful women. It was thus clear that the girls should, on their own, join study groups such as this one to further their own intellectual goals. They must recognise the benefits of the "old" system and complement their education with older values and knowledge. Religious education and knowledge must continue in order for Islamic values to be perpetuated. Clearly, 'Ā'ishah was caught between shifting social hierarchies and nostalgia for "traditional" knowledge, between the tensions arising from a desire to maintain the values and knowledge of the older generation and the authority emerging from her own new status as "educated".

For their part, the students did not all approach religion and religious education in the same way. Some of the students were more "advanced" in their abilities to recite the Qur'ān than others; some more readily answered the questions that the teachers raised. In addition to their "abilities", the students also had differing attitudes towards religion and education, some of which was marked by their dress codes. While many agreed with the way that 'Ā'ishah outlined the responsibilities of women, some also considered her style too restrictive. As the girls were responsive and considerate, this attitude was not necessarily apparent in the class.[10] In terms of the lecture on education, however, it was one that the students would have heard in different forms before, in lectures in town, on cassette-tapes and even, perhaps, in school. The issues and questions that 'Ā'ishah raised in her lecture were common enough to be "common-sensical".

Circles of knowledge: the North African legacy

In Bahlā, the girls were not only expected to be "good Muslims", but also "good Ibadis". The study circle or "circle of knowledge" (*ḥalqat al-'ilm*) in Ibadi history was one way the girls were connected to their shared identity. The girls should not only be trained in "real Arabic", the language in which God revealed Himself in the Qur'ān (and which, as 'Ā'ishah noted in her lecture, was corrupted in the Egyptian school system), but should also learn about the differences between their and other interpretations of Islam. For the most part, Ibadis – and these young women were no exception – tend to stress how similar they are to other Muslims. Discussions of differences do emerge, however, and in recent years have become intense, especially when Ibadis have felt accused of being heretics.[11]

The young women of Bahlā thought it important to define both what made their approach to Islam distinctive and what made their project of study a continuation of a tradition of scholarly endeavour. In a lecture on 13 July 1997, for instance, Mawzah explained how "people" misunderstand Ibadism and accuse Ibadis of accepting anyone who believes in God as a "Muslim". Trying to define what Ibadism is, she was only able to say what it was not, however, and to point vaguely to a connection with the Ibadis of North Africa. The efforts to define and make connections were critical nonetheless. She mentioned that although Ibadis are "moderate", which she defined as "loving people", they always have problems with other groups when they go to Mecca and Medina. Moreover, touching on the early study groups in Baṣrah as part of the establishment of Ibadism, Mawzah affirmed the importance of study circles and knowledge in Ibadism.

In order to understand the teacher's initiative better, it is necessary to mention briefly the tradition of circles of knowledge. The practice of gathering small groups of students in study circles is a popular and continually invoked practice of "traditional" Ibadi scholarly life. According to Ennami (1972: 61-4) and Grossman (1976), these circles derived from the original secret study gatherings, or *majālis*, of Ibadis in Baṣrah at least from the end of the Umayyad rule in the eighth century. They became more established during that century under the leadership of the second Ibadi Imām, Abū 'Ubaydah Muslim bin Abī Karīmah.[12] Baṣrah was the centre of the Ibadi movement at the time and young men would study with Abū 'Ubaydah or other scholars to become missionaries, spreading the message to North Africa, Yemen, Ḥaḍramawt, Khurāsān and Oman. These Ibadi missionaries would, in turn, establish schools or study groups for interested Muslims or soon-to-be Muslims. While these gatherings were first established to ensure the safety of the community and the continued transmission of Ibadi knowledge, they later became a place of refuge for students, a kind of hostel or college with rules for behaviour and organisation.[13] Still later, as the story goes, the *ḥalqat al-'ilm* became a political and judicial organisation or council in the Maghrib that replaced the institution of the Ibadi Imām.[14] This story of the gatherings and the spread of Ibadism with an emphasis on serious study is often repeated in Omani accounts of the history of Ibadism.[15]

Although Omani Ibadis, like those of North Africa, did not always have Imāms, it seems that Omanis did not form *ḥalqat al-'ilm* political councils as occurred in North Africa. Wilkinson notes that whereas in North Africa "the institution that eventually emerged to replace the Imām was the circle of the learned, the halqa[,] in Oman the position was much more fluid. There were always ulema present with a degree of open authority and the most important of these might have a pre-eminent influence" (Wilkinson 1987:162). Perhaps one of the reasons that this institution was not established is that in Oman, the Imāmate was considered to be in the state either of manifestation (*ẓuhūr*) or defence (*difā'*) rather than in a state of secrecy (*kitmān*).[16] Despite the difference in institutional histories, many Omanis are aware of North African practices of hostels and councils. At the beginning of the twentieth century when the famous North African Ibadi scholars Muḥammad Aṭfiyyash (d. 1914) and Sulaymān al-Bārūnī (d. 1940) travelled to Oman, they solidified contact between the two communities as well as a shared literature, bringing more attention to work such as 'Abd al-'Aziz al-Thamīnī's (d. 1808) influential book *Kitāb al-nīl*.[17] Not only did al-Bārūnī visit Bahlā,[18] the *Kitāb al-nīl* was popular in Bahlā too: one of my neighbours once mentioned how in the "old days" people often read it. This was the very book that another study circle, established during my fieldwork, was reading.

The participants in this other study circle consciously modeled their meetings on the Ibadi tradition, starting from the name they used to describe the group, *ḥalqat al-'ilm*. Unlike 'Ā'ishah and Mawzah's summer class, I was unable to attend this group as it was restricted to men. One of the participants, Khālid, with whom I often discussed matters of Bahlāwī history, explained some of what they did, however. He said that there were about six men who would meet in the evenings and read a particular book, taking turns in the circle to read. They would meet in a small apartment building where one of the apartments had been converted to a school for boys, rivaling the Qur'ānic school 25 metres away. Since this school, unlike the Qur'ānic school, would cater to students beyond first grade, the organisers had received official permission to proceed with the classes. When I asked who the leader of their study circle was, Khālid said there was no leader, only someone who would "comment" (*yifassir*). As the members would take turns reading, someone would raise a question and the group would discuss the point or defer to the commentator. Khālid's emphasis on the egalitarian character of the group, on the fact that there was no "leader" or "head" of the group, signaled a difference with the women's class. Certainly, while these men called their reading group *ḥalqat al-'ilm*, there were differences between their group and the rules and practices described by various North African and medieval scholars. Nevertheless, this *ḥalqah* should be understood as resonating, in some ways, with the earlier gatherings.

While 'Ā'ishah's study group seemed far from the specifics of the Baṣrah and North African *ḥalqat al-'ilm*, she, her colleagues and the students were aware of the connections between their quest for knowledge, their potential moral authority and the rich and long history of study circles. 'Ā'ishah's class was neither simply a beginner's Qur'ān class in which the students only focused on recitation, nor a gathering of equals who learned from each other, as with more advanced groups. 'Ā'ishah recognised that, while drawing on both kinds of education, her classes also resonated with, and were drawing their authority from, a political and scholarly Ibadi tradition dating to early Islamic times and practised in towns as far away as central Algeria. In fact, the emphasis on continuing this tradition was, paradoxically, tied to the emergence of the new state schools.

The state schools

At the same time as 'Ā'ishah and her colleagues were critical of the new schools and were oriented towards continuing a tradition of Ibadi scholarship, they were also replicating the methods of the state schools. The first modern state school for girls in Bahlā, the Ā'ishah Riyāmīyah school, opened in upper Bahlā in the early 1980s. At first, girls were divided by approximate age in several classes and taught the basics of writing, reading and arithmetic. Some of the girls had attended Qur'ānic schools and possessed writing and reading skills. When I was in Bahlā, there were four girls' schools in town, all outside the town walls either in the suburb of Ma'mūrah or in Jumāḥ.[19] The 12-year school system was divided into three sections: six years for primary (*ibtidā'ī*), three for elementary (*a'dādī*) and three for secondary (*thānawī*). At the time of my fieldwork, the Ministry of Education was reforming the school system and, in particular, parts of the curriculum. Most of the textbooks for English, science and mathematics were complete and the schools had begun to introduce some of them. It was unclear when and whether there would be reforms in history, social studies and Islamic studies. Although the reforms seemed to be extensive, the style of teaching and the division of subjects were expected to remain the same.

At the time of my fieldwork, students from grades one to three kept the same teachers throughout the day, and the teachers would divide the day into subjects according to a national academic schedule. After the third grade, teachers would teach particular subjects, moving from one classroom to the next. In the last two years of secondary (or high) school, the students divided between those who elected, and were selected, to study humanities and those who specialised in the sciences. The better students went to the science division or, at least, this was the assumption of the teachers and school principals. Students also assumed that the better students went to the sciences, although many thought that it was harder to do well in the humanities. While some of the textbooks were different for the two sections, the Islamic studies textbooks were the same. Islamic studies was mandatory for all students from first-year primary through to third-year secondary or, in other words, from first to twelfth grades. The twelfth-grade religious studies textbook was divided into two parts, one for each semester. The first semester textbook was itself divided into sections on the Qur'ān, *ḥadīth*, *'aqīdah*, *fiqh*, *sīrah* and the economic system. The second semester textbook was similarly divided into sections on the Qur'ān, *ḥadīth*, *'aqīdah*, *fiqh*, *sīrah*, economic system and social system.[20] The paucity of references to Ibadi history in the textbooks was indicative of concerns about Sunni-Ibadi relations in Oman. While some Sunnis complained that the textbooks assumed that Oman is necessarily Ibadi, Ibadis said that the textbooks were very vague and only emphasised a "generic" Islam. For the women's study groups in Bahlā to focus one section of their studies on Ibadi history, therefore, indicated their desire for specific attention to their distinctive religious ideologies, practices and histories – features, according to them, that were insufficiently emphasised in the religious studies classes.

As for the method of instruction, emphasis was on lecturing and, from the first grade, students' (both boys and girls) abilities to engage in direct questions and answers: students were expected to answer teachers' questions as directly and quickly as possible. Teachers asked questions and students raised their hands, hoping to be called on to answer. As the teacher called on a student, he or she stood up and attempted to "shoot back" the correct response. In the more advanced classes, the students remained seated, although they too were expected to respond directly and quickly. Students were sometimes verbally reprimanded if they paused or filled in the pauses of their answers with "umms". In the classes I observed, students who were called on were sometimes unable to answer the question or recite the memorised phrase: it was as though some of the students were pretending that they knew the answers by raising their hands, but were expecting that they would not be called on. This way the teacher might assume that the students knew the answer. As the classes averaged between 30 and 35 students, the students could count on often slipping through unnoticed. If the student did not know the answer, the teacher would ask if someone else wanted to try and, again, the students raised their hands. This would continue until a student answered correctly.

The emphasis on direct questions and answers demands what linguists call a perfect "adjacency pair" (Levinson 1983: 303, Schegloff and Sacks 1973), whereby a particular question requires and expects a particular response. In this case, it is important both that the response is composed of a certain sequence of words and, further, that it not have any interludes or "holds". While in everyday interactions strict adjacency is, as Levinson points out, "too strong a requirement" for the coherence of conversation, the concept of the adjacency pair is appropriate in these cases. Since there is a limited number of acceptable responses, including those that are dismissed because they are prefaced with a delay, such as with an "uh" or "umm", the students are trained to answer as succinctly and directly as possible.

In addition to direct questions and answers, schoolteachers in Oman employed another method, encouraging students to engage in a topic – a method similar to "high involvement repetition strategies" (Tannen 1989). Teachers began an utterance, then slowed down and raised their voices slightly before the end of the utterance, which keyed the students into finishing the phrase themselves. In the state schools as well as in the summer classes, some or all of the students would shout out the last words of the sentence in unison. This method was particularly effective after the students had heard the phrase or topic already. The students would have already been familiar with the phrase either because they would have read the chapter with the teacher in class before or because they would have had to complete their homework, which usually consisted of copying out verses from the Qur'ān or *ḥadīth* in their textbooks and then answering a series of questions at the end of the section. Sometimes the teachers made a statement and then repeated it, slowing down near the end so that the students could finish it. The students were expected to repeat the sentence they had just heard. These two methods of engaging the students in the class material – direct question-and-answer adjacency pairs and high involvement repetition strategies – were distinct from the modalities of teaching in the more "advanced" study circles.

In many ways, 'Ā'ishah's study group was unlike the classrooms of the school year. The students were less formal with the teachers, there were no grades, they all sat together in a circle on the floor and the students only focused on religious education. At the same time, however, there were clear similarities in terms of the style of instruction and the content of the lessons. The classes were divided between Qur'ān, *ḥadīth* and Ibadi history as distinct categories of religious knowledge. Although the style of the classes both invoked the traditional approach of the *ḥalqat al-'ilm* and, in some ways, replicated the assumptions of the state schools, 'Ā'ishah and her colleagues made their goals for organising these classes manifest. It was clear that their objective was to rescue religious education from its formalised context, even devaluation, and to make the students recognise that they could study Islam outside the confines of the new schools.

Good women

In the lecture about education in Egypt as well as throughout the whole summer class, 'Ā'ishah also discussed what it meant to be women and where their strengths and responsibilities lay. In the lecture discussed earlier, she had criticised notions of "liberation" by arguing that this demand was intricately tied to development politics, which would weaken the cohesion of Middle Eastern society. But the "problems" that the girls were supposed to be having and to require "liberation" from were not really problems at all. They were distractions, but distractions that could eventually sap the strength of Omani culture. Religious issues were the only serious problems. Ā'ishah argued that "problems" about "women's rights" appeared to acquire prominence precisely because Western policies are based on the knowledge that women and girls in Islamic countries are the foundation of the society and essentially powerful. God gave women, 'Ā'ishah implied, an inherent power to control men through their emotions. This strength, she told the students, is well known and one that the Western powers attempt to use to their advantage. They try and make Muslim women weak by making them un-Islamic, as in Egypt. Beware, she said to the girls, that the same does not happen here in Oman. The way to prevent this happening, the way to protect the Islamic world, is for women to study, to learn about Islam and Islamic behaviour. Knowledge is critical.

In constructing a forum for exercising their authority, for demanding respect and expounding on their religiosity, 'Ā'ishah and Mawzah also referred to women as sexual beings. A frank acknowledgement that women have sex and that men can be sexually interested in them was part of the discussions in these groups. It was suggested that avoiding places where men spend time is one of the ways of preventing illicit interaction: Muslim women become corrupt because they "go out"; or that at least is one of the ways that their corruption becomes visible. In truth, the problem is not "going out" itself but, rather, where one goes: *sūq*s and, by extension, shopping centres, 'Ā'ishah reminded the students, are the most vile places. Going to the *sūq* is not like going to the hospital, she argued; going to the *sūq* must have no other purpose than to see men. Why else would a woman go there? Everything she needs, she can ask her male relatives to get for her. The acceptable places for women to go are limited by the fact that mixing with unknown men is necessarily shameful and prohibited. By way of contrast, going to the hospital to visit sick friends and relatives maintains women's seriousness of purpose.

'Ā'ishah's brief discussion of "going out" hints at two significant tensions in her project. First, in her lecture on Egyptian education, 'A'ishah briefly noted that "in the past", in the time when women were respectable, women would study at home. 'Ā'ishah's voice lowered as she said this, mumbling the phrase to the point of near unintelligibility. One wonders if, at that moment, she recognised that her quest for public approval and authority clashed, at some level, with her vision of women's acceptability and religiosity. In fact, 'Ā'ishah quickly recovered and stated that "these were places for gathering for girls; it was OK". The teachers' desire for public approval, from both men and women, boys and girls, meant organising the classes in the schools or in the neighbourhood meeting rooms. However, this desire conflicted with the teachers' ideas about movement and limits. Second, this discussion of "going out" also hints at tensions between these young women and their mothers and grandmothers. As part of the highly structured social world, women visit each other every day in Bahlā. Women are often on the street, walking from one house to another. "Going out", therefore, also refers to the women's visiting networks and patterns.

In the class, 'Ā'ishah and Mawzah spoke about women's responsibilities in terms of strengthening the Islamic world, but also with regard to their sexuality. 'Ā'ishah's admonition to women and girls who "go out" stands less on the assumption that they might be attracted to men, however, than that men might see them and attempt to make advances. Women who "go out", then, are enticing men, even though they themselves may not be especially attracted to them. Yet, while women may flirt and attract, the object ought to be allurement, not the women's own intimacy or pleasure.

Menstruation was also an important subject of discussion. In a lecture in July, for example, 'Ā'ishah's style was matter-of-fact: she was discussing a biological topic with serious implications for ritual practice. 'Ā'ishah spoke about types of blood, from women's monthly cycles to bleeding after giving birth, as well as about the different consistencies of blood and the way blood smells. This taxonomic and legalistic style of speaking about women's bodies was markedly different from the way older women spoke when they convened in their neighbourly groups. Whereas knowledge about sex and sexualised bodies was transmitted and constructed through teasing and jokes in these older women's social gatherings, in the class women's bodies were principally legal entities. Although women in the neighbourly gatherings would sometimes tell each other what to do, what was appropriate in terms of religious norms, such reflections on appropriate practice were restricted for the most part to the bare essentials. In the study group, by contrast, bodies became objects of wonder where "blood descends from her" (*dam yanzil minhā*). For 'Ā'ishah and the class, bodies were objects of biological and legal fascination, regulated and categorised in order to maintain religious and ritual purity.

Conclusion

Through the formation and discussions of this summer class, some of the difficulties and tensions facing young women in Bahlā became apparent. On the one hand, these young women respected the way that religious knowledge was part of what it meant to be a Bahlāwī and Ibadi in the past. Many of the women felt that the dramatic changes in Omani society in the last 30 years had resulted in the loss of former religious values and awareness. The tradition of religious scholarship and the transmission of religious knowledge were, according to this idealised vision of the past, an integral part of Bahlāwī life. On the other hand, however, the young women's authority to interpret and discuss, as well as their conclusions, sometimes conflicted with older men's expectations and, particularly, older women's practices. As these young women sensed that they must participate in the formation of a public, religious good, they also considered that their participation should be through their education. Yet it was an education that was largely circumscribed by a "classroom" and focused on defining what is and is not Islam, what is and is not Ibadism and what are the prerequisites of being a good Muslim woman. While drawing from a general sense that religious scholarship must be maintained, these young women shifted what "education" meant: education and knowledge must be "useful", it must take place in sites designated for learning and it must involve the defining and articulating of absolute precepts. Just as education was required for being gainfully employed, it was required for being properly religious.

The debates and concerns of these young women were directed not only towards colonialism, Egypt and the broader Islamic world, but also specifically towards their understandings of local social practices. From their positions as "educated" individuals and using the language of devotion, these young women opposed some of the social and religious practices of their mothers and grandmothers. Although not usually stated directly, this opposition nevertheless appeared in comments about movement, place, talk and the use of time. In 'Ā'ishah's lecture about "going out", while she acknowledged that women can go out to visit the sick, she was ambivalent about what it meant to enter spaces that could be predominantly male, such as the street. While the streets of the town were not in fact predominantly male, they were, in some ways, an ambiguous place where the dynamics of male/female relationships were constantly played out. Avoiding such ambiguous spaces was a priority for 'Ā'ishah and her friends.

In addition, the young teachers were also concerned about what older women did when they convened. Part of 'Ā'ishah's determination to have the classes outside the house was tied to her concern that they would not otherwise be taken seriously. Despite her approval of women who studied at home, 'Ā'ishah acted on the idea that gatherings at home could not be serious.[21] The home was certainly safe in terms of providing security against the ambiguities of gender relations.

However, it did not provide the proper context for ‘Ā’ishah’s desire to be respected as a local intellectual. This lack of seriousness of purpose was no small matter. It was reflected in her view that “useless” (*ghayr nāfi‘*) talk is a sin that requires repentance (*tawbah*). With this brief comment, ‘Ā’ishah touched on many of the tensions in Bahlā: her tainted Euro-American/Egyptian education gave her the authority to make such comments and to act upon them, to start a study group that hoped to define what is right and wrong. But, at the same time, it put her at odds with the older women, who, according to ‘Ā’ishah and her colleagues, walked through streets and visited each other, wasting their time and engaging in pointless activity. The possibility that the older women discussed religious matters, although not in the same ways, were caring for the sick or were monitoring each other’s activities did not seem to mitigate the criticisms.

‘Ā’ishah’s opposition to the socialising practices of the older generation was related to her form of religiosity. Religion was not simply part of being a good person in the world. Rather, religion in general, and Ibadism in particular, required classes, specific definitions and lectures, study and concentration. Religion was based on defining, categorising and lecturing. It was a religiosity that stood apart from that of the older generations, who were less concerned with defining absolutes or, even, who they were. ‘Ā’ishah tended to begin by defining rules, rather than the goals of religious precepts that should be related to specific circumstances and contexts.

These generational tensions were also entwined with gender dynamics. The authority of the young women to discuss and interpret religious texts at times conflicted with their ability to achieve the recognition and respect they expected. Not finding a classroom and only being able to use the library for a few hours every week are two examples in which their relations with young men became salient. Through these tensions and negotiations, these young women were, in some ways, structuring and confronting a new discourse. Although hardly going so far as to reconceptualise doctrine, they were nonetheless questioning the limits of popular calls for returns to a scholarly tradition. Indeed, they were drawing from several styles of religious knowledge and education as well as a common political language to create a place for themselves. This new discourse was not only elaborated, but also reproduced. At the same time, however, it was as though the young women had not found the right language to make their interpretations fit their context. The language of distinction and tradition, of respect and superiority and of rejection and acceptance was not quite adequate for explaining the dynamics and limits of the world around them.

CHAPTER 9

POLITICAL ACTORS WITHOUT THE FRANCHISE

Women and Politics in Kuwait

Haya al-Mughni and Mary Ann Tétreault

In the summer of 1998, the Minister of Social Affairs and Labour appointed two women, Khawshar al-Ju'ān and Dr Nūrīyah al-Khurāfī, to the board of the 'Ārḍīyah Co-operative.[1] Liberal, that is, non-religious, women's groups hailed the decision as an "unprecedented pioneering step" and called for more state support for women's political rights (*Arab Times* 8 Aug. 1998). But what was perceived as a bold move towards bringing women into decision-making positions concealed more complicated political concerns and goals. State intervention was aimed at restricting the power of the elected board and controlling the society's budget, not only how it was spent but also how large it would be. In recent years, several co-operative boards have been criticised for unfair high pricing – and for losing money. What is interesting in this context is that the government expected Khawshar and Dr Nūrīyah, upper-class women from elite merchant families, to be both willing and able to get the 'Ārḍīyah Co-operative under control.

Although excluded from direct political participation either as members or as voters electing members of the National Assembly (parliament), Kuwaiti women play a significant role in national politics. Part of the reason for this apparent anomaly is that political parties are illegal in Kuwait. In consequence, as we discuss below, organised political activity is carried out in an array of ostensibly "non-political" institutions and organisations, including the private sphere of the home. In and outside the home, Kuwaiti women have been instrumental in the expansion of political Islam and thereby have contributed to the current balance of forces in the national parliament. Women also contribute to the stability of Kuwait through their role in the family where, lauded by the government as the "mothers of future generations", they are active participants in the reproduction of culture and traditions. This symbolic image of the mother, rather than reducing the power and influence of women as has been the case in so many other societies (Ranchod-Nilsson and Tétreault eds 2000), increases women's authority in the public sphere in Kuwait. This unusual outcome is due to women's perceived role as linchpins of national security and political stability.

We examine "politics" more broadly than simply formal political participation or, more precisely, acts of participation in electoral processes. Voting, campaigning and being elected are indeed important political activities and they help to define citizenship. However, exclusion from or denial of access to such practices does not imply lack of political influence or non-involvement in political processes. Women's participation in politics – as we attempt to show here – can and does take different forms, including involvement in social movements and political groups and serving in leadership positions in the public sphere.

Given this very real presence in the political realm, one well might ask why Kuwaiti women, so well educated and visibly involved in public life, are denied formal political rights. We argue that the lack of formal political rights is a function less of patriarchy than of the ensemble of antagonistic political interests that constitute contemporary Kuwaiti politics. The situation is complex. Many Kuwaiti women, perhaps even a majority, oppose women's political rights. In 1992, a petition signed by 300 women was submitted to the National Assembly, arguing that women should not have full political rights because it is against the principles of the Islamic *sharī'ah*. Yet the women opposed to women's political rights are not all Islamists, just as they are not all from tribal backgrounds. Moreover, not all Islamists are opposed to women's political rights. For example, two noted female Islamist leaders, Khawlah al-'Atīqī and Khadījah al-Maḥmīt, are visible and vocal supporters of women's suffrage.

State, women and gender politics

The foundations for women's role in the state were put in place during the rule of Shaykh 'Abdullāh Sālim (r. 1950–65), the first Kuwaiti Emir to channel oil revenues into distributive programmes. The rapid expansion of primary and secondary schools in the 1950s, and the establishment of Kuwait University in 1969 during the reign of Shaykh Ṣabāḥ (r. 1965–77), soon produced educated women ready to embark on paid employment and able to compete with men for jobs in the public sector. For its part, the state gave vigorous support and encouragement to the full integration of women into the labour force.

Conventionally seen as a drive for the "emancipation of women" that often is associated with modernisation, the education of women was a matter of national security for Kuwait (al-Sabah 1983). Two key trends had introduced a large number of foreign workers into Kuwait. The more important was the flood of oil revenues that began to pour into Kuwait in the early 1950s,[2] and their allocation to development programmes. The other was the establishment of the state of Israel in 1948, which created a flood of refugees – some of whom came to live and work in Kuwait. At that time, Kuwait had a very small population and, with the exception of the tiny merchant elite (some of whom educated their daughters as well as their sons), its people were mostly illiterate. Development projects, including the design and construction of infrastructure and the establishment of schools, hospitals and other social services, required the assistance of already trained foreign labour and management if they were to be accomplished rapidly. Most development jobs were filled not only by personnel from developed countries but also by skilled as well as unskilled labour from the Arab World, chiefly Egyptians and Palestinians. As Longva details in her chapter, within a few years, the influx of foreign labour made Kuwaitis a minority in their own country, and concern for the stability of Kuwaiti society and the security of the state was voiced by foreign as well as domestic observers (e.g. Daniels 1971, al-Sabah 1983).

The growing importance of foreign labour in the local economy was a particular concern for the government, which soon realised that the "need to increase the contribution of Kuwaitis to the total labour force ... cannot be achieved unless Kuwaiti women are encouraged to enlist in suitable activities" (al-Mughni [1993] 2001a: 63). Women responded to this need at all levels. The first class of engineers at Kuwait University included seven women.[3] Women went to law school and medical school, and majored in other technical fields. At the end of 2000, 82,306 Kuwaiti women were employed compared to 38,000 in 1989 (Kuwait 2001). About 49 per cent of employed Kuwaiti women are in professional occupations: teachers, doctors and engineers.

A number of women reached senior government positions. In 1993, Dr Nūrīyah al-Khurāfī was appointed president of Kuwait University. The same year Kuwait nominated its first female ambassador, Nabīlah al-Mullah, to represent Kuwait in Zimbabwe,[4] and a woman was appointed Managing Director of Administration and Economic Affairs in the state-owned Kuwait Petroleum Company (KPC). Also in the same year, the Emiri *dīwān* (the executive office of the Emir) named a woman as Director of Political Affairs. Kuwait's Under-Secretary of Higher Education is also a woman. However, all these influential posts have been confined to women from upper-class backgrounds or from the ruling family. Middle-class women as well as middle-class men are far less likely to achieve prominent positions.

Interestingly, men from tribal backgrounds resemble upper-class women in their limited but real ability to achieve positions of high visibility. This is because of the role each plays in class politics.[5] Elite women pose less of a threat to the dominance of upper-class men than upwardly mobile men from the middle class. Recruiting women from their own class allows the elite to fill vacancies caused by a shortage of qualified upper-class men and limits the encroachment of the growing middle class on their social and economic prerogatives. At the same time, a very few men from tribal backgrounds have also reached high positions. In one sense they are tokens, minorities among the upper echelons of the economy whose prominent positions are cited as evidence of the regime's openness to merit. But the bedrock reason for their high status lies in their intellectual and practical achievements. These men – and they are all men – have risen to their present positions because of their education and performance. A few have attained political power through class mobilisation, chiefly via "tribal primaries". These are clan procedures used since 1976 to consolidate tribal support for one or two candidates for parliament as a means of increasing their chances of election and, therefore, the likelihood that the group will enjoy direct representation (Gavrielides 1987, Tétreault 2000). Another path to upward mobility is a product of the mobilisation of religious constituencies into effective voting blocs (Hicks and al-Najjar 1995).

The Islamisation of Kuwaiti society became a policy of the government in the late 1970s, in response to popular criticism of the regime for having dissolved the parliament in 1976 and suspended a number of constitutionally protected civil liberties. Women were significant participants in the expansion of political Islam, not only because of their religious convictions but also their location in the public sphere. The women's organisations that the state had encouraged during the early 1960s to promote modernisation had, perhaps unexpectedly, proven to be a powerful tool for spreading Islamist beliefs. When the state moved purposefully to harness the Islamist movement and weaken the democratic opposition, it requested help from women as the guardians of national values. Appeals to women to preserve traditional values resonated especially strongly among recently settled tribal groupings whose families were given full citizenship as a means to dilute the voting power of urban constituencies. In 1981, the electoral law was changed, drawing new election districts and reapportioning representation to elect fewer legislators from urban and more from rural constituencies. Both trends contributed to the growing prominence of Islamists in the Kuwaiti parliament (Gavrielides 1987, Tétreault 2000).

Following the 1990 Iraqi invasion, Islamism became even more popular inside and outside Kuwait, a result of the relative security of the mosque as a meeting place during the occupation and the prominence of religious leaders in the Resistance (Tétreault 2000: 95). This contributed to the victory of Islamist candidates in the 1992 and 1996 elections, and produced parliaments that included first-term Islamist members prepared to challenge the regime and the secular opposition directly. Many confrontations occurred over gender issues. Islamists won important victories, the most significant of which was a law mandating gender segregation in Kuwait's post-secondary schools (Tétreault 1997, 2000; al-Mughni and Tétreault 2000).

Gender politics in Kuwait serves as a proxy for other kinds of group antagonisms. For example, gender discrimination was integral to the context in which increasing numbers of tribal men were granted formal citizenship and then enfranchised by the regime to bolster its power in what had been and continues to be an independent and often contentious parliamentary body. This history of political preference for tribal men over all women contributes to the ongoing antagonism between those men who perceive themselves as upholders of tradition and the women whom they see as dangerously modern. Economic uncertainty adds to this antagonism. The Kuwaiti economy began to falter following the crash of *Sūq al-Manākh*, an informal local stock market, in September 1982. It weakened further in response to declining world oil prices. Although oil prices subsequently enjoyed periods of recovery, pressures for economic restructuring, particularly following liberation in 1991, continue to fuel class antagonisms, some of which are managed by conducting them in the guise of gender conflicts (al-Mughni 2001a: 184, Tétreault 1999).

Family, politics and the rituals of sociability

Kuwaiti women, like women in other Gulf states, benefit from national endogamy and also from the key role of the extended family. As it is elsewhere in the Middle East, the family as an institution is extremely important in Kuwait where it is central to the social, economic and political spheres of life. So central is kinship to the political order that the head of state is symbolically conceived as the head of the national family. The Emir is often referred to as *bābā Jābir* by young Kuwaiti children; he is the father of the nation, the head of Kuwait's one united family (*al-usrah al-wāḥidah*). The state has invested a great deal of its resources to protect the "traditional" family structure from disintegration (al-Mughni and Tétreault 2000). Numerous conferences are held to warn Kuwaitis of the dangerous effects of divorce on children and society. Divorced women are penalised, with their right to social benefits substantially limited as compared to men in the same situation.

The state has entrusted women with responsibility for maintaining the family structure, and women from all social backgrounds have responded, accepting the role of repository of national identity, bearing symbols of the nation as they literally bear its children. They toil to preserve kinship ties through their organisations and daily activities. Since the early 1980s, women-only associations such as the Threshing Floor of Peace (*Bayādir al-Salām*) have sought to bring women to comply with their natural identity as mothers of future generations. These associations constantly remind women of their moral duties to strengthen family ties, to rear good children and to defend the traditions and customs of Kuwaiti society (al-Mughni 2000, 2001a, 2001b). They are not state-run, but as legal voluntary associations they are funded and licensed by the state.

The everyday lives of Kuwaiti women are also regulated by an orderly set of social rituals, all of which contribute to maintaining kin-based relations. This is more accentuated among the upper classes. Among these groups, women continue to perform *ziyārāt* (social visits) and submit to arranged marriages. Such social activities are political even if they take place in the private sphere. They sustain class relations and bring Kuwaiti families of a similar social standing closer together. Visiting follows a regular pattern. It is not confined to the kin network alone but also includes unrelated families of similar social status. In these informal gatherings, women exchange family news and make arrangements for their children's future marriages.

At the same time that the traditional family structure privileges men as heads of households, it paradoxically increases women's authority in the public sphere. As we noted earlier, upper-class women have reached senior public positions as a result of their families' location in the economic structure; meanwhile, the extensive interpenetration of kinship and public administration may hasten women's entry into the political arena as voters and candidates. One plausible explanation for the sudden decision of the Emir of Kuwait in May 1999 to grant women the right to vote and run for seats in the National Assembly was a desire to appoint female members of the ruling family to ministerial positions. The Gulf monarchies do not follow a fixed rule such as primogeniture for succession. Instead, their ruling families operate as corporate governors of their states (Herb 1999). In such dynastic monarchies, rulers are chosen by consensus from among powerful family members; others occupy strategic ranks in the state apparatus and the entire inner group rules together. Dynastic monarchies are strong because the family monopolises positions that otherwise would confer structural advantages and legitimacy on non-family members. This system allows some intra-elite competition for positions of power and authority while it also maintains a basic level of ruler competence, adding directly to the regime's security and indirectly to its legitimacy.

Women, voluntary associations and political groups

An important arena of political activity for women is the panoply of associational groups commonly known as public welfare organisations, which are authorised to collect and distribute *zakāt*. Law 24 of 1962 governs the activities of these organisations, which are limited to carrying out social, cultural, religious or sporting activities that benefit the community. The law prohibits them from engaging in "political" activity. Kuwaiti women participate actively in such organisations, ranging from women-only groups to professional clubs and societies whose members include women and men. Because they are organisations whose activities reach beyond the family to embrace explicitly political goals, despite the prohibition on overt political activity, these public-sphere groups fall under the rubric of politics as we conceive it in this chapter (see also al-Mughni 2001a: 122–3).

As early as the 1970s, women-only groups began to engage in political activities through association with men's political groups. The Arab Women's Development Society (AWDS) and Girls' Club (*Nādī al-Fatāt*) formed alliances with the Arab Nationalist opposition to promote women's rights. Hence, they campaigned and raised funds for liberal candidates to ensure their election to parliament. In the 1990s, the political activity of liberal women took new forms as they became concerned more with having an active political role across many issues rather than with merely working to gain citizenship rights for women. Hence, they became more actively involved in political groupings, perhaps trying to compensate for their exclusion from formal political roles by joining political alliances and becoming active members. The National Democratic Forum (NDF), a new political group founded in 1997, included six members of the Women's Cultural and Social Society (WCSS) among its 72 *mu'assisīn* (founding members). The NDF elected two of these women, Mūḍī al-Ḥumūd and Shaykhah al-Nuṣif, as members of its executive board. All these women are active members of the liberal WCSS.

This new female political activism was immediately visible during the first post-liberation election cycle. In 1992, women participated in unprecedented ways in the formal sphere of politics in Kuwait. Mūḍī al-Ḥumūd and attorney Badrīyah al-ʿAwāḍī were featured speakers at the campaign headquarters of Ṣāliḥ al-Yāṣīn, an independent candidate from the Rumaythīyah constituency. This event drew between one and two thousand persons, including scores of couples who listened to the speeches from their automobiles. Another woman who assumed an unprecedented public role in the 1992 election was Aymān al-Bidaḥ, who served as the campaign chair for Aḥmad Dayīn, the candidate of the liberal Kuwait Democratic Forum (KDF) in the Ḥawālī constituency. Women attended political meetings held by many urban-based candidates, although even KDF candidates found that they had to provide a separate tent for the women because so many male attendees objected to having women in the same tent as themselves. When Mūḍī and Badrīyah were scheduled to speak at Ṣāliḥ's *dīwānīyah* (social gathering), elaborate arrangements were made to ensure that women attending the event would be seated separately from the men. During the question-and-answer session following the speeches, the moderator made sure that the questioners called upon alternated between those raising their hands to speak on the women's side and those wishing to speak from the men's side (Tétreault 1993, 2000).

Women also continued to work from within the family in a number of campaigns, but 1992 brought some innovations here as well. The daughters of Sayf 'Abbās 'Abdullāh, an independent candidate running in the 'Ādilīyah constituency, had urged Sayf to take a strong public stand in favour of women's rights. Their outspoken insistence and enthusiasm angered their uncles, Sayf's brothers, who eventually forced them out of the campaign. Meanwhile, Sayf, a political scientist specialising in American politics, invited a member of the press to interview him at his home and photograph him with his family. A perfectly normal tactic to get a little free publicity when employed by US candidates for Congress, the appearance of the article, and especially the photographs, attracted negative comments from Kuwaitis who thought Sayf was wrong to breach the boundary between public and private life. Yet by 1996, when the next election took place, women's active participation already showed signs of having been normalised. A rally held in conjunction with a one-day women's strike brought more than 50 male participants to a gathering of several hundred women, and the women's tents at campaign *dīwānīyah*s throughout the city were far more populated than they had been in 1992 (Tétreault 2000: 213).

Islamist groups have also relied on women to help them expand their presence and influence in society by providing social services that attract mothers and children to their facilities. In the early 1980s, the two most influential Islamist groups in Kuwait, the Social Reform Society (*Jam'īyat al-Iṣlāḥ al-Ijtimā'īyah*), affiliated to the Muslim Brotherhood (*Ikhwān al-Muslimīn*), and the Islamic Heritage Society (*Jam'īyat al-Turāth al-Islāmī*), part of the Salafī/Wahhābī movement, established women's committees. Today, these women's groups are the most powerful in the country, with memberships far larger than those of the liberal women's groups. The activities of members of these religious groups are widely varied. Through their active role as *du'āh* ("callers" to Islam), Islamist women set up other religious women's associations, and conducted religious classes for women and summer camps for children, all of which helped them to recruit new members to the Islamist movement. Islamist female activists are also involved in raising money to support Islamic projects inside and outside Kuwait, where they assist in financing the construction of mosques, schools and orphanages. Their activities have benefited not only their organisations but also themselves, earning them respect and, for many Kuwaitis, confirming their status as moral leaders.

Although Islamist groups have long realised the utility of mobilising women to work in the political trenches, they do not include women among their decision makers. The highest position that a woman can reach is to be the head of the women's committee. Islamist women's political activism has been confined to the preaching of Islamic values (*da'wah*), and thus to transforming society from within. This has had, nonetheless, a significant impact on Kuwaiti society. The older – "feminist" – generation of women who continue to maintain a liberal lifestyle find their values being questioned by their own children who grew up during the period of Islamist revival, while veiling and observance of religious rites have increased significantly even among the upper and middle classes (al-Mughni 2001b, Ramazani 1985).

Women as participants in the national liberation struggle

Kuwaiti society excludes women from military service, but in Kuwait as elsewhere during times of crisis and national liberation struggles, it is women who often carry the burden of protecting and serving the community. Women were central actors in occupied Kuwait and were the backbone of the Kuwaiti Resistance. From the early days of the occupation, they risked their lives distributing underground newsletters urging Kuwaitis to remain steadfast, and they marched through the streets of occupied Kuwait to pledge their loyalty to Kuwait's ruling family. Iraqi soldiers opened fire on these demonstrators, killing Sanā' al-Fūdārī, a university law student, and injuring many others. But this brutal incident did little to deter Kuwaiti women from defying the Iraqi forces. Women used the mosques to distribute Resistance bulletins as well as to build support networks. They volunteered in hospitals, where they cleaned, scrubbed, nursed the wounded and brought food to staff and patients. They also took care of orphans and the handicapped, and organised regular visits to Kuwaiti prisoners detained in Iraq and Kuwait. At home, women cooked, cleaned, swept floors and took care of their children, providing them with a safe and supportive environment.[6]

Many Kuwaiti women also were actively involved in armed resistance. Because Kuwaiti men were regularly arrested and searched at checkpoints, it was women who risked their lives transporting contraband from place to place in the city, where the risk of encountering checkpoints was greatest. Like Algerian women during their struggle for national liberation, Kuwaiti women used their *'abāyāt* to cloak not only small-sized contraband such as medicines, money and documents, but also large "cargoes" of weapons and food destined for Kuwaiti families and Westerners in hiding. This last responsibility was life-threatening; simply being discovered harbouring a foreigner in hiding brought immediate death to Kuwaitis. Wafā' al-Āmīr and Su'ād al-Ḥasan were members of the "25 February" resistance group, and executed three dangerous missions: the Hassāwī Sūq explosion, the Riyad Street explosive attack and the bombing of the Safīr Hotel (al-Mughni 2001a: 154). This last mission targeted a delegation of senior Iraqi officers housed on the first floor of the hotel. Wafā' and Su'ād checked into the hotel using false identities and delivered the time-bombs to Ashraf Maḥmūd and Sālīm Abū Daghar, members of the 25 February group who were working in the hotel. The bombs exploded, killing several soldiers, but missed the delegation.

Other women engaged in unarmed resistance. Envisaging the difficulty of restoring oil production capacity after liberation if the Iraqis were to carry out their threat of setting fire to Kuwait's oil wells, KOC engineer Sārah Akbar secretly transferred detailed records from the company to her home, where she hid them in the false bottom of a wardrobe. When the Iraqis came to search her house, Sārah enlisted two nieces to pretend to be asleep in the bedroom with the wardrobe. The soldiers were reluctant to turn these young women out of their bed and made only a cursory inspection of the room before moving on.[7] The occupiers' reactions to women's involvement in resistance activities were often brutal and merciless. Female prisoners were subjected to beatings, electric shocks, rape and mock executions. Wafā' al-'Āmir, Su'ād al-Ḥasan and Asrār al-Qabandī were eventually arrested, tortured and killed. Their bodies were dumped on the pavement near their homes for their families to bury. Samīrah Ma'rafī, who volunteered as a nurse in Mubārak Hospital, was arrested in November 1990. She remains unaccounted for. Many other women suffered similar fates.

Women also engaged in resistance activities outside Kuwait. Kuwaiti "exiles" worked as members of official and voluntary organisations to locate and support other Kuwaitis marooned abroad by the invasion, and a few engaged in detailed preparations for their eventual return as part of the military and civilian liberation forces. Among the most important activities of exiles, both men and women, was to mobilise popular support for the Kuwaiti cause among the citizens of coalition countries. The most prominent woman in this group was Mūnā al-Mūsā, then an employee of Kuwait Petroleum International (KPI), who was working in London when Kuwait was invaded in August 1990. As a member of the Free Kuwait Campaign (FKC), a voluntary organisation that was not government sponsored (Tétreault 2000: 84), Mūnā worked with others in her group to monitor press coverage of the occupation. Before long, she found herself correcting misinformation and then moving gradually into the role of spokesperson. KPI staff helped Mūnā to prepare for her first few media interviews and soon she was the most readily identifiable Kuwaiti in Western Europe, an attractive and articulate representative of her country's interests, and arguably more effective than the public relations firm hired to do this job in the United States (Tétreault 2000).

Among the military forces liberating Kuwait in February 1991 were seven Kuwaiti women. Like a number of male Kuwaiti exiles in the United States, they volunteered and were accepted for military training at Fort Dix, New Jersey. One of these female soldiers was Lubnā Sayf 'Abbās 'Abdullāh, the daughter of Sayf Abbās, who was to be such a trial to her uncles the following year because of her activities in her father's campaign for the National Assembly. Lubnā's memories, recounted in September 1992, connect the resistance activities of insiders to the vicarious and actual experiences of exiles:

> We had two groups of volunteers who wanted to go back. They said women couldn't go. ... But I kept asking to join the army and they called me and said we only want a few women and we think you would be good. Training was exciting. It was hard. But we earned the guys' respect and it is very hard to earn Arab men's respect. In the end, they bragged that they were in the platoon with the girls. ... Everyone was gearing up for the air war and going back [to Kuwait]. ... I and Najāt al-Ḥusayn became the female members of the [Judge Advocate General's Corps]. They felt there would be atrocities committed against women and men couldn't interview them. I was inducted into the Kuwaiti military and attached to the US Army – I took my orders from the US Army. So I had to go for military training with [my sister] Layl, who was a medic. ... The day of graduation was the first day I cried since the invasion and the last time I ever cried in public. ...
>
> [The JAG team] got in before anybody else in our group. ... I arrived in a military plane at Kuwait Airport. It looked like Mars. And then I went looking for my mother's family and the next day Layl came. She was reattached to the war crimes documentation centre. We opened the centre but

> we were never there. We went out, house-to-house, in two-person teams. I canvassed Rumaythīyah where probably the highest percentage of martyrs were from and the highest percentage of atrocities. ... The war crimes testimony was so depressing. I would come home, break my fast – it was Ramaḍān – and file my reports. Deaths that didn't have to happen. It got to the point where Layl and our cousin could be on the other side of the house and I would feel cold and heavy and just think about all those people who died.[8]

The issue of women's political rights

In the aftermath of the Gulf war, the demand for the vote became a central issue in the Kuwaiti women's movement, providing common ground for an alliance between Islamist and liberal women activists. Suffragists invoked the heroic role of women during the Iraqi occupation as a justification for gaining political rights. They also employed a variety of strategies to win the vote, which included protest marches, press conferences and pressure on the National Assembly (al-Mughni 2001a: 180).

The most vociferous opposition to women's suffrage has come from Sunni Islamist groups. Unlike Shi'i Islamists, who support women's involvement in political life, Sunni Islamists claim that Islam restricts *al-wilāyah al-'āmmah* (leadership of the Muslim community) to men. The logical conclusion is that women have no moral justification for demanding the right to stand for office, since being a member of parliament is a form of governing and a woman governing is contrary to their version of Islam. All attempts made by liberal parliamentarians to extend political power to women were blocked. In 1992, a bill put forward by liberal Ḥamad al-Ju'ān granting women the right to vote failed to reach the floor for discussion. It was held up in the Assembly's Interior Affairs Committee, which was dominated by Sunni Islamists and tribalists. In the 1996 National Assembly, Sunni Islamists again blocked a women's suffrage bill, this one offered by three liberal parliamentarians, Sāmī al-Munāyis, 'Abdullāh al-Naybārī and Ḥasan Jawḥar. The bill was rejected unanimously by the Assembly's Legislative Committee, headed by hard-line Islamist Aḥmad Baqr, on the basis of a 1985 *fatwā* that had ruled that women were unfit for political life (al-Mughni 2001a: 176).

The hostility of Sunni Islamists towards women's suffrage cannot be explained simply in terms of patriarchy. Voting and contesting office have indeed become an integral part of male identity – sources of privilege that Kuwaiti men do not easily concede (al-Mughni and Tétreault 2000). However, this is not in itself a sufficient explanation for the Islamists' opposition to women's suffrage, especially given its utility to the achievement of their own political agenda. Indeed, their alliance with the tribalists on social issues may help us to understand their opposition. This alliance strengthens the Islamists' position in parliament and has, in the past, deprived the liberal forces of real influence.[9] Sunni Islamist groups, such as the Islamic Constitutional Movement (ICM), backed several tribalist candidates during post-liberation elections. These Islamist groups have attracted and found strength in the large numbers of badu voters newly enfranchised in 1981. Recently settled tribalists flocked to the Islamist organisations, assumed leadership positions and articulated a vision of an Islamic society that purports to mirror desert values and beliefs and has significantly shaped the post-war Islamic discourse (Ghabra 1997a). Segregation between the sexes, enforcement of a restrictive dress code for women, the prohibition of women from travelling alone unless accompanied by a *maḥram* (guardian) and amending the constitution to make the *sharī'ah* the only source of legislation constitute the core of the tribalists' demands. The prominence of tribal voters in so many legislative constituencies compelled even the most moderate political Islamists to embrace a restrictive interpretation of Islam rather than alienate a voting group that makes up more than 65 per cent of the Kuwaiti population (al-Mughni 2001a: 177–8). However, following 11 September 2001, and the terrorist attacks in Riyad in May 2003, the balance among parliamentary forces appears to be shifting (Tétreault 2002).

Also relevant is the power struggle between parliamentary conservatives and liberals, which intensified in post-war Kuwait. As we noted earlier, women's rights issues are a primary battleground on which Islamists challenge the legitimacy of liberal political groups. Sunni Islamists associate women's rights with Westernisation and secularism, and accuse liberals of waging a war against religion (al-Mughni, 2001a: 176–7) even though Shi'i Islamists do not draw this parallel and support the extension of suffrage to women. Despite their fragmentation, the liberal groups remained a potent political force in post-war Kuwait but, before September 2001, they were not numerous enough to overwhelm the combined forces of Islamists and tribalists. Since then, political and economic liberals have forged parliamentary coalitions with neo-liberal Islamists on economic issues such as privatisation (Tétreault 2002). However, it remains questionable whether they will be able to achieve similar coalitions with a different complement of Islamists to support women's political rights and, as we note below, many may not wish to do so.

Islamist opposition to women's suffrage is embedded in political platforms which promise Kuwaiti men that they will be able to find jobs in the ever-shrinking public sector through the return of women to the household, and thereby preserve male supremacy in a competitive environment where women's academic and professional achievements pose a threat to men's careers (Tétreault 1999). A newly developing coalition among political liberals and secularist and Islamist neo-liberals undermines Islamist association with this position, which in mid-2002 was occupied mainly by tribalist parliamentarians, both liberal and Islamist (Tétreault 2002). However, Islamist organisations continue to provide employment for bright male students and, as a result, a large number of young men continue to support Islamist groups. Islamist students are well represented among those elected to positions in student government at Kuwait University and work for Islamist candidates during parliamentary election campaigns.

The government and women's rights

The position of the government in these various struggles is ambiguous. In 1994, Kuwait signed the United Nations Convention on the Elimination of All Forms of Discrimination Against Women (CEDAW) but with reservations regarding several articles, including the right of women to vote and stand for elective political office. Thus it was a surprise when, on 16 May 1999, during a parliamentary suspension, the Emir issued a decree granting women full political rights. The decree was published after the dissolution of the parliament two weeks earlier, a decision taken in response to a protracted conflict over the alleged incompetence of the Minister of Justice and Islamic Affairs for failing to discover misprints in government-produced copies of the Qur'ān before the volumes were distributed. This was the third dissolution of a sitting parliament since the ratification of the Kuwaiti constitution in 1963, and the first to accord with constitutional provisions requiring a new election within 60 days. During the suspension of parliament, the Emir issued 63 decrees. The most controversial was the decree granting women the right not only to vote in parliamentary and municipal elections but also to stand for office. The decree envisaged female enfranchisement as taking effect by 2003, the year in which the next elections for members of parliament were expected to be held.

Several factors may have played a part in the Emir's decision to extend political rights to women. Most immediately, the women's political rights decree distracted popular and legislative attention from the government's poor performance in restructuring the national economy, resolving the debt crisis and dealing with national defence issues. This conclusion is supported by the large number of decrees that attempted to legislate the government's position on contentious issues ranging from privatisation to the reopening of domestic oil production to foreign participation. The enthusiasm with which the women's rights decree was greeted by many who opposed other government edicts suggests that the sudden interest in women's rights may have been a strategy to whittle away parliamentary opposition to the other decrees. A decree is nominally effective after publication in the official gazette, but one that is issued while the parliament is not in session must be approved by a simple majority of the members after parliament reconvenes. If a member could vote for this high-profile decree that was very popular in liberal constituencies, he could not reasonably assert a principled, i.e. constitutionally based, opposition to the others. Liberal members who might otherwise have supported the women's equality decree saw through this ploy immediately and a few, such as the speaker of the 1996 parliament, Aḥmad al-Sa'dūn, campaigned for re-election by vowing to oppose all the decrees (Tétreault 2000: 228).[10]

Structural factors also are likely to have played a role in the Emir's decision to use his authority to push Kuwait towards accepting women's rights. One is the government's relation to a political system in which virtually all forms of co-operation have disappeared. Repeated clashes between the government and elected parliaments throughout the 1990s made it difficult for the government to obtain needed legislation and to implement policies already in place, thereby hindering its economic reform efforts. Implicated in the decision to extend suffrage to women is the government's need to reshape the electorate as a strategy for changing the direction of Kuwait's domestic politics (al-Mughni 2001a: 174-5). Yet just what these changes would accomplish is not entirely clear. The inclusion of women in the political arena would more than double the size of the electorate, and some have speculated that the resulting loss of control by electoral intermediaries could benefit minority groups such as the Shi'ah, who make up 30 per cent of the Kuwaiti population, and small tribes unable to compete successfully against larger clans in the same electoral districts. However, both outcomes would also require redistricting and perhaps even changes in the number of persons to be chosen by each district (Tétreault 2000: 218-26).

Another uncertainty is the effect female enfranchisement could have on the power of *dīwānīyah*s. These traditionally male institutions are home-based gatherings. As Chapter 7 of this volume indicates, as a result of their private-sphere location, they have become important arenas for political activity, especially when others are blocked by regime crackdowns against public meetings and political debate in the press. Women are not welcome in most *dīwānīyah*s, even though a few women have started their own regular home-based meetings, and Rashā Āl Ṣabāḥ, a member of the ruling family, has hosted a mixed *dīwānīyah* for many years. *Dīwānīyah*s are prime venues for campaigning. But they can also be used to manipulate elections through the encouragement of campaign strategies, such as bandwagoning, and voting strategies, such as casting "one-eyed" ballots. Kuwaitis may vote for up to two candidates listed on their ballots, but by voting for only one the chance that the favoured candidate will be elected increases (Tétreault 2000). Yet diluting the voting strength of *dīwānīyah*s could limit the power of activists who work behind the scenes to promote candidates. At the same time, it could limit the influence of wealthy individuals who, operating behind a veil of secrecy, seek to control the results of elections in vulnerable districts by injecting money into campaigns.

Perhaps the greatest significance in this sudden decision to grant political rights to the disenfranchised female population is the utility of this group to the regime's future. On the elite level, Kuwait's rulers are concerned about succession, an issue that is widely rumoured to be under active consideration. Many among the ruling family's current ministers (including the Prime Minister) are old and some are also ill. Their problems are aggravated by the appointment of too many post-liberation Āl Ṣabāḥ ministers whose competence and honesty are questionable. This has led to intense pressure to appoint more competent ministers – a standard that continues to rise as more Kuwaitis from every social group demonstrate their substantive expertise and executive ability. If female ruling family members were to hold ministerial posts, the family would be seen as direct representatives of the interests of women and families throughout Kuwait, strengthening the regime's popular base.

At the mass level, women also appear likely to bolster the position of the regime because they are seen as exceptionally loyal citizens. A similar view of the badu prompted the naturalisation and enfranchisement of large numbers of tribal residents prior to the 1981 election, which marked the end of the parliamentary suspension imposed in 1976. Tribal voters were judged to be more supportive than urban voters of traditional governance and more likely to place loyalty to the ruling family over loyalty to "Kuwait" as a territorially based political concept (Tétreault 2000: 43–9). In this sense, they were thought to be "conservative". The regime hoped to "garner the badu votes for [the government's] own candidates" and also to undermine the power of the liberals by moving tribal values into the mainstream, a process that Shafeeq Ghabra calls the "desertisation" of Kuwaiti political and social life (Ghabra 1997b: 367). As we noted above, these new citizens confronted urban values with a potent combination of the desert's conservatism and Islamist populist beliefs, thus setting the stage for subsequent parliamentary impasses.

Kuwaiti women are presumed to be more conservative than Kuwaiti men as well. However, like the tribal voters whose ranks swelled the supporters of Islamists, the political choices of female candidates and voters may have a more complex outcome than supporters of women's suffrage in the ruling family might imagine. Despite essentialist views of women and their political behaviour, politically autonomous women, just as politically autonomous badu have already demonstrated, are likely to campaign and vote as their disparate interests lead them (Tétreault 2001). In consequence, expanding the electorate to include a large new population whose interests partly overlap and partly diverge from the current distribution of interests could reduce the extreme polarisation that has been such a prominent feature of post-war politics in Kuwait. To date, the National Assembly has shown itself unwilling to test any of these propositions. In November 1999, the women's political rights decree was rejected by the new parliament, first in a 41 to 21 vote on the original Emiri decree and then, on an identical bill drafted by members of the parliament, by a vote of 32 against and 30 in favour, with two abstentions.

The closeness of the second vote could reflect a significant shift in the liberal position. The liberals opposed all the non-fiscal Emiri decrees and, as a result, all were defeated. The shift in support of the parliamentary measure marked a strong departure by liberals in the 1999 parliament from the behaviour of their predecessors. Previously, parliamentary liberals did not fully support women's suffrage for fear that the preponderance of Islamist women among the female population would shift the balance of electoral forces to the advantage of the religious right. On the November 1999 parliamentary measure, however, they voted overwhelmingly in favour of equal political rights. Yet some observers are not sure that what we saw is what actually happened. Analysts such as political scientist ʻAbdullāh al-Shāyijī (personal communication) argued that the liberals voted strategically. They wanted to defeat the bill but still allow liberal and Shiʻi parliamentarians to appear to be women's rights supporters. This required that two of them abstain. This strategy maintained the appearance of a nearly even split, which suited economic and political liberals who did not want to be portrayed in the local and international press as opposed to women's rights, but who equally did not want the bill to pass. Aḥmad al-Saʻdūn and Ḥasan ʻAlī al-Qallāf supplied these abstentions, leaving observers with the impression that parliamentarians who would have voted against the measure actually supported extending political rights to women.

This ambiguity in liberal support is echoed in the population where the extension of suffrage to women is still a matter of concern to many liberal Kuwaitis. These doubters continue to believe that women's suffrage would shift the balance of forces in the electorate even further to the advantage of Islamist groups; they assume the majority of women would favour a "conservative" social and political agenda. Some support for this concern can be found in student-body elections at the university. More than 70 per cent of the student population is female and student council elections in which women participate consistently produce results favouring Islamist candidates and groups. Yet even this apparent harbinger of things to come should be viewed with scepticism. For example, as more badu girls are sent to the university by second- and subsequent-generation citizen fathers, their value as independent contributors to their natal families increases. This, in turn, may induce evolving attitudes towards women among tribal elements. Anecdotal evidence indicates that educated daughters of the tribes participate in some of their families' councils and contribute to decisions affecting their own lives. Given the results of educational opportunities for upper- and middle-class Kuwaiti women – upper-class girls gained enough self-assurance to doff their veils in the 1960s and middle-class women to lobby the National Assembly to end polygyny in the 1970s (al-Mughni 2001a: 83-9) – it seems premature to conclude that today's distribution of political loyalties among tribal women is set in stone.

Conclusion

Kuwaiti women are caught between the often contending demands of tradition and modernity, and part of their dilemma comes from the strictures embedded in the fabric of their society. The centrality of the extended family to the political order places an important value on women's domestic identity. It follows that they are honoured as mothers of the nation. Although this perpetuates women's subjugation to the traditional family structure with all its constraints, they also, by the same token, acquire public authority. But Kuwaiti women have also carved themselves explicit political roles, despite their continued exclusion from formal politics. They are integral participants in voluntary associations, social movement politics, pressure group organisations and political parties (even though formal political parties are banned, most opposition groups function as quasi-parties). Hence, women are actively engaged with not only women's issues, but also issues affecting society as a whole.

This is reflected in the political activism of Islamist women whose aim is to institute an Islamic social and political order. For almost two decades, these Islamist women played the role of *du'āh*, "converting" young women to Islam and extolling the virtues of a moral society in which the family exercises full control over its members. They succeeded in changing the direction of trends affecting Kuwaiti women by popularising the wearing of the Islamic veil and marginalising liberal feminist voices. It is not surprising that female Islamist leaders such as Khawlah al-ʻAtīqī and Khadījah al-Maḥmīt are now eager to join the suffrage movement. Having assumed moral agency and gained public visibility, these veiled activists no longer share with their male counterparts the vision of an ideal Islamic society in which women are confined to the domestic sphere. While they also support the Islamisation of society and the enforcement of strict moral norms by the state's police, a significant number of Kuwaiti Islamist women believe in the importance of women's direct political participation as they seek, in tandem with others, to establish an Islamic order (al-Mughni 2000).

The changing position of the government on the issue of women's political rights has sparked growing interest in the project among women from different social backgrounds, and also brought new vigour to the suffrage movement. Following parliamentary rejection of both women's rights measures, female activists filed six court cases against the Ministry of Interior for not allowing them to register to vote. Their intention was to force a ruling on the constitutionality of Article 1 of the Election Law that restricts the right to vote and stand for office to Kuwaiti men. Although all of these cases were dismissed on technical grounds before the end of the summer of 2000, many Kuwaiti women do not appear to regard this as a fatal setback. Rather, they continue to use their very real power in private and public life to agitate for full citizenship rights.

CHAPTER 10

MANAGING GOD'S GUESTS

The Pilgrimage, Saudi Arabia and the Politics of Legitimacy[1]

James Piscatori

> Even in the early years of this century the suffering of pilgrims did not end when they reached Makkah. Banditry, profiteering, and excessive taxation were common, medical and sanitary conditions outrageous. No such fortitude is required of today's pilgrims. The Saudi Government has invested millions of riyals in modern transport, shelter and hygiene to make the Pilgrimage as physically comfortable as is required in God's eyes. ... Less than forty years ago, the highest number of pilgrims recorded during a single Pilgrimage was a mere 108,000. Today the Pilgrimage is a miracle of faith and organization, the world's most astonishing peacetime logistical exercise. ... In the peak days of the pilgrim season, almost two million passengers land at Jeddah airport from all over the world. Many are illiterate peasants who have devoted their life savings to the journey. Some are men of wealth, and others know only poverty. Yet on the road to Makkah they are all joined in a common bond of devout servitude to God and obedience to the word of the Prophet, who said: "Know that every Muslim is every Muslim's brother. Nothing belonging to his brother is lawful to man unless it be given freely and with good grace. So wrong not yourselves ... " (Amin 1978: 21).

Each year vast numbers of Muslims travel to Mecca to participate in the *ḥajj*, the most highly charged ritual of the Muslim calendar. Fulfilling a primary obligation of the faith (Qu'rān 3: 90–1), many find spiritual solace in the seeming cosmopolitanism of the pilgrimage while also often engaging in the secular pursuit of business, diplomacy or status. The Saudi regime emphasises the pious Muslim aspiration to community and obliteration of rank, as represented by the diverse gathering and the pilgrims' common garment of simple white cloth. For the government, the pilgrimage is a self-imposed opportunity to demonstrate its paramount commitment to Islam and thus to certify its legitimacy. It is also a logistical and political nightmare that has often proved counter-productive for the custodians of the holy places. As a religiously charged, transnational force, the pilgrimage operates in a circle of contested meanings and control, complicating its patrons' quest for legitimacy.

Official narrative

The extended apparatus of the Saudi state – its bureaucracy, sponsored non-governmental institutions and directly and indirectly controlled national and transnational media – presents a uniformly self-congratulatory view of Saudi achievements. Three inter-related and general contributions, incorporated in the quotation at the outset of this paper, have been highlighted. The first and most prevalent is the provision of security. The contrast with the preceding, Hashimite, era was especially central to early claims to legitimacy, and contemporary accounts make clear that the Saudis were intent on emphasising the lax moral and security standards of late Sharifian rule.

A.J.B. Wavell's account of his success as an imposter during the *ḥajj* of late 1908 and early 1909 gives a sense of what pre-Saudi conditions were like. He depicted a Hijaz of rebellious tribes, complacent government, endemic robbery and murder, recurrent cholera epidemics, insanitary sacrificial conditions, fake beggars, harassing and corrupt *muṭawwifs* or guides, unscrupulous shopkeepers and camelmen, expensive but inadequate accommodation and filthy cafés (Wavell 1918: 74, 94–6, 112–13 and *passim*). It should be noted, however, that Wavell had a generally favourable opinion of Sharīf Ḥusayn, who appeared popular and worthy. The authorities understood that their "credit" depended on ensuring the safety of pilgrims, and to this end installed small forts on the Jiddah-Mecca road, regulated camel suppliers and often dispensed justice on the spot (ibid. 123-4, 155, quotation on 215). But these efforts were clearly inadequate, and the common sight of the armed pilgrim in this period was a vivid reminder of the government's ineffectiveness.

The English convert Eldon Rutter presents a contrasting view of the first Saudi-controlled *ḥajj* of 1925. In addition to the destruction of the tombs of the Prophet's relatives and Companions in al-Maʿlā cemetery in Mecca and at the Prophet's Mosque (*al-Masjid al-nabawī al-sharīf*) in Medina, he noted the decline in crime. This was due to the deterrent practices of the "merciless Wahhabis" (Rutter 1930: 165).[2] Not all were as sensitive as he was, for *Umm al-qurā*, the official Saudi gazette, reported that the Indian delegation of the Khilāfat movement praised the new-found security of the pilgrimage. Moreover, it urged ʿAbd al-ʿAzīz ibn Saʿūd to spare no effort in ridding the holy land of foreign influence (Foreign Office, E/4547/10/91 in Peters 1994: 360–1). It should be noted, however, that they did not endorse Saudi annexation of the Hijaz but hoped rather for an international settlement of the issue of control.

During the 1933 *ḥajj*, Lady Evelyn Cobbold approved of the King's ban on automobiles in the crowded and chaotic streets of Mecca and, in contrast with the prior "primitive" situation, particularly of the establishment of a clean and efficient hospital. The result was "perfect peace and absolute security which reign over the Hedjaz" (Cobbold 1934: 176, 196-7). She and David Chale, who made the pilgrimage in the mid-1930s, both depicted 'Abd al-'Azīz as exercising a firm but reasonable managerial hand, personally reviewing every application for a *ḥajj* visa from Westerners and normally insisting that they endure a long probationary period, part of it in Jiddah, before proceeding to Mecca itself (Rutter 1937: 132-3, 171-2).[3]

Saudi accounts routinely present Saudi pre-history in stark terms of lawlessness and irreligion: security in those days was only a "dream", and badu "plundering" was common. The stability that 'Abd al-'Azīz brought was an inestimable blessing, for it allowed the implementation of God's laws (Saudi Arabia n.d. a: 11, Islamic Center for Information and Development 2000: 79). As King Fahd emphasised in his welcoming speech to pilgrims in 2001, this in turn has ensured real security: "Each citizen, expatriate, pilgrim to the *ḥajj* and *'umrah* [minor pilgrimage] feels safe with regard to his religion, life, honour (*'irḍ*) and property" (*Majallat al-ḥajj* Apr.-May[?] 2001: 74). It is thus not surprising that "security and safety" (*al-amn wa-l-amān*) are now the standard that the government undertakes to provide for all pilgrims and, in its view, are among its proudest achievements (e.g. *Majallat al-ḥajj* Jun. 1996: 5, al-Makkī 1412 A.H: 153). Indeed, Article 24 of the Basic Law of Governance (*al-niẓām al-asāsī li-l-ḥukm*) proclaims that one of the state's duties is to provide this secure milieu for pilgrims to the holy places and to provide appropriate facilities and peace. To this end, at least 7,000 security personnel are deployed during the *'umrah* and *ḥajj*, most under the command of the Minister of the Interior (Saudi Arabia 2000a: 8, *Arabies* Jun. 1992: 62). In the more charged period of 1989, 13,000 police were on patrol and 73 video cameras were in use (*Mother Jones* Jul.-Aug. 1989: 18). In addition, directions from the *muṭawwifs*, as well as other official material, routinely invoke the Qur'ānic proscription on obscenity (*rafath*), iniquity (*fusūq*) and dispute (*jidāl*) during the *ḥajj* (Qur'ān 2: 197). They also remind pilgrims that "tranquillity" (*al-hudū'*) and respect for "the regulatory system" (*al-niẓām*) are "civilised conduct" (*maẓhar ḥaḍarī*) (Mū'assasat Ḥujjāj Turkīyah n.d).

During the *ḥajj*, Saudi television broadcasts a programme on *al-amn wa-l-amān*, produced by the Interior Ministry: "One of the essential pillars of Saudi security policies is to ensure the safety of pilgrims to the House of God, and to provide them with all the support necessary to conduct their religious duty of pilgrimage".[4] In other programmes repeated throughout the day, flattering depictions of Saudi security policy are presented against the backdrop of pictures of the Saudi kings, intercut with scenes of Mecca: "Since the unification of the Arabian Kingdom by the Āl Sa'ūd, the Kingdom has made every effort to keep and improve the security and safety of the two holy places. As the number of pilgrims has increased, the concern for safety has extended from the holy places to pilgrims' accommodation such as hotels, tents, apartment blocks (*abrāj sakanīyah*), tunnels, car parks, etc."[5] The important *khuṭbah* (sermon) at Mount 'Arafāt, following the example of the Prophet's farewell message at the end of the *ḥajj*, typically reminds pilgrims of their good fortune: "You came here today to a sacred place. It is safe and secure, and everything is available" (Wolfe 1993: 324). From the early centuries of Islam, political authorities have appointed the *imām* delivering this sermon.

A second theme focuses on Saudi munificence, leading to a massive expansion of the holy places themselves and improvements in the *ḥajj* infrastructure. Muslim rulers from far and wide have long expended great amounts of money on the central religious complexes of Mecca and Medina. Al-Walīd ibn 'Abd al-Malik, the Umayyad caliph (r. 705-15), decorated the door to the Ka'bah in gold, for instance, and in 1483, the Mamlūk sultan, Qā'it Bey (r. 1467-96), provided the bronze grill that covers the Prophet's tomb. Muẓaffar II (r. 1511-26) of the Gujarat Sultanate, who was known for sending personally transcribed copies of the Qur'ān to Mecca and Medina, built a hospice in Mecca and generously assisted poor travellers (Pearson 1996: 107-8).

Expansion of the *ḥaramayn*, owing to increasing numbers of pilgrims, has been an ongoing project from the time of the second caliph 'Umar (r. 634-44) in 638 and the third caliph 'Uthmān (r. 644-56), both of whom enlarged the Grand Mosque (*al-Masjid al-ḥaram*). The 'Abbāsid caliph, Abū Ja'far al-Manṣūr (r. 754-75), was concerned in the mid-eighth century to enlarge the area for the *ṭawāf* (circumambulation of the Ka'bah), and al-Muqtadir Billāh (r. 908-32) extended the mosque on its north side and constructed new walls and gates in 918/19. The Ottomans in the mid-sixteenth century carried out a major redevelopment that gave the holy places the form that the Saudis inherited. In 1571, 40-50,000 gold pieces were set aside in Istanbul for the restoration of the gallery of the Grand Mosque, and repairs in Medina probably amounted to 92,000 gold pieces at the end of the sixteenth century (Asad 1980: 286, Faroqhi 1994: 97-98). Sultan Aḥmad I (r. 1603-17) undertook the rebuilding of the Ka'bah itself, but the floods of 1630 exposed further weaknesses and a more extensive reconstruction was undertaken. Between 1848 and 1860, Sultan 'Abd al-Majīd I (r. 1839-61) added 1,293 square metres to the Prophet's Mosque.

At the time of the founding of the Saudi Kingdom in 1932, the Grand Mosque was able to hold no more than 48,000 worshippers at one time. In 1955, the government launched its first expansion project, enveloping the Ottoman mosque and quadrupling the size of the whole complex; it raised and covered the courtyard with white marble and added a second level for additional pilgrims. The surrounding area was "redeveloped" – to put it politely – and tunnels and culverts were constructed to guard against flash flooding. After securing an approving *fatwā*, the authorities built a two-tiered enclosure around the track of the ritual run (*sa'y*) between the hills of al-Ṣafā and al-Marwah that commemorates Hāgar's frantic search for water (Qur'ān 2: 153). Both hills are now incorporated in the mosque complex. The Ka'bah itself was shored up in 1957. Four hundred million Saudi riyals (SR) were paid in compensation to property owners whose land was confiscated, and the cost of the entire expansion came to SR800 million (approximately $213 million). The Prophet's Mosque in Medina underwent successive expansions, from 10,300 square metres before the Saudis to 16,500 square metres by the mid-1980s with the addition of spacious courts outside the mosque itself (Saudi Arabia 1993: 28–35, 44–6, *Majallat al-ḥajj* Aug.-Oct. 1999: 15–22).

The most ambitious reform project began in 1989. Over the succeeding ten years, more than SR70 billion ($18.7 billion) were expended on a vast expansion of both the Grand Mosque in Mecca and the Prophet's Mosque in Medina: "no expense has been considered too high and no effort too great" (Saudi Arabia [2000?]: 57). The former has nearly doubled in size and is now able to hold a million pilgrims; the latter has increased tenfold and is able to accommodate 700,000 congregants (ibid. 58–65, *Majallat al-ḥajj* Jul. 1997: 4–14).[6] Saudi publications are dizzyingly replete with facts and figures: numbers of escalators, air-conditioning units, marble flooring, chandeliers, new minarets and gates and ablution facilities, among other additions. Beyond Mecca and Medina, the Saudis have initiated a major redevelopment of the related pilgrimage sites of Minā, 'Arafāt and Muzdalifah, due to be completed by 2005, and have generally improved transport, utilities, communications and medical facilities. Fifty-four tunnels have been constructed, for example, to ease pedestrian and automobile traffic. In 1988, a $15 billion traffic improvement programme was begun.[7] Millions of tents are provided that are air-conditioned, fire-proofed and equipped with electrical outlets, and thousands of sprinklers, 50 feet apart from each other, constantly spread a fine mist at 'Arafāt in order to cool the pilgrims. A CNN cameraman called this a "5-star Hajj" (*Arabies Trends* May 2000: 68, Saudi Arabia 2000b: 12).

The Ministry of Ḥajj is proud of the fact that fibre optics, advanced computers and other high-technology resources are improving the administration of the pilgrimage. A sign of the times is that the passport of each pilgrim is now affixed with a trackable bar code (*shakl mulṣaq*) (*Majallat al-ḥajj* Feb.-Apr. 2000: 7-11, Jan.-Mar. 2001: 87-9), and an "e-ministry of ḥajj" is due to come into existence to facilitate the acquisition of visas and arrangements with hoteliers and local agents (*Arab News* 14 Mar. 2003). According to the government: "In order to achieve this sacred Islamic mission (*al-risālah al-islāmīyah al-muqqadasah*) [of overseeing the pilgrimage], the government of Saudi Arabia and the Ministry of the Interior have devoted great concern to the safety of pilgrims and the continuous development of the two holy places".[8] At the *ḥajj* of 2001, the King said there was no need to enumerate the extensive Saudi contributions, even as he typically outlined them (*Majallat al-ḥajj* Apr.-May [?] 2001: 74).

The third, related theme accentuates the royal family's devotion to Islamic causes as the primary rationale for its right to rule. The connection between the *ḥajj* and political legitimacy has long been obvious. The 'Abbāsids hoped to accentuate their importance by sending ornamental keys to the Ka'bah in the late twelfth and thirteenth centuries (Hawting 1993: 32). The Ottoman Sultans wrote the public transcript of their authority in alms-giving and decorative gilt, as well as in carefully designed architectural inscriptions in Arabic that were to be read by the literate and more politically active pilgrims. Congregational prayers for the distant Sultan also naturally carried a political point, especially in the 1630s when the reconstruction project did not meet with universal approval among the '*ulamā'*. Prayers for Sulṭān Murād IV (r. 1623-40) were intended to be a timely reaffirmation of Ottoman sovereignty. Sultans called themselves *khādim al-ḥaramayn al-sharīfayn*, servant of the holy places – a term that goes back to Ṣalāḥ al-Dīn in the twelfth century – and vocally proclaimed their right to protect pilgrims from across the Muslim world. The particularly vigorous defence of Central Asian pilgrims in the sixteenth and seventeenth centuries was doubtless due to the desire to enlist the Sunni Uzbek *khāns* in the fierce competition with both Shi'i Safavids and infidel Russians.

In the eighteenth century, the public display of Ottoman subventions and gifts to the Hijazis was part of the theatre of allegiance: a purposeful demonstration of the imperial centre's encouragement of client loyalty, but also a frank recognition by the locals that, having eaten "the bread of the Sultan", they had allowed themselves to be coopted (Faroqhi 1994: 139-42, 155, 184-6, quotation at 185). Egyptian rulers until the Saudi period enhanced their prestige by sending the *kiswah*, or covering of the Ka'bah, in a highly visible and ostentatious annual caravan (*maḥmal*). In the early twentieth century, Wavell records that the Turkish government objected to pilgrims taking up arms to suppress a tribal revolt in the Hijaz out of fear that the implicit acknowledgement of its inability to ensure the security of the pilgrimage would further undermine its authority: "The survivors would be likely to take home with them an unflattering opinion as to the capacity of the Sultan to be guardian of the holy places" (Wavell 1918: 111).

The Saudis today do not miss the opportunity to make an explicit link between efficient management of the *ḥajj* and their supreme qualification to rule. The King is, expectedly, "servant of the holy places", and travellers are no less than "pilgrims to the House of God" (*ḥujjāj bayt allāh al-ḥarām*) or, more directly, "guests of God" (*ḍuyūf al-raḥmān*): "Dear brothers and pilgrims to the House of God, as you have seen, the policy of the Kingdom and the main concern of *khādim al-ḥaramayn al-sharīfayn* in the protection of the *ḥaramayn* and care for the guests of God has been one of the most important principles to govern this country and people and to make Islam the dearest religion and the words of God the highest revelation".[9] Care of the holy places is a sacred trust and service to pilgrims is the Kingdom's "spiritual, material and historical responsibility" (Saudi Arabia [2000?]: 57).

If the point is not already clear to pilgrims, drinking water is distributed to them on the road in the name of the King. Many are also likely to have received copies of the Qur'ān that the King Fahd Qur'ān Printing Complex produces in Medina and that are distributed throughout the world in his name (Wolfe 1993: 244, 305). Appropriation of a divinely appointed role also allows the Kingdom to assert its moral leadership of the Islamic world. The King's annual *ḥajj* speech has become nothing less than a "state of the *ummah*" address, which affords the Saudis the opportunity not only to boast about their contributions but also to make their views on major issues such as Palestine and Kosovo appear as the "Islamic" position (Idārah al-Abḥāth wa-l-Nashr 1995: 96–8, *Majallat al-hajj* Jun. 1997: 4–9, al-Ṣawī'ah 1414 A.H.: 271–5).

Counter-narratives

Many individuals appreciate the contributions the Saudis have made to ease the rigours of the pilgrimage.[10] But robust criticism of Saudi control has also come from a variety of quarters. This has taken several forms. One is a rejection of the Saudi regime itself as fundamentally un-Islamic and thus unworthy of supervising one of the pillars of the faith. The transnational Sunni Islamist movement, Ḥizb al-Taḥrīr, argues that, contrary to Saudi propaganda, Islamic law is not the law of the land because man-made laws and courts co-exist with purportedly *sharī'ah* ones, non-Islamic practices such as *ribā* (interest) are allowed and harmful foreign influences are well established: "whoever takes a stroll near the Ḥaram will see the British-Saudi Bank, American-Saudi Bank, Arab-National Bank, the Cairo-Saudi Bank, etc.". Saudi Arabia cannot, therefore, be an Islamic state, nor can King Fahd be *khalīfah* (Ḥizb al-Taḥrir n.d.) – a not so subtle rejoinder to the *khādim al-ḥaramayn* pretensions.

Ayatullah Khomeini accentuated the customary Shi'i antipathy towards the Wahhābīs and accused them of being puppets of the imperialist West and traitors to the cause of protection of the sanctuaries (Iran n.d.: 16). A point of irritation was the Saudi opposition to distinctively Shi'i and Iranian revolutionary practices that Khomeini deemed central to Islam. Shi'i pilgrims have traditionally been more demonstrative than others at Ḥijr Isma'īl, the area in the *ḥaram* near the Ka'bah where Isma'īl is believed to be buried, and have approached the black stone (*al-ḥajar al-aswad*) with pronounced emotion. The Saudis and others have consistently urged reserve and opposed pushing and emotionalism (Saudi Arabia n.d. b: 29–30, *al-Wa'y al-islāmī* [Kuwait] 132, Dec. 1975: 29). After the revolution, Iranian "dissociation from the pagans" (*barā'at min al-mushrikīn*) demonstrations upset the Saudis because of their pro-Khomeini and anti-American slogans. Khomeini's withering riposte to King Khālid's protests accused the "government of the Hijaz" of having sold out to the United States and its AWACS and of manipulating court *'ulamā'* and "pseudo" *'ulamā'* to sustain un-Islamic kingship (Center for Research and Publication of Hajj 1988: 134–5). Khomeini argued that it was the duty of all Muslims to use the occasion to "shout their hatred against unbelievers and world arrogance and especially the criminal US at the House of Tawhid" (Khomeini 1408 A.H: 7; also see Khomeini's 1983 message in *Crescent International* 16–28 Feb. 2001).

The question of Saudi Arabia's right to control the pilgrimage grew acute after the events of 1987 when more than 400 people died in clashes between Iranian pilgrims and Saudi security officials. Saudis accused the Iranians of using the sacred occasion, when all forms of violence are doctrinally prohibited, to advance a political agenda of revolutionary upheaval, and the Iranians accused the Saudi government of deliberate murder. Charges of heresy and illegitimacy flew back and forth. The Saudi regime understood that, with events having been played out in public, the stakes were high and the consequences potentially very grave. According to Prince Nā'if, the Minister of the Interior, "the real conspiracy hatched by the leaders of Iran was to make Saudi Arabia appear unable to provide adequate security" (cited in Goldberg 1987: 590).[11] Reaction in many parts of the Muslim world centred exactly on this point, and the Saudis were thrown on the defensive. They convened a meeting of the Muslim World League in October 1987 to denounce Iran, and Iran countered with an International Congress on Safeguarding the Sanctity and Security of the Ḥaramayn Sharīfayn in November. The latter, predictably, called for the liberation of Mecca and Medina and for the holy places to be placed under international Muslim control. At this meeting, Muḥammad Ḥusayn Faḍlullāh, the spiritual leader of Ḥizbullāh, denounced Wahhābism as an Islamic deviation, and Hāshimī Rafsanjānī, then Iranian Majlis Speaker, called for the establishment of an "Islam[ic] International" (Foreign Broadcast Information Service, NES-87-228, 27 Nov. 1987: 54).

The Iranian government and its sympathisers have continued to call for internationalisation of the *ḥaramayn* – for example, after the 1990 catastrophe when over 1,000 pilgrims died (*Le Monde* 6 Jul. 1990). *Crescent International*, a pro-Iranian newspaper published in Canada and Britain, repeats the call regularly (e.g. 16–30 Apr. 1996). Arab, particularly Saudi, oppositional elements join in this demand (Jadhakhan 1990: 87). As Zafar Bangash wrote, "Not only are the Haramain not safe from the evil designs of the *kuffar* [unbelievers], but the House of Saud is also not capable of defending even its own power structure" (Bangash 1988: 84). This viewpoint builds on the recommendations of the International Ḥajj Seminar of 1982 in London when it was proclaimed that "no single nation-State or a group of States based on sentiments and philosophies of local or regional nationalism can perform the task of the liberation of Al-Quds [Jerusalem] and the defence of the Haramain" (Muslim Institute 1983: 56).

The Saudi dilemma was acute: if the Kingdom continued to allow unrestricted access, it ran the risk of further unsettling events that it might not be able to control; if it restricted the pilgrimage, it allowed its critics to claim that it had violated a basic Islamic precept – *ḥajj* at least once in the lifetime of each able-bodied Muslim (Qur'ān 3: 97). The Saudi rulers could not have been unaware of the historical irony that, in his drive to conquer the Hijaz, 'Abd al-'Azīz himself had been able to encourage *'ulamā'* support in his Najdī base and to enlist broader Muslim support precisely because Sharīf Ḥusayn had prohibited Najdīs from performing the pilgrimage (Kostiner 1993: 66).

The solution was the introduction of a quota system at the Amman meeting of the Foreign Ministers of the Organisation of the Islamic Conference in March 1988. Designed principally to limit the number of Iranian pilgrims, the measure was explained by the Saudis as due to ongoing construction and expansion work, so temporary restrictions were needed until new arrangements could be put in place. The Saudi newspaper *al-Sharq al-awsaṭ* went so far as to claim that an unrestricted large number of pilgrims entering the Kingdom was itself disorderly and thus incompatible with Islamic precepts (*al-Sharq al-awsaṭ* 25 Mar. 1988). What was intended to operate for three years is now institutionalised: the total number of *ḥajjīs* is limited to 1 per cent of the total Muslim population of each country, or one pilgrim for every 1,000 of the population.

The reaction predictably focused on the Saudi violation of the Qur'ānic precept. Critics argued that millions of Muslims would be deprived of their right to pilgrimage and, given the demographics, some Muslims would have to live a thousand years in order to qualify. "These rules are a mega-bid'ah", according to this internet criticism.[12] Suspicion was raised that the quota system would be further restrictive because it would be targeted against Muslim activists and the young, who would presumably be less amenable to normal Saudi restrictions. Although there does not appear to have been objection earlier, the very idea of *ḥajj* visas now also came under attack. They too are *bid'ah* and emblematic of a ruling house that has allied itself with the enemies of Islam (*Crescent International*, 8-22 Apr. 1997, Bangash 1988: 84). Iran boycotted the pilgrimage from 1988 to 1990, but then agreed to the negotiated figure of 115,000 pilgrims – in violation of the Saudis' own quota system. The Saudis also agreed to allow Iranians to stage demonstrations of "disavowal", as they had long demanded, but these were to be isolated from the main ceremonies of the *ḥajj* and were not to be directed against the Saudi regime.[13]

In addition to the general unworthiness of the House of Sa'ūd, criticism is lodged at specific mismanagement of the pilgrimage. Central to these accusations are numerous incidents in recent years resulting in the death of pilgrims. In addition to the 1987 incident, one pilgrim died and 16 were wounded as a result of bombs near the Grand Mosque in 1989; in 1990, referred to earlier, 1,426 pilgrims were crushed in al-Mu'aysim tunnel; in 1994, a stampede in Minā killed 270 pilgrims; in 1997, 343 pilgrims died and 1,500 were injured at a fire in Minā; in 1998, 180 pilgrims were crushed in a stampede during the stoning of Satan ritual (*ramī*); in 2001, 35 people died during that ceremony, as did 244 in 2004. Some have pointed out that such figures are minuscule in comparison to the total number of pilgrims; Wolfe says, for instance, that the number of dead in 1990 represented no more than 0.0005 per cent of the total number of pilgrims (Wolfe 1993: 275). The government itself referred to the deaths of 2001 as a "minor incident" (*ḥādith basīṭ*) given the large number of pilgrims – over a million and a half – and the advanced age of those who died. Like earlier incidents, this was to be expected (*amr ṭabī'ī*) and was part of the pilgrims' destiny (*al-qaḍā-' wa-l-qadar*).[14]

Yet many others have seen in these tragedies evidence of Saudi incompetence, indifference or, worse, malfeasance. In 1990, the Iranian government and allied groups such as the Lebanese Ḥizbullāh pointed to the large number of deaths that year as confirming the Saudi government's inability to provide for safe pilgrimage, and called again on the Islamic world to take over custodianship of the *ḥajj* (*Le Monde* 6 Jul. 1990). The Saudi government's slow response and King Fahd's initial explanation that the deaths were due to God's will infuriated many, including Turkish and Indonesian parties whose nationals constituted the majority of victims.[15] *Milliyet* caricatured the King as the devil entering a dark tunnel, and survivors noted that wire rope and Saudi soldiers blocked the exit of the 5,000 people trapped in the 32-foot-wide tunnel. Çemil Ciçek, the Turkish Minister of State, commented: "If the stairs had been open about 1,000 people could have been taken out and others inside could have been given space to breathe" (*Independent* 12 Jul. 1990). The London-based oppositional Committee for the Defence of Legitimate Rights (CDLR, *Lajnat al-Difāʿ ʿan al-Ḥuqūq al-Sharʿīyah*), contending that the number of deaths in the 1994 incident was ten times higher than the official figure, argued that the stampede was principally caused by traffic restrictions for the motorcade of the wife of Prince Badr ibn ʿAbd al-ʿAzīz (*Communiqué* No. 10, 29 May 1994). The Movement for Islamic Reform in Arabia (MIRA), a splinter group of CDLR, blamed the casualties of the 1997 tragedy on administrative chaos. There was no disaster or contingency planning, central command was absent and emergency services were ill briefed and inept (*al-Iṣlāḥ* 55, 21 Apr. 1997).

Critics have also emphasised the harm inflicted by, and the corruption of, the expansion and redevelopment programmes. Such redevelopment schemes have not been unique to the Saudis. For instance, following the Ottoman models of Istanbul, Edirne and Bursa, Sultan Murād III (1574-95) moved houses from the immediate vicinity of the Grand Mosque. The intention was to create an open courtyard. Affluent property owners, who benefited from high rents to wealthy pilgrims, naturally objected, but hostels for poor pilgrims were also demolished (Faroqhi 1994: 107-8). Although he failed to acknowledge that the *ḥaramayn* had undergone a number of important redesigns, Ayatullah Khomeini's distaste for the modern Saudi programme was apparent: "To keep the Sacred House and the mosque simple, as they were at the time of Ibrahim and the advent of Islam, is a thousand times better than decorating it and surrounding it with high-rise buildings" (Centre for Research and Publications of Hajj 1988: 210).[16]

Slimane Zeghidour, an Algerian journalist, finds the manipulation of the architectural heritage of the holy cities an aesthetic and political affront. The Saudi style is kitschy, all neo-Andalusian ornamentation and grand hotel capaciousness. The King's and other royal palaces aggressively dominate Masjid al-Ḥaram and the Ṣafā hill on Abū Qubays, the first mountain created by God where Adam's tomb is thought by many to be found and the site of Bilāl's mosque, southeast of the *ḥaram*. Pink-marbled and impossible for the congregants to miss, the palaces give the royal family a commanding symbolic presence that cannot fail to offend the egalitarian and fraternal spirit of the pilgrimage. The Inter-Continental and Hilton hotels rise high above other gates of the mosque and cater to elite pilgrims. In Zeghidour's view, local residents and mankind's heritage have been vandalised for such royal and capitalist avarice (Zeghidour 1989: 145–96, *Mother Jones* Jul./Aug. 1989: 18).

Sa'īd al-Samarra'ī laments the destruction of Muslim cemeteries, shrines and other historical sites since the Wahhābī take-over in the mid-1920s, and finds the expansion of the Mecca and Medina mosques both unnecessary and destructive. What overcrowding there is exists for only four days a year and could have been managed without massive redevelopment. Moreover, the rush to expand and reconfigure the holy places endangers valuable Umayyad, 'Abbāsid and Ottoman additions: "No destruction of heritage can be justified as development" (Samarra'ī 1993: 10). MIRA said that although the government never ceases to tout its own generosity, its spending has been wasteful and misdirected. The King and Crown Prince constructed palaces in Minā, which are used only a few days a year but cost SR6 billion ($1.75 billion). In April 1997, MIRA argued that the "recent" expansion of the Grand Mosque could have been accomplished at 21 per cent of the total spent: "Embezzlement of public funds is a crime" (*Arabia Unveiled* 6, Apr. 1977). The CDLR accused the government of *al-sariqah wa-l-talā'ub*, theft and fraud (*al-Ḥuqūq* 45, Apr. 1995). Similarly, CDLR argued that the government insults Muslims by boasting about its vast expenditures when in reality everyone knows that there is a lack of proper accounting and that the royal family takes a great deal of money in commissions (*Communiqué* 10, 29 May 1994).

Related to these accusations of profiteering from the expansion programmes is the general charge that the government is concerned above all with its own prerogatives. CDLR argues, for example, that the fees system is fundamentally dishonest, for the government takes money that should rightfully go to the *muṭawwifs* and allows friendly foreign politicians to sell extra visas for mutual profit and political gain (*al-Ḥuqūq* 47, 10 Apr. 1995).[17] Rather than reinforcing belief in the equality of all believers, moreover, the Saudis accord great privileges to VIPs. They are provided with luxurious accommodation while ordinary pilgrims must fend for themselves with sub-standard housing; places for the ceremonial "standing" (*wuqūf*) at 'Arafāt and camp sites at Minā are disproportionately accorded to members of the royal family and their guests;[18] and the attention of the police is diverted to handling royal motorcades (*al-Ḥuqūq* 45, 26 Apr. 1995 and 46, 3 Apr. 1995, CDLR 1994, CDLR n.d., *Communiqué* 10).

These themes had an echo in the controversy over the Ajyād fortress in Mecca in early 2002. The authorities demolished this 220-year-old fort on a hill overlooking the city and embarked on a $1.6 billion construction programme that would, by 2005, include residential towers, a five-star hotel and a shopping mall. The Ottomans had built the fort to ward off a Wahhābī attack on the city, and the Turkish government claimed that the new building programme was tantamount to "cultural massacre" and similar to the Taliban destruction of the Buddhist statues at Bamiyan (*al-Waṭan* 9 Jan. 2002). The Saudi government argued that it was necessary to accommodate pilgrims in the holy city and referred to it as an "endowment". But criticism grew, both within the city and outside the country, particularly as the main contract was let to the Bin Lādin Group, the construction company that had most benefited from the expansion of the *ḥaramayan* in Mecca and Medina. The government's announcement that it would rebuild the demolished fort in the vicinity of the new complex only further incensed critics, including international groups such as Patrimoine Sans Frontières. The Saudi defence was now two-fold: protection of pilgrim interests and sovereign prerogative (*sayādah*) (*al-Waṭan* 10 Jan. 2002).

Constraints and opportunities of the *ḥajj*

Beyond the discursive level, Saudi control of the pilgrimage is dogged by important problems. First, because the numbers of *ḥajjī*s have been staggering, the administrative arrangements have not always been able to meet the demand. In 1925, at the beginning of Saudi rule, there were a total of 90,662 pilgrims. The number of foreign pilgrims dipped during the world depression of the 1930s, with 25,291 in 1932 and 49,517 in 1935 (Wizārat al-Dākhilīyah n.d.). The numbers of pilgrims began to grow again in the post-war period: 100,578 in 1950 and 285,948 in 1960. In the 1970s the numbers grew dramatically. In 1970, there were 1,079,760; in 1975, 1,557,867; in 1980, 1,949,634; in 1985, 1,599,740; in 1990, 1,523,294; in 1995, 1,779,299; and in 2000, 1,839,154. There were reportedly 1,504,800 pilgrims in 2001, but the number may well have been closer to 1.8 million. The number in 2003 was 1,924,000, and 1,892,710 in 2004.[19]

Several factors account for the increase: the development of speedy and relatively inexpensive transportation, particularly by air; the growth in the numbers of Muslims worldwide; the rise in income in some Muslim countries; the general growth in religious feeling; improvements in the security and facilities of the pilgrimage; and the large numbers of expatriate Muslim workers in Gulf countries with disposable cash. Iyād Madanī, the Saudi Minister of Ḥajj, starkly outlined what, perhaps expansively, he envisaged the future demand to be: 10 per cent of the world's 1 billion Muslims may well want to perform pilgrimage, and even if only 10 per cent of these 100 million Muslims were able to do so, he thought there would soon be 10 million pilgrims at the *ḥajj* (*'Ayn al-yaqīn* 22 Mar. 2002).

The quota system of 1987 was intended to impose some order on such burgeoning numbers. Given that 3 million pilgrims were widely predicted, but did not materialise, by the early years of the twenty-first century, it has had a measure of success. Yet it is also clear that the system has been selectively applied, and informal negotiations have occurred between states and the Saudi authorities. Politics has inevitably intruded. The number of Iranian pilgrims, as has been noted, exceeds the formal quota, and Muslims in minority countries such as Britain, Australia and the United States escape in effect any quota. Some seek to circumvent their national limit by going to such minority countries; authorities at Cairo airport arrested Egyptian travel agents just prior to the 2001 *ḥajj* because they were attempting to place 114 of their clients in the German delegation.[20]

The matter of internal pilgrims has also been grating, as it turns out, to both the Saudi government and foreign ones. The growth in the number of internal pilgrims – both Saudi citizens and resident aliens – was particularly striking from the 1980s, with 1983 the peak year. Out of an official (though perhaps exaggerated) total of 2,502,855 pilgrims, 1,497,795 or 60 per cent were internal pilgrims, and of these 1,204,833 were non-Saudis (General Directorate 1984). The government felt it necessary to adopt yet another form of restriction. From 1985, internal, non-Saudi pilgrims have been limited to *ḥajj* once every five years and have to receive permission from the Ministry of the Interior. In 1988, this restriction was extended to Saudi citizens as well – a decision validated by the Council of Senior 'Ulamā' – but it appears to be honoured more in the breach than the observance. It remains a point of concern at home. In February 2000, for example, the Cabinet urged Saudi citizens to obey the restrictions on internal pilgrims, and it was later announced that Saudis living abroad must obtain *ḥajj* visas[21] and that regulations are being devised to curtail overcrowding from domestic pilgrims (*Majallat al-ḥajj* Apr. 2003: 6). But it is also a point of irritation to those outside who feel that the Saudis' relaxed attitude towards their own rules is another indication of their unworthiness to administer the holy places.

The Saudis are widely given credit for regularising the guide, or *muṭawwif* system, which was often exploitative in the past. They have adopted a number of approaches, with *muṭawwifs* now organised into six professional establishments, representing, respectively, the Arab countries, Iran, South Asia, Southeast Asia, non-Arab Africa, and Turkey, Europe, America and Australia. There are also guilds for the Jiddah-based agents of the *muṭawwifs*, the *wukalā'*; the *adillā'*, who guide visitors to Medina; and the *zamāzimah*, who supply pilgrims with water from the holy spring of Zamzam (Long 1979: 27–51).

The government's intention is to avoid unsupervised pilgrims, but practice has revealed that the system is not foolproof. It has thus encouraged individual states to take increasing responsibility for their citizens and to organise them according to strict, nationally devised procedures. The Malaysian government, which established Tabung Haji, the Pilgrims' Management and Fund Board, in 1969, is touted as a model; the Moroccan organisation is also praised. In the Indian system, a Central Hajj Committee oversaw approximately 70,000 of the 120,000 Indian pilgrims who went on the pilgrimage in 2001. Others – presumably wealthier pilgrims – made their own arrangements via commercial travel agencies. The Ministries of Civil Aviation and External Affairs co-ordinated logistical matters, and the Indian consulate in Jiddah, in return for the fees received, arranged for reception of the pilgrims, their transportation and accommodation and medical and other assistance if needed.[22]

Formally recognised *ḥajj* delegations are welcome, and even Britain has sent an official delegation, consisting of volunteer doctors, counsellors and Muslim staff of the Foreign and Commonwealth Office (FCO), to the pilgrimage from 2000 onwards. Saudi Arabia was somewhat wary at first of according Muslims from a historically Christian country the same status as others from the majority Muslim world. But both sides quickly maintained that the purpose was to provide on-the-spot consular and medical assistance, and the Saudis have also hoped to make the British government responsible for potential troublemakers without allowing interference in the Saudi legal process. The FCO makes it clear, in brochures printed in English, Arabic, Bengali and Urdu, that the British *ḥajj* delegation cannot interfere in ongoing court cases, seek release from prison, provide legal advice or investigate a crime (Foreign and Commonwealth Office 2001). But the British government uses the delegation to reach out to, and influence, home Muslim communities. In fact, Lord Ahmed, a pronounced defender of the Muslim Kashmiri cause, embarrassed officials on both sides when, as co-leader of the first official British delegation, his discretion could not automatically be assumed. Well-timed meetings of British Muslim organisations at the FCO subtly inspired the choice of the second, less controversial delegation leader (Lord Adam Patel). The *ḥajj*, not for the first time, had spill-over effects in domestic politics beyond those of Saudi Arabia.

A second difficulty the Saudis have faced is the ritual rhythm of the *ḥajj*. Traditional timing makes it difficult for the Saudi government to make changes that might render it more manageable. In addition to crowding at the obligatory *ṭawāfs* and *sa'y*, which, however, are spread out over time depending on the arrival of *ḥajjīs*, certain events must be done within particular timeframes and are thus more difficult to control. Following the example of the Prophet on his farewell pilgrimage and typically on the eighth of Dhū l-Ḥijjah, pilgrims move from Mecca to Minā and spend the night there. On the morning of the ninth, they proceed to 'Arafāt where they must be present at sunset; earlier in the day they customarily visit Nimrah mosque, and from noon to sunset they gather for the *wuqūf*, many at Jabal al-Raḥmah.

From sunset on the ninth begins the *ifāḍah* (or *nafrah*), the "rushing" to Muzdalifah, about four miles from 'Arafāt, where pilgrims spend the night and say the sunset and evening prayers. Here pilgrims gather stones that will be thrown at the satanic pillars over the next few days. After midnight but at least by dawn on the tenth, they move to Minā, about four miles from Mecca. The first lapidation ceremony occurs when pilgrims throw seven stones at Jamrat al-'Aqabah. Pilgrims are enjoined as soon as possible to return to Mecca to perform *ṭawāf* again and *sa'y* if they did not do so earlier, after which they go back to Minā, free of *iḥrām* (state of purification) restrictions, to spend the nights of the eleventh and twelfth. During these days they stone all three satanic pillars, usually not before noon. The feast of sacrifice (*'īd al-aḍḥā*) is celebrated from the tenth to the thirteenth of Dhū l-Ḥijjah. Pilgrims may make their sacrifice at any time but most prefer to do so on the first day in Minā. Back in Mecca at the end of the *ḥajj*, before leaving for home or to visit (*ziyārah*) the Prophet's Mosque in Medina and other historical sites, pilgrims perform the farewell circumambulation of the Ka'bah.

The obligatory (*wājib*) acts of the pilgrimage are *iḥrām*, *ṭawāf*, *sa'y* and *wuqūf*. In a sense this gives the Saudis latitude in which to adapt to the overcrowding and the inevitable logistical nightmare, and indeed they have encouraged spreading out the rite. The arrival of pilgrims stretches over a long time, partly out of necessity given the daily capacity of Jiddah airport – approximately 80,000 pilgrims per day – through which most pilgrims now pass, and partly in the hope of reducing the crush by the eighth of Dhū-l-Ḥijjah. Pilgrims are urged to move to Minā and 'Arafāt earlier than has been the custom. Moreover, the animal sacrifices take place over several days, and pilgrims are encouraged either to pay a bank (approximately £50–60 in 2001 for British Muslims) to arrange the sacrifice or to proceed to a government-regulated abattoir to arrange it directly. Sanitary conditions are further enhanced by the fact that, since 1983, the Islamic Development Bank has overseen the distribution of meat to refugees and other needy individuals; more than 500,000 sheep, cows and camels are packed and shipped abroad (Saudi Arabia [2000?]: 66, *Arab News* 13 Jan. 2002).

But the main problems occur at two bottlenecks – the *ifāḍah* on the evening of ninth Dhū l-Ḥijjah and the lapidation ceremonies. The first lapidation at Minā on the tenth is especially serious, but there is also a significant problem on the eleventh when some 80 per cent of pilgrims carry out the stonings (al-Yafi 1993: 29). This causes immense congestion at Jamarāt Bridge. The concentration of over 1½ million people in limited space, not to mention in the open air and often in very hot weather, is daunting. The bridge, which is over 30 years old, can safely accommodate 80,000 pilgrims an hour, but the numbers have at times risen to around 400,000 an hour. Crowd control is also exacerbated by the high emotional state of the pilgrims, particularly during the stoning ceremonies.

Although the government does not face a specific Islamic legal obstacle to adapting the rituals further to modern requirements, such change would go against the currents of tradition (Long 1979: 117). The *sunnah* is well established, formalised in hundreds of texts, handbooks and websites, many representing *'ulamā'* sentiment in the Kingdom. To tamper with it would put the regime on the defensive in the largely conservative court of Muslim opinion. Even so, religious authorities have justified innovations on the grounds of necessity. The government has introduced the cautious reform of setting a stoning schedule according to individual groups (*al-Riyāḍ* 17 Jan. 2002) and, after the deaths of 2004, announced plans to build a new nine-storey bridge that would be elliptical in form, rather than circular as it now is. The general area is also to be pedestrianised. The building programme, which would take place over 20 years, is intended to accommodate larger numbers of pilgrims on several levels simultaneously and to make the stoning ritual safer by dividing groups into a north and south side. The Grand Muftī's approval of these plans makes it clear that past practice must give way to the need of protection: "The Council [of Senior 'Ulamā'] agreed to develop the Jamarāt area for the safety and ease of pilgrims"(*al-Ḥajj wa-l-'umrah* Apr. 2004:10–13, quotation on 11).

There has been some leeway with regard to the first stoning on the tenth of Dhū l-Ḥijjah. The religious authorities have regarded the traditional timing in the morning to be "commendable" (*mustaḥabb*), rather than obligatory (al-Jazā'irī 1994: 99–100). Moreover, Shaykh Muḥammad bin Ṣāliḥ al-ʻUthaymīn, a very influential Saudi religious authority, maintained that it could be done even before sunrise if the pilgrim were unwell or incapable of facing the crowd.[23] A Saudi-approved guide in English says that stoning in the afternoon and evening is also "acceptable" (Davids 2000: 304). There is less room for manoeuvre with regard to the Jamarāt ceremony on the eleventh and twelfth. Many believe that the stoning cannot take place until after noon, and both Shaykh al-ʻUthaymīn and Shaykh ʻAbd al-ʻAzīz Bin Bāz, in effect then the Muftī of the Kingdom, specifically forbade any earlier action (al-ʻUthaymīn 1995: vol. 2, 401–2, Bin Bāz 1992: 102). The government has, however, encouraged an elongated period. The British *ḥajj* delegation, for example, was told: "The group will carry out the stoning in the early morning before fajr [early morning prayer] so as to avoid the crowds and the intense heat of the day" (el-Sawy Travel n.d.).

In addition, pilgrims are now told that, while at ʻArafāt, visits to Nimrah mosque and Jabal al-Raḥmah are not strictly necessary, despite traditional practice in the past and the exhortation of so eminent a figure as Shaykh al-ʻUthaymīn.[24] They should now exercise prudence in deciding what activity is possible in the harsh conditions. To give a sense of the obstacles involved in changing ritual procedure, the relatively less important encouragement of pilgrims to move to Minā as early as the seventh and to ʻArafāt on the eighth of Dhū l-Ḥijjah has been denounced (e.g. *Crescent International* 1–15 May 1997) as a kind of faithless jumping of the gun. In this view, it is contrary to the Qur'ānic command (2: 189) about determining the day of the *ḥajj*.[25]

Third, spatial considerations affect Saudi management of the pilgrimage. Mecca is bounded by four mountains: Jabal Khandamah to the east of the *ḥaram*; Jabal Abū Qubays to the southeast; Jabal Bakhsh to the south; and Jabal Dhāf to the north of the *ḥaram* and to the west of al-Maʻlā cemetery. The need to alleviate massive overcrowding has justified the steady expansion of the Grand Mosque, but given the physical constraints, the space available for the augmented complex and related transportation needs has been limited. Two consequences have resulted: (1) As has been noted in the oppositional narratives, the government, taking over areas adjacent to the mosque, has eliminated traditional *rawāshin* (wooden screen) houses, *sūq*s and even historical sites. Given the need for mobility, land has also been appropriated for six major pedestrian tunnels, three ring roads and a number of car parks such as the massive Kuday lot. (2) The loss of this property has both driven up the price of real estate, particularly in the vicinity of the *ḥaram*, and encouraged vertical, high-rise development. In Medina, the expansion of the Prophet's Mosque to five times its former dimensions has had similar results. The oldest part of town (Ḥārat al-Āghāwāt) and *sūqs* in the north at al-Bāb al-Majīdī have been demolished, replaced with nine-to-thirteen-storey apartment buildings.

The common effect has been to accentuate difference. The political economy of the *ḥajj* divides pilgrims according to their ability to pay. The more well-to-do stay in attractive housing or elite hotels; poorer pilgrims stay further and further away from the *ḥaram* in conditions that are often inadequate despite government regulation. In addition to the high prices, pilgrims often complain about being crowded into small flats lacking in privacy and with poor sanitation and ventilation (Ashi 1996; al-Harrbi 1998). The problem has implications for governmental control because some pilgrims, unable or unwilling to pay the going prices and hoping to avoid long walks to the mosque, sleep on the street or in the *ḥaram* in violation of government *ḥajj* rules. This phenomenon of *iftirāsh* (sleeping rough) undermines Saudi claims of guaranteed safety and sanitation for all pilgrims.

The very same constraints, however, have abetted the commercialisation of the *ḥajj* and enriched well-connected individuals. Pilgrims have long benefited from the presence of small local enterprises, and today these often take the form of fast-food restaurants in Mecca and elsewhere such as the al-Bayk and Tazaj chains or, in a less organised fashion, Russian pilgrims hawking binoculars and African women selling brightly coloured cloth and inexpensive prayer mats. Yet pilgrims have also long criticised the petty greed of hoteliers and some trinket merchants, forming what Jalāl Āl-e Aḥmad observed as the ironic "business" of the *ḥajj* (Āl-e Aḥmad 1985: 20, 91). More recently, the problem has reached a different order of magnitude. The King Fahd Building complex, owned by the King and Crown Prince, dominates the Meccan *ḥaram* on one side. In Medina, the Tabah Company, connected to 'Abd al-Majīd, the Emir of Medina, has built a new commercial development, including the 21-storey al-'Aqīq business and residential centre facing the open plaza of the Prophet's Mosque. Because of high rises the view of the Medina *ḥaram* is now blocked except from the main radial streets and from the northwest behind al-Baqī' cemetery.

In both cities middle-class Saudis have benefited from governmental subsidies, channeled through the Real Estate Development Fund, and have moved to new residential neighbourhoods further out, thus leaving inner housing to deteriorate or be exploited for commercial profit. *Muṭawwifs* have benefited by renting their houses or apartments at high prices (though leasors routinely complain that government regulations have forced them to make expensive alterations). Public as well as private investment is going into new hotels, shopping malls and rental accommodation (Bianca 2000: 232, 247). The government often distributes property to individuals to develop for commercial or "industrial" use, or builds shopping areas itself and then rents them to private businessmen at low rates.

An ironic twist of fate is that the Kingdom, once heavily dependent on *ḥajj* revenues in the pre-oil era, has recently rediscovered the pilgrimage's financial potential. The new economic policy, which seeks diversification, external investment and membership in the World Trade Organisation, has led to officially sanctioned tourism for the first time in the country's history. It is believed that the government since 1995 has invested SR25 billion ($6.6 billion) in creating a tourism infrastructure, and Sulṭān bin Salmān, son of the Governor of Riyad, directs the Supreme Tourist Commission. Pilgrimage, as has often been noted in the theoretical literature, amounts to a form of tourism, and the regulations of September 2000 make it clear that the Saudis hope to capitalise on the millions of Muslims who perform *'umrah* or *ziyārah* to the Prophet's Mosque as well as the *ḥajj*. Indeed, although one guide reminds readers of the spiritual nature of the pilgrimage, it goes on to say: "If you are one of those who 'shop until you drop' then take lots of money. There are so many things that you can buy. You name it, you will find it" (Davids 2000: 107). One report estimates that 5 million people perform *'umrah* every year, and if each were to spend $300, this would bring in $1.5 billion in revenues (*al-Ḥayāt* 15 Sep. 2000); *ḥajjī*s purportedly spent $2.7 billion in 2001 (*Arab News* 21 Jan. 2002).

As in the past, pilgrims must arrange their travel with approved local agents who will also take care of their transport and accommodation; when travelling internally, they must use Saudia, the national airline, and other government-owned transportation such as SAPTCO buses. In return, they will be allowed a month's stay in the Kingdom and, in a significant departure from past practice, are free to travel outside Mecca and Medina. The Ministry of Ḥajj approved 230 out of 1,800 companies that competed for agency licences. They were required to demonstrate that they had SR500,000 in Saudi-owned capital and a bank guarantee of SR200,000 ($53,333), were fully computerised and had offices in Jiddah, Mecca and Medina. Women are allowed to own such enterprises as long as Saudi nationals of good repute hold all the major positions. Foreign agencies need to supply one of the approved local companies with a bond of SR100,000.[26]

Although the Saudis have not yet extended this new approach to pilgrims on the *ḥajj*, the attraction of "Islamic tourism" is evident. In the past, this was virtually inconceivable. The destruction of tombs and shrines accompanied the Wahhābī take-over of the Hijaz, and the expansion and redevelopment programmes have led to the demolition of many religious and historical sites (al-Yūsuf 1996). A public toilet stands where Khadījah's house was located, the mosque of Abū Bakr, the first caliph, was torn down in 1985 to make way for a large hotel, the house of 'Abdullāh ibn 'Abd al-Muttalib, in which the Prophet was born, was also demolished and the space filled with a municipal library, and Dār al-Arqam, where the Prophet found refuge, has been torn down. One researcher asked the Dār al-Iftā' in the mid-1990s whether preservation of the Islamic heritage was enjoined. He received the artful reply that the glorification of graves was prohibited (Touba 1997: 185). One suspects that this "Wahhābī" style of reasoning is increasingly at odds with the views of the Sulṭān bin Salmāns, but to the extent that the official religious attitude towards religious tourism remains cautious – as it is bound to do – Saudi custodianship is likely to appear unfriendly to some Muslims. Many Shi'ah but others as well[27] resent the fact that, though not formally prohibited, visits to the tombs of the Prophet's Companions or Shi'i Imāms are discouraged.[28] Women are not allowed to enter these cemeteries and, generally, it is "not recommended" that they visit graves (Davids 2000: 104).

Pilgrimage in the calculus of legitimacy

The annual pilgrimage to Mecca brings together a vast number of Muslims on a spiritual journey. It is also a significant transnational force. The common received wisdom suggests that the result is likely to be integrative – on the one hand, the forging of what Victor Turner famously called "communitas" (Turner 1973: 192-4) and, on the other, the superseding of local or national authority. The above discussion, which has focused on the ability of a political authority to manage both a religious and a transnational force, can admittedly only point to part of the story, and direct ethnographic evidence from pilgrims themselves is surely needed. But the Saudi self-appointed guardianship of the *ḥajj* raises pertinent questions about the relationship between "management" of a larger, cosmopolitan force and parochial political legitimacy.

The story of Saudi control of the *ḥaramayn* is one of apparent contradictions. The Saudis say their claim rests on the provision of security, but the *ḥajj* has erupted in violence and hundreds have died from accidents. The expansion of the mosques in Mecca and Medina and the construction of an elaborate infrastructure are given as evidence of Saudi generosity, but pockets have doubtless been lined. The Āl Sa'ūd see control of the pilgrimage as validating their Islamic primacy, whereas others argue that the Islamic heritage has been changed for all time and without wide consultation. Indeed, critics at home and abroad contest the official Saudi narrative on every point.

Several tensions underlie the Saudi formula for legitimate administration of the pilgrimage:

(1) Universal/particular: The royal family's presumption is that, as custodians of the *ḥaramayn*, they represent the pan-Islamic community. The King's pilgrimage speech invokes the authority of the *ummah*, and the image of millions at peaceful prayer has become iconic of a powerful worldwide force. At the same time, however, particularisms are reinforced. It goes too far to speak of a "Wahhābī" *ḥajj*, especially at a time of rapid evolution in the thinking of both the Saudi *'ulamā'* and political authorities. Yet locally mediated distinctions are enforced: discouragement of visits to the graves of the Prophet's Companions; the insistence, contrary to Shi'i assertions, that the Qur'ānic exhortation to dissociate believers from worldly powers (Qur'ān 9: 1-3) does not require explicit ceremonial commemoration; the interpretation, proposed by Shaykhs Bin Bāz and al-'Uthaymīn and contrary to the open attitude long displayed at the pilgrimage, that men should avoid close proximity to women and that women's faces should be covered during the public rites (Bin Bāz 1992: 25, al-'Uthaymīn 1995: vol. ii, 394-5, vol. iii, 803-4, Davids 2000: 84-5); the distaste for emotional *ziyārah* to the Prophet's Mosque (Haddad 1999: 41-2).

(2) Equality/hierarchy: Like the pious literature generally, Saudi accounts make the *iḥrām* emblematic of the equality of all believers. Race, age, gender, position, sect and nationality are all irrelevant in the austere equivalence of the *ḥajj*. Pictures of a bareheaded, skimpily clad pilgrim-king, as jarring as they may be, are meant as a reassuring certification of the common subordination of mankind to God's will. Yet the Saudi formula of legitimacy inherently subverts this assertion with its intricately inter-connected claims to privilege: God has chosen the Āl Sa'ūd to provide security; this provides the essential milieu in which God's law can be enforced; the royal family thus earns its privileges of rule and Islamic primacy by its good works. In this worldview, "service" means "custodianship", "God's guests" means guests of the Kingdom. The hierarchy of host to guest and *primus* to *pares* is affirmed.

(3) Sameness/difference: The devout view of the pilgrimage is that all pilgrims are treated identically. Each has the same opportunity of prayer and sacrifice, and all are beneficiaries of the expansive Saudi attention to pilgrims' needs. But the modern organisation of the *ḥajj*

has accentuated distinctions. The Saudis strongly encourage nationally organised delegations so as to shift much of the responsibility for pilgrim conduct on to the shoulders of other states. The quota system, meant to be arithmetically neutral, is in practice subject to informal political negotiation. Restrictions are now applied to "internal" pilgrims, but these are more enthusiastically applied to migrant workers than to Saudi citizens, and the internal quota is in any event disproportionate. Travel agencies and package tours are available for pilgrims who wish to stay in more comfortable accommodation, and the rich are in effect largely separated from the poor, occupying different parts of town. Saudi expansion and redevelopment programmes, which have linked pilgrims to modern telecommunication, medical and transportation systems, have also led to escalation of property prices, the construction of ostentatious hotels and shopping complexes and individual and family profiteering. This new commercialisation of the pilgrimage, as one would expect, enhances the differences of consumerism and exacerbates a political economy of markedly differing opportunity.

Although one may be tempted to frame the tension between expectation and performance in terms of spiritual and secular, such a division is not helpful in this case. Unlike Lourdes, for instance, at which shrine officials seek to accentuate difference in order to assert their own authority (Eade 2000a: 51-76), the Āl Saʻūd hope to blur the two – even if they do not succeed – in order to legitimise their control. But here too there is a built-in problem. The Saudis have resorted to two forms of discourse – one based on religious, end-oriented credentials, the other based on technical means-oriented criteria. Qur'ānic verses, *ʻulamā'* guidelines, appeals to fraternity and solidarity make up the former; square meterage, tunnels and field hospitals, boasts of modernisation make up the latter. Both discursive forms are legitimising, but both structure expectations – Islamic probity in the first instance, efficiency in the second. To the extent that the religious script is foremost, the government, hoping to facilitate the progress of the pilgrimage and perhaps pulled in the direction of globalising economic forces, may find organisational changes clashing with purportedly authoritative theology; the ritual timing of the pilgrimage, as we have seen, imposes constraints. An entrapping principle of the "Wahhabi aesthetic", in Zeghidour's evocative phrase, is to rely on the "authentic" for purposes of legitimacy (Zeghidour 1989: 151), but this may also restrict room for manoeuvre. By the same token, to the extent that Saudi infrastructural changes appear wasteful, discriminatory or, even worse, inept, another avenue of delegitimisation becomes available.

Conclusion

This discussion is not meant to suggest that the validation of the Saudi Kingdom is entirely dependent on the pilgrimage. There are several pillars to its politics of legitimacy and, certainly, there are also a number of factors that affect the security, if not the acceptability, of the regime. But an examination of the politics of the *ḥajj* does question a number of common, theoretically generated assumptions. The transnational pilgrimage does not simply escape state manipulation, but neither does the state's manipulative strategy inevitably redound to the government's advantage. Appropriation of the "centre" – here, the critically important pilgrimage – is often a sensible part of efforts to validate oneself politically, but the centre is rarely as uniform or clear as the official imagination posits. The *ḥajj*, like pilgrimage elsewhere and as we have seen, is subject to multiple and crosscutting understandings. In the formulation of Eade and Sallnow, it is an arena for competing discourses and conflicting moves towards community and division. If not exactly a "void" in their terminology, it is also not an easily controlled structured presence (Eade 2000b: ix-xxiii). The Saudi custodianship of the *ḥajj* depends on Saudi performance, but it is also more than what the Saudis make it.

NOTES

Introduction: Societies, Identities and Global Issues

1 Ibrāhīm, S. 1982, Ibrāhīm and 'Abd al-Faḍīl 1983, Farjānī 1983a, 1983b. It is easy to forget that Khaldūn al-Naqīb's work on the "authoritarian" state, for instance, is now 20 years old.

2 In Arabic as in English, "the Gulf" can include Iraq and Iran; on the other hand, it can stand in contrast to Saudi Arabia and include only the small Arab states of the Gulf littoral from Kuwait through Qatar to Oman. The perception of the six GCC states as a set is common, however, not least among neighbours such as Yemenis and Jordanians. The inclusion of Iraq and Iran is less common except, perhaps symptomatically, in such phrases as "Gulf war".

3 Problems writing of the Gulf states (cf. Davis, E. 1991) turn constantly on the assumption that polities everywhere work in much the same way and that government is something thing-like to be described empirically. For an attempt within political science to recapture the reality of states, see the so-called "constructivism" of e.g. Barnett 1998.

4 For a summary of kinship and politics see e.g. Bonte, Conte and Dresch eds. 2001. Syria is a prime example at present of *jumlakīyah*, having managed an actual transmission of power between generations. "Monarchies" of course are a mixed set (Ben-Dor 2000), and "globalising monarchies" (Henry and Springborg 2001) include Kuwait and Qatar with Morocco, whose social forms are distinctive and whose place in the world, as exporting not importing labour, is very different. In passing one should note that "monarchy" (*malakīyah*) is not a term used much locally.

5 The term *ḥadāthah* (modernity) is not as prominent in the Gulf as in Egyptian discourse. The rhetorical package of progress and heritage, however, is at least as prominent. Globally, the markers of the modern shift almost arbitrarily, and the discourse of modernity and modernisation expresses what actually are claims about centrality and marginality (cf. Chatterjee 1997). But the Gulf shows a particular euphemistic reticence (cf. O'Brien 1977: 12, 33, 56, 92 and *passim*).

6 Fandy's analysis of Usāmah's position holds up well. But the question of identity proves volatile. It is true, and one day may be true again, that Usāmah was marginal in local terms – not thought of as really Saudi (Fandy 1999: 180). At the time of writing, however, he exerts a truly "national" fascination.

7 For depictions of the Janādirīyah see *al-Wasaṭ* 420, 14 Feb. 2000, 470, 29 Jan. 2001, 521, 21 Jan. 2002, the last of which appears under the title "Islam and globalisation, the clash of cultures and Palestine". Coverage of an earlier year featured Britain's Prince Charles dancing the *'arḍah* (*al-Wasaṭ* 24 Mar. 1997).

8 For a sample of current *'awlamah* literature in Arabic see al-Ḥamad 1999, Maḥyū 1999, Yakkan and Ṭānbūr 2000, Yūnis 1999. To document the term's prominence in the Gulf press would need a separate paper.

9 Raban 1987: 42, Khalaf and Hammoud 1988: 350, Altorki and Cole 1989: 128, Fargues 1991: 61–5, Lienhardt 1993: 35, 39, 2001: xiii–iv, al-Rumayḥī 1995: 278–9, Kapiszewski 2001: 179, 183–4.

10 Oman is something of an exception here in that key governmental posts are not held by the Sultan's kin (see Herb 1999 for the variations among states). More thought needs to be given to the actual functioning of states and families. The appearance of personal or family control of hydrocarbon wealth, for instance, is sometimes belied by quite effective, though quietly conducted, "councils". Abu Dhabi is a striking case.

11 In some measure the world was indeed transformed, but not in a way to which the Gulf was central. This was a period when the forms of US and global debt changed radically, and we entered on what some call "flexible accumulation" (Harvey 1989), with all but limitless quantities of virtual or offshore dollars (Road and Harrison 1985: 102–3). The oil exporters of the Gulf, meanwhile, went from surplus to deficit vis-à-vis their non-oil-trading partners in the space of about four years.

12 In Qatar, for instance, Zubārah is unlikely to be rebuilt since its founders are now "Bahraini" (Khuri 1980: 24ff., Crystal [1990] 1995: 116–17), but a fort at the edge of Doha was renovated for an international conference: foreign delegates to the World Trade Organisation were thus presented with evidence of Qatar's particularity (Montigny 2001). For the importance of "heritage" more generally see Davis and Gavrielides (eds) 1991.

13 The theme of rentiers "buying off" potential opposition (e.g. Beblawi 1987: 53–5, Luciani 1987: 73–8) has been much criticised, and rightly. The theme of exclusive control over major cash-flows (see also note 22) and the resulting opacity of relations with a wider world have remained oddly understated. It is this that allows us potentially to relate the Arab "rentier" states with such neighbours as Egypt or Yemen, and with the bankrupt states of Africa (Bayart 1989).

14 In recent years, one should note, the term *shabāb* has disappeared from much Arab discourse. Where 30 years ago the word denoted almost an es-

tate of the realm, it is now more likely to be used just of wild young men misbehaving.

15 Oman has a rich tradition of Islamic learning (see Wilkinson 1987). Legal practice was sophisticated in Bahrain (Khuri 1980: 68ff.). Elsewhere, there was often not the economic surplus to support more than visiting *muṭawwaʿīn*, who themselves, in the key case of Najd, may have been only ritual specialists (Al-Rasheed 2002: 55–6).

16 Sulayman Khalaf (1999) and Anie Montigny (1999) examine camel culture, and Khalaf shows well the scale of the current business. Yet the audience is hard to judge (Khalaf 1999: 89, 101, 102).

17 Older rulers, such as Shaykh Zayed of Abu Dhabi or Shaykh Jābir of Kuwait (Khalaf and Hammoud 1988: 353, al-Mughni and Tétreault in the present volume), may well be addressed as Bābā. The usual form in local tradition, however, has been the leader not as "father" but as "senior male" (e.g. shaykh), someone owed deference but not obedience (cf. Bonte, Conte and Dresch 2001). The "patriarchal state", meanwhile, has been as much a feature of recent South American history as of recent Arab history: we should not reach too quickly for "culture" as an explanation.

18 Limitation of access is not a feature only of prosperity brought on by oil: even in the 1930s, thought Bullard (1961: 198), "the days were passing when Ibn Saud could keep his *majlis* ... open to all comers." Nor was the *Majlis* ever "democratic" or a field for debate (see e.g. Khuri 1980: 36, Lienhardt 1993: 56, 102–3).

19 *Arab News* 25 Mar. 2002, cf. *al-Khalīj* 3-5 Apr. 2001, *Gulf News* 6 Apr. 2001. The current fascination with cyberspace, however, understates the way "virtual societies" can arise as much from social convention or forms of power as from technology.

20 See e.g. Yamani, M. 2000: xvi, 38, 74, 79, 88 and *passim*. The phenomenon of rulers "progressing" around their domains – Sultan Qābūs each spring in Oman, Shaykh Zayed on occasion in the UAE, Prince Sulṭān and Crown Prince ʿAbdullāh in competitive style in Saudi Arabia over several years now – has a populist value of instant communication. Pursuing what claims may be lodged is difficult.

21 The baroque city expresses state power through a series of vistas and prominent official buildings. Power is certainly expressed in something of this style by the Saudi royal *dīwān* in Riyad, built on a scale reminiscent of Albert Speer; the massive gate no doubt thins the bowels of Third World ambassadors. But the sites of actual administration and the official residences of those ruling are in most Gulf states low-rise and almost self-effacing.

22 In Bahrain oil accounts for less than 20 per cent of GDP. But even in Bahrain some 60 per cent of government revenue comes from oil. For Qatar and Oman in recent years it has been more than 70 per cent, for Kuwait almost 90 per cent.

23 The cost to the United States of "defending Gulf oil" is more than the value of the oil imported (Fuller and Lesser 1997, Losman 2001, *The Economist* 23 Mar. 2002). The political difficulty of increasing domestic taxes on American oil consumption meanwhile draws baffled comment (e.g. *The Economist* 15 Dec. 2001). For a good introduction to the issues see Blin 1996.

24 HSBC itself came third in the global rankings, after Citigroup and Bank of America Corp. In terms of assets, the top ten banks in the GCC were worth about 3 per cent of Europe's top ten; none was in the world's top 100. (For convenient listings see *The Banker* Jul. 2000.) Whatever the value of "high net worth individuals", the Gulf hardly figures in corporate banking terms and locally the area is "over-banked" (*Gulf News* 2 Feb. 2000). Indeed, by global standards the whole Middle East remains a financial backwater.

25 In the mid-1990s intra-regional trade for the Middle East and North Africa (including Iran here but excluding Turkey) was only 7–8 per cent of these countries' total trade. Given how little external trade there was of any kind (non-oil exports for the whole region were less than Finland's, with one-fiftieth the population), the figure was not thought especially skewed (World Bank 1995: 17, 30, 65).

26 The degree of openness (imports plus exports divided by GDP) is quite variable. In 2001 the UK stood at 56, the US at 23.8 and the world average at 48.3. Egypt, by comparison, was 40.2, Hong Kong 282.5 and Singapore 332.8. The ratios for the GCC were Saudi Arabia 66.4, Kuwait 92.1, Bahrain 69.5, Qatar 89.4, UAE 100.8 and Oman 92.7 (see EIU Country Data, http://countrydata.bvdep.com). In passing one might note how low the figure is for the US, the great advocate of free trade at present as Britain was in the nineteenth century.

27 Some 6 million foreign workers were thought to have sent home about $17 billion in 1995 (*al-Wasaṭ* 203, 18 Dec. 1995); the figure seems to have dropped off a little in recent years (*al-Wasaṭ* 314, 2 Feb. 1998, 405, 1 Nov. 1999).

28 Henry and Springborg (2001: 97) give a World Bank figure of $500 billion for total Arab overseas investment. This seems much too low. Others give $1.3 trillion, including perhaps $400 billion of American shares (*The Economist* 23 Mar. 2002). See also Gause 1994: 181, Yamani, H. 1997: 113, *Middle East Economic Digest* 11 Jan. 2002.

29 A common outcome of transitions elsewhere is identity by generations (the very basis of many nationalisms around the world, cf. Anderson, B. 1983: 109–10). The only chapter in the present volume which gives the theme much prominence is Limbert's on Oman, perhaps the case least exposed to recent changes.

30 *Gulf News* 5 Mar. 2002. Gross figures from the Economist Intelligence Unit country data on income, expenditure and debt are suggestive:

http://countrydata.bvdep.com. Saudi Arabia, whose borrowing (announced or otherwise) has been predominantly domestic, has never used windfall profits to draw down debt. Rather, "generosity" to citizens has been sustained and the debt of government has ratcheted ever upward.

31 For a convenient summary of Qatar's development see *Middle East Economic Digest* 29 Aug. 1997, 12 Mar. 1999, 24 May 2002. It remains the case, however, that "most of the news from Arabia is financial: the reason is ... that it reveals so little about the Arabians ... " (Iseman 1978: 42).

32 The global ideology of recent years (reflected in surprising places, e.g. Hobsbawm 1996, Evans 1997) has been that governments or states are made less important by accelerated flows of trade and finance. It depends which states. Poland, Russia, even Germany, may be less autonomous than they once were. Many Third World governments are more powerful than they have ever been. With America's dramatic if unfocused response to the attack on New York in 2001, the trend to governmental control of citizens' lives has been accentuated.

33 The WTO, formed in January 1995, took over where the GATT system ended, and membership of some states thus predates 1995. This is shown in brackets. In some cases there was a lag before subscribing to the new system. But the joining dates are Kuwait (1963) Jan. 1995, Bahrain (1993) Jan. 1995, Qatar (1994) Jan. 1996, Oman Nov. 2000, UAE (1994) Apr. 1996. For Saudi adaptation to the larger project see Henry and Springborg 2001: 179.

34 The birth rate in the UAE is said to have declined from 41 per 1,000 couples in the 1970s to 23 per 1,000 (*Emirates Weekly* 26 Feb. 2001). Saudi Arabia's birth-rate in 2000 was 5.8 births per woman and Qatar's 5.3, compared with the United States at roughly 2 and Germany at 1.3 (World Tribune.com 14 Apr. 2002).

35 It is often suggested that Gulf citizens show a certain reluctance to do kinds of work they prefer to be done by foreigners, which Gause rejects as a "racist canard" (Gause 1994: 151). Altorki and Cole (1989: 234, 239–40) are also exercised by the issue. Racist canard or not, the governments of GCC states face a real problem.

36 Twenty years ago Michael Field published an excellent and sympathetic account of Gulf merchant families (Field 1985). The members of these families are as genial as ever and as skilled at what they do: the scale of their enterprises has often grown. Structurally, however, it is remarkable how little has changed since Field's account.

37 In fact what matters for such trade is a solid legal structure. That has not emerged. Nor has the information to attract those investors who lack local *wāsiṭah* or contacts. Stock markets remain thin (Henry and Springborg 2001: 93, 180 and *passim*, cf. *Gulf News* 2 Feb. 2000).

38 Confronted with the common argument that GCC economies must become more transparent to prosper in the world, a non-academic friend

said, "Yes, about as transparent as London!" In other words, not very. The rhetoric of openness and transparency is applied often quite unthinkingly.

39 Even access to local economies by fellow GCC nationals is addressed carefully. Though in principle they are free to engage in all economic activities in any of the member states, declared the Supreme Council of the GCC in December 2000, a "restricted number of ... activities and occupations [are] reserved for nationals of the State in question" (Final Comuniqué adopted by the Supreme Council of the Gulf Co-operation Council, Manama, 30-31 Dec. 2000).

40 Gulf authors (see e.g. 'Abdullāh (ed.) 1998) tend to write of mentality (*'aqalīyah*), a term avoided on principle by Western academics. But an act of translation should be possible. What actually Gulf authors are discussing is of interest.

41 The former British Home Secretary, David Blunkett, for instance, urged British Asians to marry fellow British Asians, not import their spouses (*Guardian* 8 Feb. 2002). Those of us with longer established "British" patrilines but with, for instance, Irish mothers and American wives are as yet exempt from comment.

42 The Islamists in Kuwait do better politically almost year by year, yet few question the legitimacy of Kuwait as such. More generally, as Fandy (1999) suggested, there are not many Gulf Islamists who question the existence of their nation-states. That is left to movements such as Ḥizb ul-Taḥrīr, dismissed by most in the Gulf as a Pakistani interest.

Chapter 1: Channels of Interaction

1 Satellite channels are received centrally and distributed by cable in Bahrain and Qatar.

2 Comment by 'Ubaydlī 'Ubaydlī of al-Nadeem Information Technology at the conference on New Media and Change in Amman (Jordan), 27 Feb. 2002.

3 Interview with Muṣṭafā Karkūtī, then head of MBC Programme Evaluation, London, 17 Nov. 1997. See also the statement that "news is the primary product of MBC", made by Edwin Hart, Director of MBC News and International Operations, in *Cable and Satellite Europe*, Feb. 1998.

4 Forbes' "Richest" List for 1999, reproduced on www.news.bbc.co.uk, 21 Jun. 1999.

5 www.forbes.com, Jun. 2000.

6 Personal communication from an MBC source, 12 Oct. 1998. See also MBC press releases, 29 Oct. and 11 Nov. 1998.

7 MBC press releases, 15 Feb., 18 Jun., 18 Oct. 1999.

8 MBC press release, 7 Nov. 2000.

9 Personal communication to the author, Amman, 2 Mar. 2002.

10 Author's interviews with ART staff and associates, Cairo, 21 and 24 Feb. 1999.

11 Author's interview with ART staff, Cairo, 24 Feb. 1999.

12 www.tbsjournal.com, 1, Aug. 1998.
13 Author's interview with ART staff, Cairo, 24 Feb. 1999.
14 According to his speech to the 1998 Cairo Radio and Television Festival workshop, reported in *TV Dīsh* [in Arabic], 56, Aug. 1998.
15 Personal communication from an ART source, 7 Jul. 1999.
16 Interview with Sarah Sullivan in www.tbsjournal.com, 6, Spring 2001.
17 Personal communication from an ART source, Cairo, 21 Feb. 1999.
18 www.arabicnews.com, 14 Sep. 1999.
19 Personal communication from Rayyā al-Qāḍī on behalf of Orbit, 30 Jul. 1998.
20 Author's interview with staff at Media Production City, near Cairo, 6 Sep. 1998.

Chapter 2: Dialect and National Identity

1 *Il-Bēt il-'Ōd* means the type of house in which several generations of the same family would live, which in Bahrain, as elsewhere in the Gulf, was the normal pattern until the advent of government-built housing projects aimed at nuclear families, beginning in the late 1960s.
2 The communal distribution of sound variants in the Bahraini dialects appears in the chart of forms later in this chapter. The symbols used in the chart, transliterated titles and script excerpts have the phonetic values they normally have in the transliteration of Arabic, but the following points should be noted: the diphthongs *ay* and *aw* of other Arabic dialects are most often pronounced in Bahrain (and here transcribed) as long mid-vowels, viz ē nd ō respectively. The letter *kāf* in some words is pronounced *ch* as in English "church" (e.g. *cham*, "how much"). The letter *ẓ* stands for an emphatised *dh* (i.e. not an emphatised *z*, as in Egyptian or Syrian Arabic), and is pronounced as in the classical language. The symbol ə stands for an unstressed mid-vowel.
3 The only exception is the privately owned Qatar-based satellite news channel al-Jazeera.
4 Interestingly, in Egypt itself, the genre has moved on to address more controversial issues, and in a more realistic style. See, for example Walter Armbrust's (1996: 11-36) account of the Egyptian *musalsal*, *al-Rāya al-Bayḍā'* ("The White Flag"), where the corruption, loss of moral scruple and rank bad taste which have been one consequence of Egypt's economic *infitāḥ* are held up for the audience's inspection, though without, as Armbrust puts it, "the obligatory heavy *musalsal* didacticism".
5 Literally, "in love with the beautiful one". The title is a line from the colloquial poem *'Ēni 'Ala Naymat Ḍhihir* ("My Eye is on a Noon-time Star") by the well-known Bahraini poet, 'Alī 'Abdullāh Khalīfah.
6 This is a well-worn theme, also used in the Kuwaiti film (1964) *Bass Yā Baḥr* ("Enough, O Sea!").

7 There has not been a census which asked about religious affiliation since 1941. The Baḥārnah are not to be confused with the Persian-speaking Shi'ah who emigrated from Iran over the course of the last century, and live in the central quarters of Manama.

8 These groups used to be generically referred to as Ḥwala (sing Ḥōlī), though this term, seen by some as pejorative (the literal meaning is roughly "turncoat"), is now rarely heard and somewhat politically incorrect. The Kānō, Fakhrō and al-Mu'ayyad are among the best known Ḥwala families, and are well represented in Bahraini commerce and the public service. See Khuri 1980: 249-56 for more detail on the anatomy of human settlements in Bahrain.

9 Traditional pearl-diving ceased in Kuwait in 1959, and in Bahrain at the beginning of the 1960s.

10 The condition of the Baḥārnah at the turn of the twentieth century is summed up by Lorimer as follows: "Under the regime of the Shaikh ['Īsā bin 'Alī] and his relations the condition of the Baḥārinah, who form the bulk of the cultivating class in the principality, is unhappy. They are subject to a constant Sukhrah or corvée which affects their persons, their boats and their animals; their position in regard to the land is that of serfs rather than of tenants at will; and if they fail to deliver a certain amount of produce, which is often arbitrarily enhanced by the Shaikh's servants and relations, they are summarily evicted from their homes and in some cases are beaten and imprisoned as well. Some of the Baḥārinah are in theory landowners, having been allowed in the past to purchase gardens and obtain Sanads [deeds] for the same; but their estates are often resumed for no valid reason: even the sons of the present ruler have been guilty of this injustice. The crops of the Baḥārinah are frequently stolen by the Bedouins who range the island or are damaged by their animals. ... If oppressed beyond endurance the Baḥārinah might emigrate to Qaṭīf oasis, and a consciousness of this possibility is the principal check upon the inhumanity of their masters" (Lorimer 1908-15: 2/1: 259-60). See al-Tajir (1987: 35-70) for an account of the sectarian disturbances between 1922 and 1924.

11 This was also the case historically with the Muslim, Christian and (until 1952) Jewish dialects of Baghdad.

12 Perhaps it would be more correct to say that the Bahraini B dialects "have absorbed southern influences", as some B features link them with the dialects of southern Iraq.

13 Speakers of the A dialect often describe B speech as *qalj* ("closed, impenetrable"), and sometimes refer jocularly to the B villagers as *awlād il-'afar*, "the lads who say *'afar* ('perhaps')" in reference to a stereotypically B item of vocabulary.

14 Since roughly the mid-1960s, a similar process (though differently motivated) has resulted in the eclipse in public contexts of the dialect of Baghdadi Christians, who invariably now use the Muslim dialect except when in an in-group domestic environment (see Abu-Haidar 1990: 47).

15 Inevitably, there is a certain amount of simplification here, but the features selected would certainly be recognised by native Bahrainis as typical of the communities concerned.

16 The B village dialect forms given here are those of eastern Bahrain (Sitrah area) where the B dialect survives in its most "extreme" and unadulterated version.

17 My translation of the blurb on the box.

18 The only nod in the direction of linguistic reality I noticed was in the portrayal of a Persian sherbet seller, who spoke in the kind of broken Arabic that is the butt of Bahraini jokes about Persians' inability to speak Arabic properly.

19 *Ayāwīd* (<*ajāwīd*), "nobly descended", refers specifically, in A parlance, to the tribally descended communities, the historical "backbone" of the A community.

20 The *bayza* (Indian paise or pice) was formerly a low denomination coin, one-hundredth of a rupee when Bahrain used Indian coinage (until 1963).

21 Lit: "will get up (as strong as) a horse".

22 Khalaf is an official in the Bahrain Electricity Authority.

23 This was stated by Jāsim Khalaf in an interview in 1977 on the radio arts programme *'Ala Ṭarīq al-Fann*.

24 The producer of *Aḥmad ibn Aḥmad wa-l-Ḥajjī ibn al-Ḥajjī*, Nabīl al-'Alawī, is also, like the two actors, from the B community. The writing and production teams of all the A-dialect programmes I have mentioned are, to judge from their names, exclusively members of the A community.

25 It is certainly the case that education in the B villages, particularly of girls, has lagged behind the A areas.

26 When doing fieldwork in Bahrain in the 1970s, I wished to sample "educated" Bahraini speech, and, through the good offices of the British Council, approached around 100 literate Bahrainis who were attending English classes, making it clear that my aim was to talk to them in Arabic about Bahraini culture and language and how it had changed. The difference in strike-rate among the two communities was remarkable. More than 90 per cent of the A community members approached readily agreed to be interviewed, but the rate among the B community was only around 50 per cent and considerably less than this among those from B rural areas. All kinds of implausible excuses were adduced by the B speakers for not agreeing to be interviewed. Johnstone's *Eastern Arabian Dialect Studies* (1967), based on fieldwork done in 1958–59, has almost no information on the Bahraini B dialects, apart from occasional footnotes on one or two peculiarities of "village speech". This is an amazing but, in the social conditions of 40 years ago, entirely comprehensible gap in the description, given the extreme reluctance of the B community to open up to outsiders.

27 Holes 1983: 456.

28 *Ista'rab* when used by a B speaker in a Bahraini context means only "to adopt 'Arab (i.e. Bahraini Sunni) customs".

Chapter 3: Cultural Construction, the Gulf and Arab London

1 London-based field research formed one component of "Connection and Imagery: Transnational Cultural Flows and the Arab Gulf", part of the ESRC's Transnational Communities Programme.

2 London's real prominence as an Arab capital began with the oil boom and with Beirut's destruction as a cultural centre in the mid-1970s. A great many operations moved to London, particularly those concerned with print and television (Sakr 2001b). The Middle East Broadcasting Corporation's move to Dubai in late 2001 marks, in some ways, the end of an era.

3 For a summary of how extensive the arms trade is, see e.g. Hirst 2000. Other commercial and financial links are touched on by Field (1985) and form part of the wider phenomenon of Gulf overseas investment.

4 For London's place in the Gulf's own politics, see Al-Rasheed 1996, Aburish 1997, Fandy 1999. More generally "Londonistan" has been a node of transnational Islamic politics and debate.

5 All interviews were conducted by the author in 2000. In some cases names or details must be omitted, but I am extremely grateful to many people for their openness about careers and business.

6 Examples of World of Islam Festival publications include: Abdel Halim Mahmoud's, *The Creed of Islam*, with a foreword by Martin Lings; Janus Kirkman's *City of San'ā'* (with the Museum of Mankind); and Sheilagh Weir's *The Bedouin: aspects of the material culture of the bedouin of Jordan*.

7 David Khalili is an Iranian Jewish dealer in Islamic art who is arguably London's – and the world's – most prominent.

8 In an earlier life MacDermot taught social anthropology at the University of Durham and published a short monograph on the Nuer spear-cult.

9 In the gaps between banquets and presentations, there is a good deal of commercial and diplomatic activity. In the case at hand, the British seemed keen to promote their supposed expertise in organising "public-private initiatives", a means of drawing private-sector funds into what used to be public services: e.g. health, transport and power supplies.

10 I have not visited Highgrove myself. But reports from those who have are consistent on these points and sometimes intriguing on others. For instance, a colleague was asked over dinner, by the Prince's spiritual adviser, "Have you ever seen an angel?"

11 If Sir Donald's work appears in Oman's schools and colleges, certain other products of the same general project appear in other key locations. Al-Rasheed, in the present volume, notes for instance *Oman: a seafaring nation* (Facey 1979).

12 Museums are of obvious importance and are often mentioned in non-academic accounts of the Gulf (e.g. Graham 1978, Raban [1979] 1987). They remain understudied by academics. For the importance of "heritage" in Gulf settings see e.g. Davis and Gavrielides 1991, Montigny 1998.

13 One issue provoking a general sense of frustration – and perhaps one seen as safe to voice – was the problem of pinning down personal names. Administrators in particular argued that they often received one version of a name from an embassy, and then several different versions from the student throughout his or her course. This confusion over naming practices came up consistently throughout the day. The difficulties of being offered gifts are meanwhile touched on in print by Williams (1998: 29).

14 Examples of this "how to operate in the Gulf" literature include Rayburn and Bush 2001, Whelter 2000 and Atiyyah 1995 as well as Williams 1998.

15 The anthropological literature on this set of themes is large. For references see e.g. Dresch 2000a. Several works on the Gulf mention "hospitality" as supposedly a key Arab value (Atiyyah 1995: 32–3, Hawley 1998: 16, 17, Williams 1998: 29, 76, 85). Only Williams explores its role in everyday micropolitics.

16 The example (Atiyyah 1995: 44) is drawn from Kuwait, which provides such examples at several levels. A Western diplomat making polite conversation with a government minister in Kuwait wondered who, at a complex new traffic intersection, had right of way. His interlocutor replied, quite seriously, "Kuwaitis have right of way".

17 Anthropologists are notoriously uncomfortable with this logic, and treat "stereotyping" with elaborate care (see e.g Chock 1987). Most now treat "culture" with the same caution (Just 1995).

18 The solution to many of the puzzles discussed above (how formality and informality relate to status) is "friendship". One of the striking impressions received in the course of this work was how little simple friendship exists in the case of the Gulf and Britain. Despite the long experience on both sides, and a real affection in many cases, I found very few instances of people who felt they could drop in for coffee and share their problems. As an outsider, familiar with Britain and the Arab World but part of neither, I do not feel inclined to attribute this to anything as simple as "cultural difference".

Chapter 4: Transnational Connections and National Identity

1 For Omani history and relations with East Africa, see al-Sayyābī 1994.

2 On Omani expansion in East Africa, see the chronicles of the Grand Judge of Kenya, al-Fārisī 1994.

3 Saudi-Omani relations in the eighteenth and nineteenth centuries are discussed by ʿAbdwānī 1973. On the Ibadi movement in Oman, see Muʿammar 1994. On the general history of the Imamate see Ghubash 1998.

4 Between 1850 and 1870, the population of Muscat fell from 55,000 to 8,000. Muscat merchants moved to East Africa in search of new economic opportunities (Bhacker 1992).

5 Ho (1997) discusses the Hadrami diaspora and how it led to Hadrami *muwalladīn*, descendants of Hadrami fathers abroad (in Singapore and In-

donesia, for instance) and non-Arab mothers, who are treated as less than fully Hadrami at home. For a discussion of assimilation, creolisation and indigenisation of Arab diaspora communities, see Ho 2001.

6 The memoirs of Muḥammad bin Nāṣir al-Nadābī (2002) capture the economic situation in mid-twentieth-century Oman. He vividly describes hunger, drought and hardship, while glorifying the Islamic government of the Imamate.

7 Baluchis are Sunni immigrants who came to Oman from the Makran coast of Iran and Pakistan. The majority were brought by Omani sultans as mercenaries. They continued to play an important military role in the country until recently. The Lutis are a Shi'ah merchant community whose origins are believed to be in Sind and Hyderabad. They live in Muscat and Maṭraḥ. For further details, see Riphenburg 1998, Allen 1981.

8 In addition to tribal identity which distinguishes sub-groups within the Zanzibari community, internal distinctions stem from the use of different Swahili dialects, reflecting origins in various parts of East Africa. In present-day Muscat and among members of the community, minor dialect differences are not given serious attention.

9 In the literature on Oman, Zanzibaris are often described as the *pieds noirs* of the country (Le Cour Grandmaison, B. 2000: 31). There is some truth in this analogy. Like French colonial settlers in Algeria, Zanzibaris fought a fierce battle to protect their privileges but lost to the African majority. However, while the French government considered the *pieds noirs* as protecting and maintaining French influence in Algeria, Omani Zanzibaris never enjoyed this status as Zanzibar had been independent of Oman since the mid-nineteenth century. Furthermore, there was no government initiative in Muscat in the 1960s like that in France to organise the return of overseas Omanis. Some Zanzibaris became refugees without any valid travel documents.

10 Some Zanzibaris are found in the interior of Oman, especially in the towns of Nizwā, Izkī and Bahlā. Zanzibari employees of the government are posted to such places regularly. Also Zanzibaris working in the oil industry are often sent to the interior for special projects, after which they return to Muscat.

11 Interview with a Zanzibari, Muscat, April 2001: "You see, my surname and that of Mas'ūd indicate that we belong to a family whose Omani roots are centuries old."

12 Interview with a non-Zanzibari, Muscat, April 2000: "Zanzibaris are Africans. As far as I know, their manners and attitudes are so different from other Omanis. They have their own culture, which is more African than Omani."

13 Zahrah is a pseudonym. This biography was collected during two fieldwork trips to Muscat (2000 and 2001). But my friendship with Zahrah began in the 1980s. No words can describe her hospitality and patience, without which research in Oman would have been difficult.

[14] The anthropology of communities searching for "roots" in an age of globalisation is extensive. See e.g. James (ed.) 1995, Smith 1986, and Al-Rasheed 1998.

[15] In the context of describing the dispersal of her kinship network, Zahrah was amazed to discover that she had an Israeli cousin. Apparently a distant uncle who had lived in Zanzibar married a Jewish woman and had a son by her. He later divorced this woman, who fled to Israel in the early 1960s taking her "Omani" son with her. The child grew up in Israel and in the 1990s when Oman received an Israeli trade mission in Muscat, he came to Oman to "search for his ancestors".

[16] Zanzibaris are scattered in Muscat. While ethnic segregation is not obviously apparent, residence is determined by wealth. The old generation tend to live in the old neighbourhoods developed in the early 1970s, for example the streets around old Muscat and Maṭraḥ. Such areas are now run down, and wealthy members of the community tend to move to the new areas of Madīnat Qābūs and al-Qurm.

[17] On modern marriage ceremonial in the Arab World, see Tapper 1989.

[18] At the wedding I have particularly in mind both the bride and groom belonged to the Zanzibari branch of the Āl Bū Sa'īd family, distant relatives of Sultan Qābūs. Almost all the guests were Zanzibaris with the exception of a few Indian women, the wives of important merchants in Muscat.

[19] Noha is a pseudonym.

[20] According to a decree published in 1993, marrying an *ajnabī* (foreigner) requires permission. An *ajnabī* is someone who is not a citizen of Oman or countries of the GCC. Failure to obtain permission before marriage results in a fine of "not more than 2000 Omani riyals, exclusion or suspension from employment in the public sector, or refusal to grant the spouse an entry visa to Oman". See *al-Jarīdah al-rasmīyah* Nos. 514 (1 Nov. 1993), 515 (15 Nov. 1993), 661 (15 Dec. 1999).

[21] Interview with a non-Zanzibari nursery teacher, Muscat, April 2000.

[22] Sultan Sa'īd bin Sulṭān built Bayt al-Falaj in 1845 as his garrison's headquarters. Later the palace became the private royal residence of Sultan Fayṣal bin Turkī.

[23] *Guide to the Museum of the Sultan's Armed Forces* (n.d.). See this leaflet also for further details on Bayt al-Falaj.

[24] Princess Sālmah was no doubt one of the first adventurous Zanzibari women, initiating truly "transnational connections" not only with Africa but also with Europe. While her father's fleet roamed the Indian Ocean, with ships arriving in New York, she developed a relationship with a German citizen and eloped with him. The British arranged for the couple to leave for Aden where they organised their escape to Germany. After the death of her father, Sultan Sa'īd bin Sulṭān, Princess Sālmah travelled to London in an attempt to meet her brother, now the Sultan of Zanzibar, to

ask for her share of her father's wealth. She was disappointed when her brother refused her request. For further details, see Ruete 1998.

25 Celebrating Oman's seafaring heritage in official publications is different from acknowledging the multiple identities of Omanis. While official heritage literature glorifies Oman's African connections by publishing several chronicles and manuscripts pertaining to the historical period, the fate of the last Omani sultans of Zanzibar seems to have sunk into historical oblivion. It is worth noting that Sa'īd bin Taymūr did not welcome his relative Jamshīd, the deposed Sultan of Zanzibar, in the 1960s. Jamshīd died in exile in Britain in 1972.

26 As Sultan Jamshīd was excluded, so too was the last Ibadi Imām of the interior, Imām Ghālib, who lives in Saudi Arabia. While, in official publications, there is strong interest in highlighting the "democratic" and "just" government of previous Imāms, in social contexts there is almost complete silence on the question of the Imamate.

Chapter 5: Neither Autocracy nor Democracy but Ethnocracy

1 The only exception is the short period following the liberation of Kuwait from Iraqi occupation in 1991. For approximately one year, the Kuwaitis were a majority in their own country. By mid-1992, however, the number of expatriates was again higher than that of citizens (Longva 1997).

2 Only Kuwaiti-born men over 21 can vote and stand for elections.

3 According to Article 107 of the Constitution, "[t]he Emir may dissolve the National Assembly by a decree in which the reasons for dissolution shall be indicated. ... In the event of dissolution, elections for the new Assembly shall be held within a period not exceeding two months from the date of dissolution. If the elections are not held within the said period the dissolved Assembly shall be restored to its full constitutional authority and shall meet immediately as if the dissolution had not taken place." The Assembly was suspended from 1976 to 1981 and from 1986 to 1992. On both occasions, the clause on its restoration within two months was ignored.

4 During the 1999 elections, there were demands that the two functions be separated. The demand was flatly rejected by the Emir.

5 As a rule, Āl Ṣabāḥ men head the key ministries of foreign affairs, defence and information. Recruitment from the Assembly is rare, but has been on the increase during the past decade.

6 The term "liberal", widely used in the English-language press in Kuwait, can be misleading. The term appeared in Kuwait in the 1960s; then and throughout the 1970s, it referred to the sons of well-to-do, mostly merchant, families who went into local politics after they had returned home from studies in Beirut and Cairo where they were influenced by various versions of Arab Nationalism. A "liberal" in those days was thus a person of merchant (i.e. urban and relatively cosmopolitan) background, with left-leaning sympathies, who promoted the modernisation of society and poli-

tics and was critical, even hostile, towards the dynastic rule of the Āl Ṣabāḥ. The opposite of liberals were the tradition-bound badu, without formal education, who gave their unquestioned allegiance to the ruling family (Longva n.d.). With the rise of Islamic movements in the 1980s, the term "liberal" underwent a subtle change. From the mid-1980s onwards, what makes a Kuwaiti liberal is first and foremost his sympathies for secular politics. His opposite now is the Islamist, whose background might be urban as easily as tribal, and who is no longer uneducated. Most "liberals" refer to themselves in Arabic as *liberālīyīn*, while the Islamists call them *'almānīyīn* (secularists).

7 The National Assembly has a committee called the Public Funds Protection Committee. At present, the elected position of leader of the committee is held by the "liberal" opposition figure 'Abdullāh al-Naybārī, known as a staunchly "principled" deputy.

8 Several deputies are currently calling for charges of embezzlement to be formally lodged against two former ministers of finance, both Āl Ṣabāḥ men. Besides, the practice of appointing members of the ruling family to high offices has recently been sharply criticised in the Assembly by 'Abdullāh al-Naybārī (*Arab Times* 25 Jul. 2001). Whether the ex-ministers will be charged or whether fewer Āl Ṣabāḥ appointments will result remains to be seen. The important thing is that discontent can be publicly voiced through legitimate channels.

9 A recent illustration is the much publicised rejection by the conservative majority of the 1999 Emiri decree on women's political rights. If the Kuwaiti regime had been genuinely autocratic, Kuwaiti women might be in possession of their political rights today. Ironically, their continued exclusion is due to the Emir's willingness to respect the democratic principle of majority rule.

10 Monarchs and their families in the remaining constitutional monarchies in Europe do not have the vote. The same is true for the ruling family and military personnel in Kuwait.

11 In the Nordic countries, foreigners who have been resident and taxpayers for at least three years have the right to participate in municipal elections.

12 In the last resort, non-citizens can appeal for their own protection to principles of human rights. But human rights are a shifting and culture-bound notion whose interpretation and respect are commonly subject to manipulation.

13 Such as: the 1948 Universal Declaration of Human Rights (article 21), the 1966 International Covenant on Civil and Political Rights (article 25), and the 1967 Declaration on the Elimination of Discrimination against Women (article 4) (United Nations 1994).

14 Military service, which requires loyalty and dedication to the nation, remains ideally a matter for citizens, and few terms in most languages have such negative connotations as the word "mercenary".

15 Prior to the Iraqi invasion in 1990, the Palestinians, who numbered about 400,000, were the largest Arab expatriate community.

16 Whether the same acceptance is available to a French-speaking non-Western individual is another matter, but if acceptance is denied in this case, the kind of ethnocracy we are dealing with can no longer be called linguistic.

17 This rule does not apply to the nomads of the area.

18 Foreign husbands of Kuwaiti women are barred from Kuwaiti citizenship. The children of these couples are not considered Kuwaitis, since citizenship is transmitted through the father only.

19 Within the Arab migrant population, there has always been a minority of Christians that includes Lebanese, Iraqis, Palestinians, Egyptians and Syrians.

20 Above all, the Palestinian-Israeli conflict finds deep echoes in Kuwait, not least because of the presence, until 1990, of a large, stable, culturally influential and politically active Palestinian community. This community had, at one time, included Yasser Arafat and several other central PLO figures (Hart 1994).

21 Only workers earning at least KD400 per month are allowed to have their families with them in Kuwait or to sponsor servants. The average monthly salary of a domestic servant is KD40 (1 Kuwaiti dinar = between $3 and $4).

22 When Kuwait was invaded by Iraq in 1990, several Iraqis with established jobs in the emirate turned out to be army officers working for the Iraqi intelligence service. Another form of security risk were the violent riots that erupted in Khayṭān, a poor expatriate area in Kuwait City, in November 1999. For two consecutive days, angry Egyptians, Bangladeshis and Sri Lankans went on a rampage, burning shops and cars and clashing violently with the Kuwaiti police. The rioters were men who had been lured to Kuwait by Kuwaiti "visa traders" whom they had paid for promised work and residence permits (sponsorship). They received neither and ended up as penniless illegal aliens, hiding from the authorities yet unable to return home.

23 Throughout spring 2001 the Ministry of Labour and Social Affairs has been working on a draft to amend the provisions regarding transfer. At the time of writing, it is suggested that the period be extended to three years.

24 For more detail on the legal and social conditions under which expatriate workers live in Kuwait, see Longva 1997 and 1999.

25 Most sponsors are male, at least as far as sponsoring domestic servants is concerned. Husbands, not wives, are legally empowered to sponsor maids. Unmarried women do not live on their own, but with their parents, their brothers or their adult sons, in which case the male head of the house is the formal sponsor of expatriate servants.

26 Grandparents or an unmarried aunt are occasionally included, but they are no longer taken-for-granted components of modern household units.

[27] The "business" in question is in a large measure that of agency. Kuwait has practically no industries of its own and imports everything it consumes. The wealth of the merchants comes from their being agents for companies whose products are imported to Kuwait. The more agencies a businessman gathers, the more well known and prestigious he is and the more sought after for further business. A foreign company would not want to be represented by an anonymous, untested agent (Field 1985).

[28] Unlike Bahrain, Kuwait never had a communist party advocating more egalitarian distribution of wealth and power. The "liberal" opposition in the National Assembly, which in the 1960s and 1970s was sometimes described as "leftist", centres in fact on the heirs of some of the most illustrious merchant families. While traditionally opposed to the Āl Ṣabāḥ, their privileged social background hardly encourages them to challenge the social order fundamentally.

[29] Expatriates are an underclass not in the sense that they are all necessarily poorer than the Kuwaitis – some are richer – but in the sense that they all are subject to the power of a Kuwaiti sponsor/employer. Extremely few expatriate workers in Kuwait are their own masters.

[30] This is most obvious in the area of education: women make up 60 per cent of the students at Kuwait University. Nor are women absent from public life: there are currently two female undersecretaries, one woman ambassador and many businesswomen, and the rector of Kuwait University throughout most of the 1990s was a woman. Unlike Saudi Arabia, Kuwait has no laws forbidding women from driving, imposing on them a specific dress-code or confining their work possibilities within female-only sectors.

[31] This is the reason why the private sector obstinately refuses to employ citizens, no matter what threats and incentives the government may have issued during the past two decades since the policy of "Kuwaitisation" was first initiated.

[32] In the mid-1990s, the number of such marriages was rather stable: 838 in 1994, 903 in 1995 and 825 in 1996 (Kuwait 1997: 61). By comparison, the number of marriages of Kuwaiti women to non-Kuwaiti Arab men was lower: 605 in 1994, 602 in 1995 and 551 in 1996 (ibid.).

[33] Such legal constraints do exist for Kuwaiti women who wish to marry non-Kuwaiti men, as children from such marriages can never become Kuwaiti and the women themselves risk losing their citizenship.

[34] This is in addition to the already mentioned KD2,000 grant to help pay the brideprice.

[35] Most Kuwaitis below 40 do not treasure free education any more than do Frenchmen or Norwegians: why should they? They are brought up to believe that education is a citizen's right. This is also true for other social entitlements. What are the chances that such rights are effective means to ward off social discontent?

Chapter 6: Debates on Marriage and Nationality in the UAE

1 Fieldwork in the UAE in early 2000, and again in early 2001, formed part of the project on "Connection and Imagery", funded by the ESRC Transnational Communities Programme.

2 Ibrāhīm (1978) provides a useful compendium of Gulf nationality laws. For laws and decrees issued since then I am largely dependent on photocopies passed on by friends. As Ibrāhīm points out, Bahrain is something of an anomaly in that citizenship was given (not exclusively, of course) by place of birth; all the neighbouring states invoke primarily male descent. Legalities in the Emirates are discussed by 'Abd al-'Āl (1996).

3 This is a subject that often falls through the gap between political science and anthropology. Herb, for instance, from the former camp, says clearly enough that marriage is important (Herb 1999: 37), and then says nothing more about it. For how illusory a simple rhetoric of shared male descent is, see Baram 2001. For anthropological notes on marriage and descent, see Dresch 1998, and Conte 2000. Endogamy and close-range marriage are two different things, but there is no need to explore the issue here.

4 The fact that, for instance, Turkish or Pakistani migrants often marry closer in Europe than at home has long been noted. That a home population surrounded by foreigners might do the same is now established in the Emirati case (al-Gazali et al. 1997). Furthermore, the "closeness" is specific, not a matter of any first cousin but of *ibn* or *bint al-'amm* (cf. Fargues 2000: 139).

5 South Yemen's Marxist government around 1980 had as tight a grip on its people as any in the Arab World, and a particular enthusiasm for reforming family structure, but on bridewealth they met their match (Dresch 2000b: 136).

6 "al-'Anūsah al-qātilah", *al-Khalīj* 18 Feb. 2000. The structural complement is mothers-in-law never finding their daughters-in-law good enough, while pushing their own daughters to marry at all costs (*Kulli l-usrah* 17 Feb. 1999).

7 The use of "equality" here may need explaining. In most of the world people are unequally rich and powerful but kinship systems provide a ranking apart from this: e.g. wife-givers are symbolically superior to wife-takers, or vice versa. The Arab system, structurally, provokes questions of equality which are solved, not categorically, but always in individual terms (see Bonte, Conte and Dresch 2001).

8 Part of the issue is how one defines a family. I suspect from conversation with older people that terms such as *usrah* and *'ā'ilah* were not strongly marked: "families", so to speak, were not isolable (cf. Lienhardt 2001: 72–3). "Nuclear" families, meanwhile, appear in a recent Abu Dhabi survey (Abu Dhabi 1998: i. 26) as 60 per cent of the total and as averaging 12 persons. Subtract servants and one may well be looking at the usual

Emirati average of about 7, but what "extended" and "compound" families (*loc. cit.*) may amount to in local understanding is unclear.

9 The UAE Ministry of Planning in 1995 reckoned 35,000 local women of marriageable age were unable to find spouses (*al-Khalīj* 22 Apr. 1999). Some recent estimates run at double that (*al-Khalīj* 12 Apr. 2000). Plainly questions of definition matter here, and shifts in age of marriage can provoke a misleading appearance of crisis (Fargues 2000: 119, 142–6). A key issue not addressed in local figures is how many "foreign" marriages are second marriages and how many are sole, exclusive marriages.

10 For the region's modern history, see Heard-Bey 1996. For notes on certain of the tribes, see also Boot n.d.

11 The figures are published in *The GCC Demographic Report* (Edwards 1998) and accord with details one is sometimes slipped in government offices, save the figure for Asians tends to be slightly lower, that for Arabs higher. But the census itself may have missed people. The Ministry of the Interior is said to have had 680,000 nationals somehow registered, when the census counted only 600,000. On the other hand, illegal foreigners are very hard indeed to number.

12 See e.g. Ṣundūq al-Zawāj 1995: 75ff. To trace this theme through the press would need a separate paper, but for book-length treatments see al-Suwaydī et al. 1994, 1995. From at least 1995 to 2000, the usual salary for a live-in maid was 600 dirhams per month (Dh5 equals roughly £1; more accurately Dh3.6 equals $1).

13 Details of population structure differ among emirates and between rural and urban areas. But the last internal figures I saw for the Dubai urban area (June 2001) put nationals at 14.2 per cent of the total population. In Abu Dhabi city, figures for nationals within the workforce (not overall population) may easily be as low as 8 per cent.

14 The Kuwaiti formulation contributes whole paragraphs to those of Qatar and the Emirates. Written into the Kuwaiti law is an upper limit on naturalisation of 50 cases per year. In practice, says Fargues (1991: 57), the number has risen with absolute numbers of population but never strayed much from the original percentage. See also Longva and Crystal in the present volume.

15 A common-sense attachment to Oman has often been evident. When the Federation was first mooted it was hoped that Qatar and Bahrain would join, and practical connections with these states were close: in the Emirates' 1972 law on nationality (clause 44), fines for passport offences are quoted in Dubai-Qatar dirhams or Bahraini dinars. A separate Emirati currency appeared only in 1973.

16 A generation ago everyone would have known all the people who mattered to them, so names were in practice often simply of the form Aḥmad Muḥammad Aḥmad with no *laqab* or *kunyah*. Such common-sense links within tribes are less important than they were. Nor are tribes politically autonomous. But claiming tribal status has become much more important,

and one can think of several people with grand "tribal" names they did not have at school.

17 Some weight attaches to the *mu'arrif*, the person who supposedly "knows" in each tribe just who came from where and when. As of late 1999 the *mu'arrif* of the Āl Ḥamad, a tribe associated strongly with the offshore islands and the Iranian coast, was in prison accused of selling false certificates of tribal membership.

18 Muḥammad al-Rukn, "Naḥw i'ādah naẓar fī qānūn al-jinsīyah" (*al-Khalīj* 24 Jan. 2000), building on a paper by 'Ukāshah 'Abd al-'Āl. Naturalised citizens cannot be elected or appointed to public bodies (Ibrāhīm 1978: 204).

19 The establishment of *nasab* is a complex subject in Islamic law, a long way from simple notions of filiation. One may wonder, of course, how much the law matters. The details of *raḍā'ah* (relations produced by suckling), for instance, seemed almost a dead issue for a generation, but suddenly reappeared as a means to annul inconvenient marriages or avoid adultery charges (*Gulf News* 12 Feb. 2000). Meanwhile the reference to "blood" in discussions of nationality seems an import: common-sensical though the issue is in European law, and prominent in current Gulf discourse, it is not conspicuous in older Islamic theory (Bonte, Conte and Dresch 2001).

20 The implications of the 1975 wording of clause 3 are unclear (Ibrāhīm 1978: 84–9). The head of Nationality and Residence still spoke in 1999 as if the 1972 law applied: if the marriage lasted that long, a foreign woman married to an Emirati had the right to Emirati citizenship three years after declaring her wish for it (*al-Mawaddah* vol. 3, p. 20). The practice was far more complex.

21 For an excellent analysis of a rural Yemeni case, see Mundy 1979. Working not far from Mundy in Yemen I felt local marriage was a serious matter: *mutatis mutandis*, land and children played rather the role that mortgages and children played in my world. For a very different meaning to marriage in a (non-Western) cash economy, which perhaps sheds light on recent Gulf experience and the brevity of many marriages, see Hurgronje 1931.

22 However one defines the terms, the number of Emirati women married to foreigners is not large: one report gives a figure of 2,300 (*al-Bayān* 22 Apr. 1999). For comparison, the number of foreign wives who had gained Emirati nationality was about 18,000 (*al-Mawaddah* vol. 3, p. 22). The figures in 1980 had been about 1,700 and 8,000 (Ṣundūq al-Zawāj 1995: 78).

23 In the old days, says a recent author (Muḥammad 1999: 28), brideprice was within everyone's ability to pay, and "the spirit of co-operation reigned among all members of the group". I am more inclined to Heard-Bey's guess (1996: 148) that brideprice "has always been very high relative to income".

24 *al-Mawaddah* vol. 4, p. 25.

25 *Gulf News* 15 Nov. 1996, *Emirates News* 12 Jan. 1997.

26 Federal Law No. 47, 1992, part 1, para 3.

27 *al-Bayān* 3 Feb.1999, *Gulf News* 8 Sep. 1999, *al-Ittiḥād* 25 Feb. 1999, 28 Mar. 2000. Recently the budget has come under strain and complaints have been made about dishonest claims (*al-Ittiḥād* 26 Mar, 4 Apr. 2000, *Gulf News* 8 Jan. 2001).

28 In Saudi Arabia in the 1990s discussion began of *misyār*, a supposedly "traditional" form of marriage that few in the Sunni world had heard of since the Prophet's time (see e.g. Barakāt 1998). Unlike in the usual forms of marriage, the husband need not provide a home for the wife. Bin Bāz, Muftī of the Saudi realms, supported this as a way of absorbing unmarried Saudi women; others saw it as legitimising less than permanent connections overseas. Most Emiratis whom I know at all well dismiss it as "Sunni *muṭ'ah*", in effect no better than legalised prostitution.

29 Letter to the Federal Council, 16 Mar. 1986. Mentions of foreign marriage duly followed in the press (e.g. *Khaleej Times* 19 Mar. 1986, 20 Jul. 1986, *Gulf News* 20 Jul. 1986), and discussion predates Shaykh Ṣaqr's letter: indeed an inter-ministerial committee had been formed the year before (*al-Bayān* 21 Aug. 1985). "Pass laws" had been talked of as early as the 1970s (Sakr 1986: 70).

30 See, for instance, *al-Ittiḥād* 15 Dec. 1992. As always, the arguments had existed for years (e.g. *Khaleej Times* 7 Jan. 1986) and were redeployed, having apparently gone nowhere in the meantime.

31 I regret being unable to give the full text. The person who showed me the documents was unwilling to have me copy them. I should say, though, that both the content and the style of this first order suggest very hasty drafting. And rather than a simple law against women marrying out (Kapiszewski 2001: 52) the situation in practice has proved quite complex.

32 *Gulf News* 23 and 24 Jan. 1997. The number of Emirati women marrying non-Emiratis in Abu Dhabi in 1995 is given as 200, of whom 84 per cent married GCC citizens. As so often, however, the figures given in press reports do not add up.

33 Educational statistics can be sensitive to ask about but they are no great secret. Adding separate press reports suggests half the boys in Abu Dhabi drop out before the end of high school. The sex ratio at al-'Ain, depending on the course or faculty, can be anywhere between 2:1 and 4:1.

34 *al-Mawaddah* vol. 3, p. 31. The following quotations are from p. 29 of the same interview. The Emirati quotation earlier is from Khalfān al-Rumaydī, judge in the Abu Dhabi *sharī'ah* court (*al-Mawaddah* vol. 1, p. 48). A more traditional and scholarly view, of course, would be that Islamic law does not recognise the category "foreigner".

35 It is in the nature of local manners that dissent is not discussed publicly. Officials recently have noted people opposed to a marriage ban but "refused to name them" and spoken of major hindrances "but refused to go into detail" (*Gulf News* 25 Feb 2000). One is left guessing.

36 The interview in the same issue with 'Abdullāh 'Ubayd chose a little blonde girl for the caption, "What future does the daughter of a foreign

wife face?" Given the way that racism works in most places, one might think the answer in her case would be "pretty good", but what local readers in general made of it I do not know.

37 Document submitted to the third family seminar. For more on the seminar see *al-Bayān* 22 Mar. 1999. I am very grateful to friends for copies of the submissions and agenda.

38 A personal status law has been under discussion for many years. As yet no draft has been promulgated.

Chapter 7: Public Order and Authority

1 According to Dickson (1956: 42), in a crisis Kuwait's Ruler could raise a force of 2,000 badu and 3,000 townsmen.

2 Foreign Office, FO 371-21833: deGaury to PR, 7 Jul. 1938: 37.

3 As an observer noted in the 1950s, "there was then what was known as the Courts Department but at the same time the various departments had their own separate little 'Courts'. The Police Department, for example, tried all persons arrested by members of its force and hardly ever bothered to transfer them to the courts. The Public Security Department did the same with persons arrested by members of its force. The same was true of the Customs Department and the Municipality Department" (cited in Hijazi 1964: 429).

4 According to Mohammed al-Fahed (based on interviews with Du'ayj's son, Ṣabāḥ) in the early part of the twentieth century, Shaykh Du'ayj formed a police force to provide town security. He was succeeded by his son (al-Fahed 1989: 106).

5 India Office, IO R/15/5/206: PA to PR, 12 Mar. 1939; 74; L/P&S/12/3758: K.I.S., 1-5 Mar. 1939. See also Freeth and Winstone 1972: 120.

6 IO L/P&S/12/3758: K.I.S. 16-31 Mar.1939; IO R/15/5/206: PR to PA, 11 Mar.1939: 83. FO 371-39892: K.I.S., 16-30 Apr.1944, #130. They were released in a general amnesty in 1944.

7 IO R/15/5/206: deGaury to Fowle, PR, 6 Jan. 1939: 16.

8 An Interior Ministry official told me that in writing a report on interior ministries in the Arab World, he had requested and received information from 16 interior ministries, and of those, four lied to him about the structure of their forces. Interview, Brigadier 'Abd al-Majīd Khuraybiṭ, Planning Department, Interior Ministry, Kuwait, 10 Oct. 1995.

9 Interview, Colonel Yūsuf 'Abdullāh al-Su'aydī, director, Kuwait Police Academy, Kuwait, 25 Sep. 1995.

10 Ibid.

11 See Brown 1997: 209-16. Many of these are Asian.

12 In 2000, the government cut back on these, resulting in a further deterioration of maids' conditions (USDS 2001: 8).

13 Again in the Saudi case, Madawi and Loulouwa Al-Rasheed (1996) argue that religious and tribal traditions determined that Saudi leaders would

deal with religious (Shiʿah) opposition by force, but with tribal (Shammar) opposition by co-optation and more benign mechanisms.

14 The Kuwaiti government has detailed this violence, as have various human rights groups. See especially Human Rights Watch 1990a and 1990b, and AOHR 1990.

15 These, too, are detailed in various human rights reports. See, especially, Lawyers Committee 1993 and Amnesty International 1994.

16 Notable among the critics was Aḥmad al-Khaṭīb, who called publicly for the dissolution of the State Security police (Lawyers Committee 1993: 25).

17 Some of the data remained intact. One Interior Ministry official told me he copied much essential data, then reset the computers to read only English and format improperly. In October, he took the disks and left Kuwait. Interview, Khuraybiṭ.

18 Interview, al-Suʿaydī.

19 In 1998, the government announced that it would use DNA tests to verify the Kuwaiti lineage of some *bidūn*, Reuters on-line, 6 Jul. 1998; *Middle East International*, 18 Sep. 1998: 14.

20 Interview, Colonel ʿAbd al-Wāḥid Zayd, Legal Department, Interior Ministry, Kuwait, 24 Sep. 1995.

21 Interview, Brigadier Aḥmad al-Rājib, General Director, Assistant Undersecretary for Political Affairs, Interior Ministry, Kuwait, 23 Sep. 1995.

22 Interview, Muḥammad al-Fahd, International Liaison, Interior Ministry, 9 Oct. 1995, Kuwait.

Chapter 8: Gender, Religious Knowledge and Education in Oman

1 Research for this article was conducted between August 1996 and December 1997 and was supported by an IIE Fulbright fellowship and grants from several institutions at the University of Michigan. In order to respect their privacy, I have changed the names of the people with whom I lived and worked in Bahlā.

2 For a sustained review of Omani state discourse on education, among other popular themes, see Pridham 1986. For a more detailed examination of the history of "modern" education in Oman, see al-Dhahab 1987. This documents the changes in the curriculum of the schools over the century, the types of building that were used, how the classes were set up and who the teachers were: "modern" education has itself shifted over the century.

3 Between 1970 and 1980, for example, the number of modern state schools increased from 3 to 363.

4 The government closed all these schools in the wake of the arrests in 1995 of about 200 government officials, university professors and students who were accused of plotting against the government and spreading "fundamentalist" literature. The school's sign was still up on the Friday mosque in Bahlā while I was there, but was taken down during the summer of 1997. The Bahlā school had six subjects: Islamic studies, English, Arabic, mathematics, science and social studies, which included geography and

history. Egyptians and a Tunisian taught all the classes except English, which was taught by Hilāl, and Islamic studies, which was taught by my landlord's son by a first marriage and Jamāl, 'Ā'ishah's father. Unlike the "regular" schools, each of the five main Islamic studies subjects (Qur'ān, *fiqh, tafsīr, sīrah and ḥadīth*) had its own textbook. The three classes were taught simultaneously in different corners of the mosque, each class facing in a different direction. The students sat at desks, in straight lines, as in the "regular" schools and unlike the more advanced religious classes in the days before the introduction of mass state education.

5 El-Shibiny (1997) notes that "traditionally" in Oman, *siblah*s were used for teaching young children. While this might have been the case in other parts of Oman, in Bahlā classes were held either in or adjacent to mosques. In addition, *siblah*s were not built in Bahlā until the first half of the twentieth century.

6 A similar spatial disjuncture between the mosque and the school occurred in Ottoman Yemen in the 1860s and 1870s (Messick 1993: 104).

7 By August 1997, the library was moved to a larger house in another neighbourhood. Women were still only allowed to use the library on Friday mornings. A few things did change with the move, however. Previously, the system for checking out books was self-organised: whoever wanted to check out a book would write his or her name, the title of the book, the author and the date he or she borrowed the book in a notebook. In the new house, a man sat at the entrance and checked people and books in and out.

8 *'Abāyāt* are long, black, silky coverings worn over clothes and are somewhat different from the *chadors* worn by some women in Iran. While *'abāyāt* are usually cut as loose-fitting robes that rest on a woman's shoulders, *chadors* are less robe-like and rest on the top of a woman's head. In neither case is the woman's face covered. Face-coverings, when used, are separate articles of clothing.

9 In a similar example, Bayly (1986) describes how in mid-nineteenth-century India, certain cloths and colours did not symbolise particular things, but *were* those things.

10 The difficulty in judging peoples' responses to a lecture from within the class became clear to me one day when I went with a friend to a lecture by a male religious scholar. On that occasion, my friend wrapped her *'abāyah* round her so that even her feet were covered and then stared down at the ground in front of her for the entire hour-and-a-half lecture. One might assume that she, with her "serious" clothing and stern face, would agree with the strict prescriptions that the scholar was demanding of the women and girls in the room. As we left the room, however, she turned to me and said: "Can you believe that? What was he saying? I can't even shake the hand of my daughter's husband?!! That is ridiculous. The question about shaking hands is if there is a chance that there is a [sexual] relationship. If I don't even consider that there could be a relationship, then there is no problem."

11 The debates between Oman's national *muftī*, Aḥmad al-Khalīlī, and the late Saudi Muftī Bin Bāz became a source of discussions over who Ibadis are and how they differ from other groups. See al-Khalīlī 1409 A.H. and, for more on these debates, Eickelman 1989.

12 Ibadis consider their first Imām to be Jābir bin Zayd, who also lived in Baṣrah. There is, however, some discussion as to whether he considered himself to be an Ibadi (Ennami 1972: 40–4).

13 The first reference to such groups in North Africa dates to the tenth century and the first set of rules seem to have been established in the beginning of the eleventh century by Abū 'Abdullāh Muḥammad bin Bakr (Lewicki 1986: 95; Wilkinson 1985: 236). These earliest rules focus on the daily obligations of the '*azzābah*, or "recluses", who were the students and teachers at the hostels. Bin Bakr's rules are found in Abū l-Abbās Aḥmad bin Sa'īd al-Darjīnī's thirteenth-century work, *Kitāb ṭabaqāt al-mashāyikh*. The fifteenth-century scholar Abū l-Qāsim al-Barrādī wrote an almost identical book of rules as part of his *Kitāb jawāhir al-muntaqāt*. For a comparison of the two versions, see Rubinacci 1961. In his translation of Bin Bakr's rules as found in al-Darjīnī, Rubinacci carefully notes how al-Barrādī's version is almost identical to Bin Bakr's four centuries earlier. Although al-Barrādī changed some of the phrases, he was careful to maintain the same regulations.

14 Whereas Rubinacci suggests that Abū 'Ammār 'Abd al-Kāfī's rules reflect an evolution towards a political and religious role for the *ḥalqah*s by the twelfth century (Rubinacci 1961: 57), Lewicki insists that the political *ḥalqah*s really became important only after the fifteenth century, particularly in the Mīzāb (Lewicki 1986: 97).

15 For example, Chapter 8 of the main textbook on the history of Islam in Oman at Sulṭān Qābūs University sketches the role of the *ḥalqah* among Ibadis of North Africa ('Ashūr and Khalīfat 1993).

16 'Abd al-Raḥmān al-Sālimī (personal communication) has pointed out to me that in the classic Omani works such as *al-Muṣannif* by Aḥmad al-Kindī (d. 1162), *al-Ḍīyā'* by Salmā al-'Awtabī (d. early twelfth century), *Bayān al-shar'* by Muḥammad al-Kindī (d. 1115), and the much later *Qāmūs al-sharī'ah* by Jumayyil al-Sa'dī (d. first half of the nineteenth century), the authors focus on the categories of *ẓuhūr* and *difā'* and hardly discuss the state of *kitmān*.

17 On Sulaymān al-Bārūnī see Peterson 1987, Vaglieri 1934 and Abū l-Yaqzān al-Ḥājj Ibrāhīm 1956. On Muḥammad Aṭfiyyash, see Cuperly 1972. Imbert (1903) noted that in his time *Kitāb al-nīl* was the most important book on Ibadi law in Algeria, which the French courts in Algeria used, along with Aṭfiyyash's commentary, to decide cases involving Ibadis. He pointed out that the Germans in East Africa based their study of Ibadi law on work by the Orientalist Eduard Sachau who had one copy of al-Bisyānī's *Mukhtaṣar*, which was reprinted in Zanzibar in 1886. Al-Bisyawī was Ibn Barakah's student in Bahlā in the eleventh century. Imbert's disparaging

tone towards Sachau's limited access to Ibadi law seems to indicate a rivalry between the scholars as well as the colonial powers.

18 See Ibrāhīm 1956: 17–18.

19 At the time of my fieldwork, there were 126 schools and approximately 73,000 students in the interior region of Oman. The 'Ā'ishah Riyāmīyah High School in Bahlā had 196 students: 100 in the humanities and 96 in the science section. The principal of the school predicted that about half of the students in the science division would attend the university, a teacher training college or the medical college. There were 41 teachers, only eight of whom were Omanis. The other teachers were Egyptians, Jordanians and Sri Lankans.

20 For the relatively recent emphasis on *ḥadīth* literature among Ibadis, see Wilkinson 1985.

21 "House" and "home" are deeply ambivalent values for feminist writers (Young 2000). On the one hand, they are associated with patriarchy, domesticity and repression. On the other, they are productive spaces and might, at least in their ideal construction, provide security.

Chapter 9: Political Actors Without the Franchise

1 Co-operatives are neighbourhood-based organisations that purchase goods in bulk and market them to households. Their governing boards are locally elected by shareholders in the individual co-operatives. While women can be elected, these boards remained all-male in practice until Khawshar and Nūrīyah were appointed.

2 The rapid development of Kuwait's oil industry was spurred by the nationalisation of Iran's oil in 1951 under Prime Minister Muḥammad Muṣaddiq, and the subsequent boycott of Iran led by Britain, the former owner of the National Iranian Oil Company, and the United States. The parents of the Kuwait Oil Company were Britain's Anglo-Iranian Oil Company (now BP) and Gulf Oil (now part of Chevron), a US company.

3 M.A. Tétreault interview with Sārah Akbar, Kuwait, Oct. 1992.

4 Nabīlah al-Mullah began working for Kuwait's Ministry of Foreign Affairs in 1968. In 1973, she represented Kuwait on the United Nations Security Council.

5 "Class" in Kuwait is complicated by the persistence of status markers such as family name in the determination of social status, and the virtual absence of a citizen working class. Here we use "upper class" to denote persons from merchant backgrounds, and "middle class" less as an economic marker than a term of self-identification by those who construct personal and professional identities from their own achievements rather than receiving them by virtue of family membership. The vast majority of citizen workers are dependent on wages and entitlements from civil service employment, but most Kuwaitis reject the proposition that they constitute a proletarianised stratum. Even recently sedentarised badu men who drive the famous orange taxis (an example of those we refer to as coming from

"tribal" backgrounds) do, after all, control the means of production of their own incomes. For a further discussion of the complexities of class analysis in Kuwait, see Tétreault 2000: 129–30.

6 Studies conducted after the war on the mental health of Kuwaiti children claimed that women's role in the household had limited the psychological impact of the occupation on Kuwaiti children (e.g. Eissa and Nofel 1993, Hammadi and Behbehani 1993, Maksoud and Nazer 1993).

7 Interview with Akbar.

8 M.A. Tétreault interview with Lubnā Sayf 'Abdullāh, Kuwait, Sep. 1992.

9 Among the indications that the coalition structure in the National Assembly might be changing is the law passed in 2001 altering the rules under which the state pays subsidies to families. The new law responds to the economic liberals (including some Islamists as well as political liberals) in the Chamber of Commerce and Industry. They have been working to extend family allowances to cover men working in the private sector as a means to reduce the effective wage differential between public and private sector employment. Formerly, only men working for the government, and women working for the government whose husbands were employed in the private sector, qualified for the family allowances. Now all employed men qualify. However, the new law limits the number of children per family eligible for an allowance to five. Previously, there was no limit – a benefit to rural men with large families.

10 Another indication that the government had other aims in mind when it issued the women's rights decree is that it failed to lobby members of the newly elected parliament to support the measure until nearly all of them already had taken public positions on it. By then, it was politically impossible for those who had declared their intention to vote against the bill to change their minds.

Chapter 10: Managing God's Guests

1 I am grateful to Christa Salamandra, Jeong-min Seo, Ali Parchami, Yahya Birt and Mathias Diederich for their research assistance with this paper and to John Gurney for his helpful comments.

2 Sharīf Ḥusayn had alienated Muslim opinion in part because of the perceived mistreatment of pilgrims, particularly from Egypt, and because of his assumption of the title of Caliph in 1924. The Khilāfat Movement particularly opposed the latter.

3 Compare Cobbold 1934: 18. Chale spoke of a six-year probationary period, whereas Cobbold noted a one-year requirement in Jiddah.

4 *Al-Amn wa'l-amān*, Saudi television, Channel 1, 3 Mar. 2001.

5 *Anzimat al-kashf al-sarī'*, Saudi television, Channel 1, 6 Mar. 2001.

6 "Makkah the Blessed", http://www.jannah.org/articles/makkah.html, 17 Jun. 2001.

7 Interview with Usāmah bin Faḍl al-Bār, director of the Ḥajj Research Centre, Umm al-Qurā University, in Jiddah, 15 Jul. 2000.

8 *Al-Amn wa-l-amān*, Saudi television, Channel 1, 3 Mar. 2001.

9 Ibid.

10 For example, "One New York Woman's Thoughts About the Hajj": http://www.cnn.com/SPECIALS/2001/stories/hershey.notebook/index.html (4 Jun. 2001); "For American, Hajj is Exhilarating, Humbling": http://www.cnn.com/SPECIALS/2001/hajj/stories/salam.notebook/ (3 Jun. 2001).

11 For the official Saudi position on the 1987 incident, which was referred to as *al-fitnah*, see Saudi Arabia n.d. c: 29-67, 73-102, 134-6, 144-50, 183-92, 232, 261-2.

12 "The Hajj and the Haramain under Saudi Control": http://www.muslimedia.com/archives/editorial00/editor82.htm.

13 Although the Saudis tolerated the *barā'at min al-mushrikīn* rallies for a few years after the end of the Iranian boycott, their opposition to them is clear. They invoked the opinion of Ayatullah Mehdī Rūḥānī, who had many followers in Europe, that such demonstrations were divisive (Teitelbaum 1998: 593). Shaykh Bin Bāz denounced them as heresy (*al-Ḥayāt* 12 Apr. 1997).

14 *Al-Akhbār* (21.00 hours), Saudi television, Channel 1, 5 Mar. 2001.

15 The Saudi government said it would pay $4,000 to each victim's family (Aqsha 1995: 116-17).

16 A more polite echo of this can be heard in Murad Hoffmann's lament that the Quba' and al-Qiblatayn mosques outside Medina have been "repeatedly and recklessly rebuilt and built over" (Hoffmann 1998: 7).

17 Elsewhere, however, the group is not as sympathetic to the guides, referring to them as *al-muṭawwifīn al-intihāziyīn* – opportunist *muṭawwifs* (*al-Ḥuqūq* 45, 26 Apr. 1995). Prince Salmān, the Governor of Riyad, was accused of devising new fees for the pilgrims and thus reverting to the pre-oil period when *ḥajj* revenues were key to the public treasury (*al-Ḥuqūq* 39, Mar. 1995).

18 *Wuqūf* involves the standing of pilgrims at 'Arafāt on the ninth of Dhū-l-Ḥijjah when they listen to various sermons and engage in prayer and reflection. MIRA says that nearly 45 per cent of the camp area at Minā is reserved each year for 5 per cent of the pilgrims, the majority of whom are royals, their guests and government officials (*Arabia Unveiled* 6, Apr. 1977).

19 Statistics are often contradictory. The number from 1970 has been taken from Ma'had Khādim n.d. The 2001 figure is from *al-Sharq al-awsaṭ* 8 Mar. 2001. The 2003 and 2004 figures are from official Saudi internet sites: http://saudiembassy.net/2004News/News/HajDetail.asp?cIndex=1262, and http://www.saudinf.com/main/y6616.htm (30 Mar. 2004). One of the reasons why figures are elusive is that some compilations give an aggregate number whereas others count only pilgrims who come from outside the Kingdom.

20 "Egyptians Seized with 114 Passports" 19 Feb. 2001: http://www.cnn.com/2001/WORLD/briefs/02/19/world/ (17 Jun. 2001).

[21] "Council of Ministers Meeting", 7 Feb. 2000: http://www.saudiembassy.net/press_release/00_spa/02-07-cab.html (17 Jun. 2001). The Saudi government has formed an Establishment for Internal Pilgrims (*Mū'assasat al-Ḥujjāj al-Dākhil*) and a Committee for the Reception of Complaints from Internal Pilgrims (*Lajnat Istiqbāl Shakāwā al-Ḥujjāj al-Dākhil*). The director-general of the Establishment said that regulations for internal pilgrims have been in place for "ten years", putting their beginning somewhat later than noted above (*Jawlat al-kāmīrā*, Saudi television, Channel 1, 6 Mar. 2001).

[22] Information provided by Swashpawan Singh, director of Hajj Office, Ministry of External Affairs, Government of India, 4 Jun. 2001.

[23] Muḥammad bin Ṣāliḥ 'Uthaymīn, "How to Perform the Rituals of Hajj and Umrah": http://www.islamonline.net/English/hajj/2001/HajjRituals/article1.shtml (21 Jan. 2002).

[24] Ibid. It should be noted, however, that the Saudi government's position can be broadly sustained by the view of Shaykh Bin Bāz, who noted that visiting the three mosques in the area, inluding Nimrah, was an "innovation" (Bin Bāz 1992: 23–4). With regard to 'Arafāt, as early as 1960, Shaykh al-Azhar Maḥmūd Shaltūt stressed that, in order to avoid the press of the crowd, pilgrims need only spend an hour at 'Arafāt and not ascend the Jabal (Shaltūt 1980: 123, Wensinck 1986: 35).

[25] A Naqshabandi pilgrim also criticised the official "odd encouragement to shorten the prayer" in Mecca (Haddad 1999: 26).

[26] "New Pilgrimage Regulations Issued" 2000, *Saudi Review* 2000, Christa Salamandra interview with Hamdy El-Sawy, London, 6 Apr. 2000.

[27] Although the discussion is not framed in hostile terms and it is published by a Saudi-backed institution, a Malaysian-inspired analysis has also called for protection of various religious and historical sites (Mannan 1996: 40–1).

[28] A number of Iranian religious leaders, however, are adept at identifying unmarked graves in such cemeteries as al-Ma'lā and Khadījah in Mecca and al-Baqī' in Medina. Many of the early Imāms – notably apart from 'Alī and Ḥusayn – are buried in al-Baqī' cemetery. For an account of al-Baqī' in 1964, see Āl-e Aḥmad 1985: 28.

REFERENCES CITED

Aarts, P. 1994 Limits of political tribalism: post-war Kuwait and the process of democratization, *Civil Society* 3/6, 17-22

'Abd al-'Āl, Ukāshah. 1996 Markaz al-mar'ah fī tashrī' al-jinsīyah fī dawlat al-imārāt al-'arabīyah al-muttaḥidah, *Dirāsāt fī mujtama' al-imārāt* 12, 173-202

'Abdullāh, 'Abd al-Khāliq (ed.). 1998 *Qaḍāyā khalījīyah mu'āṣirah*, Sharjah: Jam'īyat al-Ijtimā'īyīn

'Abdwānī, Ṣādiq Ḥasan. 1973 *'Alāqāt al-dawlah al-sa'ūdīyah al-ūlā ma'a duwal sharq al-jazīrah al-'arabīyah*, Cairo: Dār al-Jīl

Abu Dhabi. 1998 *al-Natā'ij al-nihā'īyah li-masḥ mīzānīyat al-usrah* (3 vols), Abu Dhabi: Statistical Section, Emirate of Abu Dhabi Planning Department

Abu Haidar F. 1990 Maintenance and shift in the Christian Arabic of Baghdad, *Zeitschrift für arabische Linguistik* 21, 47-62

Aburish, Said K. 1997 *A Brutal Friendship: the West and the Arab elite*, London: Indigo

Adamson, P. 1991 Some comments on the origins of the police, *Police Studies* 14/1, 1-2

al-Ajmi, B. 1985 The Relationship between Guest Workers' Mode of Existence as an Underclass in Kuwait and their Rate of Crime, unpublished PhD thesis, George Washington University

Āl-e Aḥmad, J. 1985 *Lost in the Crowd* (trans. J. Green), Washington DC: Three Continents Press

Alessa, S.Y. 1981 *The Manpower Problem in Kuwait*, London: Kegan Paul

Allen, C. 1981 The Indian merchant community of Masqaṭ, *Bulletin of the School of Oriental and African Studies* 44, 39-53

Alloula, Malek. 1987 *The Colonial Harem*, Manchester: University of Manchester Press

Alnajjar, G. 2000 The challenges facing Kuwait democracy, *Middle East Journal* 54/2, 242-58

Alterman, J. 1998 *New Media, New Politics?: from satellite television to the internet in the Arab world* (Policy Paper No. 48), Washington DC: Washington Institute for Near East Policy

Altorki, S. and D. Cole. 1989 *Arabian Oasis City: the transformation of 'Unayzah*, Austin TX: University of Texas Press

Amin, H. and D. Boyd. 1994 The development of direct broadcast television

to and within the Middle East, *Journal of South Asian and Middle East Studies* 18/2, 37–50
Amin, M. 1978 *Journey of a Lifetime*, Nairobi: Camerapix Publishers International
Amnesty International. 1994 *Kuwait: three years of unfair trials*, New York: Amnesty International
Amnesty International. 2002 *Annual Report 2002*, London: Amnesty International Publications (http://www.amnesty.org) 13 Jun
Anderson, B. 1983 *Imagined Communities: reflections on the origin and spread of nationalism*, London and New York: Verso
Anderson, L. 1991 Absolutism and the resilience of monarchy in the Middle East, *Political Science Quarterly* 106/1, 1–15
Anderson, L. 2000 Dynasts and nationalists: why monarchies survive, in J. Kostiner (ed.), *Middle East Monarchies: the challenge of modernity*, pp. 53–69, Boulder CO and London: Lynne Rienner
Anderson, L. 2002 Democracy, despotism and disorder in the Arab World, paper presented at the conference on Challenges of Democracy in the Muslim World, Jakarta, 19–20 March 2002
al-ʿAnsī, Saʿūd. 1991 *al-ʿĀdāt al-ʿumānīyah*, Muscat: Wizārat al-Turāth al-Qawmī wa-l-Thaqāfah
AOHR. 1990 *al-Taqrīr ʿan ḥālat ḥuqūq al-insān fī l-kuwayt mundhu l-ghazw al-ʿirāqī*, Cairo: al-Munaẓẓamah al-ʿArabīyah li-Ḥuqūq al-Insān (Arab Organisation for Human Rights)
Appadurai, A. 1996 *Modernity at Large: cultural dimensions of globalization*, Minneapolis MN: University of Minnesota Press
Aqsha, Darul, D. van der Meij and J.H. Meuleman. 1995 *Islam in Indonesia: a survey of events and developments from 1988 to March 1993*, Jakarta: Indonesian-Netherlands Cooperation in Islamic Studies
Armbrust, W. 1996 *Mass Culture and Modernism in Egypt*, Cambridge: Cambridge University Press
Armbrust, W. (ed.) 2000 *Mass Mediations: new approaches to popular culture in the Middle East and beyond*, Berkeley and London: University of California Press
ARTICLE 19. 1997 *The Egyptian Predicament*, London: ARTICLE 19
As- Samarra'i, Said. 1993 Al Saud's heresy, *The Arab Review* (Jul.), 10–14
Asad, M. 1980 *The Road To Mecca* (4th rev. ed.), Gibraltar: Dar al-Andalus
Ashi, Sameer A.H. 1996 Accommodation for Pilgrims in Makkah: a phenomenological study, unpublished Ph.D. thesis, University of Michigan
ʿAshūr, Saʿīd ʿAbd al-Fattāḥ and ʿAwdh Muḥammad Khalīfat. 1993 *ʿUmān wa-l-ḥaḍārah al-islāmīyah*, Muscat: Jāmiʿat Sulṭān Qābūs
Assiri, A.-R. 1990 *Kuwait's Foreign Policy*, Boulder CO: Westview
Attiyah, Hamid. 1995 *How to Live and Work in the Gulf: planning your stay in the Gulf Arab states*, Plymouth: How To Books
al-Awatabī, Salmā bin Muslim. n.d. *Kitāb al-ḍīyā'*, Muscat: Wizārat al-Turāth al-Qawmī wa-l-Thaqāfah
Ayish, Muhammed I. 1997 Arab television goes commercial, *Gazette* 59 (Dec.), 473–93
Ayish, Muhammed I. 2001 American-style journalism and Arab world televi-

sion: an exploratory study of news selection at six Arab world satellite television channels, *Transnational Broadcasting Studies* (http://www.tbsjournal.com) 6 Spring/Summer
al-Azm, Sadik Jalal. 1981 Orientalism and Orientalism in reverse, *Khamsin* 8, 5-26
al-Azmeh, A. [1988] 1993 Wahhabite polity, reprinted in al-Azmeh, *Islams and Modernities*, pp. 104-21, London: Verso
al-Badrī, Fawzīyah. 1996 al-Taḥawwulāt al-ijtimā'īyah fī mujtama' dawlat al-imārāt, *al-Buḥūth al-fā'izah bi-jā'izat al-'uways li-l-dirāsāt* (Dubai: Nadwat al-Thaqāfah wa-l-'Ulūm) 7/2, 21-102
al-Bāhilī, Muḥammad. 1990 *al-Tilāfizyūn wa-l-mujtama'*, Sharjah: Maktab al-Masār
Bahry, L. 1999 Elections in Qatar: a window of democracy opens in the Gulf, *Middle East Policy* 6/4, 118-27
Bangash, Z. 1988 *The Makkah Massacre and Future of the Haramain*, Markham, Ontario: The Open Press
Barakāt, Muḥammad. 1998 'Āṣifat al-misyār, *al-Waṭan al-'arabī* 1111 (19 Jul.), 52-5
Baram, A. 2001 La maison de Ṣaddām Ḥusayn, in P. Bonte, E. Conte and P. Dresch (eds), *Emirs et Présidents: figures de la parenté et du politique dans le monde arabe*, pp. 300-29, Paris: CNRS
Barnett, M.N. 1998 *Dialogues in Arab Politics; negotiations in regional order*, New York: Columbia University Press
al-Barrādī, Abū l-Qāsim. 1885 *Kitāb jawāhir al-muntaqāt*, Cairo: Maṭba'at Bārūnī
Barth, F. 1983 *Sohar: culture and society in an Omani town*, Baltimore: Johns Hopkins Press
al-Barwani, A. 1997 *Conflict and Harmony in Zanzibar (Memoirs)*, Dubai: no publisher listed
Bayart, J.-F. 1989 *The State in Africa: the politics of the belly*, London: Longmans
Bayley, D. 1985 *Patterns of Policing: a comparative international analysis*, New Brunswick NJ: Rutgers University Press
Bayley, D. and H. Liang. 1992 *The Rise of Modern Police and the European State System from Metternich to the Second World War*, Cambridge: Cambridge University Press
Bayly, C.A. 1986 The origins of Swadeshi (home industry): cloth and Indian society, 1700-1930, in A. Appadurai (ed.), *The Social Life of Things: commodities in cultural perspective*, pp. 285-321, Cambridge: Cambridge University Press
Beaugé, G. 1986 La 'kafala': un système de gestion transitoire de la main-oeuvre et du capital dans les pays du Golfe, *Revue Européenne des migrations internationales* 2/1, 109-22
Beblawi, H. 1987 The rentier state in the Arab world, in H. Beblawi and G. Luciani (eds), *The Rentier State*, pp. 85-98, London: Croom Helm
Belchi, J.-M. 2002 Evolution of TV viewing in the Middle East 1996-2000, paper presented at the conference on New Media and Change in the Arab World, Amman, 27 February

Bendiab, A. 1991 Femmes et migrations vers les pays du Golfe - remarques sur l'état de la recherche, in G. Beaugé and F. Buttner (eds), *Les Migrations dans le Monde Arabe*, pp. 111-22, Paris: CNRS

Ben-Dor, G. 2000 Patterns of monarchy in the Middle East, in J. Kostiner (ed.), *Middle East Monarchies: the challenge of modernity*, pp. 71-84, Boulder CO and London: Lynne Rienner

Bhacker, A. 1992 *Trade and Empire in Muscat and Zanzibar: roots of British domination*, London: Routledge

Bianca, S. 2000 *Urban Form in the Arab World; past and present*, London: Thames and Hudson

Bin Bāz, 'Abd al-'Azīz bin 'Abdullāh. 1992 *Fatāwā: tata'alluq b-aḥkām al-ḥajj wa-l-'umrah wa-l-ziyārah*, Riyad: Dār Ibn Khazīmah li-l-Nashr wa-l-Tawzī'

Blin, L. 1996 *Le pétrole du Golfe : guerre et paix au Moyen-Orient*, Paris: Maison Neuve et Larose

Bonine, M. 1997 Population growth, the labor market and Gulf security, in C. Koch and D. Long (eds), *Gulf Security in the Twenty-First Century*, pp. 226-64, Abu Dhabi: Emirates Center for Strategic Studies and Research

Bonte, P. 1994 Mariage arabe: manière de dire ou manière de faire?, in P. Bonte (ed.), *Epouser au Plus Proche: inceste, prohibitions et stratégies matrimoniales autour de la Méditerranée*, pp. 371-98, Paris: EHESS

Bonte, P., E. Conte and P. Dresch (eds), 2001 *Emirs et Présidents: figures de la parenté et du politique dans le monde arabe*, Paris: CNRS

Boot, A. n.d. Tribes and families of Abu Dhabi, typescript produced for the Dutch embassy, Abu Dhabi, UAE

Bourgey, A. 1991 Les villes des emirats du golfe, sont-elles encore des villes arabes?, in G. Beaugé and F. Buttner (eds), *Les migrations dans le monde arabe*, pp. 69-91, Paris: CNRS

Bourquia, R. and S.G. Miller (eds) 1999 *In the Shadow of the Sultan: culture, power, and politics in Morocco*, Cambridge MA: Harvard Center for Middle Eastern Studies

Boyd, D. 1998 Saudi Arabia's international media strategy: influence through multinational ownership, paper presented at the Annual Meeting of the Association for Education in Journalism and Mass Communication, Baltimore MD, August

Brand, L.A. 1988 *Palestinians in the Arab World*, New York: Columbia University Press

Brown, N. 1997 *The Rule of Law in the Arab World: courts in Egypt and the Gulf*, Cambridge: Cambridge University Press

Bū Kalāh, 'Abdullāh 1998 al-Tarkībah al-sukānīyah li-duwal al-majlis ma'a l-tarkīz 'alā ḥālat mujtama' al-imārāt al-'arabīyah al-muttaḥidah, *al-Buḥūth al-fā'izah bi-jā'izat al-'uways li-l-dirāsāt* (Dubai: Nadwat al-Thaqāfah wa-l-'Ulūm) 8/1, 71-128

Bullard, R. 1961 *The Camels Must Go: an autobiography*, London: Faber and Faber

Cannadine, D. 2001 *Ornamentalism: how the British saw their empire*, London: Penguin

Castells, M. 2000 *The Rise of the Network Society* (2nd ed.), Oxford: Blackwell Publishers

CDLR 1994 *al-Ḥajj taḥt al-ḥukm al-sa'ūdī*, London: Lajnat al-Difā' 'an al-Ḥuqūq al-Shar'īyah (Committee for the Defence of Legitimate Rights), June (Muḥarram 1415 A.H.)

CDLR n.d. *A Report on the Saudi Government's Performance During Hajj*, London: Committee for the Defence of Legitimate Rights

Center for Research and Publications of Hajj. 1988 *Hajj: Politico-Religious Congress: compilation of Imam Khomeini's speeches and messages*, Tehran: Center for Research and Publications

Chatterjee, P. 1997 Our modernity, in Chatterjee, *The Present History of West Bengal: essays in political criticism*, pp. 193-210, Delhi and Calcutta: Oxford University Press

Chatty, D. 1996 *Mobile Pastoralists: development planning and change in the Sultanate of Oman*, New York: Columbia University Press

Chatty, D. 2000 Women working in Oman: individual choice and cultural constraints, *International Journal of Middle East Studies* 32/2, 241-54

Chock, P.P. 1987 The irony of stereotypes: towards an anthropology of ethnicity, *Cultural Anthropology* 2/3, 347-68

Clifford, J. 1988 *The Predicament of Culture: twentieth-century ethnography, literature and* art, Cambridge MA: Harvard University Press

Cobbold, Lady E. 1934 *Pilgrimage to Mecca*, London: John Murray

Conte, E. 2000 Mariages arabes: la part du féminin, *L'Homme* 154-5, 279-308

Cordesman, A. 1997 *Bahrain, Oman, Qatar and the UAE: challenges of security*, Boulder CO: Westview

Cordesman, A. 1998 *Demographics and the Coming Youth Explosion in the Gulf*, Washington DC: Center for Strategic and International Studies

Cordesman, A. 2001 *"Oil crash" and "oil boom": demographics and economics in the Gulf*, Washington DC: Center for Strategic and International Studies

Crystal, J. [1990] 1995 *Oil and Politics in the Gulf: rulers and merchants in Kuwait and Qatar*, Cambridge: Cambridge University Press

Crystal, J. 1992 *Kuwait: the transformation of an oil state*, Boulder CO: Westview Press

Cuperly, P. 1972 Muhammad Atfayyas et sa Risala, *Fi ba'd tawarih ahl wadi Mizab, Institut des Belles Lettres Arabes* 130, 261-303

Dalén, T. 1997 *Among the Interculturalists* (Stockholm Studies in Social Anthropology 38), Stockholm: Alqvist and Wiksell International

Daniels, J. 1971 *Kuwait Journey*, Luton UK: White Crescent Press

al-Darjīnī, Abū l-Abbās Aḥmad bin Sa'īd. n.d. *Kitāb ṭabaqāt al-mashāyikh* (ed. I. Tallay), Constantine: no publisher listed

Darwiche, F. 1986 *The Gulf Stock Exchange Crash: the rise and fall of the souq al-manakh*, London: Croom Helm

Davids, Abu Muneer Ismail. 2000 *Getting the Best out of the Hajj*, Hounslow UK: Message of Islam

Davis, E. 1991 Theorizing statecraft and social change in Arab oil-producing countries, in E. Davis and N. Gavrielides (eds), *Statecraft in the Middle East: oil, historical memory, and popular culture*, pp. 1-35, Miami: Florida International University Press

Davis, E. and N. Gavrielides (eds) 1991 *Statecraft in the Middle East: oil,*

historical memory, and popular culture, Miami: Florida International University Press
Davis, J. 1987 *Libyan Politics: tribe and revolution*, London: I.B. Tauris
Dessouki, A. 1991 Social and political dimensions of the historiography of the Arab Gulf, in E. Davis and N. Gavrielides (eds), *Statecraft in the Middle East: oil, historical memory, and popular culture*, pp. 92-115, Miami: Florida International University Press
al-Dhahab, M.H. 1987 The Historical Development of Education in Oman: from the first modern school in 1893 to the first modern university in 1986, unpublished Ph.D. thesis, Boston College
Dickson, H.R.P. 1956 *Kuwait and Her Neighbours*, London: George Allen and Unwin
Doumato, E. 1992 Gender, monarchy and national identity in Saudi Arabia, *British Journal of Middle Eastern Studies* 19/1, 31-47
Dresch, P. 1998 Mutual deception: totality, exchange and Islam in the Middle East, in W. James and N. Allen (eds), *Marcel Mauss: a centenary tribute*, pp. 111-33, New York and Oxford: Berghahn Books
Dresch, P. 2000a Wilderness of mirrors: truth and vulnerability in Middle Eastern fieldwork, in P. Dresch and W. James (eds), *Anthropologists in a Wider World: essays on field research*, pp. 109-27, New York and Oxford: Berghahn
Dresch, P. 2000b *A History of Modern Yemen*, Cambridge: Cambridge University Press
Dresch, P. 2001 The growth of Abu Dhabi, Dubai and Sharjah, paper presented at the ESRC conference on the Arab Gulf, Oxford, 24-6 September
Duncan, A. 1976 *Some Thoughts on the World of Islam Festival* (pamphlet), London: the World of Islam Trust
Eade, J. (ed.) 1997 *Living the Global City: globalisation as local process*, London: Routledge
Eade, J. 2000a Order and power at Lourdes: lay helpers and the organization of a pilgrimage shrine, in J. Eade and M.J. Sallnow (eds), *Contesting the Sacred: the anthropology of Christian pilgrimage*, pp. 51-76, Urbana: University of Illinois
Eade, J. 2000b Introduction to the Illinois paperback, in J. Eade and M.J. Sallnow (eds), *Contesting the Sacred: the anthropology of Christian pilgrimage*, pp. ix-xxiii, Urbana: University of Illinois
Eade, J. 2000c *Placing London: from imperial capital to global city*, New York: Berghahn Books
al-Easa, J. 1983 Changing family functions in Qatar, *Journal of South Asian and Middle Eastern Studies* 7/1, 50-6
al-Ebrahim, A. 1992 Perceptions of the People in Kuwait about the Performance of Kuwaiti Police and Mass Media Coverage of Police Activities, unpublished Ph.D. thesis, University of Birmingham
Economist Intelligence Unit. 2000 *Saudi Arabia Country Report* (August), London
Edwards, R. 1998 *The GCC Demographic Report*, Dubai: Middle East Research and Consultancy

Eickelman, D. 1978 The art of memory: Islamic education and its social reproduction, *Comparative Studies in Society and History* 20/4, 485-516
Eickelman, D. 1987 Ibadism and the sectarian perspective, in B.R. Pridham (ed.), *Oman: economic, social and strategic developments*, pp. 31-50, London: Croom Helm
Eickelman, D. 1989 National identity and religious discourse in contemporary Oman, *International Journal of Islamic and Arabic Studies* 6/1, 1-20
Eickelman, D. 1992 Mass higher education and the religious imagination in contemporary Arab societies, *American Ethnologist* 19, 643-54
Eickelman, D. 2001 Kings and people: information and authority in Oman, Qatar and the Persian Gulf, in J. Kechichian (ed.), *Iran, Iraq and the Arab Gulf States*, pp. 193-209, New York: Palgrave
Eickelman, D. and J. Piscatori. 1996 *Muslim Politics*, Princeton NJ: Princeton University Press
Eickelman, D. and M. Dennison. 1994 Arabizing the Omani intelligence services: clashes of culture?, *International Journal of Intelligence and Counter Intelligence* 7/1, 1-28
Eissa, J. and E. Nofel. 1993 *Screening for War Exposure and Post-traumatic Stress Disorder among Children in Kuwait, Aged 7-17* (Preliminary report), Kuwait: Ministry of Education
el-Emary, N. 1996 L'industrie du feuilleton télévision égyptien à l'ère des télévisions transfrontières, *Revue Tiers Monde* 37/146, 251-62
Emirates Center for Strategic Research and Studies. 1998 *The Information Revolution and the Arab World; its impact on state and society*, New York: British Academic Press
Enloe, C. 1980 *Ethnic Soldiers: state security in divided societies*, Athens: University of Georgia Press
Ennami, Amr Khlifa. 1972 *Studies in Ibadhism (al-Ibadhiyah)*, Tripoli: University of Libya Press
Errington, S. 1998 *The Death of Authentic Primitive Art and Other Tales of Progress*, Berkeley: University of California Press
Evans, P. 1997 The eclipse of the state? reflections on stateness in an era of globalization, *World Politics* 50, 62-87
Facey, W. 1979 *Oman: a seafaring nation*, Sultanate of Oman: Ministry of National Heritage and Culture
Facey, W. 1992 *Riyadh: the old city*, London: Immel
Facey, W. 1996 *Saudi Arabia by the First Photographers* (with Gillian Grant), London: Stacey International
Facey, W. 1997 *Dir'iyyah and the First Saudi State*, London: Stacey International
al-Fahed, M. 1989 An Historical Analysis of Police in Kuwait: prospects for the future, unpublished Ph.D. thesis, University of Exeter
Fahim, M. 1995 *From Rags to Riches: a story of Abu Dhabi*, London: The London Centre of Arab Studies
Fahy, M.A. 1998 Marginalized Modernity: an ethnographic approach to higher education and social identity at a Moroccan university, unpublished Ph.D. thesis, University of Michigan

Fandy, M. 1999 *Saudi Arabia and the Politics of Dissent*, New York: St Martin's Press
Fandy, M. 2000 Information technology, trust, and social change in the Arab world, *Middle East Journal* 54/3, 378–94
Farah, T. 1989 Political culture and development in a rentier state: the case of Kuwait, *Journal of Asian and African Studies* 24/1-2, 106–13
Fargues, P. 1991 La migration obéit-elle à la conjoncture pétrolière dans le Golfe? l'exemple du Koweit, in G. Beaugé and F. Buttner (eds), *Les Migrations dans le Monde Arabe*, pp. 41–66, Paris: CNRS
Fargues, P. 2000 *Générations arabes: l'alchimie du nombre*, Paris: Fayard
al-Fārisī, 'Abdullāh. 1994 *Āl bū sa'īdīyīn ḥukkām zinjibar*, Muscat: Wizārat al-Turāth al-Qawmī wa-l-Thaqāfah
Farjānī, Nādir. 1983a *al-Hijrah ilā l-nafṭ: ab'ād al-hijrah li-l-'amal fī l-buldān al-nafṭīyah wa-athar-hā 'alā l-tanmīyah fī l-waṭan al-'arabī*, Beirut: Markaz Dirāsāt al-Waḥdah al-'Arabīyah
Farjānī, Nādir. (ed.) 1983b *al-'Amālah al-ajnabīyah fī aqṭār al-khalīj al-'arabī*, Beirut: Markaz Dirāsāt al-Waḥdah al-'Arabīyah
Faroqhi, S. 1994 *Pilgrims & Sultans: the Hajj under the Ottomans, 1517–1683*, London: I.B. Tauris
Fattah, H. 1997 *The Politics of Regional Trade in Iraq, Arabia, and the Gulf, 1745–1900*, Albany: State University of New York Press
Featherstone, M. 1990 Global culture: an introduction, in M. Featherstone (ed.), *Global Culture: nationalism, globalisation and modernity*, pp. 1–14, London: Sage
Featherstone, M. (ed.) 1995 *Undoing Culture: globalisation, postmodernism and identity*, London: Sage
Field, M. 1985 *The Merchants: the big business families of Saudi Arabia and the Gulf states*, Woodstock NY: The Overlook Press
Finley, M.I. 1973 *Democracy Ancient and Modern*, London: Chatto & Windus
Fischer, M. 1980 *Iran: from religious dispute to revolution*, Cambridge MA: Harvard University Press
Foreign and Commonwealth Office. 2001 *Advice to British Hajjis*, London: Foreign and Commonwealth Office
Foucault, M. 1977 *Discipline and Punish: the birth of the prison* (trans. A. Sheridan), New York: Pantheon
Freeth, Z. and V. Winstone, 1972 *Kuwait: prospect and reality*, London: George Allen and Unwin
Friedmann, J. 1986 The world city hypothesis, *Development and Change* 17, 69–83
Fuccaro, N. 2001 Visions of the city: urban studies on the Gulf, *MESA Bulletin* 35/2, 175–87
Fuller, G. and I. Lesser 1997 Persian Gulf myths, *Foreign Affairs* 76/3, 42–52
Gamburd, M. 2000 *The Kitchen Spoon's Handle: transnationalism and Sri Lanka's migrant housemaids*, Ithaca NY: Cornell University Press
Gause, F.G. III. 1994 *Oil Monarchies: domestic and security challenges in the Arab Gulf states*, New York: Council on Foreign Relations Press

Gause, F.G. III. 2000 The persistence of monarchy in the Arabian peninsula: a comparative analysis, in J. Kostiner (ed.), *Middle East Monarchies: the challenge of modernity*, pp. 167-86, Boulder CO: Lynne Rienner

Gavrielides, N. 1987 Tribal democracy: the anatomy of parliamentary elections in Kuwait, in L.L. Layne (ed.), *Elections in the Middle East: implications of recent trends*, pp. 187-213, Boulder CO: Westview Press

al-Gazali, L.I. et al. 1997 Consanguineous marriages in the United Arab Emirates, *Journal of Biosocial Science* 29, 491-7

General Directorate. 1984 *Pilgrims Statistics: 1403 A.H.*, Riyad: General Directorate of Passports and Nationality, Saudi Ministry of the Interior

Ghabra, S. 1994 Democratization in a Middle Eastern state: Kuwait 1993, *Middle East Policy* 3/1, 102-19

Ghabra, S. 1997a Balancing state and society: the Islamic movement in Kuwait, *Middle East Policy* 5/2, 58-71

Ghabra, S. 1997b Kuwait and the dynamics of socio-economic change, *Middle East Journal* 51/3, 363-6

Ghubash, H. 1998 *Oman: une démocratie islamique millénaire, la tradition de l'imâma, l'histoire politique moderne (1500-1970)*, Paris: Maisonneuve et Larose

Giddens, A. 1991 *Modernity and Self-Identity: self and society in the late modern age*, Cambridge: Polity Press

Godfery, D. [1920] 1969 *The Peoples of Zanzibar: their customs and religious beliefs 1920-1969*, New York: Negro Universities Press

Goldberg, J. 1987 The Saudi Arabian kingdom, in I. Rabinovich and H. Shaked (eds), *Middle East Contemporary Survey*, vol. 11 (1985), pp. 579-614, Boulder CO: Westview Press

Golding, P. and P. Harris. 1997 Introduction, in P. Golding and P. Harris (eds), *Beyond Cultural Imperialism: globalization, communication and the new international order*, pp. 1-9, London: Sage

Graham, H. 1978 *Arabian Time Machine – self-portrait of an oil state*, London: Heinemann

Grossman, C. 1976 Aperçu sur l'histoire religieuse du Mzab en Algérie, unpublished PhD thesis (3ème cycle), Université de Paris IV

Guide to the Sultan's Armed Forces Museum. n.d. Sultanate of Oman: Ministry of Defence

al-Ḥaddād, Aḥmad 1998 Taṭawwur al-shakhsīyah al-khalījīyah, in 'Abd al-Khāliq 'Abdullāh (ed.), *Qaḍāyā khalījīyah mu'āṣirah*, pp. 83-8, Sharjah: Jam'īyat al-Ijtimā'īyīn

Haddad, Hj. Gibril Fouad. 1999 *From the Two Holy Sanctuaries*, Damascus: no place of publication

al-Ḥamad, Turkī. 1999 *al-Thaqāfah al-'arabīyah fī 'aṣr al-'awlamah*, London: Dār al-Sāqī

Hammadi, A, A. Staeher and J. Behbehani et al. 1993 *The Traumatic Events and Mental Health Consequences Resulting from the Iraqi Invasion of Kuwait*, Kuwait: Public Authority for Assessment of Compensation (PAAC)

Handler, R. 1985 On having a culture: nationalism and the preservation of Quebec's *patrimoine*, in G.W. Stocking Jr. (ed.), *Objects and Others: essays on museums and material culture*, Madison: University of Wisconsin Press

Hannerz, U. 1996 *Transnational Connections: culture, people, places*, London: Routledge

al-Harrbi, Abualziz S. 1998 The Housing of Pilgrims in al-Madina: Islamic principles and user satisfaction, unpublished Ph.D. thesis, University of Newcastle-upon-Tyne

Hart, A. 1994 *Arafat: a political biography* (rev. ed.), London: Sidgwick & Jackson

Harvey, D. 1989 *The Condition of Postmodernity: an enquiry into the origins of cultural change*, Oxford: Basil Blackwell

al-Ḥasan, Yūsuf. 1997 *Dawlat al-ra'āyah fī l-imārāt al-'arabīyah al-mutaḥḥidah*, Sharjah: Markaz al-Imārāt li-l-Buḥūth al-Inmā'īyah wa-l-Istrātijīyah

Hawley, D. 1977 *Oman and its Renaissance*, London: Stacey International

Hawley, D. [1978] 1998 *Courtesies in the Gulf Area: a dictionary of colloquial phrase and usage* (rev. ed.), London: Stacey International

Hawley, D. 1995 *Oman: jubilee edition*, London: Stacey International

Hawley, D. 2000 *Desert Wind and Tropic Storm: an autobiography*, Norwich: Michael Russell

Hawting, G.R. 1993 The hajj in the second civil war, in I.R. Netton (ed.), *Golden Roads: migration, pilgrimage and travel in mediaeval and modern Islam*, pp. 31-42, Richmond UK: Curzon Press

Heard-Bey, F. 1996 *From Trucial States to United Arab Emirates* (rev. ed.), London and New York: Longman

Henry, C. and R. Springborg 2001 *Globalization and the Politics of Development in the Middle East*, Cambridge: Cambridge University Press

Herb, M. 1999 *All in the Family: absolutism, revolution and democracy in Middle Eastern monarchies*, Albany: State University of New York Press

Herman, E. and R. McChesney 1997 *The Global Media: the new missionaries of corporate capitalism*, London: Cassell

Herzfeld, M. 1997 *Cultural Intimacy: social poetics in the nation-state*, New York and London: Routledge

Heyzer, N., G. Lycklama à Nijeholt and N. Weerakoon (eds) 1994 *The Trade in Domestic Workers: causes, mechanisms and consequences of international migration*, London: Zed Books

Hicks, N. and G. al-Najjar 1995 The utility of tradition: civil society in Kuwait, in A.R. Norton (ed.), *Civil Society in the Middle East*, vol. 1, pp. 186-213, Leiden: Brill

Hijazi, A. 1964 Kuwait: development from a semitribal, semicolonial society to democracy and sovereignty, *American Journal of Comparative Law* 13, 428-38

Hirst, C. 2000 *The Arabian Connection: the UK arms trade to Saudi Arabia*, London: Campaign Against Arms Trade

Hizb al-Tahrir, n.d. *Is Saudi a State of Islam or Kufr?*, London: Al-Khalifah Publications

Ho, E. 1997 Hadramis Abroad and in Hadramaut: the *muwalladīn*, in U. Freitag and W. Clarence-Smith (eds), *Hadrami Traders, Scholars, and Statesmen in the Indian Ocean, 1750s-1960s*, pp. 131-46, Leiden: Brill

Ho, E. 2001 Le don précieux de la généalogie, in P. Bonte, E. Conte and P.

Dresch (eds), *Emirs et présidents: figures de la parenté et du politique dans le monde arabe*, pp. 79–110, Paris: CNRS
Hobsbawm, E. 1996 The future of the state, in C. Hewitt de Alcantra (ed.), *Social Futures, Global Visions*, pp. 55–66, Oxford: Blackwell
Hoffman, M.W. 1998 *Journey to Makkah* (trans. A. Ryschka), Beltsville MD: Amana Publications
Holes, C. 1983 Patterns of communal language variation in Bahrain, *Language in Society* 12, pp. 433–57
Holes C.D. 1995 Community, dialect and urbanisation in the Arabic-speaking Middle East, *Bulletin of the School of Oriental and African Studies* 58, 270–87
Hudson, M. 1977 *Arab Politics: the search for legitimacy*, New Haven CT: Yale University Press
Human Rights Watch. 1990a *Iraq-occupied Kuwait: human rights violations since August 2, 1990*, New York: Human Rights Watch, Middle East Watch, November
Human Rights Watch. 1990b *Kuwait: deteriorating human rights conditions since the early occupation*, New York: Human Rights Watch, Middle East Watch, December
Human Rights Watch. 1995 *The Bedoons of Kuwait: citizens without citizenship*, New York: Human Rights Watch
Hurgronje, C. Snouck. 1931 *Mekka in the Latter Part of the Nineteenth Century*, Leiden: E.J. Brill
Ibrāhīm, Abū l-Yaqzān al-Ḥājj. 1956 *Sulaymān al-bārūnī bāshā*, vol. 2, Algiers: al-Maṭb'ah al-'Arabīyah
Ibrāhīm, Sa'd al-Dīn. 1982 *al-Niẓām al-ijtimā'ī al-'arabī al-jadīd: dirāsah 'an al-athar al-ijtimā'īyah li-l-tharwah al-nafṭīyah* (2nd ed.), Cairo: Dār al-Mustaqbal al-'Arabī
Ibrāhīm, Sa'd al-Dīn and Maḥmūd 'Abd al-Faḍīl. 1983 *Intiqāl al-'amālah al-'arabīyah: al-mushākil, al-āthār, al-siyāsāt*, Beirut: Markaz Dirāsāt al-Waḥdah al-'Arabīyah
Ibrāhīm, al-Sayyid Muḥammad. 1978 *al-Jinsīyah fī dawlat al-imārāt al-'arabīyah al-muttaḥidah wa-dirāsah muqārinah bi-l-jinsīyah fī duwal al-khalīj*, Abu Dhabi: Wizārat al-I'lām wa-l-Thaqāfah
Idārah al-Abḥāth wa-l-Nashr 1995 *Lamaḥāt 'an thawābit al-siyāsah al-sa'ūdīyah*, Riyad: Dār al-Āfāq li-l-Nashr wa-l-Tawzī'
Imbert, A. 1903 *Le Droit abadhite chez les Musulmans de Zanzibar et de l'Afrique Orientale*, Algiers: Adolphe Jourdan
Ingleton, R. 1979 *Police of the World*, London: Ian Allen
Iran. n.d. *Imam Khomeini's Last Will and Testament*, Washington DC: Interests Section of the Islamic Republic of Iran, Embassy of the Democratic Republic of Algeria
Iseman, P. 1978 The Arabian ethos, *Harper's* (February), 38–56
Islamic Center for Information and Development. 2000 *Kingdom of Saudi Arabia: 100 years in the service of Islam and Muslims*, Beirut: Islamic Center for Information and Development
Jacobs, J. 1996 *Edge of Empire: postcolonialism and the city*, London: Routledge

Jadhakhan, H.M. (ed.) 1990 *The Thieves of Riyadh: lives and crimes of the Al Sauds*, London: The Muslim Chronicle

James, W. (ed.) 1995 *The Pursuit of Certainty: religious and cultural formulations*, London: Routledge

al-Jāsim, Najāt ʻAbd al-Qādir. 1980 *Baladīyat al-kuwayt fī khamsīn ʻāman*, Kuwait: Kuwait Municipality

al-Jazā'irī, Abū Bakr. 1994 *al-Ḥajj al-mabrūr*, Medina: Maktabat al-ʻUlūm wa-l-Ḥikam

Johnstone T.M. 1967 *Eastern Arabian Dialect Studies*, London: Oxford University Press

Joyce, M. 1998 *Kuwait, 1945–1996: an Anglo-American perspective*, London and Westport CT: Frank Cass

Juska, A. 1999 Ethno-political transformation in the states of the former USSR, *Ethnic and Racial Studies* 22/3, 524–53

Just, R. 1995 Cultural certainties and private doubts, in W.R. James (ed.), *The Pursuit of Certainty: religious and cultural formulations*, pp. 285–30, London: Routledge

Kabbani, Rana. 1994 *Imperial Fictions: Europe's myths of orient*, London: Pandora

Kapiszewski, A. 2001 *Nationals and Expatriates: population and labour dilemmas of the Gulf Cooperation Council states*, Reading UK: Ithaca Press

Kelly, J. 1972 A prevalence of furies: tribes, politics, and religion in Oman and Trucial Oman, in D. Hopwood (ed.), *The Arabian Peninsula: society and politics*, pp. 107–41, London: Allen Unwin

Kelly, J. 1976 Hadramaut, Oman, Dhofar: the experience of revolution, *Middle Eastern Studies* 12/2, 213–20

Khalaf, S. 1992 Gulf societies and the image of unlimited good, *Dialectical Anthropology* 17/1, 53–84

Khalaf, S. 1999 Camel racing in the Gulf: notes on the evolution of a traditional cultural sport, *Anthropos* 94, 85–106

Khalaf, S. and H. Hammoud 1988 The emergence of the oil welfare state: the case of Kuwait, *Dialectical Anthropology* 12/3, 343–57

al-Khalīlī, Aḥmad ibn Ḥamad. 1409 A.H. *al-Ḥaqq al-dāmigh*, Muscat: Ṭabiʻa bi-Maṭābiʻ al-Nahdah

Khomeini, R. 1408 A.H. *The Historical Message of Imam Khomeini Addressed to the Pilgrims of Kaʻba*, [Tehran?]: Foundation of Islamic Thought

Khuri, F.I. 1980 *Tribe and State in Bahrain: the transformation of social and political authority in an Arab state*, Chicago: University of Chicago Press

al-Kindī, Aḥmad. n.d. *Kitāb al-muṣannif*, Muscat: Wizārat al-Turāth al-Qawmī wa-l-Thaqāfah

al-Kindī, Muḥammad ibn Ibrāhīm. n.d. *Bayān al-sharʻ*, Muscat: Wizārat al-Turāth al-Qawmī wa-l-Thaqāfah

King, A.D. 1990 *Global Cities: post-imperialism and the internationalism of London*, London: Routledge

Kline, N. 1963 Psychiatry in Kuwait, *British Journal of Psychiatry* 109, 764–74

Kostiner, J. 1993 *The Making of Saudi Arabia, 1916-1936: from chieftancy to monarchical state*, New York: Oxford University Press
Kuwait. 1963 Ministry of Guidance and Information, in Wizarat al-Irshād wa-l-Anbā, *Kuwait Today: a welfare state*, Nairobi: Quality Publications
Kuwait. 1997, 2000 *Annual Statistical Abstracts*, Kuwait: Ministry of Planning
Kuwait. 2001 *Population and Manpower Statistics*, Kuwait: Public Authority for Civil Information
Kuwait Oil Company Limited. 1959 *The Story of Kuwait*, Hertsford UK: Stephen Austin & Sons Ltd
Lawless, R. (ed.) 1986 *The Gulf in the Early Twentieth Century: foreign institutions and local responses*, Durham: Centre for Middle Eastern and Islamic Studies
Lawson, F.H. 1985 Class and state in Kuwait, *Middle East Report* 132, 16-32
Lawyers Committee. 1990 *Background Memorandum, Kuwait: recent human rights developments*, New York: Lawyers Committee for Human Rights
Lawyers Committee. 1993 *Laying the Foundations: human rights in Kuwait – obstacles and opportunities*, New York: Lawyers Committee for Human Rights
Le Cour Grandmaison, B. 2000 *Le Sultanat d'Oman*, Paris: Karthala
Le Cour Grandmaison, C. 1989 Rich cousins, poor cousins: hidden stratification among Omani Arabs in Eastern Africa, *Africa* 59/2, 176-84
Le Cour Grandmaison, C. 1998 L'héritage arabe, XVIIIe et XIXe siècle, in C. Le Cour Grandmaison and A. Crozon (eds), *Zanzibar aujourd'hui*, pp. 35-71, Paris: Karthala
Levinson, S.C. 1983 *Pragmatics*, Cambridge: Cambridge University Press
Levi-Strauss, C. 1985 *The View from Afar* (trans. J. Neugroschel and P. Hoss), New York: Basic Books
Lewicki, T. 1986 Halka, *Encyclopedia of Islam*, vol. 3, pp. 95-9, Leiden: E.J. Brill
Lienhardt, P. 1975 The authority of shaykhs in the Gulf: an essay in nineteenth century history, *Arabian Studies* 2, 61-75
Lienhardt, P. 1993 *Disorientations: a society in flux, Kuwait in the 1950s* (ed. Ahmed Al-Shahi), Reading UK: Ithaca Press
Lienhardt, P. 2001 *Shaikhdoms of Eastern Arabia* (ed. Ahmed Al-Shahi), Basingstoke UK: Palgrave
Lodhi, A. 1986 The Arabs in Zanzibar: from Sultanate to People's Republic, *Journal of the Institute of Muslim Minority Affairs* 7/2, 404-18
Long, D.E. 1979 *The Hajj Today: a survey of the contemporary Makkah pilgrimage*, Albany: State University of New York Press
Longuenesse, E. 1991 Raports de classes, solidarités communautaires et identité nationale dans les pays du Golfe, in G. Beaugé and F. Buttner (eds), *Les Migrations dans le monde arabe*, pp. 123-33, Paris: CNRS
Longva, A.N. 1993 Kuwaiti women at a crossroads: privileged development and the constraints of ethnic stratification, *International Journal of Middle East Studies* 25, 443-56
Longva, A.N. 1997 *Walls Built on Sand: migration, exclusion and society in Kuwait*, Boulder CO: Westview Press

Longva, A.N. 1999 Keeping migrant workers in check: the *kafala* system in the Gulf, *Middle East Report* 211, 20–3

Longva, A.N. n.d New wine in old bottles: the revival of 'hadhar' and 'badu' in Kuwaiti society and politics (unpublished typescript)

Lorimer J.G. 1908–15 [reproduced 1995] *Gazetteer of the Persian Gulf, Oman and Central Arabia*, Calcutta: Superintendent Government Printing, India [Reading UK: Garnet]

Losman, D. 2001 Economic security: a national security folly?, *Policy Analysis* No. 409, Washington DC: Cato Institute

Lowenthal, D. 1989 Nostalgia tells it like it wasn't, in C. Shaw and M. Chase (eds), *The Imagined Past: history and nostalgia*, Manchester: Manchester University Press

Lowenthal, D. 1996 *The Heritage Crusade and the Spoils of History*, London: Viking

Luciani, G. 1987 Allocation vs. production states: a theoretical framework, in H. Beblawi and G. Luciani (eds), *The Rentier State*, pp. 63–82, London: Croom Helm

al-Maamiry, A. 1988 *Omani Sultans in Zanzibar, 1832–1964*, New Delhi: S. Kumar

Mackay, H. 2000 The globalization of culture?, in D. Held (ed.), *A Globalizing World? culture, economics, politics*, London and New York: Routledge/Open University

MacKenzie, J.M. 1995 *Orientalism: history, theory and the arts*, Manchester: Manchester University Press

al-Maghiri, Sa'īd. 1985 *Riḥlat al-sulṭān khalīfah bin ḥārib ilā ūrūbā, 1937–1960*, Muscat: Wizārat al-Turāth al-Qawmī wa-l-Thaqāfah

al-Maghīrī, Sa'īd. 1995 *Juhaynāt al-akhbār fī tārīkh zinjibār* (2 vols), Muscat: Wizārat al-Turāth al-Qawmī wa-l-Thaqāfah

Ma'had Khādim. n.d. *A'dād al-ḥujjāj*, Mecca: Ma'had Khādim al-Ḥaramayn al-Sharīfayn li-Abḥāth al-Ḥajj

Mahmood, S. 2001 Feminist theory, embodiment, and the docile agent: some reflections on the Egyptian Islamic revival, *Cultural Anthropology* 16/2, 202–36

Maḥyū, Sa'd. 1999 *al-'Arab wa-l-'awlamah wa-l-taḥdīr li-l-qurn al-wāḥid wa-l-'ishrīn*, Sharjah: Kitāb al-Khalīj

al-Makkī, Muḥammad Ṭāhir al-Kurdī 1414 A.H. *Kitāb al-tārīkh al-qawīm li-makkah wa-bayt allāh al-karīm*, vol. 5, Mecca: no publisher listed

Maksoud, M.S. and F. Nazer. 1993 *The Impact of the Iraqi Occupation on the Psychological Development of Children in Kuwait*, Kuwait: Kuwait Society for the Advancement of Arab Children

Mannan, M.A. 1996 *Islamic Socio-economic Institutions and Mobilization of Resources with Special Reference to Hajj Management of Malaysia* (Research Paper No. 40), Jiddah: Islamic Research and Training Institute of Islamic Development Bank

Markaz Zāyid. 2000 *al-I'lām al-'arabī fī 'aṣr al-ma'lūmāt*, Abu Dhabi: Markaz Zāyid li-l-Tansīq wa-l-Mutāba'ah

Mazrui, A. 1975 *Soldiers and Kinsmen in Uganda: the making of a military ethnocracy*, London: Sage

MBC. 1997a Brief highlights, in MBC, *Background Information*, London: MBC Public Relations and Promotions Department, July
MBC. 1997b The Middle East Broadcasting Centre, in MBC, *Background Information*, London: MBC Public Relations and Promotions Department, July
McChesney, R.W. 1998 Media convergence and globalisation, in D. Kishan Thussu (ed.), *Electronic Empires: global media and local resistance*, pp. 27–46, London: Arnold
Messick, B. 1993 *The Calligraphic State: textual domination and history in a Muslim society*, Berkeley: University of California Press
Meyer, K. et al. 1998 Political participation of men and women in postwar Kuwait, *Research in Political Sociology* 8, 57–80
Mitchell, T. 1988 *Colonizing Egypt*, Berkeley: University of California Press
Mohamedi, F. 1997 Oil, gas, and the future of Arab Gulf countries, *Middle East Report* 204, 2–6
Montigny, A. 1998 Le *turāth* comme construction de l'identité nationale au Qatar, in N. Beyhum et al. (eds), *Patrimoine, identité, enjeux politiques* (Monde arabe contemporaine: cahiers de recherche 6), pp. 23–9, Lyon: GREMMO
Montigny, A. 1999 Ses jambes sont des ailes: le dressage de la chamelle de course, in J.-L. Jamard, A. Montigny and F.-R. Picon (eds), *Dans le Sillage des techniques: hommage à Robert Cresswell*, pp. 391–417, Paris: L'Harmattan
Montigny, A. 2001 La modernité comme reconstruction de l'identité au Qatar, paper presented at the ESRC conference on the Arab Gulf, Oxford, 24–6 September
Moody, S. 1999 Pay television in the Middle East, paper presented at the ARTICLE 19 seminar on Satellite Television in the Middle East and North Africa: Regulation, Access and Impact, Cairo, February
Moran, A. 1998 *Copycat TV: globalisation, program formats and cultural identity*, Luton UK: University of Luton Press
Morely, D. and K. Robins 1995 *Spaces of Identity: global media, electronic landscapes and cultural boundaries*, London: Routledge
Mu'ammar, 'Alī. 1994 *al-Ibāḍīyah bayn al-firaq al-islāmīyah* (3rd ed.), Muscat: Wizārat al-Turāth al-Qawmī wa-l-Thaqāfah
Mu'assasat Ḥujjāj Turkīyah n.d. *Dalīl al-ḥajj*, Mecca: Mu'assasat Ḥujjāj Turkīyah wa-Muslimī Ūrūbā wa-Amrīkā wa-Ustrāliyā
al-Mughni, H. 2000 Women's movements and the autonomy of civil society in Kuwait, in R.L. Teske and M.A. Tétreault (eds), *Conscious Acts and the Politics of Social Change*, pp. 170–87, Columbia: University of South Carolina Press
al-Mughni, H. [1993] 2001a *Women in Kuwait: the politics of gender* (rev. ed.), London: Saqi Books
al-Mughni, H. 2001b Women's organizations in Kuwait, in S. Joseph and S. Slyomovics (eds), *Women and Power in the Middle East*, pp. 176–82, Philadelphia: University of Pennsylvania Press
al-Mughni, H. and M.A. Tétreault. 2000 Citizenship, gender and the politics of quasi-states, in S. Joseph (ed.), *Gender and Citizenship in the Middle*

East, pp. 237-60, New York: Syracuse University Press
Muḥammad, Yūsuf. 1999 *al-Zawāj min ajnabīyāt wa-athar-hu 'alā abnā' al-khalīj al-'arabī* (2nd ed.), Beirut: Dār al-Wisām, Dār al-Hilāl
Mumford, L. 1961 *The City in History: its origins, its transformations and its prospects*, London: Penguin Books
Mundy, M. 1979 Women's inheritance of land in highland Yemen, *Arabian Studies* 5, 161-87
Murdock, G. 1990 Redrawing the map of the communications industries: concentration and ownership in the era of privatisation, in M Fergusson (ed.), *Public Communication: the new imperatives*, pp. 1-15, London: Sage Publications
al-Murr, Muḥammad. 1992 Hijrat al-muḥannaṭ, in *Shay' min al-ḥanān, al-a'māl al-qiṣaṣīyah*, vol.1, pp. 382-6, Beirut: Dār al-'Awdah
al-Murr, Muḥammad, 1997 *Āmāl waṭanīyah: maqālāt fī ḥubb al-imārāt*, Sharjah: Dār al-Khalīj
Muslim Institute. 1983 *Hajj – A Ritual or the Heart of the Islamic Movement*, London: The Open Press
al-Muṭawwa', Muḥammad. 1998 Ru'yah mustaqbalīyah li-l-awḍā' al-ijtimā'īyah al-siyāsīyah fī duwal majlis al-ta'āwun al-khalījī ba'd al-azmah, in 'Abd al-Khāliq 'Abdullāh (ed.), *Qaḍāyā khalījīyah mu'āṣirah*, pp. 67-77, Sharjah: Jam'īyat al-Ijtimā'īyīn
al-Muṭawwa', Muḥammad. 2001 UAE newspapers and the issue of cultural globalization, paper presented at the ESRC conference on the Arab Gulf, Oxford, 24-6 September
Naciri, M. 1997 Le role de la citadinité dans l'évolution des villes arabo-islamiques, in M. Naciri and A Raymond (eds), *Sciences sociales et phenomènes urbains dans le monde arabe*, pp. 131-47, Casablanca: Fondation du Roi Abdul-Aziz Al Saoud
al-Nadābī, Muḥammad. 2002 Dhikrāyāt shaykh 'umānī, *al-Ḥayāt* (London), 5 and 6 January
Nagy, S. 1998 Social diversity and changes in the form and appearance of the Qatari house, *Visual Anthropology* 10/2-4, 281-304
Nagy, S. 2000 Dressing up downtown: urban development and government public image in Qatar, *City and Society* 12/1, 125-47
el-Najjar M.Y. 1996 Consanguinity in Kuwait, *Colloquium of Anthropology* 20/2, 275-82
Nakhleh E.A. 1976 *Bahrain: political development in a modernizing society*, Lexington MA: D.C. Heath
al-Naqeeb [al-Naqīb], K. 1990 *Society and State in the Gulf and the Arab Peninsula: a different perspective* (trans. L.M. Kenny), London and New York: Routledge and Centre for Arab Unity Studies
al-Naqīb, Khaldūn 1996 *Ṣirā' al-qabīlah wa-l-dīmūqrāṭīyah: ḥālat al-kuwayt*, London: al-Sāqī
al-Naser, F.A. 1995 Attitudes of Kuwaitis toward the phenomenon of marrying non-Kuwaitis, *Annals of the Faculty of Arts* (Kuwait University) 15, 104

el-Nawawy, M. and A. Iskandar. 2002 *Al-Jazeera: how the free Arab news network scooped the world and changed the Middle East*, Cambridge MA: Westview/Perseus Books

Obaid, Thoraya 2002 Youth and population in the Middle East: expanding opportunity and hope, paper presented at the Washington Institute for Near East Policy, 25 April

O'Brien, E. 1977 *Arabian Days*, London, Melbourne and New York: Quartet Books

Oman. 1999 *Statistical Yearbook*, Sultanate of Oman: Ministry of National Economy

Ong, A. and D.M. Nonini. 1997 Introduction: Chinese transnationalism as an alternative modernity, in A. Ong and D.M. Nonini (eds), *Underground Empires: the cultural politics of modern Chinese transnationalism*, pp. 323-32, New York: Routledge

Onley, J. 2001 The Infrastructure of Informal Empire: a study of Britain's Native Agency in Bahrain, c. 1816-1900, unpublished D.Phil. thesis, University of Oxford

Pearson, M.N. 1996 *Pilgrimage to Mecca: the Indian experience, 1500-1800,* Princeton NJ: Markus Wiener

Peters, F.E. 1994 *The Hajj: the Muslim pilgrimage to Mecca and the holy places,* Princeton: Princeton University Press

Peterson, J. 1976 The revival of the Ibadi Imamate in Oman and the threat of Muscat, *Arabian Studies* 3, 165-88

Peterson, J. 1977 Guerrilla warfare and ideological confrontation in the Arabian Peninsula: the rebellion in Dhofar, *World Affairs* 139/4, 278-95

Peterson, J. 1987 Arab nationalism and the idealist politician: the career of Sulayman al-Baruni, in J.P. Piscatori and G.S. Harris (eds), *Law, Personalities, and Politics of the Middle East: essays in honor of Majid Khadduri*, pp. 124-39, Boulder CO: Westview Press

Piscatori, J. 2000 Religious transnationalism and global order, with particular consideration of Islam, in J. Esposito and M. Watson (eds), *Religion and Global Order*, pp. 66-99, Cardiff UK: University of Wales Press

Piscatori, J. 2003 Order, justice and global Islam, in R. Foot, A. Hurrell and J. Gaddis (eds), *Order and Justice in International Relations*, pp. 262-86, Oxford: Oxford University Press

Portes, A., L.E. Guarnizo and P. Landolt. 1999 The study of transnationalism: pitfalls and promise of an emergent research field, *Ethnic and Racial Studies* 22/2, 217-37

Pridham, B.R. 1986 Oman: change or continuity, in I.R. Netton (ed.), *Arabia and the Gulf: from traditional society to modern states*, pp. 132-55, London: Croom Helm

Prochazka Th. 1990 The spoken Arabic of Qaṭīf, *Zeitschrift für arabische Linguistik* 21, 63-70

Prunier, G. 1998 La révolution de 1964, in C. Le Cour Grandmaison and G. Crozon (eds), *Zanzibar aujourd'hui*, pp. 97-112, Paris: Karthala

Raban, J. [1979] 1987 *Arabia through the Looking Glass*, Basingstoke and London: Picador

Ralston, D.B. 1990 *Importing the European Army: the introduction of*

European military techniques and institutions into the extra-European world, 1600–1914, Chicago: University of Chicago Press

Ramazani, N. 1985 Arab women in the Gulf, *Middle East Journal* 39/2, 258–75

Ranchod-Nilsson, S. and M.A. Tétreault (eds) 2000 *Gender, States, and Nationalism: at home in the nation?*, London: Routledge

Al-Rasheed, M. 1996 Saudi Arabia's Islamic opposition, *Current History* 95(597), 16–22

Al-Rasheed, M. 1998 *Iraqi Assyrian Christians in London: the construction of ethnicity*, New York and Lampeter: Edwin Mellen

Al-Rasheed, M. 2002 *A History of Saudi Arabia*, Cambridge: Cambridge University Press

Al-Rasheed, M. and L. Al-Rasheed. 1996 The Politics of Encapsulation: Saudi policy towards tribal and religious opposition, *Middle Eastern Studies* 32/1, 96–119

Rayburn, R. and K. Bush. 2001 *Living and Working in Saudi Arabia*, Plymouth UK: How To Books

Riphenburg, C. 1998 *Oman: political development in a changing world*, Westport CT: Praeger

Road, S. and A. Harrison 1985 Gulf investment in the West: its scope and implications, in B.R. Pridham (ed.), *The Arab Gulf and the West*, pp. 80–109, London: Croom Helm

Roald, A.S. 1994 *Tarbiya: education and politics in Islamic movements in Jordan and Malaysia*, Lund, Sweden: Lunds Universitet

Robertson, R. 1990 Mapping the global condition: globalization as the central concept, in M. Featherstone (ed.), *Global Culture: nationalism, globalisation and modernity*, pp. 49–60, London: Sage

Robertson, R. 1992 *Globalisation: social theory and global culture*, London: Sage

Robinson, R. 1972 Non-European Foundations of European Imperialism: sketch for a theory of collaboration, in R. Owen and R.B. Sutcliffe (eds), *Studies in the Theory of Imperialism*, pp. 117–42, London: Longman

Ross, J.I. 1996 Policing change in the Gulf states: the effect of the Gulf conflict, in O. Marenin (ed.), *Policing Change, Changing Police*, pp. 79–105, New York: Garland Publishing

Rubinacci, M.R. 1961 Un antico documento di vita cenobitica musulmana, *Annali dell'Istituto Universale Orientale di Napoli* 10, 37–78

Ruete, E. 1998 *Memoirs of an Arabian Princess from Zanzibar*, Zanzibar: Gallery Publications

al-Rumayḥī, Muḥammad. [1983] 1995 *al-Khalīj laysa nafṭan: dirāsah fī ishkālīyat al-tanmīyah wa-l-waḥdah*, Beirut: Dār al-Jadīd

Rush, A. 1987 *Al Sabah: history & genealogy of Kuwait's ruling family, 1752–1987*, London and Atlantic Highlands NJ: Ithaca Press

Russell, S. 1989a Politics and ideology in migration policy formation: the case of Kuwait, *International Migration Review* 23/1, 24–47

Russell, S. 1989b Migration and political integration in the Arab world, in G. Luciani (ed.), *The Arab State*, pp. 373–93, London: Routledge

Russell, S. and M.A. al-Ramadhan. 1994 Kuwait's migration policy since the

Gulf crisis, *International Journal of Middle East Studies* 26/4, 569-87
Rutter, E. 1930 *The Holy Cities of Arabia,* London: G.P. Putnam's Sons
Rutter, O. 1937 *Triumphant Pilgrimage: an English Muslim's journey from Sarawak to Mecca,* London: George G. Harrap & Company
al-Saadon, H. 1990 The Role of Arabsat in Television Program Exchange in the Arab World, unpublished Ph.D. thesis, Ohio State University
al-Sabah, M.S. 1983 *Development Planning in an Oil Economy and the Role of the Woman: the case of Kuwait,* London: Eastlords Publishing
al-Sabah, S.N. 1999 Kuwait's welfare mentality must go [interview], *Middle East Quarterly* 6/1, 76-84
al-Sa'dī, Jumayyil ibn Khamīs. n.d. *Qāmūs al-sharī'ah,* Muscat: Wizārat al-Turāth al-Qawmī wa-l-Thaqāfah
Said, E. 1978 *Orientalism,* New York: Pantheon
Sakr, N. 1986 *The United Arab Emirates: one market or seven?* (EIU special report 238), London: Economist Intelligence Unit
Sakr, N. 2001a Contested blueprints for Egypt's satellite channels, *Gazette* 63/2-3, 149-67
Sakr, N. 2001b *Satellite Realms: transnational television, globalization and the Middle East,* London: I.B. Tauris
Sakr, N. 2002 Testing time for al-Jazeera, *ISIM Newsletter* 9 (January), 21
Salamé, G. 1994 Small is pluralistic: democracy as an instrument of civil peace, in G. Salamé (ed.), *Democracy without Democrats? The renewal of politics in the Muslim world,* pp. 84-111, New York: I.B. Tauris
Samarra'ī, Sa'īd as 1993 Al Saud's heresy, *The Arab Review* (July), 10-14
Sassen, S. 2001 *The Global City: New York, London and Tokyo* (2nd ed.), Princeton NJ: Princeton University Press
Saudi Arabia. 1993 *The Two Holy Mosques, 1414/1993,* London: Saudi Arabian Information Centre
Saudi Arabia. [2000?] *The March of Progress,* Riyad: Ministry of Information
Saudi Arabia. 2000a *The Kingdom of Saudi Arabia,* London: Royal Embassy of Saudi Arabia
Saudi Arabia. 2000b The hajj: a pilgrimage to Islam's holiest sites, *Saudi Arabia* (Washington, DC: Royal Embassy of Saudi Arabia) 17/1, 2-15
Saudi Arabia. n.d. a *The Two Holy Mosques,* Riyad: Ministry of Information
Saudi Arabia. n.d. b *Dalīl al-ḥajj fī khidmat ḍuyūf al-raḥmān,* Riyad: Wizārat al-I'lām
Saudi Arabia. n.d. c *Mādhā ḥadatha fī makkah al-mukarramah?,* Riyad: Wizārat al-I'lām
al-Ṣawī'ah, 'Abd al-'Azīz Ḥusayn. 1414 A.H. [1993] *al-Islām fī l-siyāsah al-khārijīyah al-sa'ūdīyah,* Riyad: Awrāq li-l-Nashr wa-l-Abḥāth
el-Sawy Travel. n.d. *Hajj and Umrah Arrangements: British Hajj mission,* London: no publisher listed
al-Sayyābī, Sālim Ḥamdī Shāmī. 1994 *'Umān 'abra l-tārīkh* (4 vols, 3rd ed.), Muscat: Wizārat al-Turāth al-Qawmī wa-l-Thaqāfah
Schechter, D. 1999 *The More You Watch, The Less You Know,* New York: Seven Stories Press
Schegloff, E.A. and H. Sacks. 1973 Opening up closings, *Semiotica* 7/4, 289-327

Scholz, F. 1997 Muscat: social segregation and comparative poverty in the expanding capital of an oil state, in M.E. Bonine (ed.), *Population, Poverty and Politics in the Middle East*, Gainesville: University of Florida Press

Seikaly, M. 1997 Bahraini women in formal and informal groups: the politics of identification, in D. Chatty and A. Rabo (eds), *Organizing Women: formal and informal women's groups in the Middle East*, pp. 125-46, Oxford and New York: Berg

Serjeant R.B. 1968 Fisher-folk and fish-traps in al-Bahrain, *Bulletin of the School of Oriental and African Studies* 31, 486-514

Shah, N.M. 1991 Asian women workers in Kuwait, *International Migration Review* 27/3, 464-86

Shah, N.M. and I. Menon. 1997 Violence against women migrant workers, *Asian and Pacific Migration Journal* 61, 5-30

Shaltūt, Maḥmūd. 1980 *al-Islām: ʿaqīdah wa-sharīʿah*, Cairo: Dār al-Shurūq

Sharafuddin, M. 1994 *Islam and Romantic Orientalism: literary encounters with the Orient*, London: I.B.Tauris

al-Sharhān, ʿAlī 1990 *Taḥawwulāt al-lughah al-dārijah: taʾthīr al-taghayyur al-ijtimāʿī ʿalā l-ʿarabīyah fī l-imārāt*, Sharjah: Ittiḥād Kuttāb wa-Udabāʾ al-Imārāt

Sheriff. A. 1987 *Slaves, Spices, and Ivory in Zanzibar: integration of an East African commercial empire into the world economy, 1770-1873*, London: James Currey

Shiber, S. 1964 *The Kuwait Urbanization*, Kuwait: Government Printing Press

el-Shibiny, Mohamed. 1997 Higher education in Oman: its development and prospects, in E.K. Shaw (ed.), *Higher Education in the Gulf: problems and prospects*, pp. 150-81, Exeter: University of Exeter Press

Shryock, A. 1997 *Nationalism and the Genealogical Imagination: oral history and textual authority in tribal Jordan*, Berkeley: University of California Press

Shryock, A. 2000 Dynastic modernism and its contradictions: testing the limits of pluralism, tribalism, and King Hussein's example in Hashemite Jordan, *Arab Studies Quarterly* 22/3, 57-79

Shryock, A. 2001 Une politique de "maisons" dans la jordanie des tribus: reflexions sur l'honneur, la famille et la nation dans le royaume hashemite, in P. Bonte, E. Conte and P. Dresch (eds), *Emirs et Présidents: figures de la parenté et du politique dans le monde arabe*, pp. 331-56, Paris: CNRS

Sinclair, J., E. Jacka and S. Cunningham. 1996 Peripheral vision, in J. Sinclair, E. Jacka and S. Cunningham (eds), *New Patterns in Global Television*, pp. 1-32, Oxford: Oxford University Press

Smeaton B.H. 1973 *Lexical Expansion Due to Technical Change, as Illustrated by the Arabic of al-Hasa, Saudi Arabia*, Bloomington: University of Indiana Press

Smith, A.D. 1986 *The Ethnic Origins of Nations*, Oxford: Blackwell

Spratt, J.E. and D.A. Wagner. 1986 The making of a *faqīh*: the transformation of traditional Islamic teachers in modern cultural adaptation, in M.I. White and S. Pollak (eds), *The Cultural Transition: human experience and social transformation in the third world and Japan*, pp. 89-112, London:

Routledge and Kegan Paul
Stacey, T. 1988 *Deadline*, Suffolk: Richard Clay Ltd
Starrett, G. 1998 *Putting Islam to Work: education, politics, and religious transformation in Egypt*, Berkeley: University of California Press
Stavenhagen, R. 1989 Communidades etnicas en estados modernos, *Américas Indígenas* 49/1, 11-34
Stouffer, S.A. and J. Toby. 1951 Role conflict and personality, *American Journal of Sociology* 56/5, 395-406
Sulṭān, Sālmah bint al-Sayyid Sa'īd. 1993 *Mudhakkarāt amīrah 'arabīyah* (trans. A. Al-Qaysi), London: Dār al-Ḥikmah
Ṣundūq al-Zawāj 1995 *Ṣundūq al-zawāj: ahdāf wa-ṭamūḥāt*, Dubai: al-Dhākirah li-l-Ma'lūmāt
Sussman, G. and J. Lent. 1991 Introduction: critical perspectives on communication and third world development, in G. Sussman and J. Lent (eds), *Transnational Communications: wiring the third world*, pp. 1-26, London: Sage
al-Suwaydī, Muḥammad, 'Abdullāh Abū Shihāb and Ṭaha Ḥasan 1994 *Khadam al-manāzil fī l-imārāt*, Dubai: Ṣundūq al-Takāful li-l-'Āmilīn
al-Suwaydī, Muḥammad and 'Abdullāh Bū Shahāb 1995 *Athar al-murabbīyāt al-ajnabīyāt 'alā khaṣā'iṣ al-usrah fī l-imārāt*, Dubai: Ṣundūq al-Takāful li-l-'Āmilīn
Swanson, G. 1975 The Ottoman police, in G.L. Mosse (ed.), *Police Forces in History*, pp. 39-56, London: Sage
al-Taher, I. 1995 *Kuwait: the reality*, Pittsburgh: Dorrance Publishing
al-Tajir M.A. 1987 *Bahrain, 1920-1945: Britain, the shaikh, and the administration*, London: Croom Helm
Tannen, D. 1989 *Talking Voices: repetition, dialogue and imagery in conversational discourse*, Cambridge: Cambridge University Press
Tapper, N. 1989 Changing marriage ceremonial and gender roles in the Arab World: an anthropological perspective, *Arab Affairs* 8, 117-35
Teitelbaum, J. 1998 Saudi Arabia, in B. Maddy-Weitzman (ed.), *Middle East Contemporary Survey*, vol. 20 (1996), pp. 580-602, Boulder CO: Westview Press
Tétreault, M.A. 1993 Civil society in Kuwait: protected spaces and women's rights, *Middle East Journal* 47/2, 275-91
Tétreault, M.A. 1997 Designer democracy in Kuwait, *Current History* 96 (606), 36-9
Tétreault, M.A. 1999 Sex and violence: social reactions to economic restructuring in Kuwait, *International Feminist Journal of Politics* 1/2, 237-55
Tétreault, M.A. 2000 *Stories of Democracy: politics and society in contemporary Kuwait*, New York: Columbia University Press
Tétreault, M.A. 2001 A state of two minds: state cultures, women, and politics in Kuwait, *International Journal of Middle East Studies* 33/2, 203-20
Tétreault, M.A. 2002 Pleasant dreams: the WTO as Kuwait's holy grail, paper presented at the *Critique* annual conference on Life and Politics in the Middle East, St Paul MN, 19 April
al-Thakeb, F. 1985 The Arab family and modernity: evidence from Kuwait, *Current Anthropology* 26/5, 575-80

al-Thamīnī, 'Abd al-'Azīz bin Ibrāhīm. n.d. *Kitāb al-nīl*, Cairo: Maṭba'at Bārūnī

Torab, A. 1996 Piety as gendered agency: a study of Jalaseh ritual discourse in an urban neighborhood in Iran, *Journal of the Royal Anthropological Institute* 2/2, 235-52

Touba, El Sayed M. 1997 Conservation in an Islamic Context: a case study of Makkah, unpublished M.Phil. thesis, University of Durham

Townsend, J. 1977 *Oman: the making of the modern state*, London: Croom Helm

Trompanaars, F. 1997 *Riding the Waves of Culture: understanding cultural diversity in business* (2nd ed.), London: Nicholas Brealey

Turner, V. 1973 The center out there: pilgrim's goal, *History of Religions* 12/3, 191-230

UNDP. 2001 *Human Development Report*, New York: United Nations Development Programme

United Nations 1994 *A Compilation of International Institutions*, vol. 1, part 1, New York and Geneva: United Nations

USDS. 1998 *Country Reports on Human Rights Practices: Kuwait*, Washington DC: US Department of State

USDS. 2001 *Country Reports on Human Rights Practices: Kuwait 2000* Washington DC: US Department of State

al-'Uthaymīn, Muḥammad bin Ṣāliḥ. 1995 *Fatāwā: manār al-islām* (3 vols), Riyad: Dār al-Waṭan

Vaglieri, L.V. 1934 Il tripolitano ibadita: Suleiman el-Baruni e sue notizie sull' Oman, *Oriente Moderno* 14, 392-6

Valensi, L. 1986 La tour de Babel: groupes et relations ethniques au moyen-orient et en afrique du nord, *Annales des Etudes en Sciences Sociales* 41, 817-38

Wagner, D.A. 1982 Quranic pedagogy in modern Morocco, in L.L. Adler (ed.), *Cross-Cultural Research at Issue*, pp. 153-62, New York: Academic Press

Wallerstein, I. 1974 *The Modern World System*, New York: Academic Press

Wavell, A.J.B. 1918 *A Modern Pilgrim in Mecca*, London: Constable & Company

Wensinck, A.J. 1986 Ḥadjdj, *Encyclopedia of Islam*, vol. 3, pp. 31-7, Leiden: E.J. Brill

Whelter, L. 2000 *Live and Work in Saudi Arabia and the Gulf*, Oxford: Vacation Work Publications

Wilkin, P. 2001 *The Political Economy of Global Communication*, London: Pluto Press

Wilkinson, J.C. 1983 Traditional concepts of territory in South East Arabia, *Geographical Journal* 149, 301-15

Wilkinson, J.C. 1985 Ibadi Hadith: an essay on normalization, *Der Islam* 62/2, 231-59

Wilkinson, J.C. 1987 *The Imamate Tradition of Oman*, Cambridge: Cambridge University Press

Williams, J. 1998 *Don't They Know It's Friday?: cross-cultural considerations for business and life in the Gulf*, Dubai: Motivate Publishing

Winckler, O. 2001 Demographic development and policies in the Arabian Gulf: the case of Oman under Sultan Qabus, *Journal of South Asian and Middle Eastern Studies* 24/3, 34-60

Wizārat al-Dākhilīyah n.d. *Al-Ḥujjāj min khārij al-mamlakah*, Riyad: Markaz al-Qiyādah wa-l-Sayṭarah wa-l-Taḥakkum

Wolfe, M. 1993 *The Hadj: an American's pilgrimage to Mecca*, New York: Grove Press

World Bank. 1995 *Claiming the Future: choosing prosperity in the Middle East and North Africa*, Washington DC: International Bank for Reconstruction and Development

World of Islam Festival Trust. 1983 *World of Islam Festival Trust, 1973-1983: the first ten years*, London: World of Islam Festival Trust

Wynn, L. 1997 The romance of Tahliyya Street: youth culture, commodities and the use of public space in Jiddah, *Middle East Report* 204, 30-1

al-Yafi, Adnan. A. 1993 *Management of Hajj Mobility Systems: a logistical perspective*, Amsterdam: Joh. Enschede Amsterdam BV

Yakkan, Fatḥī and Rāmzi Ṭānbūr. 2000 *al-'Awlamah wa-mustaqbal al-'ālim al-islāmī*, Beirut: Mu'assasat al-Risālah

Yamani, H. 1997 *To Be a Saudi*, London: Janus Publishing

Yamani, M. 2000 *Changed Identities: the challenge of the new generation in Saudi Arabia*, London: Royal Institute of International Affairs

Yiftachel, O. 1997 Israeli society and Jewish-Palestinian reconciliation: 'ethnocracy' and its territorial contradictions, *Middle East Journal* 51/4, 505-19

Young, I.M. 2000 House and home: feminist variations on a theme, in D. Olkowski (ed.), *Resistance, Flight, Creation: feminist enactments of French philosophy*, pp. 49-75, Ithaca: Cornell University Press

Young, J. 1996 Ethnicity and power in Ethiopia, *Review of African Political Economy* 23, 531-42

Yūnis, Badrī. 1999 *Mazāliq al-'awlamah al-ḥadīthah fī l-niẓām al-ālimī al-jadīd*, Beirut: Dār al-Farābī

al-Yūsuf, 'Abdullāh. 1996 *al-Masājid wa-l-amākin al-atharīyah fī l-madīnah al-munawwarah*, Beirut: Dār al-Mū'arrikh al-'Arabī

Zahlan, R.S. 1989 *The Making of the Modern Gulf States*, Reading: Ithaca Press

Zeghidour, S. 1989 *La vie quotidienne à la Mecque de Mahomet à nos jours*, Paris: Hachette

INDEX

'abāyāt (cloaks), 188, 212, 270n.8
'Abbāsids, 225, 227, 233
'Abd al-Kāfī, Abū 'Ammār, 271n.14
'Abd al-Majīd (Emir of Medina), 240
'Abd al-Majīd I, Sultan, 225
'Abd al-Majīd, Ismat, 46
'Abdullāh, Sa'd, 161, 162, 164
Abū Bakr's mosque, 242
Abu Dhabi, 4, 5, 20, 25-6, 139, 141-2, 143, 151
Abū Ghayth, Sulaymān, 179
Abū Ja'far al-Manṣūr ('Abbāsid caliph), 225
Abū Sa'ūd, Ṣafā', 41
Abū 'Ubaydah Muslim bin Abī Karīmah, 194
Action Time, 40-1
adjacency pairs, 197-8
adultery: Kuwait, 124-5
Aḥmad, Emir (Kuwait), 162, 163
Aḥmad I, Sultan, 225
Aḥmad ibn Aḥmad wa-l-Ḥajjī ibn al-Ḥajjī, 68-9
Ahmed, Lord, 236-7
'ā'ilīyah (familialism), 13, 14-15
ajānib (foreigners), 2, 122
ajnabī (foreign/foreigner), 25, 259n.20
Ajyād fortress, Mecca, 234
Akbar, Sārah, 212
Āl Bahār, 129
Āl Bū Sa'īd, 97
Āl Ghānim, 129
Āl Khalīfah, 11, 60, 137
Āl Nahyān, Shaykh 'Abdullāh (bin Zayed), 35, 45, 141
Āl Qatāmī, 129
Āl Ṣabāḥ, 11, 115, 128, 129, 137
Āl Ṣabāḥ, Rashā, 217
Āl Ṣabāḥ, Shaykh Sālim, 174
Āl Ṣaqr, 129
Āl Sa'ūd, King 'Abd al-'Azīz (Ibn Sa'ūd), 45, 48, 223, 224, 230
Āl Sa'ūd, Sulṭān bin 'Abd al-'Azīz, 82
Āl Sa'ūd, Prince Khālid al-Fayṣal, 81
Āl Thānī, 11
Āl Thānī, Shaykh Ḥamad bin Khalīfah (Qatar), 21, 28
Āl Thānī, Shaykh Khalīfah (Qatar), 21
Āl Thānī, Shaykh Sa'ūd, 77-8
al-'Alawī, Nabīl, 255n.24
Āl-e Aḥmad, Jalāl, 240
'ālimīyah (globalism), 7
Amin, Idi, 118
al-Āmīr, Wafā', 212
Amnesty International, 173
Among the Interculturalists (T. Dalén), 87
ANA Radio and Television, 39
'Anayzah (tribe), 177
AOL-Time Warner, 34, 40, 44-5
ARA Group, 38-41
Arab Bank, 76
Arab-British Chamber of Commerce, 87
Arab League, 45-6
Arab Media Summit, 36
Arab Nationalism/t, 9, 123, 158, 160, 163, 172, 176, 209
Arab Radio and Television (ART), 38, 41-4, 45, 49
Arab Women's Development Society (AWDS), 209

Arabian Gulf University, 52-3
Arabic: dialects, 56-62
Arafat, Yasser, 262n.20
'Ārḍīyah Co-operative, 203
ArRum, 78
art
  Arab, 78-82
  Islamic, 75-8
ART *see* Arab Radio and Television
aṣālah (authenticity), 4
'Āshiq fī Hawā z-Zēna, 56
Ashrāwī, Ḥanān, 46
Aṭfiyyash, Muḥammad, 195
al-'Atīqī, Khawlah, 204, 221
al-'Awāḍī, Badrīyah, 209, 210
al-Awā'il (1st Net), 41
al-'Awdah, Salmān, 6
'awlamah (globalisation), 7, 248n.8
al-'Awtabī, Salmā, 271n.16

Badr, General Zakī, 174
Badr ibn 'Abd al-'Azīz, Prince, 232
badu, 16, 122, 123, 160, 161, 167, 175, 179, 181, 218, 219, 220, 224, 272-3n.5
al-Baḥ, Jamāl, 154
Baḥārnah (Bahrain)
  community, 254n.10
  dialect, 57-62, 69, 254n.7
Bahlā, Oman: religious education in, 182-202
Bahrain
  A and B communities, 58-61, 69-70, 255n.26
  citizenship, 140-1
  dialects, 57-62, 69-71, 253n.2, 254n.12&13
  musalsalāt, 29-30, 52-7, 62-72
  police, 159-60
Bangash, Zafar, 230
Banī Yās (tribe), 138, 141, 142, 143
Banqueting House, Whitehall, 81
al-Baqī' cemetery, Medina, 240, 275n.28
Baqr, Aḥmad, 214
al-Barrādī, Abū l-Qāsim, 271n.13
al-Bārūnī, Sulaymān, 195
Baṣrah, 194, 195
Bayādir al-Salām (Threshing Floor of Peace), 208
Bayān al-shar' (Muḥammad al-Kindī), 271n.16
Berlusconi, Silvio, 44
al-Bidaḥ, Aymān, 210
bidūn: Kuwait, 120, 141, 171, 173, 174-8, 180
Bilāl's mosque, Mecca, 233
bilinearity, 31
Bin Bakr, Abū 'Abdullāh Muḥammad, 271n.13
Bin Bāz, 'Abd al-'Azīz, 13, 239, 243, 267n.28, 271n.13, 274n.13
Bin Lādin, Usāmah, 6, 248n.6
Bin Lādin Group, 234
Blunkett, David, 252n.41
Britain
  relations with Gulf states, 73-5, 257n.18
  soap operas, 54-5, 56

Cable News Network (CNN), 37, 38-9, 43-4
Cannadine, David, 74
CDLR *see* Committee for the Defence of Legitimate Rights
Cedant International, 87
CEDAW *see* United Nations Convention on the Elimination of All Forms of Discrimination Against Women
Centre for Intercultural Briefing, 87
Chale, David, 224
Chevron Corporation, 11, 15
Çiçek, Çemil, 232
"circle of knowledge" (*ḥalqat al-'ilm*), 193-6, 198
citizenship (*mawāṭanah*), 2, 8, 9-10, 24, 136
  Bahrain, 140-1
  Kuwait, 117, 119, 121-2, 141, 175, 176-8, 204, 209, 221
  Saudi Arabia, 141
  UAE, 141-2, 143-6, 151, 264n.2, 266n.20
Clark, Steve, 40
CNN *see* Cable News Network
Cobbold, Lady Evelyn, 224
Committee for the Defence of Legitimate Rights (CDLR, *Lajnat al-Difā' 'an al-Ḥuqūq al-Shar'īyah*), 232, 233

Conseil Supérieur de l'Audiovisuel, 43
consumerism (*istihlākīyah*), 27
Courtesies in the Gulf Area (Sir Donald Hawley), 93
Crescent International, 230
cross-cultural training, 87-95
culture(s)/cultural, 6, 7-8, 28, 29, 47, 60, 63, 64, 67, 73, 93-5, 121, 124, 134, 140, 143, 146, 150, 156, 199, 204, 255n.26, 258n.12, 261n.12
cultural imperialism, 35, 37, 49

Daghar, Sālīm Abū, 212
Dalén, T., 87
Dallah al-Barakah, 38, 41-4
Dār al-Arqam, 242
al-Darjīnī, Abū l-Abbās Aḥmad bin Sa'īd, 271n.13
Davis, John, 3
Dayīn, Aḥmad, 210
Deadline (Tom Stacey), 83
democracy, 12, 13, 25
democratisation, 27, 118
Kuwait, 27, 28, 31, 114, 115, 116-17, 172, 174
Derhalli, Mu'āwiyah, 90-1
Desert Wind and Tropical Storm (Sir Donald Hawley), 84-5
al-Dhawwādi, Khālid, 53
Dir'īyah, 10-11, 15
Disney Corporation, 34, 40, 45-6, 48, 49-50
dīwānīyah(s) (social gathering(s): Kuwait), 171-2, 210, 217-18
al-Ḍīyā' (Salmā al-'Awtabī), 271n.16
domestic order (*niẓām*), 7
domestic servants, 8
Kuwait, 124-5, 126-7
UAE, 140
Don't They Know It's Friday (Jeremy Williams), 87-8, 93
Dubai, 28, 139-40, 148, 151
al-Dunyā Maṣāliḥ, 55
Durkheim, Émile, 157

education: Oman, 32, 182-202
Egee, Dale, 78-9
Egee Art Consultancy, 78
Egypt
musalsalāt, 253n.4
schools, 190-2
Eisner, Michael, 34, 35-6, 44, 46
Eklund, Evonne, 79
elections, 13, 27, 32, 59, 115, 118, 160, 203, 206, 210, 214-15, 216-19, 221, 260n.2, 3&4, 261n.11
endogamy, 129, 132, 137, 151, 264n.3
ethnocracy
concept of, 118-19
Kuwait as an, 11, 31, 120-2
Euro Disney, 44, 45

Facey, William, 85-7
Faḍlullāh, Muḥammad Ḥusayn, 230
Fahd, King, 40, 48, 81, 224, 232
Fargues, Philippe, 24
Fāṭimah, Shaykhah (Abu Dhabi), 150, 151
fatwās, 187
Fayṣal, King, 10, 22, 81
Fayṣalīyah Centre, Riyad, 22
fiqh (law manuals), 187
Firjān il-Awwal ("The Neighbourhoods of the Old Days"), 53, 63-4, 65
Foucault, Michel, 167
Fox News, 44
France: as ethnocracy, 121
Fraser, Marcus, 75, 76, 77
Free Kuwait Campaign (FKC), 213
Frier, Julian, 82
al-Fūdārī, Sanā', 211

al-Ghānim, Ghānim Saqr, 161
"Gifts from the Desert" (art exhibition), 82
globalisation, 7, 22, 27-8, 33, 137, 157, 259n.14
and Arab London, 73-5
global, 6, 16, 250
and the media, 34-5, 50-1
Grand Mosque (*al-Masjid al-ḥaram*), Mecca, 225, 226, 231, 232, 233, 239
Guantanamo Bay, 179
Gulf Co-operation Council (GCC), 1, 2, 4, 11, 14, 16, 17, 18, 20, 26, 52, 73, 74, 78, 79, 80, 81, 84, 95, 138, 144, 149, 151, 152, 155, 259n.20

Gulf states
architecture, 16
arms sales to, 19, 74
banks, 250n.24
birth rates, 251n.34
citizenship, 2, 8, 9–10, 24
composition, 1, 247n.2
debt, 20
exclusive culture, appeal to, 6–7
family rule, 4, 6–7, 9–10, 11, 15, 208–9
foreign imagery in, 7
foreigners in, 8, 23
gas reserves, production and consumption, 18
GDP, 18, 249n.22
hydrocarbons, importance of, 17
identity, circles of, 25
investment, inward, 19
investment, overseas, 18–19, 250n.28
land ownership, 21, 26–7
marriage, 137–9
media, 28
merchant families, 251n.36
migrant labour, 12, 22–3, 24
national identity, 13–14, 30
oil prices, 10, 16, 248n.11
oil reserves, production and consumption, 17
"openness", 27–8, 250n.26
population, 2
public order, 4
relations between, 2
relations with Britain, 73–5, 257n.18
satellite television, 29, 34–51
share holding, 25–6
trade balances with OECD countries, 8
wealth, 1–2
women, role of, 5–6, 24
see also individual countries by name

ḥaḍārah mu'āṣirah (contemporary civilisation), 4
ḥadāthah (modernity), 4, 247n.5
al-Ḥaddād, Aḥmad, 15
ḥadīth (record of Prophetic sayings and action), 187, 188, 189, 192, 198
Hāgar, 226
ḥajj (pilgrimage), 33
accounts of, 223–4
administration, 227, 228, 237–9
commercialisation of, 240–1
delegations, 236–7
guide system, 236
numbers of pilgrims, 33, 234–6, 274n.19
Ottomans and, 225, 227–8
quota system, 230–1, 235–6
religious sites, 225–6, 233, 241–2
rituals, 237, 239
safety, 224–5, 231, 232
Saudi control, criticisms of, 228–30, 231–4, 242–4
sa'y (ritual run), 226, 237
stoning ceremony, 231, 238–9
al-Ḥajjī, Yūsuf, 179
ḥalqah(s) (circle(s) of learning), 15, 193–6, 198, 271n.14
al-Hamsan, Dhafir, 82
Handshaikh, 87
al-Ḥarakah al-Dustūrīyah al-Islāmīyah (Islamic Constitutional Movement), 179, 215
al-Ḥarakah al-Salafīyah (Salafī Movement), 179
ḥaramayn (two holy places), 225, 227, 232, 234, 243
Hart, Edwin, 252n.3
al-Ḥasan, Su'ād, 212
al-Ḥawālī, Ṣafar, 6
Ḥawār Islands, 53
Hawley, Sir Donald, 84–5, 93, 94
Hicks, Scott, 48
Hijaz, 223, 228
Ḥijr Isma'īl, 229
Ḥizb al-Da'wah al-Islāmīyah (Islamic Call Party), 171
Ḥizb al-Taḥrīr, 228–9, 252n.42
Ḥizbullāh, 230, 232
al-Ḥumūd, Mūḍī, 209
Ḥussā al-Ṣabāḥ (Āl Ṣabāḥ), Shaykhah, 77
huwīyah (identity), 30, 122
see also identity
Ḥusayn, Sharīf, 223, 230

ḥwala, 30, 254n.7
"hydrocarbon states", 3

'ibādāt (religious observances), 12
Ibadism, 12, 182, 193-6, 197, 201, 271n.17
  Ibadi(s), 13, 98, 188, 189, 198, 257n.3, 271n.11&12, 272n.20
Ibn 'Abd al-Muttalib, 'Abdullāh, 242
Ibn 'Abd al-Wahhāb, Muḥammad, 10
Ibrāhīm Pāshā, 10
al-Ibrāhīm, Shaykh Walīd, 29, 38, 39-40, 49, 50
identity, 6-7, 9, 11, 12, 13, 24, 25, 29-31, 42, 45, 52, 54, 96, 100, 105, 108, 110, 111, 113, 122, 132, 156-7, 161, 175, 176, 184, 193, 208, 214, 220, 230, 248n.6, 250n.29
ifādah (rushing to Muzdalifah), 237-8
Ikhwān al-Muslimīn (Muslim Brotherhood), 179, 210
il-Bēt il-'Ōd ("The Big House"), 53, 63, 64-5, 253n.1
intercultural training, 87-95
International Ḥajj Seminar (1982), 230
Iqrā' (Read), 42
Iran: and the *ḥajj*, 229-30, 232
Iraq: invasion of Kuwait (1990), 172-4, 177-8, 207, 211-14, 262n.22
Islam
  art, 75-8
  books, 82-5
  education in Oman, 182-202
  and marriage, 152-3
  scholarship, 12-13
Islamic Art Society, 77
Islamic Call Party (*Ḥizb al-Da'wah al-Islāmīyah*), 171
Islamic Constitutional Movement (*al-Ḥarakah al-Dustūrīyah al-Islāmīyah*), 179, 215
Islamic Development Bank, 238
Islamic Heritage Society (*Jam'īyat al-Turāth al-Islāmī*), 210
Islamic law, 146, 152, 156, 160, 204, 215, 229, 267n.34
Islamic Salafi Group (*al-Tajammu' al-Islāmī al-Salafī*), 179
Islamic Social Reform Society (*Jamā'at al-Iṣlāḥ al-Ijtimā'ī*), 178-9
Islamic Solidarity Fund, 76
Islamism, 6, 123
  Islamist, 6, 12, 32, 116, 183, 204, 210, 211
  Kuwait, 174, 178-80, 206-7, 210-11, 214-16, 218-20, 220-1, 252n.42
Isma'īl, 229
Ithna'ashari Shi'ah, 57

Jabal Akhdar, Oman, 105, 107, 184
Jabal al-Raḥmah, 237, 239
Jābir, Shaykh Du'ayj, 160, 249n.17
Jābir bin Zayd, 271n.12
Jamā'at al-Iṣlāḥ al-Ijtimā'ī (Islamic Social Reform Society), 178-9
Jamarāt Bridge, Minā, 238
Jam'īyat al-Iṣlāḥ al-Ijtimā'īyah (Social Reform Society), 210
Jam'īyat al-Turāth al-Islāmī (Islamic Heritage Society), 210
Jamrat al-'Aqabah, Minā, 237
Jamshīd bin 'Abdullāh bin Khalīfah bin Ḥārib, Sayyid, 99
Janādirīyah, 7, 19, 248n.7
Jawḥar, Ḥasan, 214
al-Jazeera, 28, 35, 37
Johnstone, T.M., 71
Jordan, 4
al-Ju'ān, Ḥamad, 214
al-Ju'ān, Khawshar, 203
Juhaynāt al-akhbār fī tārīkh zinjibār (Sa'īd bin 'Alī al-Maghīrī), 100
jumlakīyah (neologism: "monarchical republic"), 4, 247n.4

Ka'bah, 225, 226, 227, 237
kafālah (sponsorship), 23-4, 26, 32
  kafīl (sponsor), 23, 26, 139, 144-5
  Kuwait, 126, 168, 169-70, 181, 262n.25
  UAE, 139
Kāmil, Ṣāliḥ, 38, 41-4, 49
Karkūtī, 252n.3
Khalaf, Jāsim, 68, 69, 70

Khālid bin 'Abdullāh bin 'Abd al-Raḥmān, Prince, 38, 48
Khalīfah, 'Alī 'Abdullāh, 253n.5
Khalīfah, Shaykh 'Alī, 162
Khalīfah bin Ḥārib, Sultan, 101
al-Khalīlī, Shaykh Aḥmad, 187, 271n.11
Khalili, David, 256n.7
al-Khaṭīb, Aḥmad, 163
Khilāfat movement, 223
Khomeini, Ayatullah, 229, 232
al-Khurāfī, Dr Nūrīyah, 203, 205
al-Kindī, Aḥmad, 271n.16
al-Kindī, Muḥammad, 271n.16
Kingdom Centre, Riyad, 21-2
Kingdom Holdings, 38, 44-6
kinship, 13, 15, 25, 31, 48, 119, 136, 149, 264n.7
  Kuwait, 128, 134, 207-8
  Oman, 98, 104-5, 108, 110, 113, 259n.15
  UAE, 155, 156
Kirch group, 45
Kitāb al-nīl ('Abd al-'Aziz al-Thamīnī), 195, 271n.17
Kitāb jawāhir al-muntaqāt (Abū l-Qāsim al-Barrādī), 271n.13
Kitāb ṭabaqāt al-mashāyikh (Abū l-Abbās Aḥmad bin Sa'īd al-Darjīnī), 271n.13
Kuwait
  adultery, 124-5
  as autocracy, 115-16
  bidūn, 120, 141, 171, 173, 174-8, 180
  citizenship, 117, 121-2, 141, 175, 176-8
  class, 117, 118, 123, 124, 129, 130-1, 203, 206, 207, 208, 211, 220, 263n.29, 272n.5
  as democracy, 27, 28, 115, 116
  development, 127-30, 205
  dīwānīyah(s), 171-2, 210, 217-18
  domestic servants, 124-5, 126-7
  as ethnocracy, 11, 31, 120-2
  expatriates, 117-18, 120, 122-4, 125-7, 158, 168-70, 205
  "external threats", 122, 127
  the family, 207-9, 273n.9
  Iraqi invasion of (1990), 172-4, 177-8, 207, 211-14, 262n.22
  Islamisation of, 206-7, 221
  Islamist groups, 178-80, 181, 210-11, 214-16, 219-20, 220-1, 252n.42
  kafālah system, 126, 168, 169-70, 181, 262n.25
  Kuwaitisation, 175
  labour law, 170
  "liberals", 172, 203, 209-11, 214-20, 260n.6
  Majlis Movement, 161-2
  marriage, 132-3, 263n.32
  Municipality, 160
  National Assembly, 115, 171-2, 175, 178, 203, 204, 208, 214, 219, 260n.3
  National Museum, 77
  Nationality Law (1959), 121, 141, 174-5
  oil industry, 272n.2
  police, 32, 158-81
  politics, role of women in, 203-21, 261n.8
  Resistance, 211-14
  Shi'ism/Shi'ah, 120, 171-2, 179, 180, 181, 214-15, 219
  Sunnism, 171-2, 179, 180, 214-15
  surveillance, 167, 168
  University, 204, 205, 216, 263n.30
  women's resistance to Iraqi invasion, 211-14
  women's role in, 3, 6, 32, 116-17, 118, 130-3, 169, 203-21, 263n.30
Kuwait Democratic Forum (KDF), 210
Kuwait Petroleum Company (KPC), 205
Kuwait Petroleum International (KPI), 213

Lebanese Broadcasting Corporation (LBC), 35
Li, Richard, 48
"liberal(s)", 6, 32, 116, 172, 179, 203, 209-11, 214-20, 260n.6, 261n.7
Libya, 3
London: Arab presence in, 30, 73-95
London Centre of Arab Studies (LCAS), 85-7

MacDermot, Brian, 80

Madanī, Iyād, 235
al-Madanī, Ṣāliḥ, 68, 70
al-Maghīrī, Sa'īd bin 'Alī, 100-1
al-Maḥmīt, Khadījah, 204, 221
Maḥmūd, Ashraf, 212
maḥram (non-marriageable kin), 25
Mājid (bin Sa'īd bin Sulṭān), Sultan (Zanzibar), 97
majlis/majālis (council(s)), 15, 16, 194, 249n.18
Majlis Movement (Kuwait), 161-2
al-Ma'lā cemetery, Mecca, 223, 239, 275n.28
Mall Gallery, 82
MAN (*al-qawmīyīn al-'arab*), 9
manga/ wamanga (Omanis of Zanzibar), 97
Ma'rafī, Samīrah, 212
marriage, 12, 24, 30-1
  Bahrain, 59
  brideprice, 137, 146, 148, 264n.5, 263n.34, 266n.23
  expenses, 137-8, 146
  Kuwait, 132-3
  misyār (traditional marriage: Saudi Arabia), 267n.28
  Oman, 101, 108-10, 149-50, 259n.17&18 (weddings)
  polygamy, 138, 148, 149, 157
  Qatar, 149
  UAE, 31, 140-57
Marriage Fund (*Ṣunduq al-Zawāj*), 147-56
al-Marzūq, Yūsuf, 161
al-Masjid al-Ḥaram *see* Grand Mosque, Mecca
maṣlaḥah (the general good), 12, 152-3, 156
Mathaf Gallery, 80
al-Mawaddah (magazine), 151-2, 154
Mawārid Group, 38, 47-8
Mazrui, Ali, 118-19
MBC *see* Middle East Broadcasting Centre
Mecca, 225, 226, 233, 234, 237
media, 28-9
  satellite television, 29, 34-51
  Western influences on, 36-7, 49-50
  see also television
Mediaset, 44
Medina, 225, 226, 233, 237
Memoirs of an Arabian Princess from Zanzibar, 112
Microsoft, 45
Middle East Broadcasting Centre (MBC), 28, 35, 38-41, 49
Minā, 226, 231, 233, 234, 237, 238, 239
Mish'al, Khālid, 39
misyār, 267n.28
Morocco, 4, 144, 183
Mount 'Arafāt, 225, 226, 234, 237, 238, 239
Movement for Islamic Reform in Arabia (MIRA), 232, 233
mu'āmalāt (worldly actions), 12
Mubārak, Shaykh 'Abdullāh, 162, 163-4
Mubārak the Great (Emir of Kuwait), 162
Mudhakkarāt amīrah 'arabīyah (Ar. of *Memoirs of an Arabian Princess from Zanzibar*), 112
al-Mullah, Nabīlah, 205
Mumford, Lewis, 16
al-Munāyis, Muḥammad, 161
al-Munāyis, Sāmī, 214
al-Muqtadir Billāh, 225
Murād III, Sultan, 232
Murād IV, Sulṭān, 227
Murdoch, Rupert, 44, 46, 48
al-Murr, Muḥammad, 139-40, 144, 153, 156
al-Mūsā, Mūnā, 213
Muṣaddiq, Muḥammad, 272n.2
musalsalāt (soap operas), 29-30, 52-7, 62-72
al-Muṣannif (Aḥmad al-Kindī), 271n.16
Muscat: Zanzibaris in, 102-13
Muslim Brotherhood (*Ikhwān al-Muslimīn*), 179, 210
Muslim World League, 153, 230
mutajannasīn (naturalised citizens), 143
muṭawwif(s) (*ḥajj* guide(s)), 223-4, 232-3, 236, 240, 274n.17
Muzdalifah, 226, 237

al-Nadābī, Muḥammad bin Nāṣir, 258n.6

Nādī al-Fatāt (Girls' Club), 209
Nā'if, Prince, 229
nasab (line of descent), 31, 266n.19
Nāṣir al-Ṣabāḥ (Āl Ṣabāḥ), Shaykh, 77
National Council for Culture, Arts and Heritage (Qatar), 77
National Democratic Forum (NDF), 209
nationalism, 6, 24, 119, 136, 168, 250n.29
  see also Arab Nationalism
al-Naybārī, 'Abdullāh, 214, 261n.7&8
Netscape, 44-5
News Corporation, 34, 37, 40, 44, 45, 48, 50
Nimrah mosque, 'Arafāt, 237, 239
al-Nu'mānī, Aḥmad, 112
al-Nuṣif, Shaykhah, 209

Obaid, Thoraya, 5
O'Hara, Philip, 40
oil, 1, 3, 8, 9, 10, 12, 16-17, 19, 20, 21, 24, 30, 28, 55, 59, 73-4, 75, 76, 79, 83, 95, 134, 138, 139, 144, 241, 248n.11, 250n.25, 256n.2
  Bahrain, 55, 59
  Kuwait, 117, 127-30, 134, 162-3, 204-5, 207, 212, 216, 249n.18, 22&23, 258n.10, 272n.2
Oman
  Armed Forces Museum, 111-12
  badu, 16
  education, 32
  government posts, 248n.10
  Islamic learning, 249n.15
  Luti Shi'ah, 108, 258n.7
  marriage, 149-50
  migration to Zanzibar, 96-9
  nationality law, 100
  salaries, 16-17
  television, 7
  tourism, 103
  tribes, 24-5, 98, 258n.7
  women's education, 182-202
  women's role in, 32-3, 103
  Zanzibaris in, 30-1, 96-113
Oman: a seafaring nation, 111, 256n.11
Oman and its Renaissance (Sir Donald Hawley), 84, 85
Orbit, 38, 43, 47-8, 49, 50
Organisation of the Islamic Conference, 230
Orientalism, 79-80
Ottomans
  and the *ḥajj*, 225, 227-8, 233
  police, 159

"Painting and Patronage" (art exhibition), 81-2
Pan-Arab Research Centre, 35
Patel, Lord Adam, 237
patrilinearity, 31
Patrimoine Sans Frontières, 234
Petroleum Development-Oman (PDO), 103, 107
pilgrimage *see ḥajj*
police
  Bahrain, 159-60
  Kuwait, 32, 158-81
  Qatar, 159-60
  Saudi Arabia, 224, 234
Prophet's Mosque (*al-Masjid al-nabawī al-sharīf*), Medina, 223, 226, 240, 243
publishing: Islamic books, 82-5

al-Qabandī, Asrār, 212
Qābūs bin Sa'īd, Sultan (Oman), 10, 84, 102, 110, 111-12, 113, 183
al-Qā'idah, 179
al-Qallāf, Ḥasan 'Alī, 219
Qāmūs al-sharī'ah (Jumayyil al-Sa'dī), 271n.16
qarābah (kinship), 13, 15, 25
al-Qaṭāmī, Jāsim, 163
al-Qaṭāmī, Muḥammad, 161
Qatar
  building, 248n.12
  debt, 20-1
  development, 251n.31
  marriage, 149
  police, 159-60
  state museum, 77
Qur'an/Qur'anic, 188, 189, 193, 195, 197-8, 216, 222, 230-1, 244
  Qur'ānic schools: Oman, 182-202
al-Quṣaybī, Ghāzī, 87

Rafsanjānī, Hāshimī, 230
Ramdas, Khimji, 104
Ra's al-Khaimah, 5, 142, 150, 152, 154
Rāshid, Shaykh (Dubai), 141
al-Rashīd, 'Abd al-Raḥmān, 36
Redstone, Sumner, 40, 44
religious education: Oman, 182-202
rentier/rentierism, 11, 20, 23-4, 31, 139, 248n.13
Riding the Waves of Culture (Fons Trompanaar), 89
Ritchie, Ian, 40, 41
Riyad, 10, 15, 16, 21-2, 241, 274n.17
Riyadh: the old city (William Facey), 87
Rūḥānī, Ayatullah Mehdī, 274n.13
al-Rukn, Muḥammad, 157
al-Rumaydī, Khalfān, 267n.34
al-Rumayḥī, Muḥammad, 3
Rutter, Eldon, 223
al-Ruwwād (The Pioneers), 41

Ṣabāḥ, Shaykh, 204
"Ṣabāḥ al-sūq", 160
Sa'd, Shaykh (Kuwait), 173
Ṣaddām Ḥusayn, 172, 177
al-Sa'dī, Jumayyil, 271n.16
al-Sa'dūn, Aḥmad, 217, 219
Sa'īd bin Sulṭān, Sultan (Zanzibar), 96-7, 112, 113
Sa'īd bin Taymūr, Sultan (Oman), 98, 102, 183
Salafī Movement (*al-Ḥarakah al-Salafīyah*), 179
Ṣalāḥ al-Dīn, 227
Sālim, 'Abdullāh, Shaykh (Kuwait), 162, 204
Sālim, Fahd, 162, 163
Sālim, Ṣabāḥ, 161, 162, 163-4
Sālmah, Princess (Oman), 112, 259n.24
Salmān, Prince (Riyad), 11, 15
al-Samarra'ī, Sa'īd, 233
Ṣaqr, Shaykh, 150
SARAvision, 39, 41
Saudi Arabia
  citizenship, 141
  foreign debt, 20
  government buildings, 249n.21
  ḥajj, 222-45
  kinship, 13, 14
  migrant labour, 23
  oil income, 10
  population, 22
  television, 7, 28, 224-5
  tourism, 241
  Wahhabism, 11, 229, 230
  wealth, 22
  women's role in, 5, 242, 243 (gender), 267n.28
Saudi Arabia by the First Photographers (William Facey), 86
Sayf 'Abbās 'Abdullāh, 210, 213
Sayf 'Abbās 'Abdullāh, Lubnā, 213-14
September 11, 2001, 6, 36, 179
Serjeant, R.B., 58
servants, domestic, 8
  Kuwait, 124-5, 126-7
  UAE, 140
shabāb (young men), 12, 248n.14
Shammar (tribe), 142, 177-8, 269n.13
sharī'ah see Islamic law
Sharjah, 4, 139, 148
al-Sharq al-awsaṭ (newspaper), 36, 230-1, 274n.19
al-Shāyijī, 'Abdullāh, 219
Shaykh, Hadīl, 36
Shi'ism/Shi'ah, 12, 32, 268-9n.13
  and the *ḥajj*, 229, 242, 243
  Kuwait, 171-2, 179, 180, 215, 219
Showtime, 42, 43, 50
*siblah*s (meeting rooms), 186-7, 189, 270n.5
*sīrah*s (biographies), 187
soap operas *see musalsalāt*
Social Reform Society (*Jam'īyat al-Iṣlāḥ al-Ijtimā'īyah*), 210
Society for Intercultural Education, Training and Research, 87
Sotheby's, 75
Spink, Michael, 77
Stacey, Tom, 82-4
Stacey International, 82-5, 86
Star TV, 37, 48
al-Sulḥ, Munā, 45
al-Sulḥ, Riyāḍ, 45
Sullivan, Sarah, 253n.16

Sultan Qābūs University, Oman, 106
Ṣundūq al-Zawāj see Marriage Fund
Sunnism, 12, 267n.28
  Kuwait, 171–2, 179, 180, 214–15
Sūq al-Manākh crash, Kuwait (1982), 26, 207
Swahili, 103–5, 107

al-Tajammu' al-Islāmī al-Salafī (Islamic Salafī Group), 179
Ṭalāl bin 'Abd al-'Azīz, 45
tamthīlīyāt (plays), 53, 66–7
ṭawāf (circumambulation of the Ka'bah), 225, 237
television, 29, 30
  Bahrain, 30; *see also musalsalāt*
  Dubai, 28
  Kuwait, 123
  Oman, 7, 113
  Saudi Arabia, 7, 28, 224–5
  see also transnationalism and the media
al-Thamīnī, 'Abd al-'Aziz, 195
thaqāfah ("exclusive culture"), 6
  see also culture/cultural
"third cultures", 75
Thuwaynī (bin Sa'īd bin Sulṭān), 97
tourism
  Oman, 103
  Saudi Arabia, 241
transnationalism/transnational, 6, 16, 21, 24, 158, 171
  and Arab London, 73–5, 95
  and the *ḥajj*, 33, 245
  and the media, 29, 34–5
  Oman, 96, 107, 111–13
tribes and tribalism, 13, 24
  Kuwait, 120, 123, 128, 134, 160–1, 175, 204, 206–7, 216, 218–19, 220, 272–3n.5
  Oman, 24–5, 98–9, 101–2, 105–6, 258n.7
  UAE, 137–8, 142–3, 151, 265n.16
Trompanaar, Fons, 89
Turner, Victor, 242
Tydeman, John, 43

al-'Ubayd, Dr 'Abdullāh, 153
'Ubaydlī, 'Ubaydlī, 252n.2
Uganda, 118
'ulamā' (religious authorities), 227, 229, 230, 235, 238, 243–4
'Umar (second caliph), 225
Umayyad (dynasty), 225, 233
  Umayyad Mosque, Damascus, 80
'umrah (minor pilgrimage), 224
'Umrān, Ḥalā, 40
United Arab Emirates (UAE)
  citizenship, 141–2, 143–6
  domestic servants, 140
  foreign workers, 139
  kafālah system, 139
  marriage, 31, 140–57
  Marriage Fund (*Ṣundūq al-Zawāj*), 147–56
  national identity, 156
  population, 5, 139
  women, 144–5
United Nations Convention on the Elimination of All Forms of Discrimination Against Women (CEDAW), 216
United Press International (UPI), 39
USA
  as ethnocracy, 121
  interest in the Gulf, 17–18, 250n.23
  and Iraqi invasion of Kuwait (1990), 174
al-'Uthaymīn, Shaykh Muḥammad bin Ṣāliḥ, 239, 243, 275n.23
'Uthmān (third caliph), 225

Viacom, 34, 40, 42, 50

Wahhabism, 11, 229, 230
  "Wahhabi", 11, 33, 210, 223, 229, 233, 242, 244
Wales, Prince of, 81, 82, 248n.7, 256n.10
Walīd bin Ṭalāl bin 'Abd al-'Azīz, Prince, 21, 29, 38, 44–6
al-Walīd ibn 'Abd al-Malik (Umayyad caliph), 225
al-Wasaṭ, 1
Wavell, A.J.B., 223, 228
welfare state (*dawlat al-ra'āyah*), 11, 167
Wilkinson, John, 24
Williams, Jeremy, 87–92

women, 5-6, 24
  education in Oman, 32-3, 182-202
  and *ḥajj*, 243
  generational differences: Oman, 199-201
  Kuwait, 3, 6, 32, 116-17, 118, 130-3, 169, 203-21
  Saudi Arabia, 5, 242, 267n.28
  UAE, 144-5
Women's Cultural and Social Society (WCSS), 209
World of Islam Festival (1975), 76-7, 81, 256n.6
World Trade Organisation (WTO), 22, 241, 251n.33

Yamani, Hani, 14
Yamani, Mai, 16
al-Yāṣīn, Ṣāliḥ, 209, 210
Yemen, 142, 183

Za'abīs, 142
zakāt (Islamic alms), 209
Zanzibaris: Oman, 30-1, 96-113
Zayed, Shaykh (Abu Dhabi), 147-8, 150-1, 249n.17
Zeghidour, Slimane, 233, 244
Zilo, Alexander, 47, 48

www.ingramcontent.com/pod-product-compliance
Ingram Content Group UK Ltd.
Pitfield, Milton Keynes, MK11 3LW, UK
UKHW021905220326
469204UK00008B/184

9 781848 858664